'Looking for a sho~ ~.~ route, in 155~ … Willoughby a~ ¹ …d Chancellor to … passage through the Arctic to Asia. Their venture was, says Evans, one of the boldest in English history and a significant turning point in English economic and cultural development. It's also a good story, well told'

Iain Finlayson, *The Times*

'Entertaining and meticulously researched . . . *Merchant Adventurers* is much more than a reconstruction of one of the most fascinating voyages of the Tudor age. The author places the expedition in the wider context of global exploration, mercantile expansion and the establishment of the first joint-stock company. Indeed he argues that the 1553 expedition anticipated the dawn of a new era, one that would see the formation of the East India Company and England's fledgling empire'

Giles Milton, *Literary Review*

'This is the fascinating story of a forgotten few whose deeds had an important long-term impact on Britain's history'   *Good Book Guide*

'It is a heroic and tragic tale that for all the commercial and political agents at work remains, above all, a story of courage and endeavour. Evans is alert to the complexities of early modern diplomacy and cultural encounter, and the description of the survivors' experiences in Russia complements well the treatment of what they endured at sea'

Mark Hutchings, *The London Magazine*

'It's difficult to imagine the victor over the Spanish Armada as a small backward island with little maritime experience, but that's just what England was . . . Evans shows the driving force that made England great . . . A wonderful adventure story'   *Kirkus Reviews*

James Evans completed a PhD at Oriel College, Oxford, following a first-class degree and a Masters in historical research. He is a writer and producer of historical documentaries and lives in London.

www.jamesevans.org.uk

MERCHANT ADVENTURERS

The voyage of discovery that
transformed Tudor England

JAMES EVANS

PHOENIX

A PHOENIX PAPERBACK

First published in Great Britain in 2013
by Weidenfeld & Nicolson
This edition published in 2014
by Phoenix,
an imprint of Orion Books Ltd,
Orion House, 5 Upper St Martin's Lane,
London WC2H 9EA

An Hachette UK company

1 3 5 7 9 10 8 6 4 2

Text © James Evans 2013
Map © John Gilkes 2013

A CIP catalogue record for this book
is available from the British Library.

ISBN 978-1-7802-2102-1

Typeset by Input Data Services Ltd, Bridgwater, Somerset

Printed and bound by CPI Group (UK) Ltd,
Croydon, CRO 4YY

The Orion Publishing Group's policy is to use papers that
are natural, renewable and recyclable products and
made from wood grown in sustainable forests. The logging
and manufacturing processes are expected to conform to
the environmental regulations of the country of origin.

www.orionbooks.co.uk

This book is dedicated, with love and admiration,
to my two grandfathers,

Percy Evans and Jeffrey Fryer

CONTENTS

ILLUSTRATIONS

Section one

Robert Thorne, 1536 *(Nicola Pearce)*

George Gisze by Hans Holbein the Younger, 1532 *(Artothek/Bridgeman)*

John Dee, c.1594 *(Ashmolean Museum)*

The port of Seville by Alonso Sanchez Coello, c.1580 *(Album/Oronoz/ AKG images)*

Nineteenth-century copy of a portrait of Sebastian Cabot by James Herring, from an earlier original *(Bristol City Museum/Bridgeman)*

Detail from world map by Sebastian Cabot, 1544 *(British Library)*

Map of Asia by Robert Thorne, 1527

Illustration from *Arte de Navegar* by Pedro de Medina of sighting the Pole Star with a cross-staff, 1545

Illustration from *Arte de Navegar* by Pedro de Medina of sighting the sun at midday using an astrolabe, 1545

World map by Jean Rotz, 1542 *(British Library/Bridgeman)*

Sir Hugh Willoughby *(Richard Flint)*

Engraving of England's Famous Discoverers featuring Captain John Davis, Sir Walter Raleigh, Sir Hugh Willoughby and Captain John Smith, c.1589 *(National Maritime Museum, Greenwich)*

Section two

Illustration of the carrack *Lartique* from the Anthony Roll, 1546 *(Gerry Bye/Pepys Library, Magdalene College, Cambridge)*

Detail from a plan of Dover showing ships off the coast by John Thompson, 1538 *(British Library Cotton Aug. I I 23)*

Drawing of London featuring the Tower of London by Antonis Van der Wyngaerde, 1554 *(Ashmolean Museum)*

The 1553 Expedition

——— Course of the *Bona Esperanza* and *Bona Confidentia*
---------- Course of the *Edward Bonaventure*

*Atlantic
Ocean*

Senja island

Lofoten islands

Røst islands

Trondheim

Bergen

*North
Sea*

Pitsligo

Edinburgh
Lauder

Orford Ness
Bristol
London
Winchester Harwich
Calais Antwerp

N

PROLOGUE

On the coast of Russia's Kola peninsula, on the northern shore of the Eurasian continent, the cold begins finally to relax its grip. After the unbroken darkness of December, the days grow rapidly longer. By the end of April it is light until almost eleven o'clock at night. In the estuary of the river known later as the Varzina, the hard-frozen surface softens and breaks up. When sunshine pierces the scattered cloud the water glows a rich blue, contrasting with the smooth granite rocks of the fractured coastal rim and with the fresh moss and low plant-cover which clings to them. Every year, as the water defrosts, parties of Russian fishermen emerge from the throat of the White Sea, then work their way north-west, keeping the shore in view.

In the year 1554, one boat, containing just over twenty men, steers around the northern end of Nokuyev island, where the land rises steeply to a rounded summit, and snow covers the dark rock. The crew then turn sharply south, avoiding the shallows and sandbanks, and head for the river mouths which feed into a sheltered bay. Like the returning salmon they are pursuing, the fishermen pass from salt water to fresh, as they follow the estuary inland. Their boat, which they had made themselves, looks primitive. But its single mast allows them to utilise the cold wind which blows from the Pole to the north. Otherwise the men work at the boat's oars, their heads and shoulders draped in furs, clouds of steam rising from their mouths.

Within the estuary, suddenly, there are shouts. The fishermen point frantically, unable to contain their excitement, bewilderment and fear. Standing starkly out against the treeless backdrop is the skeletal outline of two large ships, anchored in the empty estuary. The sails have been hauled down, but the masts thrust upwards into a wide sky. These are

1

ships unlike any that the Russians have seen before. Cautiously, talking nervously in hushed voices, they row towards them.

Approaching one of the ships in their smaller boat, the Russians notice a complete lack of activity on board, and a peculiar silence. The wind rattles the rigging on the ship's mast, and the planks of the hull creak and groan after months of being squeezed by the ice, but when the fishermen shout out, there is no response. They draw alongside, then clamber apprehensively from their open boat up onto the deck. At first they bang on the sealed hatches, then kneel to force them open, peering, then stepping nervously down into the gloom below deck. As their eyes adjust to the half-light, a surreal and ghostly scene emerges.

There are men on board the ship, and they are dressed in thick layers of bright, new woollen clothing, stripped from boxes of merchandise to keep warm. They are in a variety of strange and lifelike postures, hunched over fixed tables, lying together in groups, bent over by cupboards of stores. But there is no movement and no noise. All of them are dead. Their bodies are perfectly preserved. They look, it is later said, like statues, adopting a variety of poses, as if they had been placed in them by some artistic creator. Among them are dogs, similarly frozen as they lived.

As the fishermen explore this bizarre scene, in a separate cabin they find the body of a tall, bearded man, seated at a fixed bench, slumped over. Even in death his clothes mark him out from the crew, and beneath his pale arm are parchments which gently lift at the corners in the wind which now blows through the forced-open hatches. But those among the Russian group who can read are unable to decipher the strange script in which he has been writing. Where have these great ships come from? Who are these dead men?

These are not questions that the Russian fishermen can answer. But when they depart back to the White Sea, they take with them all the documents they find on board, including the ship's log, which details its final movements, and allows historians to do the same.[1]

INTRODUCTION

In the first half of the sixteenth century a fundamental change was taking place in western Europe. Spain and Portugal had thrown off the shackles of ancient geography. In Asia and America they had discovered new lands, unknown to the old writers, and they had reached them by uncharted routes across the ocean.

It was a time when inventions and discoveries not only rivalled those of the ancients but exceeded them. What of theirs, asked the English scholar, translator and chemist Richard Eden, could possibly be compared with printing or with the making of guns or fireworks? Ptolemy, the second-century Alexandrian who had exerted such enduring influence on geographical ideas in Europe, had undoubtedly been an 'excellent man', but still, Eden noted, 'there were many things hid from his knowledge'. The ancients had not, as some still thought, comprehended all things. Ptolemy, after all, 'knew nothing of America'. Or consider St Augustine: would such a clever and learned man have doubted that the earth was round had he known how the Spaniards and Portuguese would sail around it, returning, by a straight course, more or less, to the point at which they had set off? The lesson was simple. No man, however brilliant, could know beyond what was tried and discovered by experience. What lay in the unexplored regions of the globe could not be calculated or imagined. Men must travel there to find out.

In this great project, England had lagged behind its rivals. This small, rather backward island had little maritime expertise or experience on which to draw. 'Ignorance has been among us,' Eden admitted, 'touching cosmography and navigation.' The country was 'indigent and destitute' of expert pilots – men who were qualified, as he put it, not only to dredge for oysters in the thick and shifting sands of the Thames estuary, but to venture out into the ocean, to 'discover unknown lands and islands'. In the past the country had relied on the proficiency of sailors and navigators from France, Portugal or Italy, who had the maritime knowledge and training that Englishmen lacked.

By the mid-sixteenth century, however, a new spirit had begun to emerge in England. A sense of possibility had been born, and the return of Sebastian Cabot, the brilliant, enigmatic and divisive navigator, who had grown up in England before spending most of his adult life in Spain, epitomised and reinforced this atmosphere. The voyage that he organised and inspired in 1553 was the ultimate expression of a changing climate.

It was now that a few Englishmen reread, usually in the account left by Marco Polo, stories about a rich and distant country they called Cathay, and dreamed.[2] They dreamed about the vast and ancient city, called 'Khan-balik', or 'Cambalu' – known now as Beijing – at the heart of which stood a magnificent palace. Its roof, they read, was 'all ablaze with scarlet and green and blue and yellow and all the colours that are, so brilliantly varnished that it glitters like crystal and the sparkle of it can be seen from far away'. They dreamed about its seemingly endless procession of halls and chambers, each richly decorated with gold and silver and with paintings of dragons, birds, horsemen and scenes of battle. They dreamed about the many wives and concubines of the great Khan who lived together in its private apartments, and in particular about its treasure rooms, piled high with his vast wealth: with gold, silver, pearls and precious stones. They dreamed about the array of luxurious goods available at the markets of Cathay, the silks, the spices, the gem-encrusted clothes. And they dreamed about the great feasts over which the Khan presided, with so much gold and silver ware on display 'that no one who did not see it with his own eyes could well believe it'.

The Iberian explorers might have reached new and rich lands, but they had not rediscovered this world about which Polo had written. Perhaps it would be possible, some Englishmen began to believe, to get there by a new route, peculiarly convenient for their northern island, which skirted Europe and Asia's upper coast and then descended gradually south-eastward. No one knew whether such a passage existed, but there were reasons to think that it might. It was true that ancient writers had insisted the Arctic was too cold and blocked in by ice. But they had also said that it would be impossible to pass the Equator, because of its intense heat, and they had been proved wrong. Why, a few dared ask, could they not be wrong again?

Crucially, for a brief period, this ethos permeated the government, who saw an opportunity to advance England's cause on a wider commercial stage. Those in senior positions co-operated with the leading London merchants, who combined an interest in profit with genuine intellectual curiosity. They promoted and sponsored experts who felt the same way. They strongly supported an expedition to explore and open up new trades that was deliberately English rather than cosmopolitan. The attitude came not just from the merchants of London. It came also, for the first time, from higher up the social scale: from the 'diverse noble men and gentlemen, as well of the council as other', who backed the resulting venture both financially and by other means.

This was a time of cultural change that extended even to the language men wrote and spoke. Then, as since, Englishmen were not natural polyglots: most did not grow up with a mastery of multiple languages, or any sense of the importance of doing so. But the many who only read English were empowered by the increasing number of translations available from Latin and contemporary languages.[3] As a side effect, the mother tongue itself was aggrandised. English, Eden noticed, was 'enriched and amplified by sundry books'. In the past it had been a mere peasant tongue. It had been 'indigent and barbarous', he observed, 'much more than it now is'.[4] One of the last acts of the young King Edward VI, on 27 June, nine days before he died, was to issue a charter to the school in Stratford at which the young William Shakespeare would learn to read and write.

It was no coincidence that a belief in careful written records was integral to the new ethos of intellectual curiosity. This, after all, was how experience could best be passed on. What was learning, Eden asked, but the 'gathering of many men's wits into one man's head, and the experience of many years, and many men's lives, to the life of one'?[5] Knowledge, no less than money, was a form of capital, to be pooled and invested. And like money, knowledge now flowed in England more freely than it had ever done before. Both could be harnessed and directed towards an important end.

From the beginning, some of those involved with Sebastian Cabot's venture were not sailors or merchants but scholars, who understood the importance of written records better than anyone. There was the brilliant young polymath John Dee, who met and developed a close friendship and a profound respect for the young sailor and instrument-maker Richard Chancellor, helping him to prepare for the voyage. There was Clement Adams, a scholar, tutor to the friends and fellow pupils of young King Edward, and a skilled cartographer, who both worked with Cabot to reissue his world map and who interviewed Richard Chancellor on his return. There was Richard Eden, who knew the protagonists well, and who translated important works by Continental scholars into English – a prolific father-figure in both the intellectual and the literal sense (with twelve children who survived to adulthood).

And there was the lawyer and scholar Richard Hakluyt, deeply knowledgeable about trade and world geography. Not only did Hakluyt directly advise the company over which Cabot presided, he also inspired his younger cousin of the same name, then a pupil at Westminster School. He talked to him with animation in his rooms at the Inns of Court about a world map that he possessed, and directed him to Psalm 107, 'where I read', the younger Hakluyt remembered, 'that they which go down to the sea in ships ... they see the works of the Lord'. The younger Richard Hakluyt resolved there and then that he would, if he had the chance, 'prosecute that knowledge and kind of literature'. Born around the time that Sebastian Cabot was planning his great venture, the principal protagonists of 1553 had all died by the time he began his mission 'to collect in orderly fashion the maritime records of our own countrymen, now lying scattered and neglected'.[6] Nevertheless, as a young man, Hakluyt spoke with many who had been involved, and he gathered together an array of such written records as had been kept, though they had not been methodically brought together. Wisely, he heeded the ancient stricture of Ptolemy: that it was first-hand travel accounts that mattered, not the bundles of speculation and hearsay which made up so many geographies, or 'cosmographies' – those 'weary volumes', as he called them, drafted by desk-bound academics.[7]

In his great work on the *Principal Navigations, Voyages, Traffiques & Discoveries of the English Nation*, Hakluyt showed that England, after a slow start, had been at the forefront of European trade and exploration. He showed that the growth of a genuine maritime culture, founded on the scientific understanding of maps and astronomy, had laid the basis for the flowering of English enterprise under Queen Elizabeth in his own day. He showed, too, that a pioneering voyage of 1553 was where it all truly began. And it was thanks to him that this story became, for a time, a staple of British imperial history.

Hakluyt was right. The voyage in search of a north-east passage to Asia in 1553, organised by Sebastian Cabot, and led by Sir Hugh Willoughby and Richard Chancellor, was one of the boldest in English history. It is an extraordinary story, with its divided outcome, and with the surviving logs and interviews that allow it to be retold in detail. While some of the participants brought English commerce to an imperial court with which the country had not previously traded, others became fatally lost and stranded within the Arctic ice.

It is a story that is remarkable too for what it reveals about the position of England at the time: in the midst of profound social and political upheaval, and in the early stages of an intellectual revolution. For the first time attitudes appeared which seem 'enlightened', scientific and almost modern. Within a seething conflict of ideas about religion and the country's political direction, a recognisably empirical way of thinking and behaving emerged.

Richard Eden, who worked for promoters of the expedition, dismissed with contempt those 'superstitious Horoscopers (Astrologers, I mean, and not Astronomers)' whose readings had been pored over in the recent past, and indeed which still were. It is impossible to read the instructions which Sebastian Cabot wrote for those who sailed in 1553, or the account of the voyage drafted by Richard Chancellor on his return, without being struck that the voice, for almost the first time, sounds familiar to modern ears.

The expedition had a human cost which is impossible to ignore. Some of the men were certainly, as it was said, 'worthy of better fortune'. At sea, perhaps more even than on land, fortune did not always favour the deserving. Few seamen, as Richard Hakluyt later wrote, lived to 'grey hairs'. Skills and ability could improve one's chances of survival, but they did not rule out misfortune. For many of the men in 1553, some with dependent family, some young themselves and in the early stage of their careers, it was a matter of luck to which ship, and to which captain, they were assigned. At the same time, it was more than simply the whim of fortune which led one of the expedition ships to return home safely while its sisters were not seen in England again.

The voyage of Willoughby and Chancellor deserves to be well known – as well known, say, as Sir Francis Drake's circumnavigation of the world or as Sir John Franklin's ill-fated attempt to navigate a north-west passage. Indeed, in many ways it is *more* deserving. Certainly it is an episode which England has more reason to remember with pride. Where Franklin's 1845 voyage is notorious for its unmitigated horror, the one Cabot had much earlier overseen, looking for a similar passage to the north-east, mixed disaster with triumph. What Drake achieved meanwhile was undoubtedly remarkable. He returned with a hold packed with spices and gold, the commodities which Willoughby and Chancellor before him had vainly hoped to obtain. But stolen treasure, while it temporarily enriched both individuals and the nation, stirred up problems for the future, and had little to offer in the way of lasting wealth.

That, as Cabot and a few others saw, was to be found in trade: in the exchange, and promotion, of England's exports, in new markets beyond the traditional networks of Europe. Where Drake's first thought was to rob, Cabot and his men looked to explore new realms in peace, offering only the 'affection' which would lead to enduring commerce. The letter they carried, signed by the young but ailing King Edward VI, acclaimed the peaceful but intrepid merchant, who wandered the world, searching land and sea, 'to carry such good and profitable things, as are found in their Countries, to remote regions and kingdoms, and again to bring from the same, such things as they find there commodious for their own Countries'. By this means, he declared, 'friendship might be established among all men, and every one seek to gratify all'. These Englishmen, he assured foreign kings, 'shall not touch any thing of yours unwilling unto you'.[8]

Dramatic and important as it is, though, Willoughby and Chancellor's story is not well known today. It features in general surveys of British maritime history. Scholarly studies exist of the trading company which resulted, and which stood as an example and inspiration to more famous successors, of which the East India Company became the most celebrated. No book has been written, however, which concentrates on the 1553 voyage, or which seeks to place this expedition in particular in the context of its time. Yet it is this context which makes the story truly remarkable. By itself it is a captivating tale: of adventure and of sharply opposed background and fortune. But it is also more than that. The voyage of 1553 marks a significant turning point in English economic and cultural history.

It is desperately hard, in the twenty-first century, to grasp the magnitude of what these men attempted. They sailed away from family and friends, into waters that were wholly unknown. They ventured into an area of the world that was widely believed to be so cold and dangerous that they could not hope to survive. Observers at the time were struck by the 'greatness of the dangers' to which the crews would be exposed: a savage climate, unknown monsters, aggressive nations. There is no modern parallel. Even astronauts on the first missions to the moon had a good idea what to expect, and remained in radio contact with their base.

It is true that these men dreamed of filling their ships with gold, pearls and spices, as the Spanish and Portuguese had been able to do, and that visions of astonishing wealth and national renown helped to allay their fears. But from the beginning these ambitions rubbed up alongside more modest ones. The leaders of the expedition sought also, from the outset, to find new outlets for basic English goods, and they hoped to find new sources of supplies, which would allow England to free herself, at last, from the suffocating grip of foreign merchants.

The fact that, as it turned out, tallow and oil from seals rather than gold were discovered, served to reinforce the central point. Lasting wealth and political power could be built on regular trade in useful low-cost articles. Cathay did prove beyond these men's reach. Even had they got there, of course, they would have found a place rather different to the one visited and eulogised by Marco Polo some two and a half centuries previously. China, and the world, had changed. None of this detracts from what these men did achieve.

Since the beginning of time, a partial but suitably impressed Richard

Eden proclaimed, no enterprise deserved greater praise than 'that which our nation have attempted by the north seas to discover the mighty and rich empire of Cathay'.

Part I

'Turning outward'

There is no land unhabitable, nor sea innavigable.

ROBERT THORNE

One

O n 6 August 1497 a fourteen-year-old boy disembarked with his father at the quayside in Bristol. Here, in front of the storehouses, cranes and residential properties which lined the harbour, crowds of excited men and women thronged the stone-paved banks. The people watching cheered and shouted as the small ship was paddled, or towed, to its mooring alongside the rebuilt church of St Stephen, where the family most closely involved had offered prayers for the success of their voyage prior to setting out. Hundreds of ordinary citizens were there, alongside emotional wives, family and friends, as well as a delegation of the town's governors, smartly turned out in livery and attempting to remain dignified in the midst of the commotion.

Hours earlier, the *Matthew* had lain at anchor in the Severn Estuary. A river pilot had come on board, and with the small crew – around eighteen men – awaited the sharp turn of the tide which would lift the ship for some six miles up the narrow, winding ascent of the Avon.[1] As they did so, news from on board had sped inland on horseback.

At first dignitaries of the town exchanged urgent whispers. Soon, Bristol's 10,000 inhabitants talked openly of how John Cabot (Giovanni Caboto), the Italian mariner who some years earlier had come to live and work with them, had succeeded in his extraordinary aim. He had sailed west across the great ocean and reached the East.[2]

Bristol mariners before John Cabot had launched into the Atlantic west of Ireland, battling winds and currents that were predominantly hostile, in the hope of finding new lands.

They had looked for the fabled Isle of Brazil, or the Isle of the Seven Cities, governed, supposedly, by the descendants of Spanish bishops and their flocks, who had fled the first coming of the Moors. Cabot's dream, though, had been different. Islands in the ocean might act as a convenient staging post. But his ultimate ambition, strengthened by the proclaimed success of another Genoan – the weaver's son, Christopher Columbus – was to reach the mainland and offshore islands of Asia.[3]

The idea had come to him while he worked as a trader, travelling from the Mediterranean to Arabia and the Black Sea, to purchase the exotic goods brought by Muslim middlemen. At the markets of Mecca, the silks, spices, perfumes and precious stones had all travelled countless dusty miles on ancient trading roads from the rich civilisations of the East. Surely, Cabot reasoned, these luxuries could be acquired more directly, and more cheaply, by a sea route which headed not east from Europe but due west across the Atlantic, following the curvature of the earth to the easternmost promontories of Asia?

It was a powerful incentive. Since the travels of Marco Polo, Europeans had obsessed about the wealth of the East. In the thirteenth century marauding Mongol armies had swept across Asia into Europe, causing devastation but making safe, in their wake, the ancient trade routes. For a period, intrepid Europeans like Polo made epic journeys to the East and returned with tales which stirred wonder and envy – of a rich civilisation they called Cathay and of a land presided over by the 'Great Chan [Khan]', on the edge of a distant ocean, whose markets overspilled with valuable goods. To try to get there, men felt, was no folly. This was not 'Utopia' or some similar imaginary place. On the contrary, wrote one explorer and sea captain, 'it is a country, well known to be described and set forth by all modern Geographers'.[4]

Meanwhile, far off Asia's eastern shore, Marco Polo had written, lay the island of 'Cipangu' – Japan. He had not visited it himself, but was assured that gold was to be found there 'in measureless quantities'. Precious stones abounded, and pearls were so numerous they were buried with the dead. The palace of the ruler was of 'incalculable richness', roofed with gold as Europeans would use lead, the floors of its halls and chambers tiled in thick, glowing slabs of the same metal. No one, he claimed, could count the island's riches. No wonder that covetous Europeans yearned to visit.[5]

By the fifteenth century, however, access to the East by land was closed off. The Mongol Empire had fragmented. A more nationalistic China had turned in on itself, refusing any longer to welcome foreign visitors. The rise of the Ottoman Empire had placed another great barrier between West and East. Europeans who set out on the path taken by their predecessors failed to return. Muslim middlemen again controlled the flow, as well as the profits, of exotic products, leaving merchants of Venice or Genoa – men like John Cabot – to collect them from Alexandria or from ports on the Black Sea.

For Europeans, the incentive grew for a new and easier ocean route to the East. The Portuguese responded by launching voyages down the west coast of Africa, into the face of unfavourable winds and unfavourable currents, trusting that it would bend northward.[6] In their search for a navigable route to the Orient, they developed the technology of seafaring. A few visionaries like Columbus and Cabot, meanwhile, dreamed of getting to the East by sailing west.

The idea was not controversial in theory. Most educated men had long believed the world to be round. In ancient Greece Aristotle had noticed the fact that different stars were visible in Egypt, say, compared with further north – a phenomenon which would not occur were the earth a flat surface. During the Middle Ages, men like Bede in England, or Dante in Italy, assumed as much. The voyages by the Portuguese down the African coast from early in the fifteenth century accumulated further empirical evidence. But it was controversial in its practicability. How vast was the ocean that men would have to cross?[7]

To many it seemed too rash an enterprise. Columbus was turned away, in Lisbon, and in London too, where the cautious and tight-fisted Henry VII listened sympathetically but politely demurred, laughing in private 'at all that Columbus had said'.[8] Eventually, however, Columbus did persuade the Spanish monarchs to support him. And once word of his success had gripped the courts of Europe, others were bound to follow.

Working in Spain himself, John Cabot yearned to make the same attempt. He was in Valencia, in 1493, when Columbus passed through, on his triumphant return to the royal court: watching, and questioning whether Columbus had really reached Asia as he claimed. For at least a year Cabot was then in Seville, working on an ill-fated project to build a new river bridge, before coming to England. He was a poor man, pursued by Venetian creditors whom he was trying to escape, but he was helped by influential clerics among the Italian community in London.[9]

Now, all of a sudden, he found a warm welcome at the Tudor court. As an old man, John's son Sebastian, who had travelled with his father as a teenage boy, recalled the time, 'many years since', when his father had moved to England 'to follow the trade of merchandises'. There, he remembered, men talked eagerly of Columbus' feat. 'With great admiration' they had 'affirmed it to be a thing more divine than human, to sail by the West into the East where spices grow'. He still recalled his first visit to the English capital, not long after Henry Tudor had defeated Richard III at the Battle of Bosworth and established the dynasty that bore his name. My father 'took me with him to the city of London', he wrote, 'while I was very young'.[10] It was lost on the boy, but it was the dawn, in England then, of a new age, which men hoped would end the warfare and instability that had haunted the country for decades.

Sensing the direction of the wind, King Henry now wanted a piece of the momentous new discoveries for himself. His realm of England lay at the end of the passage of goods from the far east of Eurasia to the west, and as such it paid the most inflated prices. Offered another chance, Henry jumped at it. There was in England, the Spanish ambassador wrote urgently home, 'a man like Columbus', who was helping the country with 'another undertaking like that of the Indies'.[11]

Henry was careful to treat his Italian navigator well. He lavished praise on his 'well-beloved John Cabot, citizen of Venice'. He granted his licence to him as well as to Cabot's son Sebastian, his two other sons and their heirs, lending his royal blessing to this attempt to discover any islands, countries or provinces of the heathen or the infidel 'which before this time have been unknown to all Christians'. He could not afford to support Cabot financially as the Catholic monarchs had supported Columbus. Bravely, Cabot sailed with only one small ship. But Henry did grant him the right to govern and exploit any new lands. He could trade with England duty-free, and need only pay the crown a fifth of 'the Capital gain so gotten'.[12]

Cabot settled in Bristol, the thriving seaport on England's west coast which had a tradition of voyaging into the Atlantic. He made one attempt which did not succeed because the spring winds blew, as they generally did, from the west. But in 1497, late in May, he tried again. He sailed 'north and then west', striking into open water from the south-western corner of Ireland. After tacking determinedly for another thirty-three days, early in the morning of 24 June he hit the undiscovered island off the coast of America which would bear the apt and lasting name: Newfoundland.

He sailed along the coast. He saw tall trees, rocky headlands and fields he suspected were cultivated. He was blanketed in impenetrable Newfoundland fogs. Briefly, and nervously, he went onshore, unfurling a Tudor banner to place the land rather insecurely under the aegis of England's Christian King. But though there were some signs of human life, he met no people, and can have found little to convince him he had struck the eastern shores of Asia. Along the underwater 'banks', where shellfish congregated, his crew found thick and valuable seams of cod, scooped up in writhing baskets from the side of the ship. But there was no wealthy civilisation: no spices, or fine silks.

Undaunted, he skimmed back on the westerly wind to assure a grateful King that he had landed in the realm of the 'Great Khan'. This was the land he expected to find, the land he fervently *hoped* to find, and so the land – pending contrary evidence – he believed he had found.

Only hours after he arrived back in Bristol, to an ecstatic welcome by local men and women crowded on the town wharf, John Cabot set off again, continuing east on the old road to London.

There, on 10 August, he had a conference with Henry VII. And though he could not on this occasion produce gold or spices, or even exotic flora and fauna, he did assure the King that he had fulfilled his ambition. He was plausible and persuasive. Brandishing the map and globe he had made himself, he showed where he had been. 'He tells all this in such a way,' one ambassador wrote home, 'and makes everything so plain, that I also feel compelled to believe him.' Mariners from Bristol who had sailed with him, moreover, 'testified that he spoke the truth'.[13]

Rewards and annuities followed, awarded 'to him that found the new Isle'. A pension was granted, 'to sustain himself until the time comes when more will be known of this business'. Cabot, though, believed that much greater wealth would follow. To a poor man, bad with money, £10 was a significant sum, and he quickly squandered it on expensive clothes.[14] He basked in widespread adoration. The common people, it was reported, called him the Admiral, and pursued him 'like madmen' through the streets. Half-drunk with the acclaim, he showered his friends with islands, and bishoprics, in this new world.

Plans for a second voyage were quickly made, and the next year Cabot set off west again. This time he went with five ships, a massive undertaking for early Tudor England. With the additional men and equipment at his disposal, he planned to establish a trading station which, he assured one ambassador, would make London 'a more important mart for spices than Alexandria'. He imagined coasting southward, along what he took to be the Asian shore, until he reached the island of Japan, where, the same ambassador reported, 'he thinks all the spices of the world have their origin, as well as the jewels'. His dream seemed, finally, so close. One of the five ships was forced by a storm to seek shelter in Ireland. It has been claimed that Cabot, at least, did reach America, and that he sailed south as he had anticipated, meeting Spanish explorers by the coast of modern-day Venezuela. But this time neither Cabot himself nor any of the remaining four ships returned, and nor did word of what happened to them. It was assumed, as one naturalised Englishman wryly observed, that Cabot had 'found the new lands nowhere but on the very bottom of the ocean'.[15]

Failing to find Cathay, or Japan, as he had hoped, he perhaps began to doubt. But probably, like Columbus, Cabot died believing he had achieved his aim: that he had sailed west across the ocean and landed in Asia.

Two

It was left to John Cabot's son, Sebastian, who had sailed west across the Atlantic with his father and who sailed that way again late in Henry VII's reign after his father had died, to confirm a growing suspicion. The new land was not Asia, or an island off its shore, but a new land mass. A passage through it would have to be sought, if England was to access the riches of the East.[1]

Many since have criticised Sebastian. It has been argued that he tried to claim for himself what was his father's achievement. As a young man he probably was jealous of his father's undoubted claim to fame. But in the world map to which he later contributed, and on which rare words of his own survive, he was open. 'This country', the legend by Newfoundland reads, 'was discovered by John Cabot, a Venetian, and Sebastian Cabot, his son.' It was Sebastian himself who ensured that John's role was remembered.[2]

Sebastian was prone to self-importance, and to affecting secret knowledge. Like his father, he was influenced, throughout his life, by offers of money, being perennially short of it himself. He was a cosmopolitan: willing to declare a national allegiance as circumstances, and offers, suited. His promises and declarations, more than one ambassador found, were not worth much. But he was of an optimistic and humane disposition. He was encouraging to younger sailors whose skills and aptitude he admired. And his undoubted skill was genuinely respected by important men, who fought hard to gain, or to retain, his services.

Cabot did yearn, all his life, to perform some truly memorable feat of his own, just as his father had done, by which his place in the history of seafaring would be secured: as a chapter, not a footnote. 'There increased in my heart,' he later professed, 'a great flame of desire to attempt some notable thing.'[3] He followed this ambition as surely as he did his financial concern. It shaped his life.

After his father's death, when he was in his twenties, Sebastian Cabot returned to the American coast. He sailed twice, as chief navigator, first in 1504 and then again in 1508–9. He was rewarded by Henry VII for the service he had done 'about the finding of the new found lands to our full good pleasure'.[4] Crucially, he seems to have realised, as his father had not done, that the land he saw was not Asia, but was an entirely new continent. He probably believed that a passage through America existed, and that, sailing into the vast expanse of Hudson Bay, he had found it. But when he returned to England, he learned that the King who had backed his family's ventures had died.

All of a sudden the focus among the English elite had changed. Where Henry VII had been captivated by global exploration, his son dreamed of military glory in Europe, and 'cared little for such an enterprise'.[5] Cabot's home town of Bristol, meanwhile, had fallen on hard times. The infectious maritime activity and ambition which had existed at the turn of the century had filtered away.

Elsewhere in England there was no interest in exploring the wider world. Foreigners – 'merchant strangers' – dominated the country's trade, and their power and privileges provoked resentment. In London they congregated in enclaves known as 'liberties', independently administered by Church authorities, as well as in the suburbs that sprouted and flourished beyond the city's walls. Like any immigrants, they headed for areas where their co-nationals had settled, creating pockets richly coloured by the culture of a particular region. French, Spanish, Portuguese, North Germans, Genoans, Venetians: all bunched together, tightly controlling certain trades and contemptuous of the unsophisticated islanders for whose needs and appetites they catered.[6]

If travel broadens the mind, the lack of it certainly constrained those of sixteenth-century Englishmen. As the practice of overseas trade languished in early Tudor England, so too did the state of geographical knowledge. At the time when the Portuguese and Spanish in particular were sailing increasing distances across the sea, and acquiring a greater knowledge of lands outside Europe, in England as a whole (in spite of the early Bristol ventures) a medieval geography still prevailed. The world was routinely divided into three conjoined parts: Europe, Asia and Africa. Of the last two, only the nearest regions were at all familiar. Few remotely grasped the concept of a new world. The drumbeat of a later imperialism misleads us. England has not always ruled the waves, nor distinguished itself as a seafaring nation. Later in the sixteenth century, the editor, Richard Hakluyt, who made the subject the study of his life, lamented 'our former gross ignorance in marine causes'.[7]

Henry VII had seen the problem, and the urgent need for England to shift course. When he came to power, late in the fifteenth century, an Act of Parliament deplored the 'decay' of English shipping and what it called the 'idleness of the Mariners'. Attempts were made to help. Throughout Henry's reign a policy was pursued of penalising imports not brought to the country in English ships. After him, however, this legacy lapsed.[8]

Cabot remained in England for a few years after King Henry's death, earning what he could as a surveyor and maker of maps. His cartographic skill, learned from his father, was rare. It was still considered worthy of comment sometime later that he could 'make cards for the sea with his own hand'.[9] But in the country in which he had grown up it was little valued. When he was employed, the nature of his appointed task spoke eloquently of the shift in focus.

In 1512 he accepted a government commission. He was to make a chart of Gascony and Guienne, in support of an invasion of western France.[10] When the English fleet which formed part of this expedition moored in Spain, Cabot slipped away. He travelled to meet a Spanish King who, by contrast with his Tudor son-in-law, was only too keen to employ a man with personal knowledge of what he called 'the island of the Codfish'. Even when Cabot subsequently returned to Bristol to collect his family and effects, no attempt was made to persuade him to stay.

Three

Approaching thirty, Cabot now settled in Seville, living there just as he may have done with his father almost two decades earlier. The city was much changed. It seemed suddenly to have relocated: from the world's western edge, it had moved to its centre. It had become the pulsing commercial heart of Spain's new empire in the lands to the west they called the Indies.

As well as the countless ships which pursued the old European trades, life was now governed by the rhythm of the great fleets. In the spring, cannon fire reverberated across the city, to proclaim the imminent departure of ships laden and bound for the New World. On their return, rich cargoes were brought upriver in barges, unloaded onto ox carts in front of curious crowds, then wheeled through the city streets to the *Casa de Contratación*: the 'House of Trade'. Silver in Seville, it was said, ran as freely as copper did in other parts.

For Cabot, the contrast with the apathy in England was stark. Here, he was immediately granted a post, a house and a salary.[1]

There were familiar faces in his new home. Living in Seville was a substantial English émigré community made up, largely, of merchants from Bristol.

For years England's western port had defied the country's general failure to reach out. Long before the arrival of John Cabot and his sons, men from the town caught fish off Iceland and traded it, along with English cloth, for the fruits, wines, oils and dyes of Spain, Portugal and southern France. Riding the high Avon tides out of the walled and battlemented town, Bristol ships pushed south-west into the Atlantic, before turning east to the hot southern rim of Andalusia. They entered the marshy estuary of Spain's only navigable river, the Guadalquivir, and transferred their goods into flat-bottomed barges for the journey upriver to Seville. When Cabot arrived, it was friends from Bristol who lent him money and gave him a hand.[2]

Among them was Robert Thorne. As a small boy, Thorne was probably part of the crowd that gathered on the bank of the Avon, squeezing through the well-dressed legs of city dignitaries to catch a glimpse of the Cabots – a father and his sons – returning in triumph from their epic voyage across the Atlantic. It seems likely that Robert's father was involved in some way. Certainly the Thornes were among Bristol's most eminent families.

As boys and young men, Robert and Sebastian knew each other well, and had much in common in spite of being a few years apart in age. Thorne, like Cabot, grew up surrounded by merchants and explorers, and by impassioned conversation about the unfolding geography of the globe. Full of natural energy and curiosity, he inherited intellectual interests as well as commercial ones: they ran in his blood. Just as some sicknesses were hereditary and were passed from father to son, he later wrote, so a burning desire to discover 'I inherited of my father'.[3]

When he was a young man, Thorne had moved to Seville to take over his late father's business, and he lived there, in his father's old house, with his Spanish mistress and their son. As well as with traditional areas, he traded with the Spanish New World, and was enriched, as Spain was enriched, by the forging there of new trades. He was successful, and became one of the leading members of the émigré community. A visiting English ambassador called him a merchant 'of great credence' in Seville.[4] Though he longed to explore, as Sebastian and his father had done, Thorne did not travel much himself. Physically, he was incapacitated in some way, and perhaps the reference to hereditary sickness was not purely metaphorical. If only he had the faculty to equal his will, he wrote, he would certainly attempt to pursue his ideas.

Cabot, meanwhile, thrived. His expertise was recognised and nurtured. Charles, the young King who inherited the thrones of the Spanish kingdoms from his grandfather in 1516, was impressed, and showed him lasting trust and loyalty.

Cabot climbed rapidly. In spite of being a foreigner, only six years after he arrived in Spain he was made the empire's Pilot Major: its head of navigation. He had responsibility for training the pilots who crossed the wide sea to colonies in the Caribbean and southern America. From a position of little consequence in England, a country which was itself of little consequence, he now had oversight of all of the trade and exploration of a great empire.[5]

Four

While some expats became effectively Spanish, Robert Thorne always remained a patriotic Englishman. In his will he left bequests to charitable causes, and invested in his country's commercial future, with money for loans to clothiers, for a grammar school in Bristol (which he had worked to found during the last year of his life), and to establish a scholarship at the Merchant Taylors' school in London.

All his adult life, Thorne yearned to push England onto the path he had seen Spain travel. Like the Spanish, he believed, the English must pioneer new trade routes to flourish. Their position as an off-shore island was ideal and the new wealth of the Indies lay there to be tapped.

If he could not explore in person, he would do so in his imagination. For hours he pored over the maps he was able to see which showed both recently discovered lands (with varying accuracy) and the continuing gaps in men's knowledge of the world.[1] Gradually, during the early 1520s, an idea took root and developed. The Spanish and Portuguese had explored to the south, the west and the east, and in doing so they had established routes of trade and pillage which they considered theirs alone to exploit. In 1494 the Pope himself had blessed the division of the world between the two countries. But they had made no attempt to voyage north. The English might do so, Thorne believed, and still make for the riches of the East.

They had sailed already, of course, west across the northern Atlantic. If they were to sail more directly north, over the Pole, he became convinced that sailors could descend towards the Equator on the further side of the new-found lands. Provided this proved practicable, as he felt sure it would, England's mariners would be in a powerful position. For by this route, as was obvious if one studied a globe, they would hit the equatorial islands of the Pacific by 'a much shorter way than either the Spaniards or Portuguese have'.

This, surely, was a path to riches which divine providence itself had marked out for the English.

In 1526 Sebastian Cabot organised, and himself led, a Spanish attempt to retrace the pioneering course taken by a Portuguese explorer, Fernando Magellan, who had sailed (and died) in Spanish service less than a decade earlier: west across the Atlantic, beneath the Americas, and on across the Pacific to the Spice Islands in the East.

The voyage was some time in the planning, and Thorne discussed it with Cabot and became involved. As a wealthy merchant and leading member of the English community in Seville, he made a substantial investment, and secured in return the participation of two of his English friends, Roger Barlow and Henry Patmer, who shared his intellectual interests.

While the Spanish wanted an immediate financial return, Thorne sought knowledge. He charged his friends to interrogate local mariners wherever they visited, and to seek to understand the maps that they used. They should try, he told them, to become 'expert in the navigation of those seas'. In particular his eye was on a route down into the Pacific region from the north, and he urged both men to discover what native peoples knew of the geography north of their own lands.

The voyage was not a success. After the flagship sank, the others diverted to explore a river estuary in what is now Argentina, and never made it into the Pacific. But if Thorne was disappointed, his natural optimism soon revived.

While Barlow and Patmer were away, a visit was paid to Seville by an ambassador of Henry VIII, Dr Edward Lee. Lee spent time with the leading Englishmen of the city, and the ebullient Thorne, then in his mid-thirties, made a significant impression. When Lee wrote home he mentioned in particular 'a right toward young man as any lightly belongeth to England called Thorne'.

Thorne seized the opportunity to talk to someone with access to the heart of English government. He spoke passionately about the geography of the world beyond Europe, expounding the theories he had developed in conversation with other Bristol sailors and merchants about how England could obtain its share of the wealth which flowed into Spain and Portugal from the Indies. Lee listened with genuine interest.

When, a few months later, Lee wanted to know more about a dispute between Spain and Portugal over their division of the newly discovered world, it was Thorne he turned to for information. What, he asked, was the significance of the Spanish Emperor's new spice trade in eastern Asia? Where did this leave English hopes for a share of the new wealth? Thorne was more than happy to oblige, and he wrote the ambassador a long letter. There was no doubt, he told Lee, that the newly discovered islands had riches in profusion. They had spices: 'Cloves, Nutmegs, Mace and Cinnamon'. And they abounded with precious metals and stones.[2]

Like most geographers and merchants of his day, Thorne believed that metals and stones, like grains or spices, were influenced by the action of heat in tropical climates. As English metals were lead, tin and iron, he wrote, 'so theirs be Gold, Silver, and Copper'. As northern conditions fostered stones like amber, crystal or jasper, so the warmth further south nurtured rubies, diamonds, sapphires 'and other like'. As Thorne's friend Roger Barlow later wrote, it was 'the influence of the sun' which 'doth nourish and bring forth gold, spices, stones and pearls'.[3]

While English ships could not follow the courses pioneered and jealously guarded by the Iberians, who by the Treaty of Tordesillas in 1494 had blithely carved up the new lands of the world between them, they did have another option. Not only did they have some claim to the lands across the northern Atlantic, which they had discovered first. They could also sail further north. Crossing the Pole and sailing down into the Pacific from above, they would not have to make for places already frequented by other Europeans. In these vast waters they would easily find new lands 'no less rich of gold and spicery'. Since the distance around the earth was greater at the Equator than on any parallel line of latitude, there must, it stood to reason, be no lack of lands rich in those commodities which abounded under a hot sun. Natives in these distant regions attached no great value to wares which fetched high prices in Europe. Why should they? It was only natural for people to prize what they did not have over what they had in abundance: 'I doubt not but to them should be as precious our corn and seeds, if they might have them, as to us their spices: & likewise the pieces of glass that here we have counterfeited are as precious to them, as to us their stones: which by experience is seen daily by them that have trade thither.'

Thorne's optimism and excitement were obvious. They spoke not only of a man of natural enthusiasm but also of one who for years had lived in Seville, who had often watched as ships returned bearing news and evidence of great wealth in unknown lands, and who was used to mixing with men and women for whom dramatic discoveries had for decades been the context of their lives.

He had a vantage point, here, on the edge of the old world, before which a new world was unfolding whose possibilities seemed almost limitless.

If the English could only establish it, there would be yet another advantage to such a northern route. On their way to and from the Pole merchants would pass cold lands which, while they could not offer exotic produce or precious stones, would provide excellent markets for those English woollen cloths which were unlikely to sell well under an equatorial sun. These cold regions, he argued, should be just as profitable for England as the Spice Islands were to the Spanish and Portuguese.

There was an obvious objection, of course, and it was not one that Thorne could afford to ignore. To sail north across the polar regions of the earth would involve all the risks and obstructions associated with a bitter climate. Here Thorne was bold enough to defy conventional wisdom.

Most experts believed, he wrote, that in the extreme north 'the sea is all ice, and the cold so great that none can suffer it'.[4] But if the Spanish and Portuguese experience in the tropics showed anything, he argued, it was that too much store should not be set by received opinions. Ancient authorities had insisted that the heat in the south was too extreme to permit human habitation, while experience had shown otherwise. In fact, Thorne exaggerated, no land was more habitable or temperate than that in the equatorial zone.

The same, he assured Dr Lee, would prove to be the case in the north. In Thorne's letter, the providentialism which would come to shape the mindset of the British Empire is already apparent. Nothing in nature had been made to go to waste. The world had 'no land unhabitable, nor sea innavigable'. England, by its position, had been offered a special role in God's plan, if it would only seize it.

To illustrate his claims, Thorne attached a rudimentary map (not one, he admitted, 'for Pilots to sail by'). It was probably based upon a map or maps he had seen surreptitiously at the *Casa de Contratación*, where Spain's accumulated geographical knowledge was kept a closely guarded secret, but where Thorne's connection to Cabot gave him a priceless link.[5]

Certainly Thorne knew what risks he was taking. In Spain none but appointed specialists were permitted to draw maps of the world, and the sort of information he discussed was banned from public conversation. He anxiously passed on the warning to Dr Lee. 'It would not sound well to them', he cautioned, 'that a stranger should know or discover the secrets: and would appear worst of all, if they understand that I write touching the short way to the spicery by our seas.' If the Spanish authorities knew that he had written as he had, and drawn the map he had, it would be 'a cause of pain to the maker'.

From surviving printed copies, it is clear both how much progress had been made since Columbus first hit land in the Caribbean a little over three decades earlier, and also how much remained obscure. Much that is featured on the map – eastern Asia, for instance, or the northeastern coastline of America – is a mixture of recognisable forms and wild approximation.

Equally significant are the map's northern and western edges, which slice through the mainland of north America before it has reached a coast. While south and central America are outlined, with a 'Mare Australe' or 'southern sea' beyond, no information indicated how far north or west the northern land mass extended, though it was certainly now considered a separate continent, for the eastern edge of Asia is clearly, if speculatively, drawn.

Thorne's idea is plain. Alongside the eastern seaboard of America, which rises directly upwards to the north rather than bearing north-east, a wide channel of open sea seems to allow passage over the Pole. While many writers had supposed that a bridge of land or ice in the extreme north connected the new world with the old – for how else had people and animals got to America? – Spanish maps seen by Thorne tended to mark only those coastlines known to exist.[6] So the way looked open. And once ships had descended into the Pacific, they would surely discover new spice islands in the ocean, and could make for the eastern shores of Cathay, by a route shorter and (Thorne argued) easier than that taken by the Portuguese.

Thorne was willing to take risks in passing information to Lee because it was a subject about which he cared deeply. He stressed that he was not motivated by personal interest. This was a private enthusiasm which had gripped him since youth, as it had his father before him, and in whose clutches he remained. 'I have had and still have', he wrote, 'no little mind of this business.' If he were able, he assured Lee, he would attempt the exploration himself.

In subsequent years, Thorne continued to promote the idea of discovery to the north. A couple of years after he wrote to Henry VIII's ambassador, he and his friend Roger Barlow tried a more direct approach. They composed a shorter, more formal letter and sent it this time to the King himself.[7]

They played on Henry's known ambition and his desire for famous triumphs. Other monarchs had pressed outward, they noted, and made possible things which previously had seemed impossible. No effort would seem too much 'where so great honour and glory is hoped for'. In the modern age, it would be strange to find a prince happy 'to live quiet [within] his own dominions'. No people would wish for such a risk-averse ruler. They would think he lacked the 'noble courage and spirit' possessed by others.

Together Thorne and Barlow reiterated the plan which Thorne had outlined to Dr Lee, for a voyage which sailed due north, over the Pole, through what they felt sure would be open sea. They did now admit what Thorne had not previously admitted, that for a short distance – two or three leagues before they reached the Pole, and as much afterwards – conditions might be difficult and dangerous. But these hazards were surmountable, and were worth braving, since in other respects the route would be both shorter and easier than those undertaken by the Spanish and Portuguese. 'From thence forth', they assured Henry, 'the seas and lands are as temperate as in these parts.'

There was a notable advantage, moreover, to which Thorne had not alluded in his original letter. If the expedition was undertaken in summer, as it naturally would be, any risk would be mitigated by almost perpetual daylight. Sailors would not have to 'go in darkness groping their way'. Once they had passed through this region of sunlit nights, and descended into the warm tropical zone, 'without doubt', Thorne and Barlow declared, 'they shall find there the richest lands and islands of the world', replete with 'gold, precious stones, balms, spices, and other things that we here esteem most'. Their timing, however, was unfortunate. By the late 1520s, Henry was absorbed in the fall-out from his determination to divorce his Spanish Queen in quest of a legitimate male heir. In Seville, as a direct consequence, the position of the English deteriorated.

England's long-standing alliance with Spain, cemented by Henry's marriage to Catherine of Aragon, the aunt of the Spanish King, was torn apart. The English heresy which unseated the Pope from his position at the head of the Church was angrily condemned by the Spanish, and pursued by the Inquisition. Merchants living in Spain faced imprisonment, interrogation and torture if they were unguarded in their speech.[8]

Thorne and Barlow, like others among the English community in southern Spain, had substantial local interests. Both owned land and invested in numerous trading concerns. Suddenly, however, there was too much to lose by remaining in Seville, and both made plans to return to England.

There is no evidence that Henry ever read the address they had written to him.

Five

Thorne did not only return to England. Soon after getting back, he left his old home in the West Country and relocated to the capital. By 1532, three years after his letter to King Henry, Thorne is described as a 'citizen and merchant of London'. As London boomed, provincial outports like Bristol struggled to compete. For the ambitious and commercially minded, the capital, increasingly, was the only place to be.

Thorne's enthusiasm for mounting a voyage of northern discovery remained strong. Prior to leaving for England he had bought an English ship that had been marketed for sale in Spain. The *Saviour* had been registered at Bristol and was, as his younger brother attested, the 'greatest and best' ship built in the West of England.

Too large for Bristol's regular trades with France and Spain, Thorne thought her well suited for the expedition of which he had dreamed for so long. He wished, his brother later wrote to the King, 'to have come into this your said realm to give your grace relation of countries to be discovered and by the same ship and others intended through your grace's aid to discover and [seek] new countries'. Excited now that the launch of his great exploit seemed imminent, it was in the *Saviour* that Thorne sailed to England.[1]

Thorne continued to seek support from central government. In London he spoke with Thomas Cromwell, who from undistinguished origins was rapidly becoming the most important man in England beneath the King. He talked to Cromwell, as he had talked to Dr Lee, and others he could trust, of 'countries to be discovered', and requested royal backing for the voyage which might allow other ships to join the *Saviour* in its attempt. Cromwell had lived and worked in trading circles during his youth, and had an affinity with merchants. He might well have wished to help. But he had his hands full. He was in the midst of managing what became known as the 'Reformation Parliament', which asserted Henry's position as 'the only head, sovereign lord, protector, and defender' of the English Church.

Nevertheless, this disappointment did not put a brake on Thorne's plans. He was a wealthy man, and could afford to fund the venture himself. His old friend from Bristol and Seville, Roger Barlow, had evidently agreed to take charge, and a window for departure seems to have been arranged, for Barlow had requested and obtained exemption from civic duties in his home town of Bristol.

Suddenly, however, on 5 May 1532, as his great project finally neared realisation, Robert Thorne died. The instigator, financier and driving force of the expedition was only forty, relatively young even then for an affluent man who had reached adulthood. We don't know what caused his death; perhaps it was the chronic ill health which had prevented him taking a direct part in expeditions, an ailment he had long known himself to be carrying. Whatever it was, without Thorne's money and energy, the enterprise lost momentum and was shelved.

For Roger Barlow, his friend's death was a massive blow. He was both intellectual and willing to be practically involved, but he was not dynamic in the way that Thorne had been. He retired to his family estate in Pembrokeshire and absorbed himself in academic pursuits.

Barlow set himself to translate from Spanish a work of world geography – the *Suma de Geographia*, of Martin Fernández de Enciso – that was permeated with a revolutionary ethos which now, belatedly, began to seep into England: the conviction that what mattered was not so much ancient authority as the acquisition of knowledge based on personal experience. Appropriately enough, in sections where he knew better, when the text talked for instance of the Bristol Channel or the Pembrokeshire coast, he used his own material. And at the end, when he considered such lands as remained to be discovered, he inserted a reworked version of the address he and Thorne had composed years earlier, calling again for an English attempt to find a new northern route to the East.[2]

It was not published, as he had hoped, but Barlow's book was put before the Privy Council. Now, almost a decade after Thorne's death, the timing was good. Rumours had been picked up that the French were planning a similar venture, and this, as always, was a certain prompt for action. The argument Thorne and Barlow had made regarding a new outlet for English exports in the north was also attractive. The Spanish ambassador, who listened to reports from his secret sources, remained alert to encroachment on his country's trades. The Councillors, he wrote, hoped that the 'extreme cold' in these northern regions would mean that 'English woollen cloths would be very acceptable and sell at a good price'.

A foreign pilot was found, but in the course of negotiations over terms, he was deemed to be too demanding. English alternatives did not exist. 'In the end', the Spanish ambassador reported, 'the undertaking has been abandoned.'[3]

One man who noticed the fatal dependence of this English expedition on a foreign pilot was the Vice-Admiral. Shortly to be promoted to Lord Admiral, John Dudley's career had progressed slowly but suddenly took off. Over the subsequent years he came to exert a crucial influence on England's maritime policy, and would become one of the most powerful politicians in the country.

Dudley was a man who reflected his times. He was a Protestant – eagerly embracing the new religious ideology which had torn deep divisions across Europe since a monk from Saxony, Martin Luther, first nailed his Ninety-Five Theses to the door of Wittenberg castle church, more than twenty years earlier. Dudley was an energetic dealer in property, for its financial returns rather than any attempt to develop a regional power base. He also endeared himself to the King by his military skills, one Frenchman hailing him as 'the most skilful of his generation, both on foot and on horseback'. And he shared Henry's new-found passion for the navy. His enthusiasm for oceanic exploration was a significant boost to those like Barlow who pushed for a more forward policy.[4]

The lack of English mariners with modern seafaring skills was becoming a recognised problem. The majority of both pilots and regular sailors on Henry VIII's ships were foreigners. As the French ambassador noted, they were a colourful mixture of Ragusans (from Dubrovnik), Venetians, Genoese, Normans or Bretons.[5] Dudley encouraged such skilled immigrants. When the French King exposed Protestants in his realm to persecution, Dudley successfully lured hundreds more sailors, shipbuilders and craftsmen from the maritime towns of Normandy and Brittany. These were men who could man English ships and, he hoped, encourage Englishmen to acquire their skills.

There remained a need, however, for someone with long experience of navigation and exploration who could oversee England's mercantile activity: someone senior and authoritative enough to advise the King's Council, and to organise voyages which would encourage merchants to attempt new trades. Not long after Dudley took up his role as Vice-Admiral, one such man did express an interest in coming back to the land which had sponsored his earliest ocean ventures.

Six

Since returning in 1532 from the unsuccessful expedition on which Roger Barlow had sailed, Sebastian Cabot had been unhappy in Spanish service. There had been investigations into his conduct, both on that voyage and in the execution of his duties as Pilot Major. He retained the strong confidence of the Emperor, and a sentence of exile was never carried out. But ongoing political and professional rivalries within the *Casa de Contratación* blighted his working life. Many in Spain had undertaken long voyages and thought they knew the business of cartography and navigation. Entrenched schools of thought feuded bitterly over both theory and policy.[1]

Cabot mused how in England, by contrast, there would be few to rival his experience or to question his authority. He was pragmatic enough to profess the national loyalty which suited the occasion and the company. But he had grown up in England, was comfortable with Englishmen, and does seem to have considered himself English. His daughter Elizabeth was the child of his first marriage to a woman called Joanna from London, while Elizabeth herself had grown up and married Henry Ostrich, an Englishman who came from another family of Bristol merchants prominent among the expat community in Spain. Cabot had made known his willingness to return to work for the English if the circumstances, and the terms, were right.

In 1538 Cabot again put out feelers regarding a possible move back to his old country. He approached an ambassador of Henry VIII's, who eagerly sent word of his conversation home. The Pilot Major was 'desirous', the ambassador reported, 'if he might not serve the [English] king, at least to see him, as his old master'. Needless to say, given Cabot's nature, money was discussed, and the ambassador was quick to note an affordable opportunity for England to poach a key figure in Spain's commercial empire, if prompt action was taken.[2]

John Dudley, who had recently taken up his post as Vice-Admiral, was sent out briefly that year to take part in the Spanish mission. He was probably introduced to Spain's Pilot Major then; certainly, he learned a great deal more about him. He must have been impressed, for he would promote the famous navigator for the rest of his life.

Circumstances, as it turned out, were not propitious in 1538 for Cabot to jump ship.

Though the English ambassador had requested an urgent response from his own government, none seems to have been forthcoming. Henry VIII still had more interest in the damage his growing navy could inflict on French galleys off the English coast than in pushing his country's commerce into new waters. After twenty years of peace, renewed war in the final years of his reign with the old enemies, France and Scotland, meant that the nation's best ships were needed at home.

From Cabot's point of view, too, compelling arguments existed against an immediate move – even if he had made the initial exploratory contact. For one thing, France and the Empire had made terms and stood united against the English, who cannot have looked like a team worth joining. For another, Cabot's second – Spanish – wife, Catalina, was a strong-minded and overbearing woman, whose enthusiasm for relocating from Seville to a cold, wet offshore island in the north of the continent was probably slight.

Over the subsequent decade, however, the rise of Cabot's admirer, John Dudley, continued. As he worked to build up England's maritime capability, he may already have had in mind the recall of a man with the expertise to guide the country onto a new path. When Henry VIII died, at the end of January 1547, his son and successor Edward VI was still a young boy of nine. The Council's influence over policy became much more decisive than it had been under the tyrannical old king. Dudley, by then, was one of its most senior and influential figures, second only to the young King's uncle, Edward Seymour, who was appointed 'Governor of the King's Person', was officially recognised as the 'Lord Protector', and who made himself the Duke of Somerset.

Almost immediately, a secret invitation was despatched to Spain. In September that year Catalina died, removing a significant obstacle to her husband's relocation. Cabot was quick to respond. Within weeks the English Privy Council had authorised a payment of £100, 'for the transporting of one Shabot a pilot to come out of Hispain to serve and inhabit in England'. Cabot was not honest with his Spanish employers about his intentions. He planned, he said, 'to go to Germany' for personal reasons. He obtained a five-month leave of absence from Imperial service and delegated his duties as Pilot Major. In the event it was his son-in-law, Henry Ostrich, who claimed the payment for shipping Sebastian to England.[3]

By the time that Cabot returned to live in England, his enthusiastic supporter, John Dudley, had been replaced at the Admiralty. His successor, the brother of the Lord Protector, had little interest in maritime expansion, and none in Cabot. Realising where matters stood, the navigator retired to his old home town of Bristol. The situation, Dudley reassured him, was unlikely to last long.

Sure enough, after Thomas Seymour's rapid disgrace and execution, Dudley temporarily resumed charge of the Admiralty and immediately brought Cabot again to the attention of the Council, commending him as a 'good and expert pilot'.[4]

The Emperor, meanwhile, was furious that his Pilot Major – a man he had stood by through scandal and controversy – had absconded to England without his permission. The Imperial ambassador in England, François van der Delft, was repeatedly instructed to make enquiries, while English envoys at the Imperial court in Brussels were similarly browbeaten. Not only had Charles V always displayed a high opinion of Cabot, but over some thirty years at the heart of the *Casa de Contratación*, his Pilot Major had acquired an intimate knowledge of the Empire's commercial practices and secrets. It was no wonder that Charles persevered in his attempts to persuade him to return to Imperial service.

Cabot, the English were firmly told, was 'a very necessary man for the Emperor, whose servant he is'. He had not resigned his post but had applied only for a short period of leave. The Empire had continued to pay his salary, not ceasing to do so until November 1548, after it was known that he had in fact taken up residence in England. 'He must clearly understand', Charles wrote to his ambassador in London early in 1550, 'that we require his services, and claim a right to them.'

Cabot himself prolonged Imperial uncertainty by customary evasions designed to keep his options open. To van der Delft he gave the impression that he would like nothing better than to return to his work in Spain. 'He often comes to me secretly,' the ambassador reported, 'to ask me to write to your Majesty so that he may be delivered from this captivity.' Unsubtly, Cabot hinted that the Emperor might want to lure him back with a financial offer he could not refuse. 'Although they offer him high wages here,' noted van der Delft (for Cabot, clearly, had told him so), 'his only wish is to die in your Majesty's service.' This, though, was merely his accustomed gamesmanship. Cabot always made himself open to better offers. He tried, as a more cynical, and more astute, Imperial ambassador in England would note, 'to make his profit out of both sides'.[5]

In truth, barring exceptional reward for returning to Spain, Cabot was happy to remain in England. Whenever necessary he soon found someone in the English government ready to obstruct any move, or to declare him, if he did not declare himself, too weakened by ill health and old age to travel abroad.

It was an exaggeration for Cabot to claim that the English were paying him high wages, but it was true that the English Council had done their best, at Dudley's bidding, to induce him to remain. Early in January 1549 he was granted a generous annuity of more than £166 – equivalent to around £35,000 today.[6] It was backdated to be paid from the previous September when, presumably, the revered navigator and orchestrator of the naval enterprise of a great empire had arrived back in the country of his childhood, tasked with launching it on a global commercial stage.

Seven

Apart from a brief visit twenty-five years earlier, it was more than thirty-five years since Cabot had collected his family from Bristol and sailed south to work in a country more appreciative of his skills. Now, in 1548, in his mid-sixties at least, he had finally returned, and he found the place much changed.[1]

Shortly before he had left, a young and confident King had assumed the English throne. His Queen, the Spanish Catherine of Aragon, had recently given birth to a son – Henry, Duke of Cornwall – which had prompted widespread rejoicing. The heavens, it seemed, were smiling on the Tudor dynasty. Sadly, the boy died when he was six weeks old, but there was no reason not to anticipate many more children for the young and enamoured royal pair.

Now, though, Henry VIII had lived out his long and notorious reign, transforming England for ever in his desperate quest for a wife who could both provide a male heir and satisfy his increasingly unbalanced sense of self-worth. In the process, a country that was part of Catholic Europe had defied the authority of Rome. The self-interest of the King (and often of others too) had coincided with intellectual currents of reform. To the horror of Spain, Henry's one-time ally, England now sat on the other side of a deep religious divide which had riven the Continent.

Soon after his return to England Cabot came to live in his old home of Bristol. He must have had fond memories of the crowds who had turned out all those years ago to welcome him back, with his father, from new lands across the western ocean.

In general the 1490s and early 1500s had been a good time in Bristol. The town's ancient trade with Bordeaux, which had collapsed when that town was lost to the French, had been replaced by lucrative relationships with Spain and Portugal. English cloth was exchanged for the products of the south. Affluent families like the Thornes had revelled in what they called their 'feats of merchandises'.

Now, fifty years later, it was a shock to find a dilapidated shadow of the vibrant place he remembered. The local cloth trade on which Bristol depended had for decades been in a deep slump. Average exports were scarcely a third of what they had been. The artisans who worked to manufacture the cloth – the shearmen, carders, dyers and others – now congregated in London, and this was where great merchants like Robert Thorne had felt impelled to make their base. '[Many] tenements', the Mayor of Bristol had recently complained, 'are fallen into decay for want of timber and stones, and the quay and town walls are in like ruin.'[2]

Since Cabot was last there, moreover, a significant slice of English society – the black, grey, brown and white habits which had brushed the streets of all major towns – had disappeared. Government inspectors had visited the religious houses, looking for reasons to enforce closure. Monks and nuns vanished from the scene, taking with them a distinctive piece of the medieval world.

The achievements of Cabot and his family did remain a source of civic pride. But most of the men and women who might have remembered Cabot personally had died. With a few old men of the town he could sit and recall a time when great ships sailed from the Avon on two or three voyages every year. Now, the old residents told him sadly, they could at best make only one.[3] Ageing as he was, though, Cabot was not a man to live in the past. When he moved to London, his mind was full of ambitious plans. For all his notable achievements, he had not himself led or organised a truly momentous voyage, and the decision to leave his post in Seville was motivated in part by this desire.

Now in England, under a new and similarly ambitious government, he had another chance – probably his last – to make his mark.

Eight

E ven in the English capital, in terms of the maritime world that he knew, Cabot must have felt that he had travelled back in time, to a world barely touched by the great ocean trades which in Seville had been his daily life. Merchants and seamen he spoke to in England were quite unversed in scientific navigation on the open sea. There was a growing demand for Eastern luxuries, but commerce was still substantially controlled by foreigners, who lived in self-governing enclaves, in London and other cities, and who dominated ancient routes through the Baltic and the North Sea.

English merchants in London might call themselves 'Merchant Adventurers'. They *ventured* some money in joining what was effectively a guild. But the route they employed, overwhelmingly, was the short sea crossing to Antwerp. They were certainly not *adventurers* in any modern sense. Nevertheless, coming to London now, Cabot could sense a change of spirit.

In recent decades the capital had thrived and expanded, often at the expense of provincial ports like Bristol. Since Antwerp (part of the Spanish Habsburg sphere) had become the trading and banking centre of northern Europe, London had expanded alongside it. In the mid-fifteenth century the capital had been responsible for around half of England's cloth exports. A century later, when Cabot returned there, the figure was 90 per cent, and for other goods the story was the same. London was becoming the place that the local historian John Stow would call 'the principal store house, and Staple of all commodities within this Realm'.[1]

The country Cabot experienced during the first summer after his return was a febrile and unsettled place. The year 1549 saw unsurpassed turbulence in Tudor England. In July the scattered rural unrest of the previous year resurfaced across wide swathes of the south and Mid-lands. The young King Edward, only eleven that summer, recorded the alarming spread of the disturbances in his diary. 'The people began to rise in Wiltshire,' he wrote; 'they rose in Sussex, Hampshire, Kent, Gloucestershire, Suffolk, Warwickshire, Essex, Hertfordshire, a piece of Leicestershire, Worcestershire, and Rutlandshire'; 'after that they rose in Oxfordshire, Devonshire, Norfolk, and Yorkshire.'[2]

These were nervous times for both the court and the city of London. Artillery was positioned at the gates, while martial law was proclaimed within the walls.[3] It was only in the country's lateral extremities – in the south-west and Norfolk – that things really got out of control. And it was Cabot's chief patron, John Dudley, who gathered a force to march against the vast rebel camp near Norwich. After storming the city and executing the ringleaders, Dudley returned to London in September, fêted by the capital's relieved political hierarchy.

By October he felt strong enough to mount a coup against Edward Seymour, the 'Lord Protector', which passed off without bloodshed but which was another anxious time for all who frequented the court. When Seymour agreed to stand down, it was Dudley who inherited the mantle, though not the title, of Regent for the young King. For Cabot, if the violence and uncertainty had been unsettling, they had a positive outcome. His most powerful patron and ally had become the dominant political force in the country. As the Imperial ambassador observed, Dudley was 'absolute master' of the Council, and he was able more than ever to sponsor the promotion of men with new ideas.[4]

Ideologically, too, it was a time of passion and uncertainty. It was in 1549 that a new Prayer Book was introduced, less radical than its authors might have wished, but steering a more Protestant direction since the death of the old king. Those who hoped Dudley's coup would mark a conservative revival were disappointed. A proclamation disavowed any intention to restore the 'old Latin service' with its 'conjured bread and water [and] such like vain and superstitious ceremonies'.[5] Not only was Dudley a reformer at heart, but he knew his power depended on being close to the young King, who was growing, under the tutelage provided for him, into an ardent Protestant.

In matters of religion Cabot remained typically wily and reserved. He made professions of belief to please a current or prospective employer – like his statements of national allegiance. From long service in Catholic Spain, policed ruthlessly by the Inquisition, he moved to an increasingly Protestant England with no sign of compunction. He later advised merchants exploring in foreign climes to pass over their religious beliefs in silence. It was certainly a practice he himself had always followed.

More important to Cabot was that the bubbling of new religious ideas in England was accompanied by a zeal for new thinking in other areas.

Nine

In 1542 a young student of only fifteen years of age arrived at St John's College in Cambridge. He was, as a later admirer put it, a 'tall, slight youth, looking wise beyond his years, with fair skin, good looks and a bright colour'.[1] Over the next few years he worked, he later said, 'vehemently', for as much as eighteen hours a day. In addition to the core subjects of grammar, logic and rhetoric, he already showed a brilliant ability at mathematics, and this was allied to a technical ingenuity, displayed, for instance, in his love of creating astonishing effects for the plays he put on. While some were delighted, conservatives muttered darkly that he must be dabbling in magic. Mathematics itself, at which the young John Dee so excelled, was often considered one of the 'black arts'. It was a contentious issue: the year he came to Cambridge, an Act against Sorcery was passed by Parliament and not repealed until five years later.[2]

Dee had come to the right place. St John's College, and Cambridge in general, were renowned bastions of reformed thought. His tutor, Sir John Cheke, who marvelled at Dee's ability, was a Professor of Greek who was also a forthright advocate of what in England were only now becoming respectable branches of learning. In accordance with the syllabus which had been extensively revised by Cheke, Dee spent his first seven months at St John's studying geometry and arithmetic.[3]

From Cambridge Dee travelled to Europe in search of a scientific education which, to his frustration, was not available in England. He studied, during the early part of Edward VI's reign, at the University of Louvain, which he later called 'the fountain-head of learning'. There he befriended and was taught by the greatest minds of his day: the Portuguese mathematician Pedro Nunes and the brilliant geographer, cartographer and instrument-maker Gerard Mercator. When he returned to Cambridge Dee brought books, globes and instruments which had never been seen in England before and which helped to sow the seeds of an interest in astronomy and map-making.

In the summer of 1550, Dee left Louvain and travelled to Paris. Already famous, at only twenty-three he was invited to lecture on Euclid, the ancient 'father of geometry', which he did in a hall so packed that students thronged outside the windows to catch his words. To an audience mostly older than himself, he invoked the unique power of mathematics to straddle worlds – from the pure world of the intellect, where it seemed to offer access to the divine, to the elemental world of physical reality. The effect was electrifying.[4]

In the audience was a substantial group of Dee's English admirers, all connected in some way both to John Dudley and to Dee's Cambridge tutor, John Cheke, who had retired from his university job to mentor the young King, and who exerted a vast influence in spreading new ideas at court. When Dee returned to England, Cheke was among those who recommended him strongly to Edward. Nobody's opinion carried greater weight with the passionate young King, and he was instrumental in securing for Dee the generous annual pension he promptly received – evidence, as with the payments to Cabot, of a new determination to cling to talent that might be commercially useful.

John Dudley, meanwhile, was so impressed by Dee that he offered him a position in his household, as a tutor to his younger sons. Over the next couple of years Dee became intimate with Dudley and his circle, forming a warm relationship with his eldest son in particular. He saw much, too, of Henry Sidney, who had been in the audience at Dee's lecture in Paris, and who had recently married Dudley's daughter Mary.

It is not recorded when Sebastian Cabot first heard about or met John Dee. He could not have remained unaware of this intellectual star who was prompting so much talk among educated circles on the Continent, and who then returned to England, to the same group, presided over by John Dudley, in which Cabot moved. The two men shared what was an unusual appreciation of the importance of geometry and arithmetic in the art of making and interpreting charts. Both shared an intense interest in cartography, and the effort to discover what seas or lands lay in the unexplored spaces on world maps.

Maps were something with which Cabot had grown up. He had learned to represent reality on paper charts from his father, who was obsessed, as his son would be, by early attempts to map the globe. Sebastian's was a rare skill in Tudor England. It was partly because cartography was so little valued that he had departed for Spain, where the subject formed a major part of his specialist work. He must have found it hard to imagine a nation developing a seagoing commerce without these essential tools.

Maritime culture in England, however, had always managed without. At the end of Henry VIII's reign, men referred to 'the want and lack of expert learned men in that faculty of making cards or maps, and the scarcity ... of such cards within this realm of England'. Merchants clung to Europe's coasts and to short, familiar routes. Pilots relied on experience, and became acquainted over long years with particular seas, coasts and harbours. 'Rutters', as they were known, were written guides passed between seamen, or at least between those who could read. They recorded the information – compass bearings, landmarks, tide times, water depths, or the make-up of the seabed – that pilots used to follow familiar coastlines or to avoid rocky shoals in the estuary mouths of major rivers. On the rare occasions when experience of new regions was required, foreign pilots were employed.[5]

Cabot saw, however, that if England was to develop a culture of long-distance trade a major change was required. The country would need to produce not pilots but *navigators*: men who relied not on the familiarity born of long years on the same short routes, but who could find their way on the open ocean using maps, instruments and the stars.

Towards the end of Henry VIII's reign England had begun, at least, to appreciate the value of maps. Here again Cabot was fortunate to have returned to a country in transition. Within the realm, officials had begun to realise, geographical knowledge enhanced central power. Taxes could be better imposed and order more effectively maintained if the country was accurately mapped. Nevertheless, it must have been a shock to Cabot to find, still, a dearth of the sort of world maps he was used to creating and updating as Pilot Major in Spain. It was no wonder that

English seamen and merchants did not aspire to sail to distant lands, without the maps to fire their imaginations and their ambitions. Cabot saw what must be his first task. He must show the English how the expanded world could be represented on paper.

Cabot no longer had access to the Imperial world map that he had been accustomed to using in his office in Seville. A few years earlier, however – in 1544 – he had contributed to a world map based on French cartography, for which he had written some of the 'legends' annotating far-flung regions of the world. It was this which he now reissued, as a means of remedying England's lack. An assistant was recommended to him: a smart young academic from Cambridge called Clement Adams. Like Dee, Adams had been taught as a student by Cheke, and had become fascinated by the new science of geography. He leapt at the chance to work with Sebastian Cabot and remained close to Cabot and his circle for some years.

With Adams doing the engraving, the 1544 map was updated and reprinted. In a country where few had seen anything like it, it caused a sensation. For years afterwards it remained popular both in high government and in trading circles. Later in the century, people spoke of 'the map of Sebastian Cabot, cut by Clement Adams ... which is to be seen in her majesty's privy gallery at Westminster, and in many other ancient merchants' houses'. One such copy of 'Cabot's table' was seen in the 1570s, at the house of the Earl of Bedford, who had been an important member of the Privy Council under Edward.[6]

The slight alterations Cabot now made to the map were designed to appeal to English curiosity about a northern route to the Indies. To the north-west the depiction of America fomented interest in a passage through the continent. Men like the young Humphrey Gilbert, who would later devote (and give) his life to exploring this region, were transfixed. 'Sebastian Cabot', Gilbert wrote in the 1560s, 'hath ... described this passage, in his Charts', which were still to be seen, he noted, in the Queen's gallery at Whitehall. 'Any man of our country, that will give the attempt,' he later chided his compatriots, 'may with small danger pass to Cathay.'[7]

To the north-east, meanwhile, though Asia is not complete, it does appear that once Scandinavia has been rounded, the coastline descends. In the accompanying legend there is a quotation from Pliny. In ancient times, it suggests, 'the whole west' and most of 'the northern sea' had been sailed over. The reason to attempt the journey is emphasised once again. In Japan, the map notes, there is, as Marco Polo had related, 'much virgin gold, which is never taken away from the said island, because ships never touch there'.[8]

Ten

The period of Edward VI's minority was one of curious flux in English affairs: a time of uncertainty and unease in the life of the nation, a time of ideological division and animosity, a time of economic hardship and complaint, but also – for those of more optimistic bent – a fertile time of new ideas and possibilities.

None focused on these, or embraced them, more enthusiastically than Sebastian Cabot. This 'most learned of all men in knowledge of the stars and the art of navigation' had overseen the reprinting of a world map to which he had contributed five years earlier.[1] Now he turned his attention to the practical business of navigation. Early in 1551, with Cabot's encouragement, a trading voyage was organised to the eastern Mediterranean.

English vessels had once sailed into this great inland sea, but with the rise of the Ottoman Empire, and the decline in English shipping, in recent years the practice had ended. A commercial voyage now would provide an opportunity for young English seamen to gain experience of sailing, and navigating, in what were unknown and often hostile waters.

The voyage was captained by a young Bristol merchant known to Cabot from Seville. Years later, Roger Bodenham was proud of the role it had played in educating the talented young men he had in his charge. Besides boys, he remembered, there had been some seventy young mariners, in addition to merchants. 'For the most part', he said, within five or six years of the voyage they were 'able to take charge of ships, and did'. Even among this large and gifted group, however, there was one mariner who stood out. Many years later, it was Richard Chancellor whom Bodenham remembered.[2]

Chancellor had been born in Bristol. He grew up in a seafaring environment, a port town. As a boy he listened to the local men who still talked of the achievements of John Cabot with his son Sebastian, who had lived in, and sailed from, the quay in central Bristol.

Chancellor became accustomed to life at sea. But he was also unusually well educated, and quickly attracted notice for remarkable intellectual gifts. In both arenas, on board ship and in the school room, he was conscientious and showed a fierce determination to succeed. He wasn't fearless, because he knew the value of human relationships. He understood what his loss, or that of others with or under him, would mean to those left behind. When he felt a cause to be worthwhile, however, he committed to it and was willing to pay the ultimate price. He was thoughtful and reflective, and sometimes the burden of expectation which he bore from a young age was a heavy weight.

When he moved to London, as men from Bristol increasingly did if they hoped to advance, he was recommended to the Sidney family. He was close in age to the young Henry Sidney, whose intimate relationship with the King looked set to secure the family's rise to prominence.[3] Whether in Bristol or in London, though, seamen of the old school were grudging. They declared themselves unimpressed by Chancellor's aptitude for mathematics, by his skill at making and tinkering with new-fangled instruments which required detailed knowledge of the stars, or by his interest in maps. 'Them that were ancient masters of ships', one writer later noted, 'derided and mocked them' that busied themselves with charts.[4] How dare this new breed, speaking the arcane language of mathematics, presume to tell them, who had been at sea all their lives, how to conduct their business?

Sometimes the charge of impracticality was fair. It was of course true, as was later protested, that 'art and reason' depended 'upon experience'.[5] Some men of academic bent did abstain from the hard life of seafaring and missed, as a result, the knowledge accrued by dealing with currents or changing winds. Sebastian Cabot had himself, as Pilot Major in Spain, stood up for seasoned pilots against unworldly and unpractised 'cosmographers'.[6] Richard Chancellor, though, was no dreamy scholar. He had travelled, and been to sea. Like few others of his generation in England, he combined the practical and intellectual gifts for which Cabot was looking.

What Chancellor did in the period immediately after the voyage to the Mediterranean under Bodenham is not known. He may have travelled to the Continent. Many well-connected young men did, and the Sidneys would have been able to sponsor him. Certainly at some point in his youth he spent time in France, and he must have had an introduction to the French court, since he later wrote of having seen the ceremonial 'pavilions' of the King of France.

It seems likely that he was out of the country, since in spite of bringing himself to Cabot's attention there is no sign that he was involved in the plans for voyages of exploration with which Cabot busied himself over the subsequent couple of years, and which were eagerly discussed by Dudley's circle within the Privy Council.[7]

Eleven

Only snippets of information cast light on Cabot's work as an unofficial adviser on nautical commerce after his return to England in the late 1540s. Many derive from foreign diplomats and spies, who were anxiously trying to work out what it was that was keeping Cabot, a figure of Continental renown, in London. After all, he held no formal position in England like the office of Pilot Major he had held in Spain, and there was no department of state responsible for maritime exploration.

The lucrative trades and still-unknown opportunities in the new worlds were fiercely guarded and contested by the maritime powers of the Atlantic: by Spain and Portugal in particular, but increasingly by France as well. Any activity by a rival was keenly watched. Imperial officials also had an added incentive. They wanted to get to the bottom of Cabot's disappearance from his post, not least since the Emperor had made repeated requests for his return. One Imperial agent, known as 'Scipperus' or 'Monsieur d'Eecke', had picked up rumours that the English under John Dudley were ambitious to push outward. That summer he wrote letters to the Imperial ambassador in London, Jehan Scheyfve. Was it true, he asked, that England was 'seeking the road to the Indies'?[1]

Scheyfve could not discover anything for certain. His predecessor had recently retired due to ill health. He was new to the post, and less attuned to whispered snatches of intelligence than an established ambassador would have been. Nevertheless, he assured Scipperus, rumours certainly abounded. On the one hand it was sometimes said that the King – a figurehead for Dudley and his ministers at this stage – wanted 'to send two of his great ships to the East', perhaps by the southern route pioneered and claimed by the Portuguese. Others talked of a royal plan 'to send a few ships towards Iceland by the northern route, to discover some island which is said to be rich in gold'.[2]

This last proposal sounds like that advanced by Thorne and Barlow, for a voyage across the North Pole which would descend towards rich, undiscovered islands in the Pacific. Although it had been discussed before in England, it surprised the new ambassador, who had evidently not heard of the idea. 'This', he commented, 'seems strange.' But it was not to be dismissed out of hand. For one thing, as he had been assured, 'the rumour has been current for six months or so'.[3]

It certainly seemed to diplomats that the English were up to something. Not only did the widespread rumours suggest as much, but there was no other explanation for the fact that they were clinging jealously to Cabot in the face of repeated requests for his return.

Another piece of information pointed in the same direction. The young French Protestant, Jean Ribault, brought to England by Dudley and subsequently imprisoned in the Tower on suspicion of spying, had been released and set to work. The Council had asked him to make a new marine chart, 'and with him', Scheyfve noted, 'works the pilot Cabot'. The ambassador could not be sure of the detail. But the rumour that had reached him was that Ribault was to sail 'to discover some islands or seek a road to the Indies, taking the way of the Arctic Pole' – further evidence, in other words, that the English were again contemplating the proposal Thorne and Barlow had made more than two decades earlier, though they still felt the need for help from foreign expertise.[4]

Robert Thorne was then long dead, but Roger Barlow was still alive, and though he had lived for some time on estates he had acquired in Pembrokeshire after the monastic dissolution, he had remained in touch with developments in geography and maritime affairs. He was a fervent Protestant, which would have appealed to those who led Edward VI's regime. And John Dudley must have been aware of his history and talents, because in November 1549 he appointed Barlow as Vice-Admiral of the Pembrokeshire coast.[5]

Now, it seems, Barlow had travelled to London in hope of taking part, at last, in the project he had espoused for so long. Ribault was to be accompanied in the northern voyage, Scheyfve wrote, 'by certain Englishmen experienced in navigation, who have been [i.e. sailed] with

Cabot'. Only Barlow and Henry Patmer, who had both voyaged with Cabot in the expedition of 1526 at Thorne's instigation, are known to have met this description.

The English plans, Scheyfve thought, were far advanced. 'Five or six ships are being fitted out,' he reported in January 1551, 'and two of them are nearly ready.' Both Cabot himself and the English Council seem to have felt confident that a historic venture was in the offing. During the previous summer, Cabot had applied to the English government for a copy – his own being lost – of the patent for discovery granted more than fifty years earlier by Henry VII to his father, his brothers and himself. Clearly, with discoveries beckoning, he wanted his rights to any discovered wealth reaffirmed. At the same time, the government made him a substantial grant of £200 (around £40,000 today), 'by way of the King's award', on top of his existing pension. The last thing they wanted at this critical stage was for their prized naval expert to abandon the country for foreign employment once more because he felt undervalued.[6]

The voyage was to depart, it seems, in company with a fishing fleet bound for Iceland, where it would continue northward while the fishermen paused to drop their nets. The fishing boats were instructed to wait until the expedition ships were ready to join them. Exactly what happened at this point is unclear, but something seems to have arisen which forced a postponement.

On 24 March the Lord Admiral received an order from the Privy Council to license the fishing fleet to depart, 'and not to stay them any longer'.[7] No northern voyage of exploration left that year. Had it done so it would certainly have set out by May, to take advantage of the Arctic summer.

Twelve

I n spite of the anxious interest of foreign ambassadors and their spies, details of the plans being put together by Cabot and the English Council remained a well-guarded secret. Alternatively, and perhaps more likely, they were genuinely changeable and uncertain.

Influential men in England seem to have accepted that Robert Thorne had been right when he said that there remained only 'one way to discover, which is into the North'. New trading ventures were organised, under the Edwardian regime, to regions like west Africa, but these sailed through crowded waters. Since the Spanish, French and Portuguese did not wish to admit interlopers, they had an inevitable privateering element. English captains who were often military men with recent experience fighting in Scotland discovered, to their satisfaction, that looting foreign ships could be more profitable than trade.

The north parts, however, were largely unexplored. Here England, by her position, was at an advantage. The difficulty only arose when it came to being more precise. Was an expedition to go north-west, along the path taken by Cabot himself many years earlier? Was it to head due north, as Robert Thorne had advised, past Iceland and Greenland, over the Arctic Pole? Or was it to forge another, little-tried and little-discussed route to the north-east – heading into a part of the world whose geography was little known, as Cabot's own surviving map clearly shows?[1]

Anxious discussions took place involving Cabot, Dudley, the members of the Privy Council and other advisers. They were long and fraught. Plans for voyages were made, debated and discarded. These were picked up and reported, in vague terms, by the foreign missions in London. Cabot himself, no doubt, confided in Continental informers who came to talk with him – but only, it seems, to mislead them. Word reached the

Continent that well-equipped ships were on the point of departure. But for three years, from 1550 to 1552, nothing actually happened.

The truth seems to be that Cabot himself was undecided as to what the exact ambition of a northern voyage ought to be, as were those who employed him. At some point, though, late in 1552, a decision was made.

One influence was the collapse of England's cloth trade to Antwerp. In a short space of time, economic conditions had worsened dramatically. The export of basic 'short-cloths', as they were known, plummeted: from over 130,000 in 1550 to under 85,000 two years later.[2] And the downturn showed no sign of easing. While men like Dudley had long shared Cabot's enthusiasm for voyages of mercantile exploration, suddenly new voices were making themselves heard.

For some time the sale of cloth from London to Antwerp had been the central pillar of England's economy. While that trade thrived, no negative impact of an unwise specialisation was felt. But wars against Scotland and France during the 1540s had been funded on credit: by loans and by repeated debasement of the currency. When attempts were made to restore the coinage, exchange rates shot up and the demand for English cloth collapsed.[3]

The slump in demand at the traditional market caused soul-searching among the merchant elite. Anxious conferences took place. 'Certain grave Citizens of London', Clement Adams reported, met to discuss 'how this mischief might be remedied'.

In response English merchants demanded an end to the privileges enjoyed by their German rivals, and Dudley's government was happy to react to their complaints. The Hanseatic traders in London were accused of abusing their position. Their privileges, it was now claimed, had 'grown so prejudicial to the state that they may no longer ... be endured'. In February 1552 they were abolished. Work which had begun on rebuilding in fine stone the city's Bishopsgate – placed in the charge of these foreign merchants – came to a halt.[4]

At the same time, alarmed for their traditional business, the capital's English merchant princes abandoned their conservative instincts and threw their weight behind Cabot's plans. Suddenly the risks involved seemed worthwhile. A number of them had traded to Spain and

Portugal. They didn't need reminding by Cabot how the wealth of the Spaniards and Portuguese had been 'marvellously increased' by the discovery of new trades. They had seen it for themselves.[5]

Adams tactfully praised the great merchants as 'careful for the good of their country', but then, as ever, it was their own benefit which probably came first. When routes were discussed, the merchants could not forget that their core business lay in exporting cloth, and with Antwerp in seizure they were anxious to find new markets.

It might be true, as Cabot believed, that a passage to the north-west offered access to rich lands in the Pacific; but these were scarcely ideal places to sell woollen cloth. And from all known experience, the route through the American continent was not promising either. It was cold enough, but the Indians encountered there were primitive people. The route advocated by Robert Thorne, meanwhile, would descend, if it were viable at all, through the thinly populated Arctic to the warm waters of the central Pacific.

A passage to the north-east, on the other hand, would be a different matter. It was known that along the northern rim of Asia lay a land called 'Tartary', described by Marco Polo as a region 'of vast plains and high mountains', where nomads lived 'on the flesh and milk' of their herds. In a bitterly cold climate, men trapped animals for their fur: sable, ermine, black fox 'and many other precious animals'.[6] If the expedition could find a route through to Cathay, this should be both a market for desirable goods and also – since it was not hot – a highly promising territory for the cloth trade.

'Our chief desire,' Richard Hakluyt later wrote, 'is to find out ample vent of our woollen cloth, the natural commodity of this our realm.' The best places, he concluded, would be 'the manifold islands of Japan and the northern parts of China and the regions of the Tartars next adjoining'.[7] Did a viable passage exist that way? If they were honest, nobody knew. It remained 'doubtful', as Clement Adams admitted afterwards, 'whether there were any passage yea or no'.

Many geographers had considered the way closed off. Some postulated an Arctic land bridge linking Asia with northern Greenland, blocking any sea route to the north-east. Others had guessed at a land connection between the north-east of Asia and north-western America, rendering impossible any of the proposed northern passages to the equatorial Pacific.[8] Crucially, though, leading geographers seem around this time to have become more positive about the route's existence.

In 1541 Gerard Mercator, the great cartographer and scientist who would become a close friend of John Dee, had produced a globe larger and more detailed than any made previously. Only three years earlier he had made a map on which the land mass of northern Asia had extended upwards to the Pole, denying any passage that way. On his globe, however, he made a significant alteration. This time the polar land mass was connected to America, but not to Asia.

Some distance along the north Asian shore the land, according to Mercator's globe, did rear up. This promontory, known as 'Tabin' and endorsed by classical writers, reached towards the Pole. It would force would-be navigators to a high latitude. But it did not close off the route. Now, in other words, a passage was open, not to the north-west but to the north-east.[9] Before the Tabin headland, moreover, entry could be gained to the mouths of mighty Asian rivers which emptied into the northern sea and which would bear travellers south-east. Getting to Cathay this way, Mercator later declared, would be 'very easy and short'.[10]

Shortly afterwards, in 1544, Sebastian Cabot had helped to produce a world map of his own. When he arrived back in England he worked with Clement Adams to reissue it. On Cabot's map, the north coast of Asia becomes indistinct as it moves east: a sign of the uncertainty that existed. It seems, however, that after Scandinavia has been rounded, the coastline descends gradually into warmer waters to the south-east. He repeated, moreover, the ancient story which gripped later geographers, of the party of Indians shipwrecked on the 'coast of Germania'. How else could they have got there but through a north-eastern passage?

If any doubt remained, the return of John Dee from the Continent was decisive. To a city and a country starved of geographical expertise came someone whose learning in such matters now surpassed even that of Cabot himself.

Dee had worked closely with Mercator, the great map-maker. Though still young, Dee was already revered by influential people in England for his understanding of mathematics and its applications. Few were in a position to speak before the Council and the leading merchants with comparable authority. And he too, like Cabot, was haunted by the tale of the shipwrecked Indians. He too now supported the radical proposal to venture north-east.

In the geography of a thirteenth-century Arab from Syria, Abu al-Fida, Dee would shortly glean vital support for his theory. This suggested that once the northern cape of Scandinavia was rounded, the upper coastline of Asia descended gradually south-east. Here was apparent confirmation of what Dee already believed. Al-Fida's words, Dee thought, were 'worthy to be written in letters of gold'.

The Council, and the merchants, were persuaded. Together a group of leading London merchants resolved that they would mount a major expedition to the north-east, in search of 'a way and passage to our men for travel to new and unknown kingdoms'.[11] But the details of the plan were shared with as few as possible. Until after the voyage's departure, its destination was kept a closely guarded secret, anxiously but vainly probed by foreign diplomats and spies in London.

Thirteen

With Cabot's help, the merchants put together a new body for the purpose. It was a 'company' of men, and they called it also a 'mystery', which could refer in the sixteenth century to a trade guild. They labelled themselves, rather long-windedly, the 'Merchant Adventurers for the discovery of regions, dominions, islands and places unknown'. They were to sail off the map that was familiar to Europeans. They were to be pioneers.

The phrase 'merchant adventurers', of course, was already employed by the English cloth merchants. 'Adventure' was a term for a commercial venture or speculation. Some of the same merchants were involved, driven to riskier undertakings by the collapse of their regular business. Any seafaring at the time was dangerous, but the old Antwerp trade scarcely seems now to merit the term. The quest for a new trading passage through the Arctic, on the other hand, was a different matter. Those involved were under no illusion. They knew that what they were attempting would be, as they called it, a 'hard and difficult matter'. To undertake the thorough planning required they set up a committee, which they called a 'senate'. On this sat those later described as the 'principal doers' of the enterprise: Cabot himself, along with men like Sir George Barne and Sir William Garrard, the commercial magnates who were close to Cabot and to the Council under John Dudley.[1] These were the leading figures of London: merchants and loyal city men. Barne was the Lord Mayor, and within a couple of years Garrard would succeed him. They, like others involved, had made money in traditional trades, particularly the old Antwerp cloth trade, before the economic downturn encouraged them to seek new investments.

The first concern was to raise the substantial sum of money required.

No private undertaking in Tudor England needed capital on the same scale as a major voyage of exploration.

In England, unlike in Spain, there was no tradition of the state funding and managing such mercantile ventures. Kings did occasionally contribute, as Henry VII had done to the voyages made by Cabot's father, but private investment had always been central.[2] Now, with the state struggling to reduce its massive debts, there was little question of significant subsidy. For investors, this was a high-risk enterprise. The discovery of new trades might secure wealth on a colossal scale. It could also, easily, lose everything.

The London merchants were men of the world. The most skilled geographers of the time, they knew, relied on indirect knowledge or even on outright speculation. The fact remained that no one had successfully sailed this way. No one really knew whether there was a viable passage to the north-east. Seafaring in the sixteenth century was hazardous at the best of times, and in the freezing conditions of the far north, without prior experience or knowledge, particularly so. None of the great merchants, individually, would underwrite the venture at such odds, for fear of finding themselves 'too much oppressed and charged'.[3]

Few, for the same reasons, fancied a place on board. And it did not make sense for them each to send factors to trade on their behalf, as was common on commercial voyages. A long-distance expedition required larger ships than were routinely used around the coasts of Europe, and to fill the hold with the goods of numerous individual merchants, each accompanied by a factor, would cause chaos.

Instead, a radical idea was tabled, possibly at Cabot's suggestion, for he knew how major ventures were organised in the Italian states. The merchants should operate as a body, raising capital and pooling it to create 'one common stock of the company'. They should hire and pay representatives – employees – who would buy and sell on behalf of the group. Trading individually was forbidden. Masters of the ships would swear a solemn oath to prevent anyone from buying, selling or bartering goods for private gain. Nor would the company be a temporary collaboration for the purpose of a single voyage, after which the spoils would be shared out. It would be an enduring entity, or 'fellowship'.[4] A corporate identity would be established independent of the individuals

involved. Those who advanced capital would own a piece of the business: a shareholding.

It was a small step, but a decisive one. This 'joint stock' operation
meant people could invest in the venture without needing to be personally involved in the trading that was carried on. They could stand
at arm's length, keeping an eye, as shareholders, on the running and
profitability of the company, but remaining aloof from its day-to-day
management. What now seems an obvious way to raise capital, and to
share risk and potential rewards, was then a revolutionary idea. No company like it had existed in England before. Only in Italy had its like been
seen in Europe.[5]

Old 'regulated' companies, like the Staplers or the Merchant Adventurers, accepted members and gave them, essentially, a licence to trade
for themselves in certain goods and over certain routes provided they
observed general rules. These company members worked together in the
sense that they shared carriage space in ships which sailed in convoy as
a defence against pirates. And they enjoyed privileges and permissions
granted by governments to the company (often in return for loans it
could make with the entry fees it charged). But they traded as individuals and anyone wishing to be involved had to be very actively involved,
as a ship-owner or a merchant.[6]

Now, a sum of money could be advanced without risk to livelihood
or to life. And, not coincidentally, the initiative was well timed. In mid-
Tudor England there were plenty of men with capital. The dissolution
of the monasteries had released vast wealth previously tied up in Church
property, and it prompted one of the great speculative property booms
in English history. Much new wealth was squandered on show, and the
soaring demand for luxury goods only fed the desire of merchants to
find a new source. Much was reinvested in property, which guaranteed
social weight and remained the standard route up the ladder. But some
was invested with an eye to higher returns, and as the tendrils of the
Church were slashed away from the nation's economic life, strictures
against usury – profit from loans – were increasingly ignored.

The committee fixed the price of a share in the venture at £25.[7] And,
in London at least, the unprecedented offer created huge interest. In no
time 240 shares had been sold, raising the substantial sum of £6,000 to

spend on buying and fitting out ships as well as purchasing merchandise.

Most of the investors were merchants of London. Among what was a close-knit community, word rapidly spread. They knew each other. They traded together. They belonged to the same livery companies, often in senior positions. They served together in the city government. They collaborated on business deals or property investments. They were connected by bonds of family and friendship. The fact that Sir George Barne's son married Sir William Garrard's daughter is merely one example of the tight nature of London's business community. Numerous city aldermen, including past and future mayors, hastened to pay up.[8]

What was unusual, however, besides the investment's financial nature – indeed largely *because* of its financial nature – was that it was not only merchants who got involved. Although it was not a royal undertaking, important men at court rushed to take part: testimony to the active role that Dudley and his fellow Councillors played in instigating the venture, and to the buzz which the poaching of Cabot and the plans and rumours emanating from his lively circle had created.

Dudley himself, as Cabot's chief patron, played an important role. Eden wrote (in an admittedly flattering preface) that he had heard Dudley to have been 'a great furtherer of this voyage'.[9] His son-in-law, the close friend of the King, Sir Henry Sidney, certainly took part. He recorded his payment of £25 in his account book.[10] So did other key allies: men like William Paulet, Marquis of Winchester, Lord High Treasurer and the most senior Councillor after Dudley; or old John Russell, the Earl of Bedford, who was the keeper of the King's personal (privy) seal.[11] The young King himself, fascinated by ships and by daring voyages at sea, took a keen interest.

Even with Dudley's backing, though, financial support for the enterprise was no formality. Times were hard, but for that reason many were averse to risk. As Cabot knew, the city was historically conservative in its ventures, and hostile to big-talking outsiders. The announcement that a major voyage would sail where none had sailed before aroused scepticism as well as excitement. Cabot might have been widely revered, but some resented or were suspicious of his renown. There was grumbling behind closed doors. Why were men so impressed by this showy foreigner, who sometimes seemed to trade on the achievements of his father?

What did he know of the north that so much should be gambled? What, indeed, did anyone?

Cabot wrote bitterly of the 'sundry authors & writers' who claimed, often anonymously, that the voyage could not succeed. They talked, these doubters, of the impossible extremity of the north, the 'perils of ice, intolerable colds, and other impediments', and denied there was a passage. Cabot derided these sceptics as dinosaurs. Echoing Robert Thorne's earlier argument, he compared them to the men who had denied there could be habitable lands beneath the Equator. The discovery of rich and temperate realms in the southern hemisphere had shown once more that experience, not ancient tradition, was 'the certain Master of all worldly knowledge'. But scepticism was a powerful and contagious force. The 'wavering minds, and doubtful heads', Cabot lamented, had not only abstained from the venture; they had also dissuaded others from taking part.[12]

Nevertheless, the lure of great wealth was too powerful, and the desire to be involved carried the day. The company raised the money it needed and quickly set to work.

Fourteen

In general those planning a trading voyage included, or at least knew, owners willing to hire out their ships. But Cabot was perturbed by the English vessels he saw.

Ships were often worked for short-term returns, and were rarely well maintained. To owners there always seemed scope for one more voyage before an expensive overhaul would be necessary. In Spain, Cabot had grown used to regulation which policed the upkeep of vessels; it was a shock to be reminded that in England there was no similar intervention.[1] Hulls became encrusted with barnacles and other marine growth, which dramatically reduced the ships' speed. More fundamentally, the basic soundness of the wooden planks, and of the caulking between them, was uncertain, meaning a crew was always at risk of a leak.

Ship design had moved on in the decades since Cabot crossed the Atlantic with his father. The strong winds and strong currents of the southern oceans had demanded innovations which were vital to the discoveries and trades of the Spanish and Portuguese.

In Henry VIII's England, though, large ships had acted usually as troop platforms. Their towering fore and stern castles, a name which reflected their design, discouraged boarders and advertised Henry's power. But on the open ocean they were top-heavy and unsafe.[2]

Smaller merchant ships also bore the mark of a people who rarely strayed far from their coast. The merchantmen drawn by Hans Holbein in the 1530s, or by John Thompson off the coast of Dover in 1538, had moved on from medieval 'cogs', as they were known, with their one central trunk. They had three masts, plus a bowsprit for another sail reaching forward at an angle from the prow. The lower aggregate sail area produced less heeling in strong winds, and less risk of capsize. But they still teetered unstably high above the waterline.

There was change afoot, however. In the mid-1540s all the ships of Henry's navy were painted on three rolls of vellum. Their military intent is evident. Cannon bristle from gun-ports. Flags and pennants of England and the Tudors decorate the decks and snake in coiling lengths from the masts. But the basic design was no different to merchantmen, and the illustrations show the direction in which nautical architecture was moving. Older 'carracks', with their rearing castles, sit alongside hybrids called 'galleasses' which were lower in the water (allowing them to be rowed if necessary), must have sailed faster, been safer in bad weather and easier to manoeuvre.[3]

It is not surprising, then, that Cabot and his board chose to fund new vessels. With the money they had raised they could afford to provide three – well manned and well provisioned.

There was the *Edward Bonaventure* – the largest, at 160 tons.[4] 'Edward' referred of course to the young King, while 'Bonaventure' meant 'good luck', a commodity which all owners wished on their ships. Next in size, at 120 tons, was the *Bona Esperanza*, a name which also invoked good luck, while the smallest, at 90 tons, the *Bona Confidentia*, seemed to invite the discovery of a wonderful secret. The *Edward* was perhaps a little over sixty feet long and twenty-five feet wide at its broadest point, the *Confidentia* fifty by twenty-one and the *Esperanza* in between.[5] The names are a mixture of Italian and Spanish, with which one assumes Cabot was involved. They testify to the anticipation and nervousness surrounding a voyage for which so much was hoped.

Elm was often used for the keels, since the wood was hard and durable in water.[6] For the bodies of the ships the merchants went to some trouble, according to Clement Adams, to obtain strong and well-seasoned planks, probably of oak from the Weald. The straight-growing conifer trunks used for the masts had to be imported from Scandinavia. The shipwrights worked fast, under pressure from the dignitaries who backed the expedition, to build the ships, to caulk them (hammering hemp fibres as a seal into the gaps between the planks), and then to waterproof them using the dark resin known as pitch.

Most of these marine supplies had to be imported, often by Hanseatic merchants from the Baltic. When the London historian John Stow listed commodities brought to England by Germans, many of them were primarily naval: 'Cables, Ropes, Masts, Pitch, Tar, Flax, Hemp'. Ropes, made usually from hemp, were an expensive but indispensable product for maritime activity, used for everything from attaching sails to lowering anchors, from 'breeching' – that is, securing guns as they recoiled – to 'wolying' or 'woolding' – winding ropes tightly round masts or beams to strengthen a joint or split. Traditionally, they were obtained from the Dorset town of Bridport, which had built up a virtual monopoly of domestic manufacture since medieval times. But by the sixteenth century the town's prices were uncompetitive, attempts to promote rope production elsewhere in England do not seem to have thrived, and London shipbuilders preferred to buy in bulk from abroad.[7]

With sail canvas, the story was similar. It too was a product vital to the country's maritime affairs. Under Dudley, the first attempts were made to stimulate domestic manufacture as the most reliable source. The links he established with Protestant seafaring communities in Brittany meant that in 1552 he was able to bring to London two craftsmen who could train local artisans to make the durable sheets of canvas known in England as 'poldavies', after the Breton village of Pouldavid. In later years Ipswich would become the hub of a national industry. But in the 1550s most canvas still had to be imported, from France or, again, from the Baltic.[8]

On one ship an innovative technique was tried in England for the first time. The idea was probably Cabot's. In Spain, measures were taken against the teredo 'shipworm' – a mollusc which eats unseen into the hull of a wooden ship and which damaged Spanish ships in the Caribbean. The problem did not arise in the cold waters of the Arctic, but it was hoped, of course, to sail through these to the warmth of the mid-Pacific. Cabot unnerved the merchants with stories of these 'worms' which 'pearceth and eateth through the strongest oak'. A technique was copied therefore from the Spanish. The ship's keel, its central spine, was lined with thin sheets of lead.[9] This added to the ship's weight, and was an expensive measure. But it illustrated the lengths to which organisers went to maximise the venture's chances.

Fifteen

As important as the soundness of the ships was the choice of men to lead 'so great an enterprise'. The appointment of captains was left until late in the day, but not because there was any lack of willing applicants for the role.

As the foreign ambassadors noticed, London hummed with talk of an English venture to rival those of the Spanish and Portuguese. In those difficult times, numerous men put themselves forward, attracted by rumours of adventure and rich reward. But this was new territory for England, and men with suitable backgrounds were barely to be found. Most of those in line, as Adams observed, were 'void of experience'.[1] It was paramount that the captain be a man of authority.

The morale and discipline of the crew would waver during the trials ahead, as Cabot knew from personal experience. More than once, while exploring the New World, he had been frustrated by crew members who refused to venture further through strange waters and an unforgiving climate. He was prone to vanity, but perhaps admitted to himself in old age that leading men in adversity was not what he was best at. As he surveyed those who volunteered for the post now, his principal consideration was that the captain of the fleet should be a man who commanded respect and obedience.

One man stood, literally, head and shoulders above the competition. His 'tall stature' was particularly remarked upon. And there is no doubting the presence of the man who stares out of the huge portrait still in the possession of his family: his dark beard and thick hair swept back, his resolute gaze and impressive physique. Though not wearing military attire, Sir Hugh Willoughby looks every inch the career soldier knighted for valiant conduct during years spent campaigning against the Scots – an honour he received in the service of Henry VIII just as his father, Sir Henry Willoughby, had done in the service of the King's father. Hugh had arisen as Sir Hugh on Scottish soil in May 1544, with more than fifty other English soldiers, having distinguished himself in violence 'at the burning of Edinburgh, Leith and others'. He marked the occasion by adorning his coat of arms with a dragon, a symbol of his family's service to the Tudor dynasty.

Willoughby was 'well born', a gentleman, with the natural authority bequeathed by his social status as well as by his military record and commanding personality. He might have lived a relaxed life of inherited privilege, but since the family seat at Middleton passed to the son of his older half-brother, he had to rely on connections to make his way. His family were linked by marriage to the powerful Grey family, and such patronage secured him some significant roles at court, not least being one of those appointed to receive Anne of Cleves, Henry VIII's fourth wife, when she arrived in England in 1539. With the return of sporadic warfare in the 1540s, he turned to the military career that suited his temperament. Only when peace was restored by a cash-strapped government a decade later did he cast around for alternative employment, and jumped at the chance to lead Cabot's great expedition (though in doing so he left behind a son, a daughter and possibly a wife).[2]

Willoughby's appointment now was another sign that this was no ordinary commercial voyage. Trading runs were not generally led by members of the gentry. Even successful ship-owning merchants preferred to appoint someone well experienced at sea to captain a vessel on their behalf. As an exploration deemed vital to the national interest, however, Cabot's plan enjoyed the high-level attention given to an important naval undertaking. And in the navy, newly esteemed after the attention lavished on it by Henry VIII, it had become customary for men of standing to command ships-of-war, regardless of their previous experience at sea.[3] It seemed natural, if not for Cabot then certainly for his fellow organisers, to give 'greatest account' to Willoughby's distinguished family as well as to his 'singular skill in the services of war'.

It was still not an easy decision, however, or one quickly reached. 'At the last', Clement Adams wrote, the committee chose him as the voyage's general, though he had in reality little naval experience. Like others of his class, he had commanded a privateer in Scotland. He had, the Imperial ambassador noted, 'served the King of England at sea during the last war with the Scots'.[4] His mettle was undoubted, as was his stature and his dignity of birth and bearing. But that was it: one maritime role which had revolved more around marshalling men and fighting than sailing a ship, which would have been left to the master and crew. He was, we must assume, entirely ignorant of those new sciences, of navigation and shipcraft, which had enabled Europeans to undertake long voyages on the open sea, and so to present themselves before a wider world.

On the one hand this is no surprise, since naval or privateering expeditions were accustomed to scavenging along the coasts of France and Spain, but not to venturing into waters that would be unfamiliar to the crew. The voyage planned now, however, was a deliberate departure, not simply in its projected route but for the English as a seafaring nation. The bad old days of pilots with little navigational expertise beyond that born of long familiarity with a particular patch, and of captains whose military experience barely extended to time at sea, were supposed to be over.

As so often, though, an abrupt break proved impossible. Qualified Englishmen simply did not exist. The decision to appoint Willoughby speaks eloquently of a lack of more suitable candidates.

Some of the merchants involved did not appreciate the demands of long-distance exploration. Cabot, however, certainly did, and he knew the sort of man he was looking for to lead not only this voyage, but also a more general blossoming in England of oceanic trade and exploration: a man who could link the academic world of mathematicians and geographers with the practical world of the sea.

Fortunately, for Cabot and for England, he had met just such a man. And it was not only Cabot who was impressed. Old-school sea pilots might have been dismissive, but educated men recognised a man of enormous potential. A practical merchant like Roger Bodenham could vouch, after the voyage he had captained to the Mediterranean of 1551, that Richard Chancellor might like gazing at the stars, but he was certainly not starry-eyed.

Chancellor had never held a position of such responsibility. But he was travelled and ambitious, and determined to acquire the skills of the best modern sea captains. There was none of the doubt or delay with his appointment that there was with that of Willoughby. There was no dispute among the committee about nominating him as Pilot Major of the voyage, and entrusting him with the captaincy of the *Edward Bonaventure*, the largest ship of the three. Once again, there were numerous applications for the role. 'Diverse men', Adams wrote, put themselves forward. But it was by 'common consent' that Chancellor was given the position.

With the job of Pilot Major came recognition that the task of seamanship, of navigating the flotilla to the limits of known geography and beyond, would be his. Here was a man who personified the new world of the sea as surely as Willoughby did the old. He was 'a man of great estimation for many good parts of wit in him'. In Chancellor, Cabot saw the pre-eminent example of those 'young and lusty pilots and mariners of good experience' whose ambition and presence in England he found so heartening.[5]

Dreams of great success for the expedition rested largely on his shoulders. In him alone, Clement Adams wrote, 'great hope for the performance of this business rested'.

Sixteen

From the moment of his appointment, Chancellor prepared conscientiously for the voyage. He had evidently been talking to Cabot and other leading figures for some time, and expected to be involved.

Through his patron, Sir Henry Sidney, he was introduced to the remarkable young scholar who had blazed such an astonishing trail on the Continent: John Dee. Since the legendary lectures he gave in Paris, Dee had returned to England and taken up a post as tutor in the household of John Dudley. Dee came to know Dudley and his family well, including his son-in-law Sir Henry Sidney. Through Sidney, Dee and Chancellor were introduced.

The two men hit it off from the beginning. They were both still young – Dee only twenty-five, and Chancellor not much different – though Dee's unparalleled intellectual brilliance and remarkable early career must have rendered the sailor from Bristol somewhat in awe. Both had a passionate interest in the new geography ('cosmography', as it was known) which used mathematical as well as empirical methods to chart the globe with unprecedented accuracy.

As a friend and collaborator of the great Continental geographers, Dee's knowledge and insights must have seemed extraordinary to Chancellor. Nevertheless, Chancellor's great natural gift for mathematics, combined with his practical ingenuity in the construction and adaptation of instruments, meant that as time went on theirs became a partnership of equals. Dee, certainly, was impressed. Years later, he would look back nostalgically on the time he had spent working with a man he called 'the incomparable Richard Chancellor'.[1]

The two shared a fascination with astronomy, which is difficult to differentiate, in this period, from astrology. It was generally believed that there was a close relationship between events in the heavens and events on earth. Anything unusual in the sky was certain to have its corollary in the human world.[2] Men like Dee were much in demand for their astrological readings, which seemed to offer an insight into mundane prospects. And Chancellor, too, after initial studies of the humanities, wrote the bibliographer John Bale, 'focused his concern purely on the study of the stars, and is said to have delved into almost all areas of astrology'.[3]

For men who closely watched the sky, this was a time of upheaval and excitement. In the traditional view, the earth lay stationary at the centre of creation, surrounded by invisible concentric spheres, wrapped around each other like the layers of an onion. Attached to successive spheres were the moon, the sun and each of the planets. Then, fixed like studs on the outermost, crystal sphere, rotating in unison around the earth, were the stars. Beyond them lay the heavens.

Now, however, it was ten years since a Polish canon, Nicolaus Copernicus, had argued – in a work he finally dared to publish a day before he died – that the sun, not the earth, was at the centre. The earth was catapulted into a spinning orbit. For hours Dee had discussed these ideas with friends like Gerard Mercator, and he endorsed the Copernican model. He discussed them too, no doubt, with Richard Chancellor, as the two men studied the sky, their eyes gleaming with intellectual excitement.

As much to the point, though, the study of the stars was integral to the science of navigation on the open sea. It was a subject that Dee had written about, and whose practical methods were unchanged. However little the knowledge had been used by English sailors, it had long been known that by accurate measurement of the angle above the horizon of either the sun or of certain fixed stars, a reading for one's latitude on the earth could be obtained. One needed to know in advance, though, the expected positions of these heavenly bodies at particular times of the day – of the sun at noon, for instance – and on particular dates in the year. What Chancellor needed were carefully compiled tables, known as 'Ephemerides', which recorded the positions of the sun and of notable stars on particular dates.

He asked Dee to assist him. Dee, since his time in Louvain, had become absorbed by astronomy. He recalled how, in 1547, he had begun to make observations of the heavenly bodies, making 'some thousands in the years then following'.[4] Now back in England, Dee duly produced a work which offered Chancellor the help he needed. Though no copy survives, it was later published, under the wordy but useful title: *Astronomical and logistical rules and Canons, to calculate the Ephemerides by, and other necessary accounts of heavenly motions: written at the request, and for the use of that excellent Mechanician Master Richard Chancellor ...*

Chancellor's reputation with Dee as a 'mechanician' derived from instruments he had made in order to take astronomical measurements, in preparation for this major voyage. Years later, Dee remembered 'certain rare and exquisitely made instruments mathematical' which he had preserved in his library. Among them was a quadrant: the brass quarter-circle used to measure the altitude of a star. It had been adapted since, he wrote, but it was 'first made by that famous Richard Chancellor'. It was 'excellent, strong, and fair', Dee remembered, and also unusually large, 'of five foot semi-diameter', which was critical given that the accuracy of which the instrument was capable was directly proportionate to its size. Ever innovative, Chancellor was also credited by men who knew him with inventing what were known as 'transversals' – parallel lines inscribed on the scale which allowed more accurate, fractional readings of the angles measured.[5]

Having a second person to assist was a considerable advantage. This was not so much with holding the instrument (since presumably, as with the ten-foot-long cross-staff also in Dee's collection, the quadrant had some sort of frame to allow a man to use it easily) but with measurement. It was difficult, with even a smaller quadrant, to sight the sun or star in question along one radial edge of the quarter-circle while simultaneously reading off the angle from the plumb-line which fell vertically downwards.

Chancellor did have someone, of course. Together he and Dee noted figures carefully, for the position of the sun and a few major stars. Often the two men remained long into the night after others had retired, taking advantage of the deep, pre-electric darkness to record the positions of heavenly bodies in detailed tables.[6] They also knew that, heading as

Chancellor was into the far north, the hours of light would be long and the stars would for much of the time be invisible. The sun, as a result, was more dependable as a reference point. At midday too, therefore, Dee recalled, with Chancellor's magnificent quadrant, 'he and I made sundry observations meridian of the sun's height'.[7] They carefully recorded the results as they did so, in Ephemerides which Chancellor could take with him on board.

Sebastian Cabot would have known the pair well, and taken a keen interest in their studies. Few others in England could advise from experience on the use of astronomy for the purposes of navigation. And there is no doubt that Cabot was increasingly taken with Chancellor in particular as the Englishman the country had lacked for so long, who could be a true ocean navigator of the modern kind.

Seventeen

At some point in the spring of 1553, the merchants and others with a stake in the venture held a rowdy meeting to discuss their plans. Clement Adams was there, perhaps as an assistant of Cabot's, and he later wrote a rather stylised account of what took place.

Top of the agenda was affirmation of the choice of individuals to act as Captain and Pilot Major. Richard Chancellor was much discussed, because he was young and not widely known. Those like Cabot who knew him had sung his praises. A decision had probably been made by the inner committee to approve his appointment. But Cabot was aware of a vein of distrust among the London merchants towards himself personally, with his foreign blood and long service in Spain, and wished to reassure them. So Sir Henry Sidney, who knew Chancellor better than anyone, was asked to attend the meeting, to provide what amounted to a character reference.

Sidney certainly had significant influence with the assembled merchants. Not only was he a member of the King's intimate circle, but he was close to the head of Edward's Council, John Dudley. Not only had Richard Chancellor lived for some time in his household, but the two men were close in age. In spite of Sidney's social superiority, they had formed a bond. As he rose the merchants hushed respectfully, and with anticipation, to hear him speak.

Tactfully enough, Sidney began by flattering his audience. He praised the merchants for an undertaking which he hoped would prove 'profitable for this nation, and honourable to this our land'. He spoke on behalf of the nobility, he said, who were willing to do whatever they could – to give up anything – in order to advance so worthy a cause. He could speak as someone making a considerable sacrifice himself. He gave up Richard Chancellor to lead the voyage, he told the merchants, not because he found him a financial burden, because he did not value him, or because he would not miss him. Quite the contrary. He parted with Chancellor without complaint to show support for a venture he backed, and because he believed that by doing so he would boost its chances of success. He was pleased, too, to see such a gifted young man given the opportunity to make his mark.

No one, Sidney assured the merchants, was in a better position to recommend Chancellor. The merchants had had the chance to learn of him through reports made by others, and through his own words when they met him. They were practical men of business, though: they knew how some men could talk a good game in an interview. He knew Chancellor through his deeds as well as his words. By the 'daily trial of his life' over a long period, he said, he had acquired a 'full and perfect knowledge of him'. And he was delighted now to see him accorded the authority and respect that he deserved. All the same, he hoped the merchants would not forget the risks Chancellor was running on their behalf:

> We commit a little money to the chance and hazard of Fortune: He commits his life (a thing to a man of all things most dear) to the raging Sea, and the uncertainties of many dangers. We shall here live and rest at home quietly with our friends, and acquaintances: but he in the mean time labouring to keep the ignorant and unruly Mariners in good order and obedience, with how many cares shall he trouble and vex himself? ... We shall keep [to] our own coasts and country: He shall seek strange and unknown kingdoms. He shall commit his safety to barbarous and cruel people, and shall hazard his life amongst the monstrous and terrible beasts of the Sea.

If Chancellor returned safely from such dangers, Sidney told the merchants, it was their duty to reward him liberally.

His speech made the impact that he, and the leaders of the enterprise, had hoped for. Meaningful looks were exchanged among the assembled merchants. A hubbub broke and grew in the room as whispered conversations increased in volume and excitement. Those who knew Chancellor congratulated themselves. Perhaps this man really would justify the hype and, as Adams said, 'his virtues already appearing and shining to the world would grow to the great honour and advancement of this kingdom'.[1]

Perhaps, less loftily but more to the point, he would make them rich?

As the chatter subsided, the leading men focused the group's attention on the business in hand. There was much else to be discussed. For one thing, as those of 'greatest gravity' present insisted, every attempt should be made to learn in advance of the 'Easterly part or tract of the world' where the ships would be heading, of which so little was currently known. Someone mentioned that two Tartars who had travelled to England were working in the King's stables. Perhaps, he suggested, they could provide useful information? The idea was welcomed, and the two men were sent for, along with someone capable of interpreting.

After a delay, the men arrived. They were subjected immediately to a barrage of questions. What was their country like? What were its manners and customs, its wealth and commodities? What could they tell the group about its northern coast? How easy was passage by sea from there to Cathay or to the offshore islands further east?

It was soon obvious, however, that the merchants were wasting their time. Quite probably the men came from nowhere near the northern seas. In any case, they were barely coherent and could answer 'nothing to the purpose'. Someone present loudly quipped that the men seemed to be more acquainted with 'toss pots' – that is, with drink – than with 'the states and dispositions of people', and at this, mounting frustration among the organisers and investors gave way to laughter.

The two Tartar men may have been angered at being made the object of ridicule. Certainly a commotion seems to have ensued. As Adams discreetly noted, there was then 'much ado', and 'many things passed about this matter'. Eventually, though, calm was restored and the meeting moved on, none the wiser about the state of the East.

Attention was directed once more to a practical matter of great urgency. Spring was already far advanced, and still no departure date had been fixed. Many were well aware of the importance of utilising the summer months for an expedition into the north. Several voiced their concern that if the matter were delayed much longer, the intended exploration would be impossible that year: 'the way would be stopped and barred by the force of the Ice, and the cold climate'. It was an argument that spoke keenly to the pockets as well as the minds of the prime movers and investors. So a deadline was agreed. 'By the twentieth day of May', it was settled, 'the Captains and Mariners should take shipping, and depart from Ratcliffe upon the ebb, if', of course, 'it pleased God.'[2]

Eighteen

The fixing of a deadline for departure added to the pressure on those who were assembling the crews.

The Captain General, Sir Hugh Willoughby, and the Pilot Major, Richard Chancellor, had been appointed. Others, probably, had been found to fill the most important remaining posts on the voyage. William Gefferson, an old hand at sea, was master of Willoughby's ship – with full responsibility for sailing it, given Willoughby's own lack of experience. On Chancellor's ship, the *Edward*, the post of master was given to a man from Devon called Stephen Borough. Chancellor, of course, certainly did know what he was doing, so it was a less responsible job. But Borough was twenty-seven years old, had been sailing for over a decade and was another, like Chancellor, who took an unusual interest in the intellectual side of seafaring. His younger brother William, only sixteen, was taken on as one of the regular mariners to gain experience, as boys his age often were. Command of the third and smallest ship was allotted to Cornelius Durforth, a man who sounds Dutch in origin, and who also had a brother or other relative among the mariners. (Then, as now, contacts were a vital way to get on.) Each of the three masters had a mate. On the *Edward* it was John Buckland.

Some of the men on board took little part in sailing the ships. On the *Bona Esperanza* there were six merchants, on the smaller *Bona Confidentia* three. On the *Edward Bonaventure*, the largest, there were merchants, like John Hasse and the 'Cape' or head merchant, George Burton, but also men like James Dallaber who were described simply as gentlemen: present to add dignity when visiting foreign courts, and a sign of the increasing interaction, and intermarriage, between merchants and gentry. Unusually, of course, merchants on board were not there to operate independently, but were employed by the company. Together they were responsible for selling company goods and for buying or bartering for stock with which to return to England. Their trades were overseen by the company purser, Robert Gwinne, who travelled with Willoughby, and whose role it was to supervise the expedition's commercial activity and to deal with foreign governments over such matters as customs and trading rights. Numerate as well as literate, he handled company money and issued salaries to the crew.

Also on the *Edward* was John Stafford, a minister of religion.[1] Twice daily, in the morning and in the evening, he was expected to take prayers, as well as 'other common services' prescribed for particular days by the King or the laws of England. On two of the ships there was no minister. This was common enough on a trading ship, but instructions offer a glimpse of the Protestant ideology then increasingly dominant in England. For Protestants, readings from Scripture in the vernacular were what mattered; less importance was attached to an ordained ministry, to liaise between men and God. Services were not to go unsaid. Rather a merchant, 'or some other person learned', was to take them. The Bible, in English of course, was 'to be read devoutly and Christianly to God's honour', while His grace was to be obtained 'by humble and hearty prayer of the Navigants'.

Cabot's instructions imply that Stafford was to have sailed on the admiral: that is to say, on Willoughby's ship, the *Esperanza*. In fact, for whatever reason – a last-minute practical matter of space or numbers, or so that he could minister to the largest number, or to the gentlemen – he sailed, according to Hakluyt's list, with Chancellor on the *Edward*.

The regular crew proved harder to assemble. A voyage into the northern seas offered additional risks without the high returns anticipated by investors and company merchants. By May 1553, with the date fixed for departure impending, pressure was mounting and anxious enquiries were made by the company's most senior men.

Merchants, particularly those who had been ship-owners themselves, were familiar with the problem. In recent years securing reliable crew had become an increasingly difficult matter. The long-term decline of English merchant shipping had forced many, especially in the provincial ports, to abandon seafaring for an inland trade. There simply weren't enough jobs at sea to go round. More recently, the growth of the navy, the country's wars with France and Scotland and the parallel rise of a semi-official privateering industry had created the opposite problem: more jobs, now with fewer people to fill them. Good seamen, as a result, were often already engaged.

The early 1550s was a time of peace, but still it was hard to find qual-ified men willing to crew three ships for a dangerous venture heading into an entirely unknown part of the world.[2] Senior government figures became worried. After urgent discussion, measures were taken which were generally associated with military service, by land or sea, rather than with a privately funded commercial voyage, and which illustrate the extent of government interest. The Lord High Admiral despatched a letter to the Clerk of the Admiralty. If necessary, he wrote, men to work on the ships, and to serve on the 'voyage to seek the land un-known' – 'ship masters, mariners, shipwrights, gunners, and other such persons' – could be seized and forcibly 'impressed'.[3] It is not known whether the strategy – which was to have a long and ignoble history in the British Navy – was used. No further reference to it is made, and the official authorisation may have come too late. The disadvantages of a begrudging and potentially under-skilled crew are obvious. Men who were impressed, it was said, were 'the scum and dregs of the country'.[4] In any case, men were found.

Merchantmen were at least much less heavily manned than naval ships. In spite of the development of cannon, the business of fighting at sea still revolved primarily around grappling, boarding and hand-to-hand fighting, placing a premium on sheer numbers of armed soldiers. Where commerce was the aim, financial considerations kept the crew down. The combined total carried by the three ships in 1553 was fewer than 120. A single naval vessel of comparable size would have carried more.[5] Even this, though, meant that the ratio of men to tons served (370) was approximately one to three, a level of manning that would have been considered extravagant for most ordinary commercial ventures.[6]

The fact is of course that this voyage was anything but ordinary. It was heading into dangerous, uncharted waters. The ships needed to be able to defend themselves, not only against pirates but also against the sea-power of unfriendly states along their route. And they wished to discourage hostility by making an imposing appearance wherever they arrived. No less significantly, the organisers knew the other dangers to human life, from accident as well as disease. The simple fact that the voyage was likely to last much longer than most substantially increased the risks. Both in the far north during winter, and in the tropics if they made it that far, the mortal threats were known to be severe. It was natural, therefore, to crew ships with extensive fatalities in mind, and for promoters to wish to be confident that even a much-depleted crew could sail home.

There were thirty-seven men on the *Edward* who belonged to the 'mariners and officers, according to the custom and use of the Seas', a category which did not include the captain, the master and his mate. There were twenty-one ordinary mariners, among whom were Miles Butter and the young Arthur Pet. On the *Esperanza*, on which there were more men in other positions, there were ten ordinary mariners, including Thomas Allen and George Blake. On the *Confidentia* there were eleven, among whom was John Durforth: probably, given the unusual name, a relation of the captain.

As the lowest level of sailor, many would have been young and some, like William Borough, were only boys. It was normal for well-connected youths to begin their maritime careers as apprentices at eleven or twelve years old. In his strictures about on-board hygiene, Cabot required the men to show their juniors a good example: 'the gromals & pages', he wrote ('gromal' being a term for an adolescent boy on a ship), 'to be brought up according to the laudable order and use of the Sea'.[7] If lasting life was to be breathed into English commerce, moreover, it was stressed that attention be paid to their 'learning of Navigation' as well as to the performance of the menial tasks which were their lot.

The sailors' names sound English, by and large, a fact which might occasion surprise given the cosmopolitan nature of the maritime community.[8] This, however, was a peculiarly English venture. The national interest was kept firmly in mind, and unusual effort may have been made to give experience to an English crew. Though recruited in London, they would have originated from all over the country. Young men in many lines of work travelled in search of employment – journeymen in the literal sense – and sixteenth-century London exerted a strong draw. As a major port, it was the destination of ships from around the coast of England as well as from abroad. Crews often passed time in the capital, spending their wages and waiting for the next opportunity.

Such men had a bad reputation: for drunkenness, for fighting and for being difficult to govern. As Pilot Major and a leader of the voyage, Richard Chancellor, it was said, would have a battle on his hands 'to keep the ignorant and unruly Mariners in good order and obedience'.[9] Certainly in part, and at times, the reputation was earned. But these men covered a wide spectrum: from the rough and trouble-making ne'er-do-wells who could find no other employment, to well-connected and often capable boys and men marked out for rapid promotion. Many, of course, were neither. They were not born to the sea but were willing to take wages wherever and however they were offered. They were hard-edged, by experience if not by nature, inured to violence, but willing to toil and to accept the rigours of what was dangerous and punishing work because nothing else was available – and certainly nothing that was not equally tough.

Sixteen men on the *Edward* held more specialised positions. They helped to sail the ship, but also had additional tasks, with proportionately higher pay.

This was a merchant vessel, not looking for trouble; but the state had taken a keen interest in the venture and security was a concern. Four men, therefore, were responsible for artillery, including Robert Stanton, the Master Gunner.[10] On the smaller *Esperanza* there were two gunners and on the *Confidentia* only one. The expedition ships, Hakluyt wrote, were 'well appointed with all manner of artillery', and Adams noted that they were provided with 'armour and munition of all sorts'.[11] There would have been brass cannon – minions perhaps – with smaller, wrought-iron guns which could be operated by one person, as well as handguns.

All of the ships would have carried barrels of gunpowder: either primitive black 'serpentine', rather unreliable and dangerous to use, or powder that was 'corned', that is to say set using liquid and broken into granules to prevent the separation of constituent parts. Iron shot was used by the larger guns, stone or lead shot by the smaller. There would also have been conventional items of weaponry. As well as the artillery, it was said that the ships carried 'other things necessary for their defence': pikes to fend off boarders, and bows made of yew, with plenty of arrows and spare strings.

Other men had particular skills. Each ship had a carpenter; on the *Edward* it was Griffin Wagham. On a wooden vessel, he was an important man. He would have been formally trained, and his salary reflected his status. He was expected to keep a careful eye on the sides of the ship, on the masts, the rudder, the decks and the ship's boats, to spot any damage before it caused a problem. Emergency repairs would be his responsibility. The cooper, meanwhile – William Every on the *Edward* – also worked with wood. He specialised in the construction and maintenance of casks of all shapes and sizes, holding liquids, foodstuffs, trade goods and commodities like gunpowder which it was essential to keep dry. Since water quickly became ridden with algae and undrinkable, weak wine or beer were vital resources and wastage could not be afforded. With the money raised, the merchants decided to supply the ships with food for eighteen months: allowing six months for the outward voyage, six to see out the winter if the weather prevented an immediate return, and another six to sail back the following year. Inevitably, there would be protracted intervals between opportunities to restock.

The cooks had a limited array of ingredients with which to work. On the *Edward* this was Austen Jacks.[12] The instructions refer to fish and 'meate' (bacon or beef, well salted to last), as well as to biscuit, bread, beer, wine, oil, vinegar and 'other kind of victualling'. In the latter category, cheese, butter and 'pease' were common supplies, while beans, wheat or oatmeal might bulk out this protein-rich diet and help to provide the calories needed by a crew working for long days in the extended daylight of a northern summer. Fresh fruit and vegetables were not on the menu unless they happened to be picked up at a port en route, and there was no understanding yet in any case of their preventive role where diseases like scurvy were concerned. On small merchant ships, cooking was often done on a metal stove kept on deck. On larger naval vessels, and probably on those of the expedition too given the cold conditions expected, a stove was constructed on bricks deep in the hold among the ballast – often a dirty, smelly and unhygienic place to be, though less so on a new-built ship – with a metal flue to carry smoke and sparks clear of the wooden decks. A steward was responsible for the potentially inflammatory task of dishing out rations, and it was he, with the cook, who accounted, weekly, for the food consumed.

Four quartermasters oversaw a designated area, or quarter, of the ship. Meanwhile the boatswain or 'bosun' – Peter Palmer on the *Edward* – was the link between the captain or master and his crew. He worked with the men, but spoke regularly to the captain, ensuring that orders were transmitted and carried out, often possessing a whistle by which if necessary he could communicate with the crew. He was responsible for checking the ship was well maintained, and took particular charge, often, of the sails, the rigging and the ship's boats. It was also his job to supervise the packing of cargo, an important task on a merchantman, in which heavy commodities would be stowed low and centrally to act as a counterweight to the tipping moment of wind-filled sails. In the event that there was too little cargo, or too little that was heavy, ballast of sand or stones would be used. Reporting to the voyage's purser, the bosun logged all cargo on board, in his bosun's book, and registered its unloading at its destination, to try to prevent the theft and private trading rife among seamen alive to any chance to enhance their meagre earnings. It was an important position, accorded to a man who was on the way to taking overall command of a ship himself.[13]

Also on the *Edward* was a surgeon: Thomas Walter. If there was no intention, on this voyage, to engage deliberately in violence, nevertheless it could not be ruled out. Accidents, moreover, were an ever-present cause of injury at sea. Medical attention, in the sixteenth century, could be as dangerous as the wound or illness that required it. Some naval surgeons, however, had made worthwhile advances in the treatment of common injuries, like the wounds and burns from artillery, or substantial splinters from wooden planks. Methods for extracting foreign bodies, for debriding (that is, removing dead tissue), for stitching open wounds and for amputating limbs using tight tourniquets to reduce pain and blood loss, had improved, and could be better than nothing. Fastidious surgeons made some attempt at cleanliness, which was known to be healthier and to improve the chances of recovery in spite of the absence of any bacterial explanation.[14] Everything depended on the knowledge and skill of the man involved, and the best that can be said is that again, given the nature of the voyage, Thomas Walter was probably more qualified than most.[15]

He was the only surgeon to set sail with the expedition, a sign that the role was not yet considered indispensable, and that the intention was for the ships to stay together so that a surgeon could tend, at a convenient moment, to any man on the voyage. In other respects, too, regular contact was assumed.

Nineteen

At the top level, a council was selected from the leading men which would meet to discuss progress and to make important decisions. The council had twelve members, since twelve, or a multiple thereof, was considered the prudent biblical number. With Willoughby and Chancellor, its members included the masters of the three ships – Cornelius Durforth, William Gefferson and Stephen Borough – and their three mates, along with George Burton and Thomas Langlie for the merchants, James Dallaber as a 'gentleman' and the minister, John Stafford. The operation of such a council, of course, required that 'the fleet shall keep together, and not separate themselves asunder, as much as by wind & weather may be done or permitted'.

For all that Willoughby's authority with the mariners was vital, life on an English ship in Tudor times was less autocratic than it later became. A ship, or a fleet of ships, was no democracy. But it was often an oligarchy rather than a dictatorship.

Significant decisions were voted on by the council, who were expected to gather on board the admiral whenever Willoughby wished to consult them 'concerning the affairs of the fleet and the voyage'. Willoughby's pre-eminence at these meetings was affirmed only by the fact that he received a 'double voice', two votes to the one of his fellow members, to ensure there could be no split decisions. Twelve plus one, of course, also had a biblical ring. For the community of more than one hundred men who would be living on board the three ships for the coming months, the council were effectively the government. All would be bound by their orders and regulations, duly written down in a hefty, leather-bound book provided for the purpose, most of whose pages were blank.

As the crew assembled early in May on the bank-side at Ratcliffe, the book was brought by Sebastian Cabot and presented to Willoughby and the other leading men. Already neatly inscribed in the first part of the book was a list of thirty-three general rules which Cabot had drawn up, with the help of his fellow board members, to govern the conduct of all those taking part in the expedition. He described them as 'ordinances, instructions, and advertisements'. These were to be read aloud regularly, every week, to the men: 'to the intent that every man may better remember his oath, conscience, duty and charge'. They were a sort of constitution by which the enterprise should be regulated.¹ It is a list full of the practical wisdom accrued by an old man who had taken part in, led, or organised such expeditions for most of his life.

Much is shrewd common sense. There are articles, for instance, about ship management. Cabot advised that careful records should be kept of food and drink consumed, while 'waste or unprofitable excess' should be avoided. Tabs should be kept too on other equipment and supplies. Guns and powder, for instance, should not be wasted or misused, but 'preserved for the necessary defence of the fleet and voyage'. Navigational instruments should be scrupulously maintained. Order and cleanliness were to be ensured. 'No liquor,' he instructed, 'to be spilt on the ballast, nor filthiness to be left within board: the cook room, and all other places to be kept clean for the better health of the company' – a directive which shows surprising wisdom in an age often assumed to be ignorant of the link between hygiene and health. Anyone who did become sick was to be carefully tended, and others were to cover his work without complaint. The clothes and belongings of any who died should be kept for his wife and children (or other beneficiary specified in his will) along with whatever salary the man was owed until the day of his death.

Some articles invoke the lessons of Cabot's own prior misfortune or miscalculation. Great emphasis, for instance, is given to the need for unity among the leadership. The Captain General, the Pilot Major, the masters, merchants and other officers should be 'so knit and accorded in unity, love, conformity, and obedience' that no damaging differences should emerge, to be exploited by the mariners. This sort of dissent,

Cabot wrote, had 'overthrown many notable intended and likely enterprises and exploits', and he was certainly including his own. When he returned to the theme in the last article, he passed on the wisdom of bitter personal experience. 'Item', he wrote, 'no conspiracies, partakings, factions, false tales, untrue reports, which be the very seeds, and fruits of contention, discord, & confusion, by evil tongues to be suffered.'

Articles regarding encounters with natives drew on his own with Indians in America. 'If you shall see them wear Lions or Bears skins, having long bows, and arrows,' he advised, 'be not afraid of that sight: for such be worn oftentimes more to fear strangers, than for any other cause.' Nevertheless, crew should remain alert when anchored close to inhabited land, and keep 'diligent watch' both day and night. 'There are people', he warned, 'that can swim in the sea, havens, & rivers, naked', who might attempt to assault an unguarded ship and – since Europeans had a perennial fear of and fascination with cannibalism – might attempt to kidnap men whose bodies 'they covet for meat'.[2] He didn't anticipate such threats in the freezing waters of the Arctic, though even here the map legends of 1544 had warned that 'no ship dares to ride at anchor near the coast' for fear of what it called the 'night people' who lived through months of darkness and who killed and robbed any visitors.[3] And the intention, of course, was to return to the Equator, where it was hot.

Four articles reminded the party of the oaths they had taken, of obedience to the King and his realm, as well as to the leadership of the voyage. They had promised, he wrote, to uphold all the orders 'contained in this book', including any added by the ship's council. They had bound themselves to pursue their aim with determination, and not to give up until they had succeeded: 'so far forth', at least, 'as possibility and life of man may serve or extend'. Again, the memory of expeditions of his own on which sailors refused to go further came flooding back as Cabot wrote. The whole crew had sworn obedience to the Captain General and his council. Both had the authority to punish negligent or dishonest behaviour, 'after the laws and common customs of the sea'. A guilty man might be demoted, or even unshipped, with the proportion of his salary to which he was entitled. But justice, Cabot stressed, should be even-handed, and so less likely to provoke hostility. Punishment should be ministered 'moderately, according to the fault or desert of his offence'.

Symptomatic of the new spirit of the enterprise, and critical to the business of exploration, was the emphasis Cabot placed on the keeping of written records. In this his articles were revolutionary. Nowhere in the history of ocean-going navigation had anything comparable been seen.

Records of earlier voyages, if they existed at all, had been haphazard, incomplete and often retrospective, written sometimes by the captain in the form of a letter to his ruler.[4] But the clear aim now was to forge trade routes, which by definition would be repeated, and not necessarily by the same men. So they needed to be meticulously mapped. 'Item,' required article seven, 'that the merchants, and other skilful persons in writing, shall daily write, describe, and put in memory the Navigation of every day and night, with the points, and observation of the lands, tides, elements, altitude of the sun, course of the moon and stars.'

For centuries coastal pilots had relied on rutters, containing basic landmarks, drawings and information about water depths and tides. All this was useful, but Cabot wanted more. He wanted a scrupulous record of astronomical observations which could help to provide a definite location on the earth's surface. This was another reason for the members of the council to meet regularly on board Willoughby's ship, to ensure their instruments were similarly adjusted and to compare observations. 'Once every week (if wind and weather shall serve)', Cabot proposed, the three masters should pool their notes, examining points of agreement or disagreement. In the process they should create 'a common ledger, to remain of record for the company'. The fact that this now seems a rather obvious suggestion belies its radicalism.

For all that human agency – the right preparation and the right skills – would help, no one doubted that God's support would ultimately decide the success of the venture and the safety of the crews. None were more conscious than sailors of the precariousness of their existence. Under God's merciful hand, Cabot wrote, 'navigants above all other creatures naturally be most nigh'. And as such, religious observance was fundamental. Regular prayers and services were to be conducted and the Bible read aloud. Just as importantly, all behaviour was barred which might jeopardise His support. There was, Cabot urged, to be 'no blaspheming of God, or detestable swearing', no 'ribaldry, filthy tales, or ungodly talk'. There should also be no gambling from which quarrels might ensue: 'neither dicing, carding, tabling, nor other devilish games'. These wouldn't only cause 'poverty to the players'; they could also lead to 'strife, variance, brawling, fighting, and oftentimes murder'. The outcome would not only be the 'utter destruction' of the parties concerned, but would also affect them all, by 'provoking of God's most just wrath, and sword of vengeance'.

Here, of course, God's taste in shipboard conduct matched that of a judicious captain (even were the captain not anxious to placate Him). We know from Cabot's own flexibility when it came to the articles of religious belief, that it was their impact in the material world that concerned him. As he admitted, religious observance and godly behaviour served a dual purpose: they were important for 'duty and conscience sake towards God' but also 'for prudent and worldly policy'. Certainly the captain's 'just wrath' would be provoked as surely as God's by a significant lapse in standards. After fair warning – 'the offenders once monished, and not reforming' – all such 'pestilences' were to be punished.

In another way, too, the practice of religion was to be pragmatic. This was a commercial venture. Little benefit was to be expected from the sort of aggressive proselytising carried out by the Spanish and the Portuguese. Rather the opposite. Far better, Cabot advised, 'not to disclose to any nation the state of our religion, but to pass it over in silence'. Instead, the crews should conform with the traditions of their hosts, religious and otherwise. (God, surely, would understand.) They should avoid provoking a foreign people 'by any disdain, laughing, contempt, or such like'. Every nation and region was to be approached 'with prudent circumspection, with all gentleness, and courtesy'. This was not, needless to say, a template for imperial conduct which the English would always honour. But it stands, nevertheless, at the outset of English expansion, as a proclamation of the better side of the impulse.

The merchants involved, and Cabot too, hoped to find markets where transactions could be conducted that were immediately profitable. More important in the long run, though, as Cabot saw, was the acquisition of knowledge which might promote lasting trade. What was required was an inquisitive commercial eye. 'The names of the people of every Island', he instructed, 'are to be taken in writing, with the commodities, and incommodities of the same, their natures, qualities, and dispositions.' Detailed records should be kept, listing for each people 'what things they are most desirous of, & what commodities they will most willingly depart with, & what metals they have in hills, mountains, streams, or rivers, in, or under the earth'.

Information was better obtained, he advised, by politeness, discretion and if necessary by guile than by aggression. If, for instance, people were spotted on the shoreline, 'gathering of stones, gold, metal, or other like', the crew should approach cautiously in their smaller boats to observe what it was they were collecting. No hint of menace should be displayed, 'no ... sign of rigour and hostility'. On the contrary, men who knew how to use them should reach for the instruments which had been provided, as was common at sea. The crew should sing, and together they should make soothing, captivating music, to send the natives into a reverie or to make them want to come closer, 'to see, and hear your instruments and voices'.[5] If possible, an individual should be lured or persuaded on board, so that as much as possible could be learned of these people. Violence, Cabot stressed, was unacceptable, and would only prove counter-productive. If it was a woman, strictly no advantage was to be taken. She was not 'to be tempted, or entreated to incontinency, or dishonesty'.

One well-trusted strategy which he did recommend, though, was alcohol. 'If the person taken may be made drunk with your beer, or wine', he advised, 'you shall know the secrets of his heart'.

At all times Cabot urged caution and a cool distrust. He had heard, if not credited, fantastic rumours from Roger Barlow of people like the Scythians, who lived in northern Asia and who received strangers 'lovingly' before killing them, eating them and drinking their blood mixed with milk.[6]

He had come across tribes in southern America who genuinely were cannibals, albeit of a sparing and ritualistic kind, and the legends of the 1544 map cautioned of the 'very wicked people' who lived in these lands, deserted by the sun for months on end, who killed and robbed all who visited.[7] At any rate, he now urged the English not to 'credit the fair words of the strange people, which be many times tried subtle, and false'. They should not venture too far inland, for fear they might be unable to get back to their pinnaces or ships. If invited to the house of a local lord or ruler, they should go, but only armed and in numbers.

Cabot knew what effect the lust for precious things could have on men. Great caution should be taken that a desire for gold, silver and other riches did not lure them into peril. In any case, good commercial strategy was to mask enthusiasm for any goods on offer: advice that stemmed, perhaps, from one of the experienced merchants on the company board. It was much better to feign lack of interest. 'Esteem your own commodities above all other', article 25 recommended, 'and in countenance show not much to desire the foreign commodities.' The men should take them, of course; but only as if 'for friendship'.

Not surprisingly, Cabot wrote articles which reminded the merchants in particular of the unprecedented nature of the enterprise. As never before, he reminded them, they were trading not individually but as a company. And as such, the 'common stock of the company' was to be given priority over any private trading. No person was 'to hinder the common benefit'. If it should happen, as men dared to hope, that jewels, pearls, precious stones or metals became available, it must be the company's transactions which came first, and guidelines then issued by the Captain and his council should be strictly followed.

In trading on behalf of the company, merchants should obtain consent from the Captain General, the Pilot Major and the Cape Merchant prior to any deal, whether it involved buying, selling or trucking (as bartering was known). Goods acquired were to be stored in one place, 'well ordered, packed, and conserved', until they could be presented in due course to the governor, consuls and assistants in London. Meticulous records were to be kept, so that all business was transparent. On return, 'the truth of the whole voyage' was 'to be opened, to the common wealth and benefit of the whole company'.

If possible, the company hoped to receive word of progress *during* the expedition. Cabot's natural optimism is obvious. Urgent information might include, he suggested, the 'likely success of the voyage', the finding of a passage or the advancement of a fruitful new trade. In this case the on-board council should send a messenger or two, if it seemed possible, by land or sea, so that the company could begin to make appropriate plans. The men would know how many back home, from the top down, were anxious for positive news: 'the king's Majesty, the Lords of his honourable Counsel, this whole company, as also your wives, children, kinsfolk, allies, friends and familiars'. All would be desperate to know how things went, to be reassured that their loved ones were well, and to learn how likely it was that they could achieve 'this notable enterprise', which it was hoped would be as rewarding as the East and West Indies had proved to the rulers of Spain and Portugal.

Cabot pleaded for good conduct. The men should remember, always, to what lengths the company board and subscribers had gone to furnish and equip the ships with 'plenty of all necessaries', the like of which, he said, had never been known in any realm for such an exploit. As ever in Tudor England, when social mobility, and disorder, was everywhere apparent, the key to stability and success seemed to be for men to stick dutifully to their stations. 'It behoveth every person in his degree', Cabot wrote, 'to remember his said charge, and the accomplishment thereof.' And on a voyage, no doubt, if not in life, this was true enough. Beyond that, the men could only pray to 'the living God' that He 'prosper your voyage, and preserve you from all dangers'.

'In witness whereof,' he concluded, 'I Sebastian Cabot, Governor aforesaid, to these present ordinances, have subscribed my name, and put my seal, the day and year above written.'

Part II

'INTO THE FROZEN SEA'

… dar'st thou lay
Thee in ships' wooden sepulchres, a prey
To leaders' rage, to storms, to shot, to dearth?
Dar'st thou dive seas, and dungeons of the earth?
Hast thou courageous fire to thaw the ice
Of frozen North discoveries? …

JOHN DONNE, *Satire III*

Twenty

On the morning of 10 May 1553, more than a week ahead of deadline, the three newly built merchant ships were launched off the low sandbanks of Ratcliffe into the turbid waters of the Thames. Beneath the sullen gaze of the Tower of London, its familiar outline looming over the marshland and recently reclaimed fields of Wapping, the ships anchored midstream to await the turning of the tide.[1]

For the community of this small but burgeoning 'sailor town' downstream of the capital – one of the 'tower hamlets' overseen directly by the Constable of the Tower, who had the right to call up residents to serve in his local militia – this was a momentous day.

Shipwrights, chandlers, coopers, carpenters, blacksmiths: for months the marine craftsmen and suppliers of Ratcliffe had laboured to prepare the three ships for their perilous voyage. They had been under intense pressure from the promoters of the expedition, who knew, or had been made well aware, how dangerously narrow was the window of the Arctic summer. The inhabitants of Ratcliffe, for whom the river was their primary outlet to the world, were out in force to witness the completion of their task – proud to have played a part in what, they had been confidently assured, would be an historic undertaking.

On shore, captains and crews – 115 men, all told, though some of them were only boys – said goodbye to wives, children, parents and friends. For merchants and sailors used to the perils of sixteenth-century seafaring, such leave-taking had become habitual. But for even the most hardened, this departure was out of the ordinary. Previous journeys would have followed established trading routes which traced Europe's temperate and well-mapped coastlines. This time they were to broach uncharted waters and traverse untravelled territories in the extreme climate of the Arctic and (it was hoped) in unknown climes beyond.

Organisers and investors with feet planted firmly on dry land exuded confidence: the route would prove manageable, perhaps even straightforward. In fact, as all present knew, there was every chance that this leave-taking would be a final one. But qualms were suppressed; for such is the timeless lure of imagined wealth.

Sebastian Cabot, the leading organiser of the expedition, was prominent among the crowd. He was now around seventy, had white hair and a long beard which fell in a fork on his chest. He had reached a rare age for the Tudor period, but was still energetic and alert. His voice was unusual, mingling notes of the Mediterranean with a Bristolian twang. But few would have mistaken him for a provincial Englishman. His appearance was distinguished, his clothes expensive and well made. He was, as Clement Adams wrote, a man 'in those days very renowned'. He was treated with obvious reverence by the departing crews and bystanders alike.

Cabot knew well enough that his own days breasting the oceans were over. 'Waxing old,' he had said, 'I give myself to rest from such travels.'[2] But he had never resigned himself to nostalgia, still driven by ideas and ambition. He wanted to organise, if he could not take part in, voyages which redrew the world map and the landscape of European trade. As the crews prepared now to make for the open sea his pulse quickened, amid memories of his own departures.

He busied himself overseeing the final preparations and engaged in intense last-minute conversation with the leading members of the expedition – particularly, of course, with Sir Hugh Willoughby and Richard Chancellor. The three men made a contrasting group. Next to Cabot, somewhat stooped, inevitably, with age, Willoughby stood tall and strikingly upright. It was easy to see why his physical presence, as well as his reputation, had impressed those choosing the leadership of the venture. It was Chancellor, though, the third man, who had earned Cabot's particular confidence and affection, and it was their final discussions which were the most animated.

One would never have guessed that Chancellor was a junior party – not, at least, in any sense other than his age. As he examined charts and tables with Cabot, he talked confidently and with passion. Since returning to England over four years earlier, Cabot had warmed to a new breed of young and strong-minded English mariners. But of these it was Chancellor who stood out as the most gifted. Certainly Cabot showed obvious respect and affection for a man less than half his age. He could see in him something of his younger self. Chancellor was intellectual and ambitious. He was interested in astronomy, in using instruments and in reading and drawing maps. His background was among the maritime community of Bristol. And he shared, too, an urgent desire to transform the fortunes of a nation.

As the tide swelled to high-water then slackened and began to ebb, the anchors of the three vessels were hauled in. In front of banks thickly packed, the three ships were towed downriver by their pinnaces. In these smaller boats mariners of the crew rowed, smartly dressed in the crisp, sky-blue uniforms which had been issued to them by the company for special occasions. Conscious of their noisy audience, they worked hard at their oars.

As they rowed, they relished the admiring looks and comments they drew from smaller vessels on the water. The Thames was not yet the super-highway it would become, but it was already a busy commercial route. Its high tides acted as a conveyor belt, bearing in and guiding out the trading ships of England's chief town and port. On the waters which flowed through Southwark, London and Westminster, John Stow guessed, over 2,000 wherries and small boats, at least 3,000 men, worked ferrying passengers and goods. And that didn't include 'great ships, and other vessels of burden'.[3]

Although there was activity on the water, along the two miles south down Limehouse Reach the crews rowed rapidly away from the commotion of the capital and the squalid but vibrant suburbs which spilled along the riverside east of London. As the tide flowed gradually out, glistening mudflats were exposed at the river's edge between the rushing water and the reeds, paused and picked over by wading birds.

The banks of the Thames here still felt wild, though remains of ancient flood defences were a reminder of earlier attempts to tame the waters. Stepney Marsh, or the 'Isle of Dogs' as it was already known, had been drained and planted in the thirteenth century but abandoned to nature once more when flood water crashed through the medieval river wall in 1449, destroying the small settlement of Pomfret with its chapel, St Mary in the Marsh, whose tumbled remains were still just visible amid the long grass.[4]

As they began to sweep round the great meander of Greenwich Reach, however, the crews reached the settlement of Deptford, a fishing and boat-building community on the southern bank which had grown rapidly since Henry VIII chose it as one of his new naval shipyards. Places like this were the most significant industrial plants in the early modern world. Some naval parts were still imported, but increasing effort was made to be self-sufficient. There were forges and workshops, mast ponds, brickyards and sail lofts. There were timber pounds, saw houses and dry docks, launchways, rope walks and all the buildings required to house a large community of labourers and craftsmen. Yards like Deptford were a major catalyst to the river economy, and to the fast expansion of suburbs east of the city.[5] Here the three ships paused and dropped anchor for the night.

Twenty-One

W hen the three ships set out again the following day, the focus of all on board was less the watching inhabitants of Deptford than the imposing mansion a short distance further along the same shore.

Its numerous spired towers were embellishments to an older core. Its principal entrance opened through an ornate gatehouse directly onto the river. And its three quadrangles, banqueting hall, tilt yard, armouries and other outbuildings backed onto an expansive deer park which stretched up the hill to an old watchtower on the crest. Recently restored for the use of Henry VIII's young family and mistresses, the tower boasted uninterrupted views of the coiling Thames, west towards the Tower of London and the spire of old St Paul's, east over the marshy floodplain bisected by the glinting sheet of the broadening river.[1] This was the royal palace of Greenwich, still known sometimes as 'Placentia' – pleasant place.

It had been rebuilt by Henry VII and was the birthplace of his second son, Henry VIII. More so than the palace upriver at Hampton Court, this was the favourite residence of successive Tudor monarchs. Here Catherine of Aragon gave birth to her daughter, Mary. Here Catherine was later kept prisoner, refusing to accept that her marriage was void. Here her usurper, Anne Boleyn, gave birth to another girl, Elizabeth, who would also be Queen, baptised next day in the adjacent monastic church with Thomas Cranmer standing as godfather. Here, not long after, at the May Day tournament held annually in the park, Anne was accused of dropping a handkerchief as a signal to her lover.

It was from Greenwich that Anne was swiftly taken by water to the Tower and at Greenwich that her enraged husband affixed his seal to her death warrant. Here Henry married by proxy his fourth wife, Anne of Cleves. And it would be here too that Elizabeth, who as Queen used Greenwich as her principal summer residence, would tread a flirtatious shoe on the cloak laid out by Sir Walter Raleigh.

Now, as the expedition ships were rowed past in the late spring of 1553, the crews turned out once more in their ceremonial clothes, Greenwich Palace was the stage for one of the sadder stories of Tudor royal history.

A month earlier, King Edward, now aged fifteen, had been brought downriver from Westminster for the sake of his health. He had become ill during the previous winter, probably with tuberculosis, as he began to assume the mantle of power.[2] At the Tower as well as on the Ratcliffe bank, where preparations for the voyage were nearing completion, cannon were fired to honour the stricken King as he passed on the royal barge. Henry Machyn, a merchant tailor of London, recorded in his diary:

> The eleventh day of April the King removed from Westminster by water to Greenwich, and passed by the Tower, and there were a great shot of guns and chambers, and all the ships shot off guns all the way to Ratcliff. And there the three ships that was rigging there, appointed to go to the Newfoundland. And two pinnaces shot guns and chambers, a great number.[3]

Even in Greenwich's clean air, Edward's condition worsened. The Imperial ambassador, who had an informant in the King's household, filed lurid reports of the royal sputum: 'the matter he ejects from his mouth', he wrote with relish, 'is sometimes coloured a greenish yellow and black, sometimes pink, like the colour of blood'. The chronic coughing, and the swelling of his legs and head, increased. He was becoming weaker as time passed, Scheyfve reported, 'and wasting away'.[4]

Anxious Councillors scrambled to avert the trouble ahead, when the death of a Protestant King looked set to bring to the throne a Catholic heir in the person of his half-sister Mary – who had persisted, in the teeth of Edward's protestations, in hearing the Mass.[5] In her wake would come the likely ruin of all who had presided over Edward's regime, and already plans were being hatched, in which Dudley and Edward both connived, to rupture the succession.

Those on board the expedition ships, familiar with the journey down-river from London, noticed an unusual congregation of naval vessels on the Thames – downstream at Woolwich, at Deptford and near the city itself. Carpenters worked hard to repair any damage to the royal ships. Londoners had seen the strengthening of the military presence in the Tower and within the city, while armour and ammunition were moved around in carts and stockpiled by members of the Council. Upriver at Windsor Castle, meanwhile, and at key points along England's southern coast, precautions were also being taken lest a disputed succession tempt an opportunist invasion or an internal revolt.[6] Those setting out from England now sensed the climate of fear and uncertainty, and wondered what threats or changes the country would face in their absence.

For most of the thriving Greenwich community who catered to the demands of the court, however, such issues were merely sensational rumours. Those who spread them were brutally punished. 'Such things were being said,' Scheyfve reported, 'that three citizens who were accused of saying that the King was dead or dying had their ears torn off.' But people talked all the same.[7]

Word of the passage of the expedition ships, about which so much had been heard during the preceding months, was a different matter: crowds rushed to the riverbank to watch, standing 'thick upon the shore'. Courtiers and commoners alike jostled for a view of the river. Those within the building who were not immediately engaged ran to the uppermost towers to look out. Among them were Edward's closest friends and confidants – his tutor, Sir John Cheke, who at Cambridge had taught and been so impressed by John Dee, and his best friend, Sir Henry Sidney. Sidney in particular felt a mixture of pride and trepidation as another man dear to him, Richard Chancellor, waved from the largest of the three ships.

Even the Privy Council, deep in anxious deliberation, broke off to watch the scene from the palace windows. Nor was this idle curiosity, since the Council, from the outset, had taken a keen interest in plans for the voyage. Such interest had been superseded by the pressing question of the succession. But many of the Councillors, including some of the most senior, had personally invested in the venture.

None could easily have missed the commotion, for on board the mariners marked the occasion in the traditional manner, by firing their cannon. On the *Edward*, under the supervision of the master gunner, Robert Stanton, the gunners cleaned, loaded and packed the cannon before the powder was lit. As they did so, the tops of the hills resounded:

> ... the valleys and the waters gave an echo, and the mariners they shouted in such sort that the sky rang again with the noise thereof. One stood in the poop of the ship, and by his gesture bids farewell to his friends in the best manner he could. Another walks upon the hatches, another climbs the shrouds, another stands upon the main yard, and another in the top of the ship.

To the beholders, thought Clement Adams (and no doubt he was one of them), 'it was a very triumph'.[8]

The events were missed, however, by the young man in whose honour they had been arranged. Confined to his bed, the King heard the noise of the guns and the excited cheering of the crowds, but did not see the celebratory departure of the voyage he had keenly sponsored. Sidney, Cheke and others who were with him described a scene he would greatly have wished to witness, passionate as he had long been about ships and seafaring.

Edward did not leave Greenwich. Ambassadors reported his rapidly deteriorating condition. 'It is held for certain that he cannot escape', wrote Scheyfve: 'He is beginning to break out in ulcers; he is vexed by a harsh, continuous cough, his body is dry and burning, his belly is swollen, he has a slow fever upon him that never leaves him.'[9] He made only one further public appearance, on 1 July, at a window of the palace. During the days that followed crowds continued to gather, hoping to catch a further glimpse; but in vain. Five days later, having whispered to Sir John Cheke that he was 'glad to die', the suffering King passed away.[10]

With them the crews were carrying a letter that Edward had signed, in a weak and shaking hand. It was addressed to 'Kings, princes and other potentates inhabiting the north-east parts of the world toward the mighty Empire of Cathay'.[11] With the English version were bound additional copies translated into Greek as well as 'divers other languages' thought likely to assist interaction with the peoples along a northern route to China. Given his ill health, as well as his youth and status, the letter was not written personally by the King. Quite likely it was drafted by Cabot, the expedition's leader and its driving influence. Certainly it is suffused with an idealistic spirit similar to that found in the navigator's instructions to his crews.

The letter is a plea, to any foreign leader or government they should encounter, that those on board the three ships be treated respectfully and well. It professes an optimistic view: that God had instilled in all men the desire 'to join friendship with other, to love, and be loved', and that men should more particularly display this kindred sympathy to those who had 'come unto them from far countries'. It suggests, rather doubtfully, that only ardent fellow feeling would have driven men to embark in the first place on a long-distance voyage.

The letter is also a hymn to trade, the rock on which English expansion would be based. Particular respect, it argues, should be due to merchants, whose role in distributing the fruits of the earth – and so in bringing together, in peace, its various peoples – was clearly aligned with the divine plan:

> For the God of heaven and earth greatly providing for mankind, would not that all things should be found in one region, to the end that one should have need of another, that by this means friendship might be established among all men, and every one seek to gratify all.

If commerce had any less noble motive, such as the desire for personal enrichment, this was passed over in silence. It was this humanitarian goal – 'the establishing and furtherance of ... universal amity' – which motivated this group of men to 'voyage by sea into far Countries', just as the Lord had intended.

By trading, the letter promised, the English merchants hoped to establish 'an indissoluble and perpetual league of friendship' with peoples they encountered. Their intentions were benevolent, and they hoped only for the same respect that foreigners from distant lands would certainly be accorded in England. Cabot, of course, must have listened to the argument in Spain over the treatment accorded to Indians in the New World. His letter is imbued with a universal humanitarianism unusual at the time. 'Consider you', the letter implores any foreign ruler, 'that they also are men':

> If therefore they shall stand in need of anything, we desire you of all humanity, and for the nobility which is in you, to aid and help them with such things as they lack, receiving again of them such things as they shall be able to give you in recompense. Show yourselves so towards them, as you would that we and our subjects should show ourselves towards your servants, if at any time they shall pass by our regions.

The letter endorses in practice the philosophy Cabot had espoused in his instructions. The religion with which it is suffused is of the most general kind, to avoid giving offence. Repeated reference is made to 'Almighty God', creator of 'all things that are contained in heaven, earth and the Sea', but none to His son, Jesus Christ, and certainly none to tangled matters of doctrine or observance.

The date of authorship is given not in a Christian time frame, but in one that derived from the Hebrew Old Testament and which seemed universal. The letter was written, it concluded, 'in London, which is the chief City of our kingdom, in the year from the creation of the world, 5515, in the month of Iyar' – that is, the second month of the biblical calendar which fell in April and May.

Twenty-Two

A mile and a half downriver of Greenwich the three vessels paused again – but not, this time, for the tide. A slipway of dark, impacted mud allowed large ships to be grounded here for repairs, with materials brought by barge from London. For six days the crew waited in this marshy district, a delay which suggests that further work must have become necessary. The place was known as Blackwall – a name derived from the 'blackness or darkness of the banks or wall at that place'.[1] It was a period of deep frustration for the leaders of the expedition, who were anxious to make progress northward before the summer drew on.

When finally afloat once more, the crews continued past the mouth of the River Lea, through open country, along wider, gentler bends with the run of the tide towards Woolwich – an insignificant Kentish village with a minor reputation for shipbuilding until Henry had chosen it, too, as the site for a naval shipyard.[2]

Night was drawing in as the ships arrived at Woolwich. It was nine o'clock.[3] In May there was still some light, but the shadows reached long across the river as the sun set behind the crews, while insects swarmed in clouds above the water. Moored here – its tall masts dimly outlined against the dark eastern sky – was a great ship, the greatest of Henry's, now Edward's, navy: 165 feet long, more than 1,000 tuns in volume, and carrying under sail almost the same number of men.[4]

The *Harry Grace à Dieu* had recently been rechristened the *Edward* in honour of the young King. Though increasingly outdated, with her rearing and ungainly castles, she had been a floating statement of intent: a declaration of England's, and King Henry's, confidence and ambition on the wider stage. She was a flagship of what had become recognised as a truly national navy: a purpose-built warship, among the first in

111

England not expected to double up as merchantman and military vessel according to circumstance.

As with other vessels recalled to the capital in 1553, the *Harry* – or the *Edward* as she now was – provided a measure of security at a time of danger. But it would be the last sighting the crews would have of this famous ship. Shortly after they departed she caught fire accidentally here at Woolwich and was destroyed, in the same year that the King for whom she had been renamed passed away. With the accelerating speed of change on the seas, she would in any case soon have become redundant: as overweight and immobile as Henry himself became.

As the water level dropped, exposing broad, dirty expanses of Thames beach, the three ships cast anchor to 'tide over'. But those on board were anxious to progress, and if some of them grabbed a few hours' rest they were woken in the dark after the influx of a single tide, setting off again in the small hours. They were anxious too for a favourable wind which would allow them to raise their sails on a river which now opened out to a mile or more wide at high tide.

In spite of clean new sails hauled up on a broadening river, however, the three ships made sluggish progress through the flat, little-populated marshlands on the Kent–Essex border. They stayed overnight at the small town of Erith, yet another place on the Thames at which Henry had built naval facilities, and then at Gravesend, where the chalk downs of southern England descend to a narrow neck in the river and where departing sailors traditionally felt their journey into open water began.

Out in the estuary they followed channels through the submerged shoals and banked mud and sands, shaped by the river and the tides. No doubt a number of the mariners on board were experienced at navigating these tricky waters, and the captains would have had both a chart and a rutter, with its clear written instructions.

As they left the Thames behind, the crews steered not south towards the Channel, but north-east up the Essex coast.

Where were the ships heading? To a degree that seems surprising, the secret had been kept. Foreign ambassadors observed the preparations for the voyage. They watched the ceremony of the leave-taking. But the reports they sent home remained anxious and uncertain.

For at least a couple of months prior to the departure, the Emperor's representative in England, Jehan Scheyfve, had tried to learn what he could of the English plans. Early in March he reported that three vessels were being fitted out. His sources were well informed. They would be, he wrote, of 180, 120 and 60 tons respectively, and would be ready within between four and six weeks. They were to be sent on a voyage of discovery, and were 'to steer their course towards Iceland, and thence towards the east, making a few ports'. He could not, however, be more precise. And he confused these preparations with others taking place in Portsmouth (involving a Portuguese pilot who had fled to England) for a voyage to the African coast.[5]

The Imperial government was anxious for more information. The very fact that the endeavour seemed 'of such importance' to the English meant that it should be taken seriously. On 2 April the Emperor, Charles V, wrote to his son and heir, Prince Philip. He forwarded the information he had received from his ambassador in England. This 'seems to us', he wrote, 'a matter of importance'. It should be 'dealt with in good time' and be 'well weighed and considered'. 'You will order,' Charles told Philip, 'that all due consideration is given to it, and that a suitable remedy be provided, so that they may not obtain what they are trying for.'[6]

A month later Scheyfve updated his government with the fruit of further enquiries. 'Since I last wrote,' he said, 'I have been able to ascertain that they will follow a northerly course and navigate by the Frozen Sea towards the country of the great Chamchina' (that is, the country of the great Khan of China). He had had a visit, he wrote, from Cabot himself, who had been to see him about a financial matter he was still pursuing in Spain.

Naturally enough, the ambassador had taken the opportunity to quiz him on the subject of the English venture. As was his wont, Cabot had given the impression of confiding in the Imperial representative. He could help to confound the English ambition: 'he knew a means of thwarting them', he assured Scheyfve, 'if he could go to his Majesty's Court'. And as ever he professed to have 'great secrets' to unfold in which 'many millions were at stake'. He expressed his willingness to leave England for Spain, if so commanded.

In truth, though, this was Cabot's accustomed artifice. And despite an impression of candour – 'he enlarged', Scheyfve wrote, 'so much' – he plainly gave little away. The ambassador's report of the voyage's 'northerly course' was scarcely informative, nor was its ultimate destination a surprise. Perhaps Cabot was ingenuous only in the confidence he exuded. 'At last I asked him if the said voyage was as certain as it seemed', Scheyfve reported; 'he replied, yes, it was.'[7]

Even on the expedition's departure the ambassador remained uncertain, for all that Londoners like Henry Machyn had inevitably gossiped about the venture. In a letter sent on 11 May, as the ships made their way downriver from London, Scheyfve described a conversation he had had with a Portuguese messenger in which they had discussed the English plans. He had been guarded, he said, taking care 'to speak of the enterprise in general terms'. He alluded to the different stories circulating on the streets – pointing out 'that it was variously spoken of'. It is clear, though, that his uncertainty was genuine enough:

> I said it was rumoured that they would follow a north-easterly route, or possibly a north-westerly one. Some said they would steer to the north-east and pass the Frozen Sea, and others that their plan was to follow a westerly course and enter the Strait of the Three Brethren, or pass Cape de las Parras [Barra Head, the southernmost point of the Hebrides], and proceed thence to the Great Cham's country or the neighbouring places.[8]

Still, in other words, it was not generally known whether Willoughby and Chancellor intended to lead their expedition north-east, north-west or over the Pole.

Twenty-Three

Twice, out in the North Sea, favourable winds bore the three ships northward, only to swing sharply round and beat them back.

On the first occasion the men had reached Lowestoft, England's most eastern point, before spending a night at anchor three leagues (nine nautical miles) off Great Yarmouth. The following day, 31 May, Willoughby's log records that they sailed 'into the sea six leagues Northeast, and there tarried that night, where the wind blew very sore'. Their cables held as they rode out a restless night on the violent swell. But the following day brought only frustration. The wind was resolutely unfavourable, firmly 'at North contrary to us'. Reluctantly, unable to progress, the order was given for anchors to be raised and sails set to take them back to Harwich, on the northern Essex coast – the only safe estuary between the Thames estuary and the Humber.

Days passed without any change. For over two weeks – the whole first half of June – the crews remained in the English port 'tarrying for the wind'. 'All this time,' Willoughby wrote, 'the wind was contrary to our purpose.' It was an infuriating delay, and an unnerving one, given the pressure the expedition was under to sail through any north-eastern passage before the end of summer closed it shut. Willoughby and his council met, regularly, to vent their frustration. Prayers were said. But nothing else could be done.

With little to do, Chancellor indulged his regular habit and watched the night skies – perhaps kept company by the few men on board, like Stephen Borough, who were interested in astronomical navigation. For practice he took a measurement of latitude at the mouth of the Orwell. It is correctly recorded in Willoughby's log as 52 degrees.

Planning to travel through the Arctic, the leaders of the present voyage felt unusually anxious about the passage of time. The delay, though, was scarcely uncommon: for captains and crews, waiting on conditions was a normal part of life at sea.

Ships of the sixteenth century demanded a following wind. The mainsail and the foresail were square. In spite of the bowline, introduced by Norsemen, which did at least help to trim a square sail, ships were ill suited to making headway into the wind.[1] Facing contrary wind while out at sea, sails often had to be lowered entirely to avoid the ships being 'taken aback': blown literally backwards. Only the rear, or 'mizzen', sail was 'lateen' rigged – that is, it used a triangular sail suspended from a yard mounted at an angle on the mast which was able to provide momentum somewhat closer to the wind.[2]

In port an anxious watch was maintained, through the night as well as during the day, so that any change could be immediately exploited. Willoughby thought it worthy of note that they had remained at the village of St Osyth 'all that night', because arriving, or leaving, during the hours of darkness was common practice. If the owners of ships, and the products being shipped, had any flexibility, a change of destination was often called for, to make use of the wind that there was. Fervent prayers were said for an improvement in conditions; for sailors, of all people, were bound to read in the shifts of the wind and the mood of the sea the visible expression of God's favour.

On 15 June anchors were weighed once more and the ships battled for two days some fifteen miles north-east up the coast. But early on the 17th, at five in the morning, the wind forced them back to Orford Ness. There, for two days, they clung to the wild expanse of shingle and mudflat under vast East Anglian skies.

The 18th was a Sunday, and though religious services were held twice daily, in the morning and the evening, no doubt the crews were assembled to mark the Sabbath under the leadership of John Stafford, the minister, intoning 'humble and hearty prayer' in order that God's grace be obtained. The following day, with no immediate improvement, they headed back to the shelter of the Orwell, where once again they 'abode there three days tarrying for the wind'.

Willoughby was not easily flustered. On the outside, Chancellor too remained confident. But internally he was prone to anxiety and was worried. His unease may be read between the lines of the account he later gave to Clement Adams. At Harwich, he said, 'they stayed long, not without great loss and consuming of time'.

It was fortunate, perhaps, that Protestant Englishmen were already beginning to acquire a serene assurance of their standing in the celestial estimation. For the Almighty's stalwart support for their venture must have been difficult to discern.

Nor was the wind the only problem to beset them so early. More worrying still, perhaps, for the leading members of the expedition, was the discovery that some of their stores of food, intended to last many months, were already rotten to the point of being inedible. Some of their casks of wine, furthermore, turned out on inspection to be badly made and leaking.

The two coopers on board – William Every on the *Edward* and Laurence Edwards on the *Bona Esperanza* – did their best to make good the barrels. If some of the salted beef, pork or fish had not been cured as it should have been, there was little that could be done to salvage it. The provision of foodstuffs for ships was generally put out to contractors, and shoddy preparation and fraud were widespread. It was common enough, for instance, for pipes of salt beef to contain only a fraction of the actual meat that they were supposed to.[3]

It was fortunate that the decision had been made, and the investment been available, to stock the ships generously for an eighteen-month voyage. Even so, Chancellor himself was more concerned at this point than he let on. It was a nervous time, in any case, at the outset of a major expedition, without fearing for the state of their supplies. He later admitted to being 'not a little grieved' with anxiety that they would run short of food. In the circumstances, however, the passage of time was a still greater threat and they could not afford to wait for fresh supplies.

To add to the woes of Willoughby and his council, problems of crew health and discipline had already raised their heads. Three men were discharged while the ships were delayed at Harwich. George Blake and Nicholas Anthony, two men of Willoughby's ship, had become seriously ill and were set ashore. It was expected that the captain would find and fund lodging on land for the sick men, and provide a local woman, if he could not spare one of the ship's boys, to tend them. He would pay for food and candlelight, along with any salary that the men had earned – though deductions might be made according to the expense of the care provided. It was not expected that the ship would wait for a resolution, by death or recovery, and clearly it did not, in spite of the long delay caused by the weather.[4]

We don't know what the problem was: perhaps it was related to the rotten foodstuffs, perhaps to the marshy, unhealthy environment of the Thames basin (where they spent many weeks, and where malaria – albeit of a less serious kind than was encountered in the tropics – had become endemic), perhaps to any number of possible complaints.[5] The council, plainly, were concerned lest the illness break out more widely among the men. At Harwich they took on two additional crew members, surgeons, who joined Willoughby's ship at the same time as the sick men were discharged. But of course there was little even such 'qualified' men could do in the face of disease; prayer that the problem did not break out more widely was at least as effective.

Meanwhile another man of the *Bona Esperanza*, Thomas Nash, was caught indulging in petty theft ('pickerie' as it was known). For a merchant company paranoid about the cumulative impact of pilfering and personal trading, a firm line was mandatory. Discipline continued to be founded on the ancient laws of Oléron – inscribed on parchment and taken, for reference and admonition, on every voyage, and named after the island off France's Atlantic coast.[6] A case would be heard by the council sitting together in judgement, but they were guided by what seems now a fierce and unbending code, with punishment and deterrence the pre-eminent aims. A murderer was bound to his victim's corpse before being flung mercilessly overboard. For theft, a dishonourable discharge was preceded by traditional naval punishment.[7]

The unfortunate Nash was 'ducked at the yards arm'. His hands were tightly bound, and a rope fastened under his arms and around his waist. He was then hoisted, his fellow seamen hauling on the rope, to the end of the yard – the horizontal beam to which a square sail was attached. From there, dangling precariously from the outer edge over the frothing swell, he was plunged several times into the sea. He was left submerged, helplessly tied, until close to drowning, before being reeled up once more, gasping and flailing like a hooked fish, for a repeat dunking.

Serious offenders might also be 'keel-hauled': dragged, at a leisurely rate, under the keel of the ship from one side to the other. As with many punishments of the period, the practice served the watching and excited crew simultaneously as edification and entertainment. At last Nash was towed ashore behind the ship's boat, still bound and struggling for air, before being discharged.

The purpose was to discourage further offences, and no doubt it was an effective disincentive, though opportunity and temptation might remain.

Twenty-Four

'At the last,' wrote Adams, 'with a good wind they hoisted up sail.' It was now 23 June, more than six weeks after they had set out from Ratcliffe. Finally the three ships headed north, and this time they left England's shores behind.

On each ship, shouts came first from the captain, then, more loudly, from his bosun – unless he used a whistle. Two seamen climbed nimbly to the yard on the forward mast to release the foresail. Then, more shouting, before, to the accompaniment of a throaty shanty, the crew hoisted the heavy main yard: 'Haul all and one, Haul all and one, Haul him up to us, Haul him up to us.'[1] The mainsail was unfurled and 'sheeted home' – that is to say, the ropes attached to its lower corners were drawn tight and secured. Topsails were set and hauled taut, and, in the stern, the mizzen was hoisted and adjusted. A strong, invigorating pull was felt as the wind filled the canvas. As they picked up speed, the ships lifted and rolled faster on the swell.

The predominant emotion was relief. At last the long, frustrating wait seemed over. Nevertheless, the moment when a confident course was finally set away from the home shore towards the open sea was a poignant one for all on board. They were entirely separated now from families and friends, and had no further imperative to mask their fears, other than from each other:

> ... they ... committed themselves to the sea, giving their last adieu to their native country, which they knew not whether they should ever return to see again or not. Many of them looked oftentimes back, and could not refrain from tears, considering into what hazards they were to fall, and what uncertainties of the sea they were to make trial of.[2]

For Chancellor, on whose shoulders the success of the venture largely lay, it was a particularly gut-wrenching moment. Not only did the lofty hopes of investors and the political community at large rest on his expertise, but he was leaving behind him two sons. The boys' mother, plainly, had already died, because Adams remarks that 'if he sped not well' – if some mishap befell him – they would be left as orphans. Pride at the esteem which had earned him prominence in this path-breaking expedition must have jostled sorely both with trepidation for himself at the unknown ordeal ahead and fear for the fate of his children should he fail to return.

The stakes were high: there was much to be gained in terms of wealth, prestige and knowledge of the world, but also everything – more than a hundred lives, including his own – to be lost.

Even now that they had at last left the English coast behind, the three ships continued to battle out in the North Sea against changing and often unfavourable conditions.

The voyage's council had met at Holmhead before the fortnight's stay at Harwich. There, Willoughby recorded, they had 'consulted which way, and what courses were best to be holden for the discovery of our voyage, and there agreed'. But intent was one thing; they could only set the courses that the wind permitted.

At first they headed broadly north. On 27 June they attempted to steer slightly to the west, to pick up the coast of Scotland, but before they could do so the wind 'veered to the West' (that is, it blew from the west), preventing them from doing so. As they sailed further, they continued to be beset by jagged winds that swung about the compass, with the three ships at their mercy:

> Then we sailed north 16 leagues by estimation, after that north and by west, and north-north-west, then southeast, with diverse other courses, traversing and tracing the seas, by reason of sundry and manifold contrary winds.

How, now that they were out of sight of any land, did they keep track of their position? More than ever before on English ships, there was an emphasis upon careful measurement as an aid to location-finding – but at sea its limitations remained.

Speeds through the water could be roughly assessed by the eye of an experienced captain. More scientifically, it was at about this time that the English began to use the log-line. A flat piece of wood designed to remain more or less stationary was thrown overboard on the end of a line. One seaman then counted the evenly spaced knots which passed through his fingers as the line unfurled. Another kept an eye on the steady fall of sand through the ship's glass.[3] The resulting measurement in 'knots' (that is, in nautical miles per hour) could then be married to the compass bearing on which the ship was heading to plot an approximate course.

To keep record, a traverse board was used, its lines of peg-sized holes radiating to each point of the compass and allowing progress to be marked up with each watch. This technique had become established – by the 1550s most 'ancient masters of ships' relied on such a board, and they did not need to be literate to do so. Distance, increasingly, was measured in leagues, each of which was reckoned as three nautical miles.[4] Pilots in France and the Mediterranean sometimes transposed such a board onto a chart of the region, a practice that was still rare in England, and rather scorned by older and perhaps illiterate men of the sea. Chancellor, of course, was not one of the latter. He was a rare navigator, and in Cabot he had a mentor with long experience of Spanish practice. He did not, though, have a chart of these northern seas that was accurate enough to be reliable.

Either way, using this method to keep tabs on progress – 'dead reckoning', as it was known – was an imprecise art. Tides and currents could have a significant impact on the ship's speed and course. Since the long voyages of Columbus, Cabot and others, moreover, it was recognised that compass readings could mislead. In the Atlantic and the seas of the north, much more so than in the Mediterranean, there was a significant difference between the direction of magnetic north, indicated by the needle, and that of 'true' north. Efforts were made to measure this 'variation' and to understand it – but on this first English foray into the waters of the far north, its impact on compass navigation was not known. As the wind forced Willoughby, Chancellor and their crews into repeated changes of course, errors of this nature accumulated.

There was another method of establishing one's latitude (though not longitude) on the earth's surface, and this was a discipline in which Chancellor, at least, was highly skilled. By measuring the altitude above the horizon either of particular stars, or of the sun at noon, and with reference to tables that carefully predicted these angles for each day or night of the year, a latitude reading could be obtained.

With him Chancellor had his trusty instruments, which allowed him to conduct these measurements: astrolabes, cross-staffs and quadrants. Which instrument was used depended on conditions and personal preference. An admired 'mechanician', as Dee had called him, Chancellor had built and fine-tuned them himself. The trouble, though, was that it was extremely difficult to use these instruments with any degree of accuracy on a ship's deck rolling on an open sea. He may have tried – only Willoughby's ship's log survives. But reliable measurements needed to be made on land.

Certainly, on board the admiral of the fleet, attempts to keep track of position by dead reckoning must have been wildly inaccurate given the changeability of the conditions and the multitude of courses taken. Willoughby probably had little idea how far north the three ships had travelled when finally, on 14 July, the shout greeted him from boys perched high in the rigging that land could be seen to the east.

The sun, Willoughby noted significantly, had just passed into Leo – the 'fire' sign (ruled by the sun) which favoured bold, determined behaviour.[5] Perhaps he had convinced himself, in spite of all the unfavourable winds, that the heavens smiled on his expedition.

Twenty-Five

The three ships had now been at sea for twenty-two days. As the evening moved on and midnight neared, the sun lowered in the sky before dipping below the horizon for an hour. But even then a warm, reddish glow remained to mark where it had fallen and there was nothing in the way of deep darkness to impede their approach. Towards the land, Willoughby recorded in his journal, 'we sailed that night as much as we might'.

Before a backdrop of mountains up which the snowline had retreated beneath the summer sun they found a coastal region of dramatic inlets and shallow water which lapped at innumerable islands. On the low ground, woods and green fields basked beneath clear skies in a climate that was remarkably warm for the northerly latitude. In places the high hills and mountains spilled out from inland ranges to the sea, rising sharply from the water's edge. Some of the islands were flat; others reared suddenly up in thrusts of rock from the water. Everywhere, glaciers had torn fierce and unusual shapes.

With the sea floor as irregular as the visible rock, and with the coastline and the tides unknown, regular measurements were necessary of the water beneath the ships to avoid shoals and reefs. The 'lead and line' was one of the oldest instruments used at sea. A weight, attached to a rope, was thrown overboard to 'sound' the depth. The rope was subdivided at regular intervals by distinct and consistent 'marks': a knot of black leather at two and three fathoms, white cloth at five and fifteen fathoms, red cloth at seven and so on. Close to shore, as they were, a short sounding line was used with which measurements could be taken regularly as they proceeded. (They also had with them a longer deep-sea or 'dipsie' line.) Plugs of tallow would be added to the weight to bring a scraping of the sea floor to the surface for inspection – information which, in familiar waters at least, might assist with fixing a location.

Eventually, leaving the larger ships and some of the men anchored in a sheltered bay, the crews took to their pinnaces, from which they could wade ashore. On land they saw clear evidence of a small settlement: 'little houses to the number of 30', tended and lived in. But when the crews approached they found them deserted. The inhabitants, they surmised, had seen the large, unknown ships drawing near across the water and 'were fled away ... for fear of us'.

Now that he was standing on firm land – a disorientating feeling at first after more than three weeks of pitching with the waves on the open sea – Chancellor was able to take measurements which helped in fixing their position. At this time of year, when the sky remained bright for almost all of the day, it was difficult to sight stars for which he had tabulated positions. Twenty-five years later, furthermore, the son of one man who sailed this way with Chancellor wrote that in the Arctic, far to the north, the Pole or North Star was too high in the sky to be accurately observed. 'Therefore,' he commented, 'we always use the staff and the sun, as fittest instruments for this use.'[1] A clear reading could be obtained of the angle between the sun and the horizon at midday. Often Chancellor was able to set up the supports for his quadrant or astrolabe to ensure that the instrument remained steady while he lined up the sun through the small viewing hole, squinting as he did so, and read off its altitude.

With this information, and consulting his ephemerides or 'sun tables', he calculated the party's position as 66 degrees of latitude, which without any reference to a specific town or landmark it is impossible to verify, though it may have been a slight underestimate. They later established that they were in the district of Helgeland, more than halfway up the Norwegian coast. They must have been close to the Arctic Circle – the point at which twenty-four-hour sunlight may be experienced for at least a day in summer.[2]

Returning to their ships, they sailed, by Willoughby's reckoning, a further twelve leagues – thirty-six nautical miles – north-west. They came across many more islands clustered in the sea, most of them merely uninhabited rocks.

The more southerly of the larger islands were flat, spotted with lakes and low-lying meadows. Here, on 19 July (by an old-style reckoning), the crews dropped their anchors into the shallow water and parties took to their pinnaces to row or sail to shore. It felt warm in the summer sun, in spite of their northerly location; the Norwegian coast benefits from a substantial temperature anomaly for its latitude. Exploring the land, they found 'people mowing and making of hay', capitalising on the long hours of daylight in preparation, already, for the rapid onset of autumn and then winter, when the sun would all but disappear from their lives.

These people were more curious, or less alarmed, and came down to the shoreline to greet the strange arrivals. The English crews were now, they quickly learned, in the Røst islands – at the southern tip of an extended archipelago which curves gently south-west from the northern tip of Scandinavia, now 'under the dominion of the king of Denmark', as was all of Norway between the end of the fourteenth and the early nineteenth centuries. The islanders retained a communal memory of previous strangers who had washed up, blown wildly off-course, on their shores – of a Venetian merchant in the fifteenth century, and later, thirty-odd years prior to the present expedition, a Dutch princess, whose visit was still remembered by the older inhabitants.[3]

As they came ashore the wind swung about the compass, preventing any immediate progress northward; but no doubt it seemed a bearable misfortune that the crews were obliged to remain where they were for three days, given the unknown hazards that lay ahead. Vast colonies of seabirds – puffins, cormorants and others – thronged the rocks and cliffs of the numerous islets. If their beauty was admired, their flavour was likewise, and hungry sailors clambered in pursuit of them with bows strapped to their backs.

All added variety to the monotonous shipboard diet, lamented as 'rotten and unwholesome' by one naval surgeon. Even the beef which hadn't gone bad was typically 'of a most loathsome and filthy taste and savour', while fish, butter and cheese were all 'wonderful bad'.[4] Men in Tudor England were accustomed in any case to catching and eating birdlife in all its variety, harbouring none of the fastidious and rather arbitrary discrimination of a later age.[5] Here in Røst there was 'an innumerable sort of fouls of diverse kinds', wrote Willoughby, 'of which we took very many'.

Food stores became more exotic. Alongside the bacon and dried beans were stuffed dead puffins and other seabirds.

On 22 July the wind changed again and the crews were ordered to prepare for a prompt departure.

For five days they sailed north-north-east, keeping the island chain known as the Lofoten to their east. From Røst they travelled, Willoughby calculated, another thirty leagues – passing near (though they did not mention and presumably did not encounter) the great whirlpool formed by the tide and the seabed near the rearing, uninhabited rock of Mosken.

When they next approached an island that looked inhabited and sent a pinnace to investigate, they found good harbours for their ships and inhabitants who were a 'very gentle people'. Chancellor again set up his instruments and used the sun to make an accurate measurement of the latitude as 68 degrees north of the Equator. After another short stay, at about midday on 30 July, they weighed anchor once more and 'went into the Seas', continuing to follow the string of islands north-north-east.

At around this time Willoughby ordered a flag to be hoisted on the *Bona Esperanza* summoning the three English ships together so that the council could meet. Perhaps cloud banks had begun to mass on the horizon, suggesting the onset of bad weather. The wind may have been picking up, or other signs, carefully watched by mariners, have been considered ominous: the behaviour of birds, flying low, of fish, jumping out of the sea, or the pattern of wind on distant water. With the ships anchored close by one another, council members on the *Edward Bonaventure* and the *Bona Confidentia* were able to use their ship's boats to meet on board the admiral.

Thus far the three ships had followed Cabot's injunction that 'the fleet shall keep together', even during their difficult crossing of the North Sea. But it was crucial, Willoughby urged his fellow councillors, that they each knew what to do if the ships were forced by extreme weather to separate.

The men naturally agreed. Just off the coast of Finnmark, the most northerly province of Norway which bent over the top of Sweden and Finland, was a small island fortress well known as the principal place in the region: Vardøhus, or 'Wardhouse' as the English knew it. This, as Willoughby noted, was 'the strongest hold in Finnmark', and the 'most resorted to by report'. It was agreed that 'if any great tempest should arise at any time, and happen to disperse and scatter them', each ship would make for this castle, and 'they that arrived there first in safety should stay and expect the coming of the rest'. It was a sensible plan, but uncontroversial, and Adams is being a little generous in deducing that the captain was a man of 'good foresight'.

On 2 August the three ships sailed in close to another island, large and with high, rugged mountains rising hard up from the sea, to check their position. As they did so a small local skiff came out to meet them, drawing alongside, allowing Willoughby and others to interrogate its pilot, perhaps in German or French. The fleet was now, they learned, by 'Seynam' (Senja) island, close to the mainland.

Loyal to Cabot's instructions, the leaders shouted enquiries about the types of products which were available for trade. Willoughby was evidently disappointed in the response: 'there was', he wrote, 'no merchandise there, but only dried fish, and train oil'. These were valuable products, but the English had plentiful sources of fish elsewhere, and in any case the local fishermen had an established market; having plundered the cod which massed in winter in the waters off northern Norway, in summer they sailed south to sell their dried catch to the Hanseatic merchants who were based in the southern Norwegian port of Bergen. Train oil was made from the blubber of whales and seals and was used, among other things, for making candles and for oiling wool. It was not a well-known product in England. Willoughby makes no mention of sightings of whales in his journal, though some are quite likely. Four years later an Englishman sailing off Senja reported seeing 'many whales, very monstrous, about our ships, some by estimation of 60 foot long'.[6]

Willoughby told the local man that the expedition wished to get to Finnmark – the region which spanned the northern tip of the Scandinavian peninsula. He asked whether it was possible to find a local pilot who could come on board to help them navigate along an unfamiliar coastline for which they had no accurate chart. He got a positive response. 'If we could bear in,' he noted in his log, 'we should have a good harbour, and on the next day a pilot to bring us to Finnmark, unto the wardhouse.' If.

Already, however, the men had to raise their voices to communicate. The wind picked up and, even quite close to the shore, the waves grew in size and noise, their tops white with foam which was whipped in streaks across the decks.

The English ships tried to follow the skiff as it threaded its way through gaps in the jagged cliffs. But the attempt to do so became increasingly treacherous. 'The land' here, Willoughby observed in his log, was 'very high on every side', and the sheer rock plunged directly into the water. The wind continued to blow harder, in spite of shelter from the island, and it gusted in unpredictable directions as it cascaded off the rocks – rocks into which the ships might at any moment be fatally hurled.

Twenty-Six

I t was the afternoon, about 'four of the clock' by Chancellor's memory.
Even in the near-perpetual light of the Arctic summer, the sky grew
dark and visibility reduced dangerously. The seas swelled, becoming 'so
outrageous', Chancellor recalled, that it was impossible to steer their intended course. 'Flaws of wind and terrible whirlwinds' battered the ships
unpredictably and they could not bear in further towards the island.

Reluctantly a decision was taken to head back out into open water –
'to take the sea again' – to ride out the storm away from the hazardous
rocky coast. At first the three ships remained together. Leaning from the
stern of the admiral, Willoughby yelled to Chancellor across the water,
above the dreadful noise of the wind and waves, urging the *Edward* to
remain in view.

Chancellor heard him. He later told others of Willoughby's words.
But he was powerless to comply. All three captains were at the mercy of
the elements: 'some were perforce driven one way, and some another' in
the strong and shifting gusts. As the wind picked up, the mists and fog
common to these northern waters descended, making it harder for the
captains to keep track of their fellow ships. The waters reared higher,
dark and impenetrable apart from the white foaming crests which battered into their flanks.

So severely was Willoughby's ship, the *Bona Esperanza*, thrown about
that its pinnace, hoisted and roped on deck, was wrenched free and fell
with a crash into the water. Helplessly the three ships were blown north
and slightly east in the direction of the wind, which continued to get
stronger. Desperately Chancellor on the *Edward*, as well as Cornelius
Durforth on the *Bona Confidentia*, tried to keep together with Willoughby, their captain, but the latter's ship flew forward too fast before

the wind. The *Esperanza* was the fastest sailing vessel of the three, and somehow ('I know not by what means', Chancellor later confessed in bemusement) it kept its main- and topsails up even in the howling wind.

On the *Edward*, the largest of the three ships, not only was Chancellor unable to keep up but he thought it rash even to try, 'if [Willoughby] sailed so fast'. The bosun and quartermaster shouted Chancellor's orders through the spray, and boys clung desperately to rigging high on the masts while the topsails were lowered on a pitching sea. Its leaders and its crew, meanwhile, were forced to watch their fellow ships become enveloped, far ahead, by the cloud and mist.

Willoughby 'was carried away with so great force and swiftness', Chancellor later recalled, 'that not long after he was quite out of sight'. Nor could they stay in touch with Durforth. 'The third ship also', Chancellor remembered, 'with the same storm and like rage was dispersed and lost us'.

For the moment, there was little opportunity for regret. The mariners of the *Edward* were too busy riding out the elements and desperately willing the gale to pass.

Darkness which accompanied the descent of the sun was short-lived, but in the thick fog it made little difference and the ship reared, plunged and drifted, blanketed by cloud and by the noise of the elements in a world of its own. Only when, the following day, conditions eventually eased was there time to reflect on what had happened.

Now that Chancellor's ship and company were left alone in the far northern ocean, the Pilot Major was struck by the melancholy to which he was prone. He became, as he later admitted to Clement Adams, 'very pensive, heavy and sorrowful by this dispersion of the Fleet'. The sea seemed vast and empty after they had become accustomed to sailing in convoy. And it was impossible not to dwell on the fact that they had failed to adhere to Cabot's clear instruction to stay together.

Nevertheless, what was an understandable depression was never, with Chancellor, a weight that constrained him. The council's collective decision had been clear enough. If they were separated, each ship should make for Wardhouse. And it was there, accordingly, that Chancellor immediately 'shapeth his course' – in no significant doubt about his position – 'to expect and abide the arrival of the rest of the ships'. With sails taken quickly down as the wind picked up, the *Edward* had avoided being swept too far north of the Scandinavian land mass.

No description of their voyage to Wardhouse survives, but they must have skirted within view of the fractured coast and myriad islands as these trended east and reached a northernmost point. Three years later Stephen Borough, Richard Chancellor's master in 1553, sailed this way again. Passing the 'North Cape', he commented that he had himself named it thus on the earlier voyage.[1]

Certainly the square, flat-topped cliffs must have seemed to mark the point the crew had expected to pass, the northernmost extremity of Europe, just as Bartolomeu Dias, sixty-five years earlier, had rounded a southern cape beneath Africa.[2] It is significant that the same word, 'Cape', was used to describe it. A continent had been rounded, and with luck, or God's will, the English, like the Portuguese before them, were en route to the East.

There was no sense, though, that the dangers they faced had passed. Not long after they had rounded the cape, the *Edward* reached Wardhouse, the small island fortress just off the Norwegian shore. The other two ships of their party were not there, as they had hoped that they would be. But Chancellor weighed anchor to wait for his fellows, as the council had agreed.[3]

For a full seven days they remained with the tiny community which manned and serviced the fortress. Many times every day they scanned the horizon for the *Bona Esperanza* or the *Bona Confidentia*. The sea was calm now, and visibility was good. Regular prayers were cast upwards for the safe delivery of their friends.

There was, though, no sign of Willoughby or Durforth and their crews, and with every day that passed hopes for their arrival grew weaker.

Robert Thorne was an early enthusiast for English exploration to the north. His portrait is owned by Bristol Grammar School, which he founded after his return to England.

English trade in the first half of the sixteenth century was dominated by wealthy foreign merchants such as George Gisze, shown here in a portrait by Holbein.

As a young man, the great polymath John Dee was an expert adviser to the organisers and leaders of the 1553 expedition.

eville was awarded exclusive rights to trade with the New World. It was
ere that Sebastian Cabot lived and worked for much of his career before
e returned to England.

Sebastian Cabot, the brilliant, enigmatic and divisive navigator, was the driving force behind the 1553 expedition.

Cabot worked on this map in 1544 before republishing it in England. The north-eastern corner shown here refers to Indians allegedly shipwrecked above Asia in classical times: proof to some of the existence of a north-eastern passage.

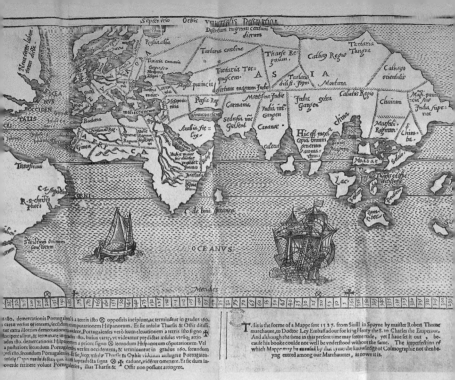

his map, which was attached to Robert Thorne's letter advocating a northern discovery, nows both the passage he believed to exist directly over the Pole, and the limits of uropean knowledge.

or navigators like Richard Chancellor, the sighting of astronomical objects offered the ey to pinpointing a location on the earth's surface. Here an astrolabe is used to measure he altitude of the sun at midday while a cross-staff is used to sight the Pole Star.

his world map was made by a French cartographer for Henry VIII. The empty paces along the north of Asia reveal the lack of knowledge about this part of the lobe.

SIR.HUGH.WILLOUGHBY
FROZEN.IN.THE.NORTH
SEA.IN.1553.

Sir Hugh Willoug[hby]
was a fearless
gentleman soldier
who volunteered
to lead the 1553
expedition, despit[e]
limited navigation[al]
knowledge or
experience.

This late sixteenth
century engraving
showing 'England['s]
Famous Discovere[rs]'
features Willough[by]
alongside other
explorers made
famous by Richar[d]
Hakluyt's histories[.]

England's Famous Discoverers

Twenty-Seven

As he watched the skies, Richard Chancellor was anxiously aware how much time was passing. It was August now. It was still summer, but the solstice had long passed. Each night lasted noticeably longer as the winter grew nearer. Reluctantly, he decided that his crew should press onward with their voyage.

As he was making preparations for departure, Chancellor fell into conversation with some Scots – merchants, or mercenaries – who happened to be at Wardhouse. They asked about his plan. When he told them, they assured him they wished him well and tried to dissuade him from the attempt he had in mind. Further east, they told him, his ship would encounter great dangers. Their words were certainly unnerving. Chancellor worried, as ever, about the responsibilities of his position. It was not only his life that was at stake, but those of all his men. He knew they were afraid and that now, more than ever, they felt fearful and exposed.

The separation from the other ships of the expedition enhanced the uncertainty, hanging over the crew from the start, about the course they were to take. Decisions which had been for the council as a whole, with Willoughby at its head, now rested with Chancellor personally. The fact that his crew showed unbending loyalty in spite of their unease only increased his inner trepidation: he was grateful to them, felt deeply his own personal responsibility, and in the privacy of his own cabin (a luxury afforded only to the most eminent men on board) 'feared lest through any error of his, the safety of the company should be endangered'.

He was aware, though, that there could be no turning back. He believed in the venture he had undertaken, and had a strong sense of its importance. And, for all his tendency to reflect, Chancellor was a man of resolution. Fears could better be quashed by action than by continuing to perch anxiously on this northern edge of the world. Later, in conversation with Clement Adams, he downplayed any doubts he might have had. 'A man of valour', he said, could commit no more dishonourable act than 'for fear of danger to avoid and shun great attempts'. He claimed not to have been discouraged by what the Scots had told him, and certainly, if not true of his innermost thoughts, this did reflect his outward demeanour. He was determined, he said, to succeed in his task, or else to 'die the death'.

Chancellor had learned well from Cabot the impossibility of compelling men to proceed who had vowed among themselves to turn back. In front of them he showed nothing but this steely resolve. Partly as a result, the men of the *Edward* retained great confidence and trust in their captain. Discipline never seems to have been a problem, in spite of the dangers they faced. Under him, Adams later wrote, the crew were willing 'to make proof and trial of all adventures'.

At some point early in August, a favourable wind allowed the *Edward* to lift its anchor, to raise its sails and to make once more for the open sea. Its prow cut through waters that were surprisingly warm given how far north they were, sweeping as they did with the Gulf Stream from warmer, more southerly regions across the Atlantic. Now, in the summer, they were mercifully free of ice.

On Chancellor's instruction the helmsman set his course east, making 'towards that unknown part of the world'.

Twenty-Eight

It was now, Adams thought, that they entered the realm of the midnight sun, where they found 'no night at all'.

In reality, the year was too far advanced. The period when at their latitude the sun literally did not fall below the horizon in twenty-four hours had already come to an end. As they followed the coast now south-east, the nightly spells of half-light lengthened, as John Dee had assured them that they would. Nevertheless, it was bright most of the time, and as they sailed on under clear skies the 'continual light and brightness of the Sun' did shine, as Adams wrote, 'upon the huge and mighty Sea'.

For days, when the wind allowed, the *Edward* followed a coast that was largely treeless and barren, its grey tongues of rock washed smooth by the sea and brushed only with green and yellow scrub. There was little to see, and Chancellor recalled nothing of note in his later account.

Eventually, their south-east course bent round to the south and then south-west as they found themselves funnelled into the long throat of a great inland sea. With the benefit of almost perpetual light, experienced crew members took turns at the helm as they hugged now the further shore as it trended south-east again, bringing them, as 'it pleased God', into 'a certain great Bay' which they thought – with only a little overstatement – must be 100 miles across. Deep within it they cast anchor, near the mouth of a large river which branched into a delta of channels and small islands.

With no clear idea any more where they were, the crew looked apprehensively about for signs of human settlement or activity, readying themselves, if need be, for an unwelcome reception. Before long, a lookout spotted a small fishing boat far off on the water. Immediately the *Edward*'s ship's boat was lowered and Richard Chancellor himself, with a few of his men, climbed down into it to sail across to make contact, hoping to discover what land this was and what people lived in it.

For the fishermen of the White Sea, accustomed only to the small local boats, the *Edward* must have been an extraordinary and terrifying sight. Frightened by 'the strange greatness of his ship', they attempted to flee. Chancellor's faster boat, however, caught them up, and a meeting took place either on board one of the boats or on land nearby. The fishermen were greatly alarmed and made frantic gestures of submission. 'In great fear, as men half dead,' Chancellor remembered, they 'prostrated themselves before him, offering to kiss his feet'. In accordance with Cabot's instructions, meanwhile, Chancellor did his best to ease their concerns, confined as he was to signs, since they had no language in common: '... he (according to his great and singular courtesy), looked pleasantly upon them, comforting them by signs and gestures, refusing those duties and reverences of theirs, and taking them up in all loving sort from the ground'. It was an attitude that had its reward, just as Cabot had hoped.

The local communities were 'Pomors' – that is to say, they were Russians who had settled by the sea and who earned a livelihood fishing, whaling and trading with the coastal towns of northern Norway. Word among them quickly spread of the arrival of a party of strange people on a ship of unprecedented strength and size. But the reputation of Chancellor's men became, as intended, one of 'a singular gentleness and courtesy'.

As a result, people in the small settlements nearby came forward freely, offering the Englishmen food and other commodities. The locals first came out in small boats to the *Edward*, and members of the English crew were able to row ashore. But, apologetically, the Pomors professed that they were forbidden to trade or buy foreign goods without explicit permission from their ruler. Who was this powerful ruler, the English wanted to know, who instilled such fear and obedience in a small and distant community?

The English ship anchored by an island near the mouth of the great river. They called it 'Rose Island', for the obvious reason that they found it, in late summer, before the frost came, 'full of Roses, damask and red, of violets and wild Rosemary'.

On the mainland close by, fir and birch trees massed in great forests. There was a monastery near the shore, built entirely of wood, and named after St Nicholas. Some twenty monks lived there in low, small houses, along with a tiny number of other residents, reminiscent, in their dress, of the orders of pre-Reformation England. They wore black hoods, one Englishman later reported superstitiously, 'as ours have been'. And their church, while simple and pleasing from the outside, was 'full of painted images, tapers, and candles'.[1]

Coastal communities, Chancellor later wrote, 'used to boil the water of the sea, whereof they make very great store of salt'. They fished. And they also produced train oil. As the air began to feel colder, large numbers of small boats set off towards the bay's eastern edge. Many of them were left floating there, at anchor, to be frozen in by the coming of the ice.

When winter had set in the local men would return, across the solid surface of the sea. Dragging their boats and using them as houses, they located and surrounded the large colonies of thousands of seals congregated, lying 'sunning themselves' on the ice and unable to escape. As the slaughter began, the seals clustered in terrified groups, jumping in unison in a desperate attempt to break through the ice. Hundreds were clubbed for the blubber, which was boiled down in great pits dug on the shore to make the oil. The carcasses were discarded and the blinding white landscape was stained a violent red.[2]

A century earlier the sparsely populated lands around the White Sea had lain under the loose control of the Republic of Novgorod, the ancient city state which ruled a vast swathe of north-eastern Europe. During the latter half of the fifteenth century, however, Novgorod's territory had been absorbed by the rapidly expanding state of Russia, which had cast off its allegiance to the 'Golden Horde', the western region of the Mongol Empire. For the people who fished and lived largely in isolation on these northern shores, the hand of an increasingly assertive government was felt for the first time. It reached all the way from Moscow, more than 600 miles to the south.

So Chancellor's men learned now that they were in a country called Russia, which lived under a great King called Ivan. It was six years since

Ivan IV had been crowned in Moscow and assumed the title, new to his dynasty, of 'Tsar of All Russia'. Even in remote regions, his was a real not a nominal control. As Chancellor noted, he 'ruled and governed far and wide in those places'.[3]

England had had no previous diplomatic contact with Russia. Some word of the country had reached this north-western European island, for in the reign of Ivan's grandfather, Ivan III, ambassadors and architects from the Italian states had come to Moscow – and news filtered, in vague fashion, northward. But it was as the archetype of a strange and distant land, about which little that was at all reliable was known, that Russia 'or Russland' was chosen as the theme for a masque put on at the court of the newly crowned King, Henry VIII, in 1509.[4] News of it, and general awareness, only lessened over the decades that came after.

According to a Russian chronicle, it was 24 August when the *Edward* anchored at the mouth of the River Dvina. The long days were growing rapidly shorter. Soon the harsh northern winter would descend like a shroud over these shores. Since it was too late in the year to proceed with the voyage east, Chancellor decided that his ship would remain where it was until spring, and in the meantime he would attempt to make direct contact with the Russian King.

The Russians were equally eager to know where Chancellor and his men had come from, and what was the purpose of their voyage. They learned that these were Englishmen, carrying important letters from their own King, Edward VI, to convey to the Russian Tsar. The letters, they were told, expressed England's desire for friendship and trade, from which both nations would benefit. By this time Chancellor had gained the trust of the coastal community, who told him that he would need to travel south, up the Dvina, to meet the local governors at the regional capital of Kholmogory.

This river was large, but it separated at its delta into channels, and the water was shallow. Chancellor and his men embarked therefore in their pinnace, while the larger ship, the *Edward*, was anchored in a small bay nearby at the suggestion of locals. Most of her crew stayed with her to see out the winter. Chancellor bore in mind Cabot's cautionary words, and remained distrustful. He requested that a few Russians remain on board the *Edward* with his crew, as security for the well-being of himself and his fellow leaders.[5] He then set out to make the 100-mile journey upriver.

A Russian chronicle recorded the arrival in Kholmogory of 'one named Richard', who was 'an envoy of the English King Edward'. Chancellor and his men were taken to meet those who comprised the regional government. There was the governor, who was effectively Ivan's viceroy, who may have been away on campaign. There were also two elected officials, whose 'election' in practice was far from democratic in the modern sense. Filipp Rodionov and Feofan Makarov regretfully reiterated to Chancellor the law of the land.[6] They could provide him with food, but they could not freely trade with foreigners without royal permission. Nevertheless, Chancellor reported that the Russians had heard what he had to say 'very gladly' and promised to help by sending word to their King of 'so honest and reasonable a request'.

A message was accordingly despatched to Moscow, telling Tsar Ivan IV 'of the arrival of a strange nation', and asking what response he would wish to be made to them.

Twenty-Nine

Leaning from the rear castle of his ship, Sir Hugh Willoughby had yelled back to Richard Chancellor to remain in view. But the accumulating noise of the wind and the waves had swallowed even his strident voice, and the *Edward* rapidly vanished back into the mist which had descended – a suffocating blanket draped over the raging sea.

From this point, the accounts written by Chancellor himself, and that worked up by Clement Adams after speaking to Chancellor, offer no clue as to the fate of the other two ships of the expedition. When the *Edward* eventually returned to England, its crew brought no word concerning the well-being of their companions. 'As for them that are already returned and arrived,' wrote Adams, 'they know nothing of the rest of the ships what has become of them.'

Together with Chancellor and his crew, he could only speculate and hope:

> But if it be so that any miserable mishap have overtaken them, if the rage and fury of the sea have devoured these good men, or if as yet they live, and wander up and down in strange countries, I must needs say they were men worthy of better fortune; and if they be living, let us wish them safety and a good return, but if the cruelty of death hath taken hold of them, God send them a Christian grave and sepulchre.

It is only because, months later, the ships were found, while at the same time the log was recovered which Willoughby had kept in his cabin on board the *Bona Esperanza*, that we know something of what became of them.

For most of the men, it had been an arbitrary matter of luck – a cast of the die – as to which ship, and which fate, they were allotted. The minister, John Stafford, was transferred at the last minute from Willoughby's ship to Chancellor's. The sickness which had struck down George Blake and Nicholas Anthony, and caused them to be discharged at Harwich, may have saved their lives, if it didn't take them first. At the same time, the surgeons Alexander Gardiner and Richard Molton joined the expedition belatedly, on Willoughby's ship, having not previously been involved.

The theft, meanwhile, which caused Thomas Nash some serious temporary discomfort as he was plunged, lungs bursting, into the water, before being sent ashore, secured him a reprieve not granted to his more honest colleagues.

As his ship flew helplessly north and east before the wind, Willoughby lost sight not only of the *Edward*, with Chancellor on board, but also, subsequently, of the *Bona Confidentia* under Cornelius Durforth. 'By violence of wind, and thickness of mists,' Willoughby wrote later in his log, 'we were not able to keep together within sight.'

Left alone on the raging sea, Willoughby's crew were obliged, when they found it possible, to haul down their sails in order to ride out the bad weather, as Chancellor had already done in anticipation. Though they had initially kept their sails up, somewhat to Chancellor's bemusement, conditions only grew worse, until his ship too, Willoughby recorded, was unable 'to bear any sail'. He ordered his crew to take them in so that they might lie adrift, 'to let the storm over pass'. There was little that could then be done, beyond struggling to keep the ship heading into the wind.

Most of the mariners lay helpless below decks as the *Bona Esperanza* was tossed about. Around midnight its pinnace, which had already been ripped from its position on deck and thrown into the churning water, broke free from the rope which held it to the ship. Previously the crew would have hoped to mend it in due course, as the carpenter was equipped to do. This time, however, it was lost altogether – a handicap to those on board, who could no longer use it to explore in shallow water. It was, Willoughby admitted, 'a discomfort unto us'.

The thick fog that was the primary bar to visibility lifted. When it did so, officers and crew anxiously scanned the horizon. With a shout, and a widespread sense of relief, they spotted to the leeward – in a downwind direction – another of the expedition ships. The wind remained strong, but by spreading a small expanse of sail, a 'hullock' as Willoughby called it, they were able to close the gap. They realised, with disappointment, that it was the *Confidentia* they could see. The *Edward*, Chancellor's vessel, was nowhere in sight.

For several long days conditions remained bad, though visibility at least improved and the two smaller of the expedition ships were able to remain together, drifting with the currents and the wind. Finally, on 4 August, five days after the storm initially hit, the dangerous gusts eased significantly and the ships were able to raise their sails once more. Willoughby's first thought, communicated to Durforth on the *Confidentia* by the raising of a prearranged flag, was to make for Wardhouse, the island fortress beyond the northern cape where the expedition's council had agreed that they would meet should they become separated in bad weather.

They were now out of view of land, and Willoughby had to take a reading from his compass and estimate their position on the inaccurate charts in his possession. He assumed that they had further to travel up the Scandinavian peninsula, and set a course north-east and by north (that is, between north and north-east), 'to the end to fall with the Wardhouse, as we did consult to do before, in case we should part company'.

For two days the crews followed Willoughby's roughly north-easterly course. He estimated that they had travelled fifty leagues, or 150 nautical miles. But still no land was seen, and he and the other senior officers on board both ships began to feel increasingly anxious. On 6 August Willoughby ordered that a sounding be carried out. When they tried first, however, with the shorter lead and line, its 100-fathom length was paid out entirely without the seabed being reached. They tried again using the longer 'dipsie' line, marked first at twenty fathoms and then at ten-fathom intervals.[1] The weight was cast into the dark, heaving water and immediately disappeared, rapidly pulling the line down with it. Shouts were raised as the marks passed through the hands of the sailor paying out the line. Eventually the pulling ceased and a depth measurement was proclaimed: 160 fathoms.

There was no firm rule which linked the depth of water under a boat to the proximity of the coast. From Cornwall, ships sailed southwest for many miles before clearing the relatively shallow Continental shelf, while to the west of Spain or Ireland, very deep water – in which the ocean bed plummeted thousands of fathoms – lay a short distance from land. Nevertheless men presumed, not unfairly, that the two were correlated. 'Whereby', Willoughby wrote after recording the depth in his log, 'we thought to be far from land.' And in this instance he was right.

As Chancellor had quickly lowered his sails before following the bend of the land around to the east when the wind finally dropped, the *Bona Esperanza* and the *Bona Confidentia* scudded along before the howling winds and must have sailed well beyond the Scandinavian land mass, to the north of what their friends on the *Edward* called the North Cape. For Willoughby and his crews, 6 August was a long and anxious day. The nights were now lengthening but here, far to the north, the sun still set only briefly. In every direction there was open water. Men leaned from deck rails, their eyes straining, as shifting banks of cloud or mist on the horizon caused confusion and false hope.[2]

In his cabin Willoughby looked repeatedly, and with mounting frustration, at the map of the region in his possession. He probably had a copy of the globe produced in 1541 by Mercator, the great mathematician and maker of maps and instruments who was a friend of John Dee. According to this, immediately to the north of Scandinavia Greenland stretched east at the base of a polar continent, leaving only a narrow channel through which ships could pass above Europe. The fact that here, in these unexplored northern waters, the map was largely conjectural, was no comfort to Willoughby, who had little choice but to assume that it was substantially correct.

Willoughby would have imagined that sailing too far north of Wardhouse, marked on Mercator's map to the west of this channel, could only result in sighting Greenland, after which the error could be easily corrected. But instead the ships passed through mile after mile of open ocean.

The confusion and frustration may easily be read into the Captain General's brief inscription in his log. 'The land', he wrote, 'lay not as the Globe made mention.'

Thirty

A misleading map was not Willoughby's only difficulty. Navigation was complicated, too, by a fact that was recognised by learned men like Cabot, Dee or Chancellor, but was scarcely measured or understood.

Immersed in thick cloud or mist, with little guidance from the sun or other celestial bodies, ships depended for information regarding their course on the readings of their compass: 'that extra pair of eyes', as the instrument was labelled, 'which enabled a pilot to see in the dark of a cloudy day or in a starless night'.[1] These readings, however, were beset by serious inaccuracies.

Introduced to the Mediterranean in the twelfth century, the compass had quickly become established as an essential instrument for the pilot at sea. In a procedure which seemed magical or divine, its iron needle was first magnetised by a 'lode-stone', which the pilot kept in a brass case to remagnetise the needle as required, since the effect was impermanent. Initially the needle had then been allowed to float freely in a bowl of water, before in later years being set to rotate on a pivot over a card marked with a graduated display of bearings. These points – north, south, east and west – were commonly known as 'winds', since a compass was often used initially to measure the wind direction and only indirectly the course of the ship. The north point was indicated, as it still is, by a fleur-de-lis. The east was shown not by the letter E but by a Cross, in honour of the Holy Land which, from the Mediterranean at least, lay in this direction.[2]

The box containing the compass was placed within a pair of brass rings known as 'gimbals' which rotated freely within each other, on different planes, to maximise stability on turbulent water. These were then secured within a wooden case known as a 'binnacle', held together with wooden pins rather than iron nails, in which the compass sat where it could be clearly seen by the helmsman steering the ship.

For pilots in the Mediterranean, such a compass proved accurate enough. In much-sailed waters, in which men used rutters whose authors had themselves depended upon measurements from the standard compass, instructions could be followed with reasonable confidence. But as navigators of the fifteenth century pushed further out into the Atlantic, it was increasingly observed that the compass needle did not in fact point directly north, as indicated by the Pole Star, but significantly west or east of it, depending on one's location. Columbus noticed it when he voyaged west, and so did John Cabot and his son Sebastian.

The 'variation' of the compass remained a controversial matter. Some navigators refused to believe in it, attributing the errors to inaccurate manufacture of the compass or to faults with its use, both of which problems certainly did occur. At a time when coastal charts were often misleading, and tides and currents imperfectly known, it could be as reliable to follow bearings without regard for variation, particularly in foreign waters when one did not in any case know what the variation ought to be. But Sebastian Cabot had given the question considerable thought and had strong views which he had advanced to King Edward VI himself and must surely have discussed with Willoughby, Chancellor and other leading men involved. Mistakenly, he was convinced that the phenomenon offered the secret to the calculation of longitude at sea.[3]

In the northern waters of the Arctic, explored and charted now by the English for the first time, experienced pilots did observe a significant variation. Attempts would be made to measure it using a 'compass of variation' which compared the direction indicated by the magnetic needle with the shadow produced by the sun lying due south at midday – though this, of course, relied upon clear conditions. Stephen Borough, second-in-command to Chancellor now, went on to record numerous measurements of variation in these waters. Willoughby, however, makes no reference to the phenomenon, and one can only assume that he ignored the problem – a fact which further confounded attempts to pinpoint his location.

The figures recorded by Willoughby in his log are incomplete, and allow only a provisional re-creation of the course taken by the *Bona Esperanza* and the *Bona Confidentia* during the late summer and autumn of 1553. Nevertheless, the outline is clear enough.

On 6 August, in response to the alarmingly deep reading from the plumb-line, as well as the lack of any sighting of land, contrary to what was expected from the map speculatively drawn by Mercator, Willoughby ordered the course to be changed. Now, he commanded, since the wind allowed, the ships should sail south-east and by south, 'thinking thereby to find the Wardhouse'. He continued to exude the authority and confidence which had got him the job, but inside he was plainly nervous.

For the next two days they maintained the new course, sailing, Willoughby thought, forty-eight leagues, or 144 nautical miles, before the wind once more became very strong. It blew from almost directly behind them, from west north-west, and Willoughby ordered the ships to strike their sails and drift, 'not knowing how the coast lay'. Expecting land at any time, he was naturally afraid that they might be blown at speed onto rocks that were submerged in shallow water or reared up out of it. But in fact there was no sign of land. When they took another sounding, to their surprise the crews again measured 160 fathoms of water beneath their hull.

On 9 August the wind swung round again, 'veering to the South Southeast'. Since they could no longer continue in a southerly direction, where they assumed land to lie, they raised their sails once more and sailed north-east. Early the next morning, when another sounding was carried out, even the 'dipsie' line, 200 fathoms long, could not reach the seabed. Men lined the deck rails and climbed the masts in an effort to make out land on the horizon, but none could be seen in any direction – 'whereat', Willoughby anxiously recorded, 'we wondered'. No amount of staring at Mercator's globe could make it align with the geography they were experiencing.

When the wind changed again, blowing now from the north-east, they sailed south-east, on a 'reach': that is, at a 90-degree angle to the wind.

Over the next few days the two ships moved further east, and soundings began to reveal much shallower water. On 11 August they were in forty fathoms, while the seabed, Willoughby recorded, from a sample brought up on a plug of wax attached to the plumb-line, was of 'fair sand'. Early in the morning of the 14th the crewman on watch shouted from his position high in the rigging: for the first time since the great storm had separated the three ships, further to the east he had made out what was certainly land.

Excited and relieved, Willoughby ordered the ships to make towards it, and when the water began to become dangerously shallow the small ship's boat (the larger pinnace having been lost) was hoisted down from the deck into the sea and a few men clambered aboard, to attempt to row to the shore. They struggled to do so, however. As they grew near, reefs, barely submerged and breaking the surface of the shallow water, frustrated them. There were bays with good anchorages, as it happens, to the south and the north, but not where they were.

From what they could see, there was little to lure them. The land nearby was a low and featureless plateau, bleak and empty and all the more dreary for the thick cloud which massed overhead and blocked out the sun. The tundra was dusted with green now, in late summer, but also – already – with ice and snow. In the water too there was 'very much ice', Willoughby wrote. The thick slabs spun and ricocheted, white and often faintly green in hue, causing patches of clear water to open and, just as suddenly, to close shut. On the adjacent land, meanwhile, there was 'no similitude of habitation'.

Their exact location has been the source of much debate, and certainty is impossible. They were probably, though, near the south of the western coast of the crescent-shaped islands of Novaya Zemlya: the New Land, as it was already known. Here the water was calm enough for Willoughby to attempt the only latitude reading that he recorded in his log, other than one in England when he was still with Richard Chancellor, and the figure he came up with of 72 degrees accords exactly with this supposition. Deep in the interior, particularly to the north, reared inhospitable ice-fronted mountains which continued the Urals chain on the continent further south. Closer to hand, the expanse of sandbanks and shallows thronged in summer with breeding birds – numerous species of ducks, geese and swans – which filled the air with their cries and which would lend this southern peninsula the label 'Goose Island'.[4]

Unable to reach land, and not greatly tempted by what they saw, the two ships tacked laboriously against the wind – tacking, for square-sailed ships, was always laborious – inching slowly, for three days, northward along the coast. There was little alteration in the weather, and the *Bona Confidentia* was increasingly troubled by bilge water, which leaked into the lowest section of the hold running along the keel.

Attempts to resolve the problem at sea were unsuccessful and, after communicating with Durforth, Willoughby noted that 'we thought it good to seek harbour for her redress'.

On 18 August Willoughby ordered a radical change of course.

The wind continued to blow from the north-east, unfavourable for progress north, and an icy chill already accompanied these northerly gusts, which blew off the Pole. Slowly they turned about and sailed south-south-east, much faster with the wind now almost behind them. The unpromising shore of Novaya Zemlya slipped from view as they made for what, as they assumed, must be the north Asian coast. For three days they travelled in that direction, covering, Willoughby calculated, seventy leagues or 210 nautical miles.

On 21 August a sounding was carried out and, to the crew's surprise, revealed that they were in only ten fathoms of water. When they sounded again shortly afterwards, they found only seven fathoms. The water was shallower and shallower, Willoughby noted in bemusement, and yet no land could be seen. The leading men anxiously deliberated together but could make no sense of it. 'We marvelled greatly', Willoughby wrote in his log. He felt that they could not continue in their current course, for fear that they might strike the seabed or a submerged rock, and do damage to one or both of the ships which could prove fatal. So he ordered yet another significant change. All that night, he recorded, 'to avoid this danger', they headed north-west and by west, into what they were sure was deeper water.

For two days the ships now sailed west, sounding once more and finding a reassuring increase in depth to twenty fathoms, before, on the 23rd, sighting land again. But it looked no more promising: low, as before, and barren, with long, monotonous cliffs of mud and snow collapsing occasionally into the drifting fields of ice below. Small inlets and river valleys cut into the cliffs but were inaccessible on account of the ice. Mists descended without warning, causing the temperature to plunge. Flocks of ducks and other waterbirds – a sign of land nearby – splashed and dived near the boat, then took to the air en masse and blew past like clouds of snow. But Willoughby and his men were in search of humans rather than birds, and this land looked depressingly unhopeful. 'It appeared unto us uninhabitable', Willoughby recorded.

Over the course of the next five days the wind shifted sharply and often. For a time, with the wind gusting from the west, they tacked effortfully alongside the shore of what was probably Kolguev island – a near-circular wilderness of marsh and very low hills.

Contrary winds blew the ships about, north-east, north-west, then south-west, before they saw the land again and drew close enough to inspect it. They advanced cautiously through the shallows until the depth reduced to just three fathoms, when they steered out into deeper water while following the coastline as it curved round to the west. After sixteen leagues, or just under fifty nautical miles, they encountered a 'fair bay', where Willoughby and some of his crew were able to land using the ship's boat.

As they suspected, the land seemed entirely uninhabited. But this time they did at least find evidence of recent human presence. Mounted on the flats by the shore were crosses 'and other signs', primitively made, one assumes, from stones (there being no trees at this latitude from which to derive substantial timbers) but which plainly showed to the Englishmen that 'people had been there'.[5] Willoughby recorded the fact in his log after they had rowed back out to the *Bona Esperanza*. After weeks of solitary wandering in the northern ocean, spirits were perhaps a little buoyed as they sailed further west along the island's coast.

At last, and at least, in this vast and far-northern sea, human life had been detected.

Thirty-One

As the two ships under his command sliced a jagged course through these unfamiliar waters, Willoughby's thoughts drifted at times back to the England he had left behind. He had known, as his home shores faded finally away, that the King's life was in danger. He surely never guessed, though, that in his absence a young lady he knew, who was his own kinswoman, had, briefly, become Queen.

When tuberculosis killed King Edward on 6 July, the leading politician in the land, John Dudley, who was also of course the senior sponsor of Willoughby's expedition, hastened to act on the deceased King's stated wish: that the first in line to succeed him should be not his Catholic half-sister Mary, as convention and statute dictated, but rather his Protestant cousin (once removed), Lady Jane Grey. Aware of this plan, Dudley had married his own son, Guildford, to Lady Jane, in what was pointedly described at the time as 'a display truly regal'.[1]

Jane and Edward were descended alike from Henry VII. While Edward was grandson of the founder of the Tudor dynasty, Jane was his great-granddaughter, through Henry VII's daughter Mary. Though a generation further down the family tree, Jane was actually a year or two older than Edward, owing to the length of time it had taken Henry VIII to father a boy who lived beyond infancy. Jane's father, meanwhile, was Henry Grey, the 1st Duke of Suffolk: a leading member of the powerful Grey clan, to which Willoughby was also related.

The link between Sir Hugh and Lady Jane might not now seem a particularly close one. Henry Willoughby, the son of Hugh's elder half-brother, had married Anne Grey. This Anne was the sister of the Henry Grey who with Frances Brandon, a descendant of Henry VII, fathered Jane Grey. But the connection was close enough for Sir Hugh to feel himself strongly connected to the Grey family, which guarded its relations' interests more determinedly even than many other major families. It is possible, indeed, that it was the Grey connection that had helped Sir Hugh to land his current job, of captaining Cabot's expedition, for which he was scarcely well qualified by naval credentials alone.

Members of the Grey family paid regular visits to the Willoughby households at Wollaton and at Middleton. When Sir Hugh's nephew Henry and his wife both died young, it was Anne's brother, Henry Grey, who supervised the interests of their children. Sir Hugh was often away, forging his own career as a soldier on campaign in Scotland. But he remained in touch with his extended family. He certainly knew Henry's daughter, Jane, and the family must have been somewhat in awe of this imposing man who appeared back from battles in the north with frightening stories and a burgeoning military reputation.[2]

On 21 June senior judges and crown lawyers produced a patent which named Jane as Edward's heir. On 10 July, four days after Edward VI's death – as Willoughby battled with his three ships through the North Sea towards the Norwegian coast – in London Jane Grey was formally declared Queen of England.

In ceremonial procession she was escorted to the Tower, traditional residence of kings and queens before their coronations. After reminding the Council that they had all backed his move, John Dudley left London a few days later to attempt to apprehend the Princess Mary, who in East Anglia had already proclaimed that she, not Jane, was the rightful Queen and was busily rallying support. But already, by 19 July, Dudley could see that the game was up.

Considerable men, with considerable forces, had flocked to Mary's side. For this largely pragmatic reason the Council in London had reneged on its promise, and transferred its allegiance from Jane to Mary.[3] And there were clear signs that popular opinion resented an attempt to sabotage what seemed the rightful path of the succession. Confronted by the inevitable, Dudley conceded defeat. On 20 July he too proclaimed Mary Queen.

In a matter of hours, Willoughby's young relation saw the Tower in both its principal guises. From being an uncrowned Queen, she became a prisoner. Others joined her, also under guard: among them her own father, the Duke of Suffolk, her husband of about six weeks, Guildford Dudley, and his father, John, the Duke of Northumberland, who had so recently been the most powerful man in the kingdom.

For the time being Mary was inclined to spare young Lady Jane, who had clearly been the tool of others in the plot rather than the prime mover. For John Dudley, however, there was no such concession. His trial began on 18 August, as Willoughby and his crews sailed past the inhospitable shore of Novaya Zemlya, and on the 22nd – after an unprincipled but futile declaration of his return to the Catholic faith – he, like his father before him, was executed.

Thirty-Two

In Kholmogory, Richard Chancellor and his fellow Englishmen were treated with generous if primitive hospitality. In a region that was wholly unused to passing traffic, they were honoured guests. They were provided with houses, built, as all here were, from straight, narrow trunks of fir, roofed with bark and insulated with moss that was stuffed into the cracks. They were small and square, divided internally into four rooms, with narrow windows covered with translucent sheets of animal skin to let in some light while keeping out the cold. Wooden benches lined the walls, which by most were used to sleep, 'for the common people know not the use of beds'.[1] To a degree that was almost embarrassing, they were supplied with food and drink, as well as with servants who both took care of their needs and kept a watchful eye on what they did.

Days and weeks passed, however, and no word arrived back from Moscow. The local governors insisted that no further progress into Russia was possible until it did. Repeated entreaties were shrugged off with ever-changing excuses: permission needed to be obtained from all members of the government; the delay must have been caused by 'great and weighty affairs of the kingdom'. The Tsar may have been away from his capital on pilgrimage to a remote monastery, as he often was, and as he had particular reason to be. But the delay may also have been, as the local officials surely suspected, merely the standard practice of the Muscovite state.

Foreign delegations wishing to see the Tsar were generally held near the border until permission was obtained, until supervision and preparations for the journey could be arranged and, crucially, until the government could discover as much about its guests as they were likely to know or to learn about them. The sudden and entirely unforeseen

155

appearance of men representing the King of England must have prompt-ed frantic enquiries in Moscow.[2]

To Chancellor and his fellows waiting with mounting frustration and impatience in Kholmogory, however, the half-understood excuses only grated and aroused suspicion. As the weeks and months passed it seemed clear to them that they were being fobbed off. Nowhere, moreover, was the passage of time more obvious than it was here.

For Richard Chancellor, it was a long-ingrained habit to observe the position of the sun in the sky, as a guide both to the time and to a man's position on the earth. He had brought with him from his ship a portable instrument with which to take rudimentary readings of his latitude. Now that the solstice was well passed, he watched the sun rise each morn-ing significantly later above the horizon, and shine more weakly on a landscape increasingly encased after the bitter night by a thick film of frost. Daily, the hours of light diminished. Anxious and conscientious by nature, Chancellor could not suppress his unease at the fact that he and his crew were making no progress towards the goals they had been given.

As autumn gave way rapidly to winter, the changing of the season was marked much more dramatically than it ever was in England. When the wind swung through the compass and blew from the north, it brought with it thick snow and air that cut sharply, plunging the region into a state of torpor. The wide river on which they had travelled from the White Sea, along whose bank sprawled the cluttered buildings of Kholmogory, became dotted with pieces of floating ice which grew and congealed into bumping, spinning slabs before its surface froze entirely solid. From the beginning of November the river was entombed beneath a thick, broad sheet. The English had learned that most of those who journeyed from Kholmogory to Moscow used the river to travel much of the distance by boat. Now, however, with winter set in, this, for boats at least, had become impossible.

Around them the local people began to wear the thick furs which kept out the snow and the wind and allowed them to survive. No doubt they offered some to Chancellor and his men, for the clothes provided by the company for the crews – even with cold weather in mind – were scarce-ly adequate for the plunging temperatures. To the English it seemed another sign of God's providence and care for mankind that creatures abounded in the dense northern forests with luxurious thick coats: sables and foxes, squirrels, hares and ermine (as the larger stoat was known), which in these latitudes donned a thicker white coat during the winter.

Whenever they could the men followed their hosts' example: they remained indoors, by stoves replenished with a limitless supply of wood that was chopped and piled in readiness for the frozen months ahead. As the evenings grew longer and the temperature outside dropped, the men sat and talked by the dim, flickering light of their stoves, and perhaps that of a few candles. Internally, they were warmed by plentiful liquors. Mead, made from the honey that was widely available in the region, was provided by the local officials in what seemed vast quantities. Englishmen were bemused by the level of Russian drinking. 'Drink is their whole desire,' one wrote home shortly afterwards to a friend: 'the soberest head doth once a day stand needful of a guide.'[3]

Perhaps the intense cold fostered other means of attaining warmth. The people of Kholmogory, a fellow Tudor Englishman noted contemptuously, were not only unsophisticated and given to drunkenness. They were also prone to 'all other kind of abominable vices', though he was too diplomatic to name them.[4]

Chancellor was inquisitive and observant, so his time was not wholly wasted. The Englishmen were able to conduct their own religious services, based on readings from their Bible. But they also visited the churches in Kholmogory, built, like everything else, from wood. Towns, Chancellor noted, often had two: one designed to be kept warm during the winter and the other for use in summer.[5]

Chancellor came from an England in which religious reform was now a more contentious issue than any other. He was interested in the practice of faith in Russia, as he knew others would be. He had known he would be travelling to places where life was different in all respects, and he had absorbed Cabot's advice about the need not to be outwardly critical or disapproving. But he was young enough not to remember a time when England was loyal to the Pope and, close as he was to Sidney, Dee, Dudley and their circle, was committed to the new Protestant faith. It made it more difficult, if anything, that Russia was a Christian country. He looked with grave distaste on much of what he saw which, with its images, ceremonies and similar 'superstition', reminded Protestant Englishmen of the Catholicism they had come to detest.

In Russia, Chancellor noted, men observed the Greek Orthodox religion, 'with such excess of superstition, as the like hath not been heard of'. They eschewed 'graven' – that is, sculpted – images. But they worshipped painted ones with 'such idolatry', he thought, that even under the old faith 'the like was never heard of in England'. Churches were full of nooks and niches inhabited by these images, before which people prostrated themselves, pleaded and cried out for help, and banged their heads upon the ground so fervently, as another Englishman wrote, 'that some will have knobs upon their foreheads with knocking, as great as eggs'.[6] These 'saints' were felt in a sense to be real, not merely representations. They were lit by numerous candles, or splashed with water, just as they had been in English churches. But in recent years many Englishmen had been persuaded, and bullied, into abominating all such supposed sacrilege, and Chancellor and his companions were shocked.[7]

It was not only in church. In all private houses painted icons were hung by law. They were treated with extraordinary reverence. The Englishmen watched in bemusement as visitors to a house, before any living person was greeted, first blessed themselves several times and flung themselves down before the icons, striking their foreheads on the ground.[8] The icons might not even be visible. For the most part, as Chancellor told Adams, household saints were placed in the darkest corner. 'He that comes into his neighbour's house', he said, 'doth first salute his saints, although he see them not.'

It was true that in church services Russians used the vernacular, a practice that was close to the Protestant heart. But Chancellor was unimpressed by the practical engagement with Scripture that he encountered. On the contrary, he found 'superstition is no less'. Priests deliberately sought to be obscure, while their congregations merely talked among themselves. Religion in Russia was pervaded with ceremony – 'with more ceremonies', Chancellor proclaimed, 'than I am able to declare' – and while the priests conducted their service, men and women stood around and gossiped. They 'gaggle and duck', he observed with disgust, 'like so many Geese'.

He was acute enough to notice, though, that however laxly observed or ill understood it could seem to an educated Englishman, their faith was integral to Russian people. Every Wednesday and Friday they kept their fasts, in commemoration first of Christ's betrayal and then of his Crucifixion, abstaining from meat and dairy products and eating only herbs and preserved fish. During the year, he discovered, they fasted for prolonged periods not only during Lent, as observed in England, but also at three other times, in honour, each time, of saints venerated in Russia. They believed that any who broke St Peter's Lent, for instance, would be denied entry to heaven by St Peter himself who stood on duty at its gates.

Death surrounded the men here, as it did in every sixteenth-century community. In winter the ground was too hard to permit burial. But dead bodies remained magically preserved by the cold. When people died, they lay in pinewood coffins – a luxury denied to many in England, where wood was less cheap – until late spring thawed the ground. They were provided with a written slip, which was enclosed in their hands, ready to be presented to St Peter at heaven's gates. It affirmed that the individual was a 'true and holy Russian'. At a time when the English already saw themselves as men and women from the land of England, with a sense of national identity that was secular and patriotic, Chancellor sensed how for Russians national identity and faith were so tightly entwined as to be inseparable. They believed they were superior because their religion was superior.

'Very ridiculous', was the reaction of Clement Adams after speaking to Richard Chancellor. He scoffed at the Russian Orthodox believer's idea that:

> ... his glory and place is higher and greater than the glory of the Christians of the Latin Church, reputing themselves to be followers of a more sincere faith and religion than they; they hold opinion that we are but half Christians, and themselves only to be the true and perfect Church – these are the foolish and childish dotages of such ignorant barbarians.

Eventually, Chancellor's patience gave out. Fearing, as he later told Clement Adams, an attempt to delude him – for 'they posted [put] the matter off so often' – he visited the governor and gave him a direct ultimatum. If he and his men were not allowed to set out at once for the Russian capital, they would simply leave and continue their voyage.

In some ways, of course, it was an empty threat. Where would the English have gone now that a winter beyond their experience had set in? How, indeed, would they have gone anywhere? Soon the cold which set firm the Dvina would freeze solid the surface of the White Sea itself. Not for many months would the *Edward Bonaventure* be able to sail back towards the throat of the sea and out into the northern ocean.

Nevertheless, the governors of Kholmogory were alarmed at the consequences for themselves if the Tsar should expect these exotic visitors in Moscow, with their rich cargo of cloths and letters from a fellow king, only to be disappointed because they felt they had been mistreated and would not, or could not, come. Certainly Chancellor noticed, and reflected upon, the palpable fear the local governors felt for the man who ruled them from such a distance.

Thirty-Three

Reluctantly, though permission from Moscow had not yet reached them, the Russian authorities arranged sleds for Chancellor and the merchants and gentlemen who were with him. Moving onwards by boat from Kholmogory had become impossible at this late stage in the year. It was around the same time, however, that travelling by land did become feasible.

Throughout the warmer months the terrain of northern Russia made it effectively impassable. Numerous lakes, vast, thick woods and endless marshy plains made travel desperately difficult and slow. 'In summer,' wrote one of Chancellor's companions, 'the way is dangerous by means of marshes and bogs, and not safely then to be passed.' Travellers overland could be limited to struggling through the mud for a frustrating few miles in a day.[1]

As snow fell and the ground froze, however, roads which had been hopelessly wet, rutted and muddy hardened into smooth sheets over which sleds could run, pulled by horses, at considerable speed. Sometimes large rivers themselves, thickly frozen, could be used as highways for sleds: 'winter roads', as they were known. To the English, used to roads which were drier, faster and easier in the summer, it was a counter-intuitive phenomenon, unusual enough to be noted, as it was by the traveller and ambassador Anthony Jenkinson, who followed Chancellor to Moscow a few years later:

> In the wintertime ... the road is firm and smooth from the snow; all the water and rivers freeze, and one horse harnessed to a sleigh can take a man as much as 400 miles in three days; but in the summertime the roads are covered in deep mud and travelling is very hard.[2]

Progress could also be more direct. Broad rivers traversed the country but they often took a circuitous route, and carriage overland might be necessary as people and goods moved from one channel of water to another. One of Chancellor's companions now was the adventurous young merchant Arthur Edwards, who later observed that the journey of about 700 miles from the White Sea to Vologda by river took a fortnight – travelling day and night, rowing against the current, or sailing if the wind was favourable, in long Russian boats cut directly from the trunks of large trees. (It could take longer; when the current was strong and the wind hostile the boats had to be towed slowly upstream, and in 1568 the journey took a frustrated English ambassador five weeks.)[3]

During the cold months of the year, by contrast, the trip was easier. 'By horse and sleds', Edwards remarked, 'in 8 days you may pass it in Winter.'[4]

Western Europeans were impressed by Russian horses which, while not large, were resilient and fast: 'shorter than average, strong, and fast-going', as a Venetian ambassador later remarked.[5] They could be exchanged at post stations, which although more numerous in the central Russian heartland, were present in northern regions too now that these had been integrated into the system of state control. Settlements on routes between major cities, which regularly provided such a service to passing delegations, were granted tax advantages in return for keeping fresh horses standing by.[6] In general it was not found necessary to shoe horses unless, like those pulling the English party now, they were used to 'ride in post upon the frozen floods', in which case shoes were used to prevent them slipping.[7]

Chancellor was probably accompanied on his journey by most if not all of the merchants and gentlemen indicated on the crew list. There were ten in all, who together were equipped both to accumulate the commercial information about unknown realms that the company required and to provide the necessary dignity and experience essential in visiting a foreign court. They would have been accompanied also by Russians, to guide the sleds, to offer some protection against the bandits or 'cut-purses' who proliferated in the outlying regions of the realm, to provide logistical assistance with overnight accommodation and with the provision of food and fresh horses, as well as to function as minders.[8]

Foreigners were invariably treated with suspicion in Russia, as potential spies, and while great hospitality might be extended, they were not permitted to travel without supervision, but were held 'under a manner of honourable arrest'.[9]

Chancellor's mission was a curious one for the Russian court to know how to deal with. He was not, strictly speaking, the ambassador of a monarch, with the requirements in terms of etiquette and treatment that that entailed. But at the same time, he did bear letters from the English King, as well as offerings of fine cloths which the company hoped would appeal to any foreign ruler. Unlike most formal embassies his arrival was entirely unexpected, and it came via a distant, outlying region of the country which up until now had not acted as a port for international visitors, even though it currently provided the only direct access by sea, before Russia had fulfilled its ambition of establishing itself on the Baltic or the Black Seas. Previous European delegations – from the Italian states, the King of Poland or the Holy Roman Emperor – had arrived at Russia's western border, where they were met by officials of the Tsar and then formally escorted to Moscow.

For distinguished ambassadors the Tsar might send his personal sled, lavishly decorated in the manner of the finest coach, its interior insulated against the cold and made comfortable with expensive skins. On this occasion, however, the vital question of status was uncertain, and in any case Chancellor and his men departed from Kholmogory before any response from Moscow had arrived. As such they must have had to make do with the best the regional governors were willing to provide.

Thirty-Four

As London recovered from the seismic events of the summer of 1553, and as the *Edward*, captained by Richard Chancellor, sailed into the White Sea and dropped anchor by the Dvina River, its sister ships, the *Bona Esperanza* and the *Bona Confidentia*, were some 200 miles to the north-east. They left behind the shores of Kolguev island, with their votive marks, in search of living communities.

On 4 September they followed the coast of the island west, Willoughby wrote, then struggled with 'contrary winds' which caused them to lose sight of the land. They were forced, presumably, to tack once more. Progress was painfully slow, and they were pushed north, out to sea. On the 8th, Willoughby recorded, they briefly saw land again but quickly lost sight of it once more.

The land they had seen was probably the barren Kanin peninsula, where low, rolling grasslands, intercut by small streams and girdled by rocks, thrust north from the Eurasian mainland, on the eastern flank of the entrance to the White Sea. The crews ran 'west and by south' – that is, a little to the south of due west – for thirty leagues, or ninety sea miles. They lost sight of the coast, then picked it up again and sailed in closer as the sun set.

They quickly realised, however, that this was what was known, and feared, among sailors as a 'lee shore': a shoreline towards which the wind was blowing. For square-rigged ships in particular such a coast was perilous. All too easily, mariners lost the ability to steer clear and found themselves blown into ever-shallower water, onto rocks or the seabed. Anxious to prevent this happening, Willoughby immediately ordered his helmsmen to make once more towards the north. 'We got us into the sea', he wrote, to ensure that they had what he called 'sea room', or space in which to manoeuvre.

On 12 September, in 'indifferent wind and weather', Willoughby watched from the rear castle as the *Bona Esperanza* sailed cautiously once more towards the shoreline. As they approached the coast, they worried not only about the wind but also about the tides, about whose pattern here the English crew had no information. They had to be cautious not to sail into water which was sufficiently deep at high tide only to find themselves beached and at risk of damaging the keel or hull as the water flowed out. Willoughby and his leading men watched the changing depth of the sea carefully and concluded that the tide was 'almost spent' when the crew were instructed to drop anchor in what they measured at thirty fathoms of water.

On the 13th they sailed towards and along the coast of the wide Kola peninsula which jutted, like a thumb, from north-west to south-east, above the White Sea. They had missed, however, the narrow channel to its east, through which Chancellor had already passed.

On the 14th they anchored, with safety in mind, two leagues, or six nautical miles, from the shore, in deeper water, and launched the ship's boat from there to allow a few of them to explore the coastline at closer proximity. When those who had done so returned to the ship, they reported that the land that here edged the sea seemed in general un-promising: 'rocky and high'. They did, though, Willoughby noted in his log, row into 'two or three good harbours'.

What they could not report was what they longed most to find: signs of human civilisation. 'As for people,' Willoughby wrote in frustration, 'could we see none.' This was a windswept landscape of Arctic tundra. In the early autumn the air was cold though not yet freezing, but above the rocks the terrain was grassy and devoid of trees, which refused to sink roots deep into soil that was permanently frozen beneath the surface. For three days the Englishmen pushed west along the coast, away from the White Sea, in hope of finding a settlement, but there was none to be found.

With the wind becoming unfavourable, progress was painfully slow. Eventually, disappointed and exasperated, Willoughby made a decision: the two ships should cut their losses and turn about, heading back to the deep-water harbours that they had found previously.

On the 18th, he wrote, 'we entered into the haven', and there they dropped anchor in six fathoms of water. The inlet they had found was a substantial one, pushing two leagues, or six miles, into the mainland, Willoughby thought, and half a league – a mile and a half – wide. It was one of several huge openings which reached like splayed fingers into the land mass from a coastline which fractured suddenly behind Nokuyev island. Low, rocky hills descended gently to the water's edge, green with scrub and grey with scattered stone but bare of trees or larger plant life.

In their smaller ship's boats, the crew explored the inlet. Into the gulf, at its southern end, flowed a river – the Varzina – and around them the men saw rich wildlife: a great many seals, or 'seal fishes' as they called them, as well as 'other great fishes', salmon in particular.

Exploring on land they saw bears, as well as 'great deer' – reindeer – which came down to the water's edge in herds to drink, foxes and other 'strange beasts', such as animals they called 'guloines'. These last must have been wolverines: stocky, aggressive members of the weasel family with thick, glossy fur, resembling small bears and known scientifically as *gulo gulo*. The men saw other animals too with which they were not familiar – 'to us', Willoughby noted, 'unknown, and also wonderful'. Their hold was already well stocked, and with the abundance of wildlife there was clearly plenty of food for the crews to survive the winter.

The calendar now moved towards the end of September and here in the Arctic the year already seemed 'far spent', abbreviated as it was by the impossible conditions of winter.

The hours of darkness rapidly increased: the sun, so recently in view for most of each twenty-four-hour day, now set at around half past seven in the evening and rose again at around half past seven in the morning. Several hours of daylight were being lost each month, and more time was spent by the crews hunkering below deck. For a week the two ships remained sheltered within their haven, and already as they did so the weather seemed to deteriorate, faster and more significantly than they expected, even taking into account their high latitude.

The days began with thick frosts which coated the timbers of the ships in a slippery, glistening film. From densely clouded skies fell billowing veils of snow and storms of hail which stung the faces of anyone not below deck. Such was the 'very evil weather' that it seemed already, Willoughby wrote, as though it were the depth of winter. Soon the water in the haven itself would begin to freeze.

Willoughby met to discuss the situation with the other council members on board the two ships: Cornelius Durforth, the master of the *Bona Confidentia*, William Gefferson, the master on his own ship, Roger Wilson and Richard Ingram, the two masters' mates, and the merchant Thomas Langley, all of whom were officially members with Willoughby of the expedition's council. Together they agreed on a course of action, or rather of inaction.

It was decided to remain where they were, to batten down the hatches and to see the winter through before attempting to move on.

There is no hint in Willoughby's journal of any discord among the men about what must have been a controversial, if perhaps unavoidable, decision. Certainly, if anyone questioned his authority, Willoughby did not feel the need to record it. But he was a man of natural presence whose view was not lightly questioned. In a different context, he had been in a similar position before, and his ability then to command the loyalty of a potentially disruptive group of men had proved indispensable.

Three and a half years previously, towards the end of the 1540s, Willoughby had been tasked with governing a new fort at Lauder. Sitting astride the ancient road running north through hostile border country to Edinburgh, Lauder was one of four thrown hastily up to improve security for English garrisons in south-east Scotland. It was a daunting assignment, not made easier by the fact that the fort was under-manned and under-gunned. The man who had overseen its construction had warned the government that the four artillery pieces and 120 men assigned to it were inadequate given its key location: 'it needs a larger number,' he wrote, 'as it will be the first place the Scots will have to do with'.[1]

For governors in such isolated outposts, the number of troops at their disposal was not the only concern. As often a cause for complaint was the unreliable nature of the men with whom they were quartered: scarcely less alarming, at times, than the encircling Scots. To the north, at Broughty Castle near Dundee, the beleaguered governor had lamented the state of his garrison in terms Willoughby would have recognised. 'Never,' he complained, 'had a man so weak a company of soldiers given to drinking, eating and slothfulness.' Those Scottish soldiers considered allies and brought in as part of the garrison – for the Scots fought each other first, and the English second – were divisive and dangerous: 'ready to mutiny as I would not suffer their harlots here, they will put hand to nothing, but spoil and destroy everything'. 'What with them and my own men,' he lamented, 'I cannot eat, drink, nor sleep.' The following year, his successor received orders from London to dismiss the German mercenaries under his command who, more so even than the Scots, were a liability rather than a reassurance.

The job of governing a remote fort in hostile territory had not, Willoughby may now have reflected, been far removed from that of commanding a ship in unknown seas. (Perhaps Cabot and his employers on the company board had thought the same when Willoughby first presented himself.) Close at hand was a fearful, restless garrison of mercenaries and 'pioneers', confined and quarrelsome; beyond there was only the rolling darkness of Lauderdale forest, beneath the barren Lammermuir Hills. As winter advanced on the *Bona Esperanza*, the threats from outside came from the hostility of the elements rather than a besieging army, but the situation, for a captain with a potentially mutinous crew, was similar.

The threat from allied Scottish and French armies outside Lauder steadily increased, until the castle was subjected to a prolonged siege. 'Lauder being besieged by the Scots', King Edward VI himself noted in his journal.[2] Food supplies were critically restricted and ammunition ran dangerously low. In desperation, the starving soldiers were reduced to melting down the pewter cups and vessels in their possession in order to make shot.

Amid the cold of a Scottish winter, with interminable nights ceding only to drifting blankets of mist, lookouts struggled to keep track of the encircling enemy. Word of savage assaults on other English castles caused panic. Hunger sapped morale. But in spite of any real hope of relief, Willoughby's garrison clung on, fortified by the resolution of their governor, until all Scottish forts in English hands were surrendered by the Anglo-French Treaty of Boulogne.

On 10 April 1550 the ensign was struck and the beleaguered garrison marched from the site, their personal pride intact. Though he returned initially to London, by 1551 Willoughby was back in action in the Eastern Marchlands. None could doubt his steel.

Now, once again, Willoughby prepared to sit out a siege, with an at times querulous garrison, while hostile elements moved across the hills outside. This time it was the weather which was his enemy – the snow, the howling wind, the hail and the frost. But he was well supplied, at least. As had been the case in Scotland, fear was often as much a danger as the reality, and it prompted unease and disquiet. Neither he nor any of his crew were sure what the climate at this latitude might have in store.

Thirty-Five

Riding in convoy, Richard Chancellor and his men glided smoothly along frozen rivers, through open expanses of flat country, bleached white by snow which was banked many feet deep in places, and along ice-packed roads which ran through barren wasteland and dark coniferous forests. For hours on end there was an eerie silence, broken only by the men's voices, the strangely muffled thump of the horses' hooves and the incessant, sibilant scrape of the runners beneath the sleds.

Cabot and his fellow organisers had guessed their crews might have to winter in cold regions of northern Europe or Asia. Chancellor could not help but reflect, though, as the snow and thick, unpeopled forest flashed by, how different this environment was to the warm lands of spices and silk which were his intended destination.

Nothing, certainly, was more painfully apparent to the Englishmen than the intense cold. They were used to somewhat lower temperatures than today. The mid-sixteenth century is often considered to mark the onset of a 'Little Ice Age' – a period of sustained colder weather. But the men knew nothing like the climate in northern Russia. Here winter's grip was unremitting. It seized the country, and for months on end did not let go, seeming only to grow fiercer 'by a perpetuity of cold'.

In the account he wrote based on conversations with Chancellor, Adams reported that a man could lay a moist stick on an outdoor fire and see the damp frozen solid at one end while the other end burned in the flames. Similar stories were told elsewhere, of post boys lying down to rest while a colleague drove the sled and being found frozen to death on arrival, or of water thrown in the air only to shatter, frozen, on landing.[1] Passing along tracks which ran through great forests or along iced-over rivers, it did not seem that there was much agriculture. In the north parts of the Tsar's dominions, Chancellor recorded, 'the cold will suffer no corn to grow, it is so extreme'.[2]

As a result, the diet of northern Russia, as sampled in winter by the Englishmen, was low in agricultural produce. There was little in the way of bread, that staple of the English table. The shortfall was made up by consumption of lichens, of roots like those of the bog arum, and of the ground bark of the fir tree.[3] There was plenty of game in the warmer months, and fish all year round, which was often eaten preserved. The regular consumption of fish that had been pickled when far from fresh appalled Chancellor. 'I have seen them', he wrote, 'eat the pickle of Herring and other stinking fish' and even 'praise it to be more wholesome than other fish or fresh meat'. But men here, he noted admiringly, were hardy.

Most of the wild animals which inhabited the endless forests had disappeared into hibernation to escape the bitter winter conditions. Only the occasional set of tracks in fresh-fallen snow excited interest and enquiries of the Russian mentors. Buffalo, bears and black wolves, they learned, were among the creatures who haunted these woods. In more clement conditions, the buffalo was hunted by men on horseback, while the bears were pursued by men on foot armed with wooden forks.

Clement Adams repeated the story of a strange animal known as the 'rossomakka' – a Samoyed name for the wolverine – which gave birth, he claimed, by squeezing itself between two closely positioned trees.[4] Such tales appealed to readers of travel accounts, which historically had been full of surprising and outlandish creatures: men with one leg, or the lamb which grew like a vegetable and hung as it ripened from the branches of a tree. Even in the legends on which Cabot had co-operated, on his map of 1544 there are claims of exotic monsters in the north-east – of humans with the heads of pigs, of men with ears so large they covered all their bodies, or of others without joints at the knees.[5]

Chancellor was more sceptical, as Cabot surely was himself. He insisted on personal experience, or at least a reliable authority, and left any mention of such creatures out of his own account.

For long hours Chancellor and his men travelled in their sleds, endeavouring to make good time across the huge distance, capitalising on the fresh horses which were available for payment at post stations in the towns. At lunchtime fires were made over which food could be cooked, and snow and ice melted for the horses to drink.

In towns they paused overnight. 'There is small succour in those parts,' Anthony Jenkinson wrote shortly afterwards, 'unless it be in towns.'[6] Post stations often provided facilities for travellers to rest, to escape the perishing temperatures.[7] Near settlements there were also often religious communities, which played an important role in putting up travellers – even non-Orthodox, who might be housed in separate buildings so as not to corrupt the faithful.

The English had encountered one monastery devoted to St Nicholas almost as soon as they set foot on Russian soil, and they quickly noticed how widespread such institutions were in Russia. Everywhere, Chancellor wrote, there were 'a great number of Religious men', known, after their clothing, as Black Monks.[8] Monasteries, he noted, owned more land than the ruler – the source of an acrimonious dispute in Russia between monks known as 'Possessors', who believed in such ownership, and 'non-Possessors', who did not. Older members of the group were reminded of the way England had been prior to the dissolutions of the 1530s.

There was little sense, though, of nostalgia. English government propaganda had entrenched the belief that such places were sinks of the most appalling vice and corruption. Monks, to Protestant Englishmen, were a byword for ungodly conduct and this attitude coloured their view of the Russian examples they saw. Lodging at monasteries, the English had a chance to observe their practices at first hand. They saw the regular attendance at services, and the strict fasts during which they ate nothing but 'Coleworts, Cabbages, salt Cowcumbers [cucumbers], with other roots, as Radish and such like'. But 'as for whoredom and drunkenness', Chancellor reassured his audience, 'there be none such living: and for extortion, they be the most abominable under the sun'. 'Now', he concluded, 'judge of their holiness.'

After they had reached Vologda, some 650 miles from Kholmogory, the journey became easier and the landscape less barren. Forests were often mixed. Beech and larch, as well as firs and pine, carpeted the gently rolling hills.[9]

As they made progress into Russia's central lands, the population and number of settlements on their route noticeably increased. Vologda itself was a flourishing town, and between it and Moscow there were twelve post stations on a journey which took about six days and which passed through three other great towns: Yaroslavl', Rostov and Perejaslavl'.[10] In the latter stages of the journey in particular, the density of population grew markedly. The party visited numerous villages 'so well filled with people', Chancellor noted, 'that it is a wonder to see them'.

These Russian settlements struck the English as rather primitive by comparison with those of their own experience. Houses were haphazardly clustered, and continued, almost invariably, to be constructed from wood, while roofs also were made from shingle boards. In towns the streets were 'not paved with stone as ours are' – though this they could only have learned by asking, because the ground now was thick-packed with ice and snow. Here too, as further north, sleds were the only feasible form of transport; during the winter, Russians barely knew 'any other manner of carriage'. It was still bitterly cold: 'very extreme and horrible'. Nevertheless here – unlike the windswept wilderness from which they had come – there was regular traffic, of which Moscow, like London, was the centre. 'You shall meet in a morning', Chancellor reckoned, 'seven or eight hundred sleds coming or going thither', carrying corn or fish to or from the capital city.

At some point on the road towards Moscow they were approached by a messenger who was travelling in a sled in the opposite direction. Word had reached him of the English party on the road and he hastened to meet them because he was carrying a message for them from the Tsar – the long-delayed response to the report despatched some time earlier by the governors in Kholmogory. He apologised and claimed, rather implausibly, to have set out in the wrong direction. He had expected, he said, to find the English ship on the coast he knew, in the country of the Tartars to the south of Russia: an excuse that was probably intended as cover for the time it had taken the imperial court to glean significant information about these unexpected visitors.

In any case, the letters he was carrying from the Tsar were favourable and warm. They granted belated permission to his own subjects in Kholmogory to trade with the English merchants. And they extended an invitation to the latter to visit his court in Moscow, if they were willing to make the long journey. There were formal instructions to his own subjects that, should Chancellor and his men decide to do so, fresh post horses be provided for them on the road at each station without any charge, for which he himself would cover the expense.

Armed with this letter, Chancellor reported, men working in the post stations practically fought each other for the chance to attach their horses to the sleds. Keeping hold of their saddle blankets and bits, the English were given the choice of a great number of horses. The Russian postal system entitled them to drive the animals at all possible speed, seizing with impunity, should they need to, horses belonging to any householder en route or any traveller on the road, with the exception only of the Tsar's couriers.[11]

In the depth of the Russian winter a speed of travel was possible greatly in excess of anything known in western Europe. Again, the English were amazed at the extent to which Russians were in thrall to their emperor.

Thirty-Six

In all, the journey to Moscow from Kholmogory took about two weeks. Since they set out on 25 November, it was about 9 December when they arrived.

Since they had let it be known that they bore a letter from the English King, Chancellor and his group were treated, probably, as a junior embassy. As such, they would have been made to wait at the outskirts of the capital city. There may also have been a brief stay at another monastery outside Moscow, to allow time for Ivan himself to be notified of the Englishmen's arrival. One of Ivan's officials arrived to meet them and to explain the sequence of events involved in a formal audience, before taking word back to the Kremlin.

Initially, on entering the city the men were shown to houses where they could stay – wooden again and sparsely furnished, with benches around the walls and some skins and rugs.

There they were visited by bailiffs of the Tsar who ensured that they were well provided with food and drink and anything else they should require. (The supply of food for visitors could be so embarrassingly large that a later English ambassador even attempted to have it reduced.)[1] Candles were another important resource since daylight was brief and there were long hours of darkness only slightly mitigated, on the rare occasions when they braved the cold outside, by moonlight reflecting from the snow-filled streets. No doubt the men were not averse to putting their feet up for a few days while they took stock of their surroundings. Including the enforced stay in Kholmogory it had been, as Adams put it after talking to Chancellor, a 'long and most troublesome' journey.

They were not, however, free to explore. Guards were provided by

Ivan on the pretext of protecting them, but they were evidently intended quite as much to keep these foreigners, curious in both senses, contained and under surveillance in the houses provided. Numerous ambassadors in Russia complained of being kept, in effect, under house arrest. The Englishmen were notified only that they would be told when the Tsar was ready to see them. The interlude in fact was significantly shorter than many formal embassies were required to wait. Ivan was anxious, perhaps, to hear what these strange visitors had to say, and to learn how they might be able to help him.

After twelve days, Chancellor noted – shortly before Christmas – word reached him from the secretary who dealt with foreign visitors that the Tsar wished him to bring 'the king's my master's letters'.[2]

Travelling through the city towards its heart – the central citadel known, as others were in Russian towns, as the 'Kremlin' – Chancellor and his companions were impressed by its size. 'The Moscow itself', he wrote, 'is great.' He judged it larger even than London with all their home city's suburbs and recent expansion.

In other respects, though, he found it less impressive. Here again the English were struck by what seemed, even by sixteenth-century standards, a chaotic lack of planning. Buildings clustered and sprawled 'without all order', and in their design they seemed 'very rude'. Here too wood predominated as a building material. Even the churches were predominantly wooden, heated now, in winter, by stoves. And as a result, the English visitors immediately thought, the city was very vulnerable to that great scourge of cities of the time: fire.

Charred timbers protruded from the snow, and the odd ruined building still remained as evidence of the terrifying fire which had devastated the city six years earlier, during the summer of 1547. As this conflagration spread, thousands had been killed.[3] Fires happened 'very oft and in very fearful sort', an English visitor later noted, 'by reason of the dryness and fatness of the fir, that being once fired, burneth like a torch, & is hardly quenched till all be burnt up'.[4] Nevertheless, as they neared the centre, buildings in brick and stone did begin to predominate, for the first time since they had been in Russia – testimony to the remodelling of Moscow undertaken by Ivan's grandfather, Ivan III, who aspired to assert the pre-eminence of his duchy, and his dynasty, among the states which jostled for supremacy in the lands presided over until recently by a Tartar overlord.

Watched by curious citizens of Moscow, to whom word had filtered out of an exotic delegation from further afield than had previously visited the Russian court, Chancellor and his companions passed with their escort through the huge open field and market place recently cleared in front of the Kremlin's eastern wall. This was known as the 'Great Market', or was called after the Trinity church which stood here, having not yet acquired the name – Red Square – by which it would later be known. Around the Trinity church, against its walls, the English noticed, a curious series of smaller, wooden churches or chapels had been erected.

From the outside, the great brick walls of the Kremlin towered over the surroundings. Within, the buildings rose up from the hill on which the complex was built. Aspects of its exterior were impressive, and Chancellor describes it as a 'fair Castle'. Beneath its walls, running close along one side, was the hard-frozen River Moskva which headed south into Tartary before falling into the Caspian Sea. On its solid surface market traders worked, steam following them as they moved, their shouts filling the cold air.

Defended by artillery of all kinds, the Kremlin's fortifications seemed impregnable. In places, the Englishmen were assured, the outer walls were eighteen feet thick, though without any visible confirmation; as a man who rated personal experience in all matters over the word of authority, Chancellor inclined to be sceptical. Foreigners, he cautioned, were denied access to see for themselves. 'I do not believe it ...', he commented, 'notwithstanding I do not certainly know it: for no stranger may come to view it.'[5]

To enter the Kremlin the party crossed a bridge over a wide moat quite recently dug out along the eastern wall and lined on both sides by low, thick walls of brick. They were then formally welcomed through the great Saviour gate.

With its jumbled assortment of churches, monasteries, royal residences and other houses, the Kremlin was practically a city in its own right. Once entirely wooden, Ivan III had left it transformed. He had imported

Italian master builders to inject Renaissance sophistication into parts of the royal palace – give me, he had demanded, a castle like that of Milan – as well as into the design of great cathedrals built of white stone, like the 'Dormition', where coronations took place, or the 'Archangel Michael', where members of the ruling family were buried. There was a place, too, for the baptism of the Tsar's offspring. The rites of passage which marked out the Tsar's life were built into the very architecture of the Moscow Kremlin.

The English passed through this 'Cathedral Square' on their way to the audience hall. Having been at both the English and the French royal courts, Chancellor was disappointed at the Tsar's own buildings. The Kremlin seemed as much a religious complex as one devoted to an earthly king. Church and court here were fused together. Everywhere there were 'religious men'. Chancellor noted the Kremlin's full complement of 'nine fair Churches'. Its cathedrals were grander and more eye-catching than the royal palace, which failed by contrast to rise above its surroundings. On the contrary, its structures were low-built, reminding him, he said, of old buildings in England, with small, narrow windows letting in little of the Moscow winter's subdued light.

Everything was disjointed and jumbled. Buildings of quite different sizes and styles, with windows or roofs that did not match, were connected by corridors, staircases and galleries – thrown together, as Russian towns in general often seemed to be, without regard for symmetry or order.[6] To an Englishman familiar with the great royal palaces of England and France, which pronounced the unparalleled earthly glory and majesty of the monarch and projected the grandeur of his rule, there was little here that could easily be recognised or understood.[7]

Henry VIII was the only adult king under whom these Englishmen had lived. He had expressed unambiguously in architecture, as in words, his emphatic supremacy over his realm and his Church.[8] No one could doubt whether king or archbishop held ultimate sway. Here, for all that ordinary Russians clearly regarded their ruler with awe, Ivan's own palace was overshadowed by the gilded cupolas of the churches. The message seemed plain: the Tsar was less God's powerful representative on earth than his servant.

As they passed into the palace, the impression remained unchanged.

The Tsar's public quarters were not, Chancellor commented, 'so sumptuous as I have seen'. There were few of the rich tapestries and other wall coverings which embellished palaces and the private houses of the wealthy in England. Rooms tended to be smaller, often for the simple reason that it was easier to heat them in winter. But, for the English, size mattered.

Instead, the Russian court relied for its glamour on large numbers of human models who were draped with all the extravagance and luxury that was missing from the fabric of the building. As they were led into the first, outer reception chamber, the Englishmen were dazzled by the rich attire of some hundred or more courtiers, or men they took for courtiers, seated on benches which were built, as in smaller private houses, around the edges of the room.

This large and glittering company, Chancellor remembered, was 'all apparelled in cloth of gold down to their ankles'. As he and his men were met by officials, the watching men sat so astonishingly stationary and silent that it took repeated glances to be sure that they were alive, and were not in fact merely inanimate decoration. Pure decoration, in fact, was what they were, for it was later discovered that rich clothes were distributed by the royal wardrobe to ordinary Muscovites recruited to take part in such reception ceremonies.[9]

Here in this chamber, awe-struck by the rich human display by which they were surrounded, the Englishmen waited until the Tsar was ready to receive them, and an official who could act as an interpreter and intermediary came to usher them through into the inner reception chamber.

Thirty-Seven

For the man who had been Chancellor's Captain General, and who had expected to head any visits to foreign courts, circumstances – almost 1,000 miles north of Moscow – were rather different.

Before Willoughby and his leading men resigned themselves to hibernating in their ships for the winter, they wanted to make every effort to reach human settlement. Since they had failed to do so by sea, they resorted to looking by land.

Three men volunteered to set out on an exploratory mission. They carried provisions with them, and the plentiful clothing they needed to sleep rough in increasingly wintry conditions. Leaving their companions on board ship, saying farewells they knew might be their last, they walked south-south-west in the hope of finding other people.

For three days they trudged, across the barren, open tundra of the northern Kola peninsula, a region left scarred and pitted by lakes after the relatively recent retreat of glaciers. Already, snow piled into deep drifts in the numerous depressions.[1] But they met no other person, nor any evidence of human presence.

They must have reached Lake Yanozero, the huge freshwater lake which filled the irregularly shaped crevices left in the landscape by tectonic shifts and which was the source of the River Varsina, flowing north into the gulf in which the two English ships were now anchored. They passed it probably on its eastern side. They may have ascended to a ridge which runs along the spine of the peninsula. They would have noticed a dramatic transition as they passed from the tundra to the taiga zone: that is, from the windswept, open region to the north where trees did not grow, into the strip of northern (boreal) evergreen forest of spruce and pine which reached to an east–west line running across the peninsula.

We can only guess how far they went. The walking was not always easy. Perhaps they covered thirty, even forty, miles per day. Probably, in these difficult conditions, it was far less. In any case, it was not enough. In the direction they were heading, it was about 150 miles to cross the peninsula to reach the northern shores of the White Sea: further than they could possibly make in the time available. A decision had clearly been made with Willoughby and his fellow councillors beforehand that the group should walk for three days before turning back. They probably carried with them enough food to last six days, but not more.

One can only imagine the relief they must have felt on seeing again the skeletal outline of the two ships. But it was a cold, exhausted and deeply disappointed party who returned, without positive news to convey.

Anxious as Willoughby and the other leaders were to hear what the first party had found, there was no time to waste. Promptly after their return three more men were despatched, this time in a westerly direction. This group carried additional provisions and they walked solidly for four days as the weather worsened, the temperature fell and the hours of darkness grew almost perceptibly longer from one night to the next.

Theirs, however, was a near-hopeless quest. Heading west they walked into the empty central region of the peninsula, struggling across rivers, diverting around numerous small lakes and scrambling, always, across the peculiar, twisted rock formations left by glaciers on this wounded landscape. There were no settlements to find and they found no people nor any sign of them. After four fruitless days they turned about, disheartened, and retraced their steps.

By now it was well into October. The nights were longer than the days. Snow was falling regularly and banking up, many feet deep in hollows in the land. With every step the men were uncertain how far their feet would sink. Water in rivers and in the gulf in which the ships lay anchored was gradually freezing solid.

One more time Willoughby sent out a party. Another three men were this time tasked to walk south-east, again for three days, in search of human life. For another six days the crews remained huddled in the holds, praying for news of a nearby settlement. But on the sixth day this last group reappeared at the haven. Their faces, and the weary dejection with which they trudged, conveyed their news long before they reached the two ships. They had walked, it was obvious, and they confirmed it soon enough, 'without finding of people, or any similitude of habitation'.

The cold wind spiralled, spinning snow and particles of ice. Soon the darkness would be perpetual, lightening only to a murky gloom at midday. There was nothing for it, it seemed, but to batten down the hatches and to hope to see through an extended polar winter.

Was it inevitable that they found no one? In fact they were probably a matter of weeks too late. A short while earlier they would have encountered what they were looking for: not settlements as such, but groups of nomadic Lapps encamped by the estuaries of major rivers along the northern coast, like that within which they were now anchored.

But these people were migrants, who moved with the reindeer that were their livelihood; and as the year drew on and the nights outlasted the days, they moved south to winter in the taiga forest which reached only into the lower half of the peninsula. Behind them they left no traces that were noticed and recorded by the Englishmen, who thought themselves, as indeed they now were, in an uninhabited wilderness.[2]

Known as the Sami, this population fanned across the north-western extremity of Ivan IV's Russia and into the uppermost part of the Scandinavian peninsula. They lived by fishing on the coast and in the many inland rivers and lakes, and by herding reindeer which provided them with food, temporary shelter (their hides being used to make tents) and warm clothing. For centuries they had worshipped heathen gods, using runes and shamanistic rituals which struck those Christians who witnessed them as diabolical, and these traditions remained strong in spite of attempts by missionaries from the advancing Russian population to convert them to Christianity.

The man who came to be known as Saint Tryphon was living now, with the monastic community he had established, near the mouth of the River Pechenga some 200 miles up the coast to the west. In the 1530s, as a young man, he had travelled north from Novgorod, hoping to show that Orthodoxy could flourish even in these cold and thinly populated wastelands. From the wooden monastery he constructed, he tirelessly spread the Gospel among the Sami peoples – successfully, too, even if this new religion mingled with traditional beliefs rather than supplanting them. He would continue to do so until his death in the 1580s.

The Sami spoke languages which were related to those of another fishing and reindeer-herding population in northern Russia: the Samoyeds. These people lived further east, along Russia's northern fringes to the east of the White Sea. A false etymology of their name had led them to be classed as cannibals – 'self-eaters' – and it was this reputation which had reached sixteenth-century Europe. Richard Chancellor's second-in-command, Stephen Borough, would later encounter one of them while exploring further east and would recount with disgust the idols and the remains of a bloody sacrifice. Attitudes, of course, were strongly influenced by the Russians to whom they listened. The merchant John Hasse, who also sailed with Chancellor and accompanied him to Moscow, wrote of the rich furs obtained from the Samoyeds, 'that are counted [by the Russians] savage people'.[3]

Thirty-Eight

Attempting to remain calm and confident, Chancellor and his fellow merchants and gentlemen followed the Russian official, at a stately pace, into the throne room.

Here, raised on elevated benches which were again fixed in ranks around the edge of the room and covered with rich velvet, sat nobles and other councillors. Chancellor estimated there were about 150 of them in all. They too were resplendently dressed. Four years later Anthony Jenkinson described the rich winter attire of a Russian nobleman: 'His upper garment is of cloth of gold, silk, or cloth, long, down to the foot, and buttoned with great buttons of silver, or else laces of silk, set on with brooches, the sleeves thereof very long, which he weareth on his arm, ruffed up.' Under this, he wrote, men wore a long garment with a brightly coloured collar which stood upright, over a shirt of red or gold silk. Boots, meanwhile, were of leather, dyed red or yellow. 'On his head he weareth a white Colpeck, with buttons of silver, gold, pearl, or stone, and under it a black Fox cap, turned up very broad.'[1] The height of these caps indicated the status of the wearer. They showed that the men were sat according to a strict hierarchy, which governed all aspects of Muscovite court life.

Meanwhile, in a corner of the room, on a carpeted platform raised three or four silver steps higher than all others present, was the Tsar himself. He was seated beneath a canopy on a gilt throne, decorated richly with engravings and stones. Unlike the palace as a whole, which underwhelmed, this impressed the English immediately as 'very royal'.

Ivan had not yet acquired the sobriquet 'Grozni' – 'awesome' or 'terrible', as it is slightly misleadingly rendered in English. But he was certainly an awe-inspiring sight. From his shoulders fell a glistening robe of beaten gold, draped over multiple layers of fur-lined garments, all visible and carefully co-ordinated, whose accumulated bulk filled the wide expanse of the throne. On his head was an imperial crown which may have been the famous 'cap of Monomakh' – thickly trimmed with sable, encrusted with precious stones and surmounted by a golden Cross tipped with pearls.

The crown's skullcap design, quite different to those of western Europe, was derived from the Muslim khans of the steppe, but it symbolised too the status claimed by the rulers of Russia as heirs to the Western, Christian Empire. Alleged to be the direct bequest of an emperor of Byzantium, it embodied the transfer of divine authority on earth from the imperial thrones of Rome and Constantinople to that of Moscow, which the Tsar and others close to him claimed had now become the 'third Rome'.[2] In his right hand Ivan held a sceptre of crystal, gold and precious stones, while his left lay prone upon the arm of his throne. Beside him, on a ledge or special stand, sat a golden orb surmounted by a Cross: the symbol both of Christ's universal dominion over the spiritual world and of the Tsar's over the physical realm. Near to the throne were icons, the Tsar's proximity to which emphasised his closeness to God. Like Christ, the message was clear, Ivan was both a man, afflicted by mortal ailments, and divine.[3] He was merciful but he was also awesome.

Even seated on his throne, it was obvious that Ivan was tall and physically imposing, particularly with all his thick clothing. He was young – still only twenty-three years old – and growing into the full authority of manhood, entirely confident in his position as God's appointed ruler on earth. His demeanour was welcoming, for there were reasons why this unexpected delegation struck him as useful and timely. But his eyes were cold and penetrating – a sign of the unpredictable cruelty to which he was already prone. 'There was a majesty in his countenance', Adams later wrote, that was 'proportionable with the excellency of his estate.'

Standing close by were four men – two to each side – silent and motionless as statues, dressed in white robes with tall white caps, and draped in golden chains. They were young, without the long beards worn by elder nobles present, and were strikingly handsome. Unusually for diplomatic situations in Europe, they were visibly armed. Each, on his shoulder, held a gleaming silver axe, its blade turned menacingly outward.[4] The Englishmen had been required to hand over any weapons prior to entering the royal presence.

Meanwhile, nearer still, the Tsar was flanked by two men who were also impressively turned out in cloth of gold. One was referred to by Chancellor as Ivan's 'Chief Secretary'. Probably this was the man who had risen to preside over the Tsar's office of foreign affairs, Ivan Mikhailovich Viskovatyi, though Viskovatyi had become embroiled, that year, in allegations of heresy – for his outspoken criticism of new icons and murals designed for the Kremlin. The other was a young man called Aleksei Adashev who had risen fast at Ivan's court, owing to a family connection to Ivan's wife. A senior court usher, Clement Adams referred to him by the distinguished-sounding title: 'Great Commander of Silence'.[5]

Close, too, in a position of high status, was a man now known as Simeon Kasaevich. Chancellor does not mention him, but his background and perhaps his physical appearance set him apart from other members of Ivan's council. In February 1553 he had been granted the status of a prince in Ivan's service. At the same time he had been ordered 'to see the eyes of the Tsar', meaning that his presence at Ivan's court was required.[6]

Born Ediger Mohammed, he had briefly been recognised as Khan of Kazan, a Muslim region on Russia's southern frontier left independent after the collapse of the Golden Horde. From Kazan devastating annual attacks had been launched into Russia. In response, Ivan had organised three unsuccessful campaigns to conquer the region, an ambition which, for the zealous Tsar, was steeped in anti-Islamic fervour.

The previous year had seen his fourth attempt. With more than 100,000 troops Ivan had marched south into what he later called this 'godless and most unbelieving land'. Accompanying his traditional cavalry were new permanent units specialised in the use of firearms, created in reforms Ivan had overseen in 1550. Six companies of musketeers, whose concentrated firepower was a significant advantage to the Russian forces, were paid a fixed salary, were not disbanded after a campaign, and were less hampered by arguments about precedence than the bulk of the army. Ivan had also introduced regimental artillery, and though in many respects his army had changed little since medieval times, it was no co-incidence that this time, after a long and brutal siege of the walled town of Kazan, Ivan succeeded. As a result of the Russian victory Ediger was carried into captivity by the returning Russian troops, who were greeted with jubilant celebrations in Moscow.[7]

In the churches of the Kremlin Ivan gave fervent thanks, and had an emotional reunion with his pregnant wife. It was a seismic moment in Russian history. The conquest of a khanate reinforced Ivan's claim to have inherited the imperial mantle. The old relationship, by which Ivan's ancestors had paid homage for their rule in Moscow at the court of the Tartar khans, had been reversed. The seemingly inexorable expansion of the Russian Church and state continued. Orthodox Russian colonists were moved into Kazan, though large numbers of non-Christians were also absorbed.[8]

The successful campaign against Kazan was marked by the erection of additional wooden chapels against the walls of the Trinity church outside the Kremlin, seen by Chancellor and his fellow Englishmen as they approached the Kremlin gate through the snow. Soon construction would begin here on a great cathedral, built in honour of Kazan's subjection – its brightly painted cupolas licking the heavens like flames – and dedicated to St Vasily, St Basil.

Ediger, meanwhile, had agreed to convert to Christianity and to be baptised. He adopted a new name, Simeon. He had married recently into a Russian family, a union overseen by Ivan, who strongly encouraged the integration of Tartar leaders at his Moscow court where they became his service people, as his ancestors had once been theirs.

All was certainly not yet calm in Kazan. As Chancellor and his men waited in Kholmogory for permission to travel to Moscow, they had learned that the governor of this northern province was away. Prince Semen Ivanovich Mikulinsky-Punkov, described as 'a man of great bravery and skilled in deeds of valour', had been sent by Ivan with other leaders to Kazan to quell ongoing unrest.[9]

Meanwhile a decision had been taken by Ivan and his council to launch an assault on the neighbouring khanate of Astrakhan, and preparations were already under way.

*

In the audience chamber of the royal palace, older, more experienced members of the English party were concerned their younger colleagues might be overawed and fail to conduct themselves with appropriate dignity. Chancellor himself was relatively young and inexperienced, of course. But he had been to royal courts before, and remained outwardly composed.

As Chancellor approached the throne, Ivan reached across to his right to an ornate basin of water with a pitcher where he ostentatiously washed his hands, a traditional custom in Russia which emphasised the purity of the Tsar's intentions. In front of Ivan, Chancellor paid his formal respects. He did his duty to the Tsar, he later said, after the English manner, indicating presumably that he removed his hat, if he had not done so already, bowed low and kissed the Tsar's right hand. He addressed the Tsar, as he had been warned by Russian officials to do, using his full array of titles, some of which were as much a reflection of aspiration as reality:

> Great Duke Ivan Vasilivich, by the grace of God great lord and Emperor of all Russia, great Duke of Volodemer, Mosco, and Novograd, King of Kazan, King of Astracan, lord of Plesko, and great duke of Smolensko, of Twerria, Joughoria, Permia, Vadska, Bulghoria, and others, lord and great duke of Novograd in the Low country, of Chernigo, Rezan, Polotskoy, Rostove, Yaruslavely, Bealozera, Liefland, Oudoria, Obdoria and Condensa, Commander of all Siberia, and of the North parts, and lord of many other countries.[10]

He explained the purpose of his mission, then presented to the Tsar the letters he bore from Edward VI.

Taking them, Ivan rose to his feet – towering, from his considerable height and on his raised platform, over his English visitors. The Tsar spoke slowly, allowing time for the interpreter who had been found to relay his words. He welcomed Chancellor and his men to his court. As was customary, he asked after the health of Edward, their King. Chancellor had been warned in advance that no one should talk before the Emperor unless he had been directly addressed, but now he was free to respond. 'I answered', Chancellor later wrote, 'that he was in good health at my departure from his court, and that my trust was that he was now in the same.'

Did he hold Ivan's steely stare as he said this? Chancellor was a man who cared about truth, whether it concerned the thickness of the Kremlin walls or the health of the English King. He did not know, of course, that Edward had died some time since, while the ship named in his honour had battled through the North Sea towards the Norwegian coast. He did know, however, that as he readied to depart from London, Edward was seriously ill. There had been some signs of improvement. Far from being in good health, however, his life was widely believed to be in grave danger.

Perhaps Edward had been well when Chancellor had last visited the court. He could have convinced himself, if so, that he was not lying to the Tsar. For now, he could only hope that the young King had indeed made a recovery. The requirements of diplomacy dictated that, since he did not know otherwise, he should affirm Edward to be in good health.

The Englishmen must, though, have wondered. Had Edward pulled through? And if he had not, had his demise plunged their country into political and religious turmoil? Just as those back in England who were in some way connected to the venture longed for news of its fate, so too did those involved think about events in the country they had left behind, whose outlook had been so uncertain when they left.

Thirty-Nine

H ad the Russians known of the true situation in England when the expedition departed, it would have seemed uncannily familiar. In the early spring of 1553, as the three ships captained by Sir Hugh Willoughby were made ready to depart, Ivan, like Edward, had become suddenly and dangerously ill.

At the same time as Edward showed increasing symptoms of the tuberculosis that would kill him, Ivan languished with a heavy fever from which it was feared that he would not recover. Both in England and in Russia prayers were said for a beleaguered monarch, as the unpredictable vagaries of death and disease – the inscrutable hand of God – plunged the political class into crisis.

Like Edward, Ivan had ascended the throne as a young boy, having been left an orphan by the premature death of his parents. Later he bitterly lamented the deprivation he had suffered; without his mother in particular, he claimed, he had received 'no human care from any quarter'.[1] Though it was some years since Ivan's father had died, Edward and Ivan were crowned within a month of each other, early in 1547, when Ivan became the first of his dynasty to be formally anointed, using the title the Russians derived from 'Caesar', as the 'Tsar of All Russia'.[2] He exploited every opportunity to emphasise and embellish his connection to the emperors of Rome and Constantinople. Bogus genealogies were constructed which traced his family's descent from the brother of the Emperor Augustus. His grandmother – who was herself connected to the dethroned imperial family of Constantinople – introduced rituals to Moscow derived from this second Rome.[3]

Like Edward, Ivan was the son of a marriage made by his father after a controversial divorce. At almost the same time both Ivan's father,

Vasili III, and Edward's father, Henry VIII, had become frustrated by the failure of their first wives to provide the male heirs they longed for to secure their dynasties' futures. Both, during the 1520s, resolved to respond to what seemed a clear message from on high. In the teeth of vehement clerical opposition, they would dispense with one, ill-starred, wife and take another.

At the time of their near-simultaneous coronations Edward was only nine, while Ivan was sixteen. One was still a child, the other approached adulthood. But both, at first, were figureheads rather than rulers, dominated by charismatic men in their entourage. In Russia, as in England, men were haunted by the unstable politics of a minority, when relatives and advisers intrigued to become the power behind a juvenile on the throne. Nevertheless, by 1553 prominent individuals in both countries looked forward to the stability that a mature and strong monarch could bring.

Now, suddenly, and in unknowing unison, they contemplated the further upheaval of a disputed succession. In Russia there was the possibility of another long minority, for Ivan's young son, Dmitri, was not yet six months old. Men feared the power this would give to the family of Ivan's wife: 'your son is still in swaddling clothes,' they protested to the Tsar, 'the Zakhar'ins will rule us'.[4]

In both countries factions manoeuvred desperately around an ailing young monarch, trying to protect their interests in the event that he failed to recover.

As in England Edward himself, in collaboration with his close advisers, had driven an attempt to alter the succession in favour of his Protestant cousin, Jane Grey, so in Russia a group of nobles plotted – this time against Ivan's vehement wishes – to bring about a similar change to the succession in favour of Ivan's adult cousin Vladimir. Both sets of conspirators believed that by succeeding they would save their country, as well as themselves, from unwanted turmoil.

To the English it might have seemed that the succession in Russia was more straightforward and irrefutable: there was a son, for all that he was an infant. But in Russia, unlike in England, it was not an automatic presumption that the eldest son would inherit, in preference to a brother or other family member. (This was why, just as at the Ottoman imperial court, a succession to the throne was so often followed by the ruthless spilling of family blood.) Ivan, meanwhile – wise to their schemes even as he lay ill – forced his nobles and courtiers, including Vladimir, to kiss the Cross and swear an oath of loyalty to the infant Dmitri.

Unlike Edward, Ivan recovered, but as Chancellor and his men stood before him in the Kremlin, the terrible ramifications of his illness were only beginning to be felt. Like his royal counterpart in England, Ivan was intensely, zealously religious. Soon after his recovery he was anxious to give thanks by making, as he often did, a pilgrimage to a distant monastery. With his wife and young son, against the advice of some, he travelled north, crossing the waterlogged summer terrain by river.

God, however, seemed not to appreciate the gesture. The boat carrying the royal party was overturned by an unexpected wave. Dmitri, who was being held by his wet-nurse, was dropped, with a shriek, into the murky water. By the time he was retrieved, he had drowned.

Oblivious, of course, to the progress being made by the *Edward*, alone now, along the northern fringe of Russia towards the White Sea, Ivan stood with his wife, consumed by grief, as their baby son Dmitri was interred beside his royal ancestors in the Cathedral of the Archangel in the Kremlin.

Although he had recovered his health, the episode of his sickness left a profound mark on Ivan. He could have further sons, of course. The death of a baby was not the unusual event it is now. And for one who believed fervently in the hand of the Almighty, this, surely, was His will, however inscrutable it might be. But the realisation that nobles had been plotting against him while he was gravely ill – defying him at his most vulnerable – shook him deeply. He reacted with venom towards those who had sought to betray him. Those standing close to him now, men like Viskovatyi and Adashev, were men who had been quick to display their loyalty by taking the oath to be faithful to Ivan's son.

Over the coming years Ivan brooded on what had taken place. Much later it still pained him to think of those who, 'thinking that we were no longer alive', rose up 'like drunken men' to destroy the infant 'given to us by God'.[5] The paranoia which resulted, and the determination to impose himself, had a serious effect on his later reign. The consequences, for many, were gruesome.

During the same pilgrimage, it was alleged, a former bishop now in retirement as a monk gave Ivan some advice on ruling by divine right. 'If you wish to be an autocrat,' the monk whispered in Ivan's ear, 'keep not a single adviser wiser than yourself; for you are better than all.'[6] Ivan took the suggestion to heart, and the subsequent years saw his relations with hitherto trusted counsellors gradually deteriorate, and his paranoia worsen – even to the extent that in dark moments, beset by imagined plots, he planned his own escape to England.[7]

Forty

At their audience in the Kremlin, Ivan said he was pleased to hear that Edward was well. One of Chancellor's men then came forward to proffer a gift. A sample of fine English cloth was handed either to the Master of Ceremonies or to the Chief Secretary – having been stowed on board to encourage the leaders of unknown states and islands to deal with England's adventurous new company. Before the ships departed, on 10 April 1553 the Imperial ambassador had noted that 'the said vessels are well-found and carry scarlet kerseys and velvets of excellent quality, besides other pieces (of cloth) to give away as presents'.[1]

It was at the presentation of a gift that the Secretary removed his tall cap. 'Before,' Chancellor noted, 'they were all covered.' This was an important symbolic moment. Throughout a formal visit in Russia, matters of precedence were given the utmost care and scrutiny. Only on the presentation of a gift was the ambassador considered to have proclaimed his monarch's inferior status, and to have testified to the great esteem in which his master – in this case, King Edward – held the Russian Tsar. Without such a statement, it was impossible for the Russian officials to remove their hats, since being the first to do so would amount to an admission of inferior status. Emperors, in the secular world, ceded to nobody.[2]

With hats removed, it was possible to see that the men present had closely shorn heads. This was the fashion in Russia, except for anyone unlucky enough to be out of favour with the Tsar. Exiled to his estates, away from the Tsar's watchful gaze, the disgraced individual would let his hair grow long as a clear sign of his outcast status.[3]

Ivan accepted the gift graciously. (Declining one was a weapon reserved for a diplomatic stand-off.) Only then, with the matter of respective status resolved, would an ambassador with business to discuss have been ushered to a bench draped with a fine rug and placed, in preparation, before the Tsar, to allow him to continue his discussion from a seated position.

There was not, of course, any ongoing relationship between England and Russia to talk about. Generally, letters from monarchs would have been taken, read and translated in advance, so that an answer, if required, could be provided. If in these unusual circumstances, however, it had not been, it required some careful thought.

In any case, Chancellor and his men were dismissed from the Tsar's presence. First, though, the Tsar had issued the English party with a formal invitation to dine with him that day in the Kremlin. This was a routine which, as subsequent English visitors discovered, formed a central part of hospitality at the Russian court.

When Ivan himself was engaged, by a religious ceremony, for example, at one of the Kremlin cathedrals, he compensated by ordering that lavish quantities of food and drink from his hall be delivered to an embassy at their lodgings. On this occasion, however, since Ivan was not otherwise committed, the Englishmen were dismissed from his presence to await a summons. They bowed again and left the room, walking slowly backwards to ensure that they did not turn their backs on the Tsar.

Chancellor and his fellows were led from the audience chamber by the Chief Secretary, who escorted them to his own room where they waited for what seemed like a couple of hours. This sort of interval was customary, and often an ambassador and his entourage were taken to a chamber where there were displays of luxury items – silver bowls and gilded objects – which allowed the party to spend the time marvelling at the Tsar's wealth and taste. Only then, when curiosity was utterly exhausted, did a messenger arrive summoning them to dinner.

Generally, when the Tsar gave a formal state dinner for an ambassador, it took place at around six o'clock in the evening.[4] In this case they must have eaten earlier, perhaps soon after noon, because Chancellor mentioned to Adams that night had fallen while they ate. Deep in the Russian winter it grew dark midway through the afternoon, and this sort of detail he is unlikely to have mistaken.

The official led Chancellor and his fellow Englishmen this time to another palace – probably the 'Palace of Facets', overlooking the Cathedral Square, which was named after the faceted white-stone bricks which decorated its eastern facade. Like much of the stone building commissioned by Ivan's namesake and grandfather within the Kremlin, this was the work of Italian Renaissance architects rather than Russians. Here again, though, Chancellor professed himself unimpressed. He had, he said, 'seen many fairer than it in all points'.

First the party was led into a hall whose scale they found disappointing. It was 'small', Chancellor noted, 'not great as is the Kings Majesties of England'. To one side of the hall was a large table draped in a clean white tablecloth, at one end of which sat an official he referred to as a marshal, carrying in his hand 'a little white rod'. On the table stood a large assortment of golden cups and pitchers, some of them very ornate and clearly intended for show rather than for any practical use. On the other side of the hall was what he described as 'a fair cupboard' – a term referring to a side table intended for display purposes, which if it had shelves at all were usually left open. It was generously stacked with plate: all manner of bowls, dishes, drinking vessels and decanters.

In Russia, just as had long been the case in England, the display of gold and silver plate of all kinds was considered an important way to advertise wealth and status.[5] Visitors were deliberately led past the gleaming array, with time to take in the prestigious collection and to draw the appropriate conclusions about the eminence of their host.

Chancellor and his companions were then led into a dining chamber beyond. Here eight long tables were set up – four on each side – dressed again in clean white tablecloths, and 'full set' in a manner that may have been customary for a visiting embassy, since Russians were generally expected to bring their own knives to such occasions. Spoons were also provided, though not forks. Salt and bread were on the table.

All of the tables were mounted on platforms, 'higher by two steps', Chancellor reckoned, 'than the rest of the house', and at them, on benches, sat some 200 men dressed in thick furs underneath linen robes. Though fireplaces provided a little warmth, the cold remained penetrating. The Englishmen may have been given over-garments by their Russian hosts; certainly such loans were often made by the Russian treasury to visiting embassies, as indeed to their own courtiers – partly to deal with the cold and partly to ensure a certain standard of appearance was maintained in the Tsar's presence. There were no women in attendance. The Tsaritsa and her ladies rarely dined in public, eating separately in their own quarters.[6]

Substantially higher again, meanwhile, was another table some distance apart from the others where the Emperor sat on a 'high and stately seat'. There was not this time, over his head, the ornately decorated canopy or 'cloth of estate' under which he had been seated before, and which was commonplace for royalty and great nobility as another mark of their rarefied status. (It was the absence of such a canopy, rather than its presence at their first audience, which Chancellor thought worthy of comment.) Ivan had changed his clothes, however, and was majestically dressed now in a silver gown – perfectly judged to reflect the glow of countless candles when they were lit in the gathering darkness – and on his head he wore a different imperial crown. This he changed again during the meal, 'so that I saw', Chancellor remembered, 'three several crowns upon his head in one day'.

In the middle of the room there was another large table or 'cupboard', so heavily packed with Ivan's finest plate that even the stout wooden furniture bowed under the weight of it. Innumerable large goblets were interspersed with other vessels, all of 'very fine gold'. Among them were four vast tureens, silver and gold, which Chancellor and his men reckoned must have been five feet high, as well as several silver casks, the size, Chancellor thought, of English firkins (that is, quarter-barrels carrying seventy-two pints) which were used to hold drink for the personal use of the Tsar. Next to the cupboard two men stood stationary and formally dressed, with napkins draped over their shoulders. In front of them each held a large and ornate golden cup, inlaid with pearls and precious stones, which, the company later learned, were reserved for the use of the Tsar.

Following their guides, the Englishmen mounted the platforms to take their seats at places of honour left for them at a table relatively close to Ivan, where he could see them and they him. As would have been customary at other royal courts, the tables were so arranged that no man sat with his back to the Tsar. On occasions an ambassadorial party would sit at a table that was 'curved', that is to say, semicircular, in order that there be no position of precedence, but Chancellor makes no mention of this and no doubt it was he who occupied the predominant position among the English party. In acknowledgement, the heavy, decorated salt cellar which stood on their table would have been placed in front of his position.

It seems, from Chancellor's account, that on this occasion Ivan dined alone. This was often but not always the case. Sometimes Ivan ate with his disabled younger brother, sometimes with the emperor of Kazan, or with senior members of his privy council, though space, and height, always emphasised the Tsar's superior status.

Englishmen who followed in Chancellor's footsteps soon afterwards, and who ate at similar dinners with the Tsar in the Kremlin, referred to a man who sat on a table close to Ivan who was also alone, and who was treated with almost equal deference. In contrast to Ivan's ornate and glittering robes and crown, this man was dressed in a simple habit. 'At another table near unto the Emperor's table,' reported one of Jenkinson's companions in 1557, 'there was set a Monk all alone.' This plainly dressed man, to the astonishment of the English, was treated with the honour accorded to the Tsar, being 'in all points as well served as the Emperor'.

Such a presence would surely have struck Chancellor as worthy of note. Indisposition, or a religious commitment, may have forced his absence that afternoon, for there is no doubt that in 1553 Sylvester was a leading power behind the throne and a strong influence on Ivan. He was 'all-powerful', according to a Russian chronicle; 'all obeyed him'.[7] Sylvester helped to keep a check, during the 1550s, on the violence, cruelty and licentiousness to which the Tsar had been, and would later again become, prone. Realising Ivan's tendencies, he deliberately terrified the Tsar with tales of miracles and apparitions, and bullied him, telling him what clothes to wear, how to behave, how often to worship in church and even how often and when to have sex with his wife.[8]

As with other influential clerics, Sylvester's rise to prominence had been enabled by Ivan's intense religiosity and willingness as a young man to take advice from ecclesiastical advisers who won his trust. His oratory had made a great impression on the young Ivan, who sought the priest's 'spiritual counsel' and help.[9] All his life the Tsar had been surrounded by monks and priests, and regular religious services had profoundly shaped his view of the world.[10]

Unlike the metropolitan bishops, however, Sylvester's power derived from his personal relationship with Ivan rather than from his position. The same was true of others among the group of advisers who shaped government policy in Russia during the 1550s and who were associated with Sylvester: men like Adashev, who had acquired his influence through proximity to the Tsar as a gentleman of the bedchamber. In Russia, more than in England, government was personal rather than institutional.

Only later in life did Ivan rage that a divinely appointed Tsar like himself should have been left 'at the mercy of the priest', as he came contemptuously to label Sylvester, and the 'wicked designs' of those close to him. A true Tsar, he would claim, should rule outright, with 'fear and suppression and bridling and extreme suppression'.[11]

Forty-One

Initially, before any other food was brought, Ivan ordered his serving staff to take a hunk of bread from him to each man present, as a gesture both of his nurturing attention and their submission. He started, no doubt, with his English guests – a means of commencing which, Chancellor was informed, was an ancient custom at the Muscovite court.

As each piece was bestowed the servant loudly proclaimed the bequest. To the English captain he pronounced, in Russian: 'John [Ivan] Basilivich, Emperor of Russia and great Duke of Muscovy, doth reward thee, Richard Chancellor, with bread.' The person honoured then promptly rose to acknowledge the gift, bowing in Ivan's direction, before everybody else in the room stood likewise. Guardians sitting with the English at their table made sure that they were kept abreast of customs or rituals with which they were unfamiliar.

When all those seated had been served, a piece of bread was offered to the master of ceremonies, who ate it in front of the Tsar before bowing low in homage and retreating.

When the bread had been solemnly distributed, the Tsar's Gentleman Usher entered the room followed by a large company of servants, all splendidly dressed in cloth of gold and wearing the traditional 'colpecks', as the tall Russian caps were known. These were not mere servants, of course, but relatively important members of the Tsar's council, assigned to serve their lord, and honoured, rather than insulted, to do so (as indeed was often the case at the table of an English king or lord). There was not, as there was later, any simple division between diner and servant, with a substantial social gulf in between. Those serving were also offered bread, and later meat and drink, by the Tsar.

With them, as they entered the chamber, they carried an array of large dishes, steam spiralling thickly in the cold air, brought from the palace kitchens. The first plates contained the signature dish of any Kremlin banquet: young swan, which was formally presented to the Tsar before being taken to his official carver and his assistants to divide.[1] The dark meat was presented first to the Tsar, and then to the attendant guests, on heavy golden platters which, like the cups provided, impressed Chancellor with their weight and design: 'very rich', he observed in appreciation, referring to the tableware rather than the flesh of the swan.

Men helped themselves directly from the platters, individual plates playing no part in sixteenth-century Muscovite dining.[2] After the swan came numerous other dishes, in succession rather than at once, but all left on the tables until there was no space for more. There were baked meats of all kinds (little cooking being done over an open fire in Russia). There were also pies, and root vegetables cooked with onions and garlic. There must have been some 140 men serving at the banquet, Chancellor thought, and three times, he reckoned, they appeared reclothed in new and equally luxurious outfits.

Numerous toasts were made. The consumption of alcohol, as well as that of food, was prodigious. In truth, the English were more impressed by the quality of the drink than the food. The latter was unimaginative – a relentless sequence of baked meats, remarkable principally for their quantity. 'As for costly meats,' an Englishman remarked soon afterwards, 'I have many times seen better.' But, he said, 'for change of wines, and diverse sorts of meads, it was wonderful'. A seemingly endless supply of different liqueurs continued to arrive, and the table top became cluttered with ornate beakers. 'There was not left at any time', it was observed, 'so much void room on the table, that one cup more might have been set.'[3] The Russians, as Chancellor and his men had already noticed during their stay in the country, were 'notable toss-pots'.

Offerings both of food and of drink were sent, at the Tsar's bidding, to Chancellor and other individual members of his party – a mark of great honour. The recipient made sure to follow the Russian form: to stand up, and bow in all directions, before, in the case of drink, draining the vessel dry. This was the Russian way; watching the Tsar himself the Englishmen noticed that whenever he summoned one of his fine drinking vessels to be brought, 'he drunk them off at a draught'. For an esteemed and relatively abstemious ambassador, who might receive several dozen such offerings during a meal, the occasion could be arduous.

Naturally curious about the behaviour of the Tsar in particular, the English watched him intently. As well as the impressive thirst which he shared with his countrymen they noticed signs of his intense religiosity, which seemed worthy of comment even in a religious age. Whenever he reached out to grasp either some bread or his knife, the men observed, he first made the sign of the Cross with his finger on his forehead. A few years later another Englishman made the same observation: 'The Emperor never putteth morsel of meat in his mouth, but he first blesseth it himself, & in like manner as often as he drinketh: for after his manner he is very religious, & he esteemeth his religious men above his noble men.'⁴ Levels of relaxation were helped, at least, by the fact that conversation was permitted – which often at formal dinners it wasn't.

The occasion would have lasted several hours. As the dinner itself was concluded, in what must have been the early part of the afternoon, at around three o'clock, darkness fell. Large numbers of candles were brought in and placed on the tables, their flickering light dancing on the silver and gold dishes and platters beneath, while further candles were lit in the great chandeliers which hung from the ceiling. Towards the end of the meal the Tsar made a point of calling each of his guests – the noblemen and courtiers as well as the visiting Englishmen – by name, a feat which made a great impression. 'It seems miraculous', wrote Adams, after talking to Chancellor, 'that a prince, otherwise occupied in great matters of estate, should so well remember so many and sundry particular names.' Russians emphasised how much importance was placed upon the Tsar knowing his household – no mere matter of courtesy, since by knowing their names Ivan showed that these men were under his subjection.

As the feast reached its conclusion – countless platters lying untouched, finally, by the sated throng – the Tsar ordered that a cup of mead be conveyed to each of his English guests: the traditional way to finish a formal meal. Only when this too had been downed did the Englishmen make their way, unsteadily, back through the palace and out into the darkness which had long since descended, though it was still the late afternoon.

Outside, the thick snow and the pale, almost white stone of the Kremlin palaces and cathedrals reflected any light from the moon or the stars. Crunching through the powder that was cleared from frequently used paths and stairs, the men's alcohol-scented breath formed thick clouds in air that was stingingly cold.

It was an hour, Chancellor reckoned, to his lodgings – which may imply that these were in the outskirts of the city, and that they walked, thinking, perhaps, to clear their heads. If so, the intention may have been in vain, since after a banquet the Tsar ordered further supplies of mead to be conveyed to the house of a visiting delegation to keep thirst at bay.

As Chancellor and his leading men returned drunkenly to their stove-warmed accommodation, their crew saw out the cold and the near-relentless dark of midwinter on board ship, making do with the plain provisions with which the *Edward* had been stocked. Sheltering below deck, they did all they could to remain warm as ice spread across the bay of the Una, where they were, and the White Sea beyond.

They were quick, later, to tell their captain of the hardship they had suffered. 'Our mariners which we left in the ship in the meantime to keep it,' Chancellor told Adams, 'in their going up only from their cabins to the hatches, had their breath oftentimes so suddenly taken away, that they eftsoons fell down as men very near dead, so great is the sharpness of that cold climate.'

Forty-Two

For Sir Hugh Willoughby and his men, meanwhile, with no community nearby to provide help if it was needed, basic survival was the only issue that mattered.

In autumn nature's offerings had still been abundant. In and around the cooling waters of the Varzina, fish and game were plentiful – seals and salmon in the water, reindeer, foxes and bears on land. Willoughby had been sufficiently struck by the quantity as well as the unusual appearance of the animal life to make a particular note of it in his journal, and he was not one to labour over unnecessary detail. On shore men could still have foraged for berries and mushrooms.[1]

As winter advanced, wildlife became much less common. Animals hibernated or moved inland. The river itself was sealed by thick ice which denied access to its fish.[2] Snow covered any edible plant life on the ground. But food would have been easy to preserve in the sub-zero temperatures, or by using the oil from seals, even if salt supplies were running low. Stores on board were plentiful, and Willoughby and his men had reason to be grateful for the decision by Cabot and the venture's other leading men to stock the ships with food for eighteen months.

Hunger, then, was not a major worry. As the weather deteriorated, the primary concern for Willoughby and for all of his crews was keeping warm.

Certainly, as they contemplated the winter ahead, after the final three-man group returned to the ships without human contact to report, this must have caused considerable apprehension. No English crew had experience of an Arctic climate in winter. None of the men on board now knew quite what they would be forced to endure.

Men had passed on what they had heard, of course, and the crews knew to expect severe cold. The accepted wisdom had been relayed years earlier by Robert Thorne, even as he doubted it himself: the 'general opinion of all Cosmographers', he had written, was that in the far north the sea was 'all ice' and 'the cold so much that none can suffer it'.[3] The organiser of this expedition, Sebastian Cabot, had himself sailed west as a young man, pushing into the northern region of the American continent where it grew cold at a latitude substantially lower than it did in Europe. There he had experienced large blocks of ice floating in the sea, which were a serious threat to his ship. But he had never been obliged to winter there.

As the weeks passed, conditions became dramatically worse. The hours of daylight dwindled and the temperature fell. Remaining on board ship, rather than attempting to make shelters on land, the men listened nervously to the freezing north-easterly winds which blew snow and ice across the water and rattled the ropes in the rigging. Before long most of their days were spent below deck, in near darkness, listening to the weather and to the angry creaking of the ship timbers as they were squeezed by the expanding ice. Always there was the underlying fear and uncertainty: how bad would things get?

Willoughby was a man of natural authority, but seamen were tough and strong-minded. There were arguments, and tempers frayed. Ultimately he was in charge, and under his captaincy they had carved around the northern ocean with no precise idea of their location, and now faced death in an Arctic wilderness, hundreds of miles from home. Perhaps Willoughby even wished himself back at the besieged fort of Lauder.

After the return of the third search party, Willoughby's log comes suddenly to an end. Having made entries regularly, if not at great length, his pen fell dry. No further entries describe the time he and his crews spent moored in the Varzina estuary or their attempts to remain alive.

There was of course no decision, or movement, to report. While Richard Chancellor and the few men he had selected were travelling by sled to Moscow, and the crew of the *Edward Bonaventure* were seeing out the winter moored near the Dvina estuary of the White Sea, no more than a day or two's sail away, the men of their fellow ships sheltered in a river haven on the northern shore, lost and entirely deprived of human contact.

Forty-Three

Exactly what happened to Willoughby and his two crews over the winter will never be known. Some, at least, of the men remained alive on board during November and December as the days, measured in a lightening of the sky, shortened to nothing and the ice thickened on the water.

They were still alive in January 1554, more than three months after the two ships had cast anchor in the estuary – or some of them were, because a will was later found, signed and dated to that month. It belonged to Gabriel Willoughby, a merchant who was on board and who was probably a relative of the captain. Perhaps as a result of the family connection, it was Sir Hugh himself who had signed it as a witness.

The Captain General, in other words, was also still alive. It would be strange if Gabriel had not made a will before he first embarked on a voyage of exploration which was quite likely to run into trouble, either with the elements or with aggressive mankind. But perhaps he had not; and if he had, perhaps he had reconsidered the terms. Either way, the document was surely an indication that the men's thoughts, in those weeks of perpetual cold and darkness, were turning, naturally enough, to the prospect of death.

Sir Hugh could not have known it, but that same winter, back in England, his young kinswoman Jane Grey – the centre of such an extraordinary crisis after the death of Edward VI – was facing a very different end, much before her time.

Initially, when Mary was welcomed in London as the rightful Queen, Jane had been spared. Some had expected her to die, but Mary saw in her only the unknowing tool of politicians who sought desperately to protect Edward's Protestant reforms. Jane 'knew nothing of it', Mary had insisted, 'nor was she ever a party, nor did she ever give her consent to the duke's intrigues and plots'. Her conscience, Mary declared, 'would not permit her to have [Jane] put to death'.[1]

Although Jane was kept in the Tower as a prisoner – evicted, of course, from the royal apartments she had initially inhabited – she was well treated, attended by three gentlewomen and a manservant.[2] In August she was walked in shame through the city streets to her trial, where she was found guilty of high treason and condemned to death, along with her husband, Guildford Dudley, and the former Archbishop, Thomas Cranmer. But her sentence was exemplary: few expected it to be carried out.

From her captivity in the Tower Jane heard reports of Mary's lavish coronation at the beginning of October, for which consecrated oil – untainted by the sinful religious policies of the previous reign – was imported from Flanders.[3] It included a ceremonial procession through London. The parade passed through elaborate arches provided by, among others, the foreign merchant communities of the capital, anxious to win favour with the new regime and to express their gratitude; for Mary had already ordered that the penalties placed upon the Hanse merchants under her half-brother were to be rescinded, and the German merchants were again to enjoy their former advantages.[4]

Did Sebastian Cabot watch in dismay? The events of recent months had certainly damaged his prospects, old as he was. The young King who was enthused by his schemes had died prematurely. His powerful patron, John Dudley, had fallen spectacularly from grace and died a traitor's death. And there was not yet, though he would not have expected it, any sign or word of his major expedition, which might win over a new regime with other concerns, and so promote once more a lasting revival in English commercial fortunes.

As the months passed, Jane Grey took comfort in the deep Protestant beliefs she had shared with her late cousin, King Edward. She knew that, under Mary's rule, Edward's religious reforms were being reversed. Statutes which had compelled the use of Cranmer's revised Prayer Book, and which had reduced the seven sacraments to only two, were repealed. The Mass Jane hated was restored.[5]

To Jane's disgust, her father-in-law, the Duke of Northumberland, had recanted his views and attended Mass prior to his execution. Did he, an ageing man who could have little time to live, value life so much, and principle so little, that he would seek to save his skin this way? 'Should I, who am young and in my few years,' she wrote, 'forsake my faith for the love of life?'[6]

Among the populace at large, though, there was little doubt that a return to the traditional and comfortable practices of the late years of Henry VIII was broadly popular. What was not popular was the fact, kept secret for a time, but whispered and spread first among the court and then in London more generally, that the Queen intended to marry a Spaniard.

The heir to the Habsburg throne, Philip was both a Catholic and a foreigner.

Men feared and assumed that Mary's authority would be subsumed by that of her husband, and that the interests of England would be relegated beneath those of Habsburg Continental lands. For a number of prominent men this, more than the undoing of Edward's religious reform, was an urgent reason to depose her, and they plotted to rebel. Among them was Henry Grey, the Duke of Suffolk – Jane's father.[7]

Their plan was to organise regional rebellions in areas in which they had influence. When word of the impending trouble leaked out, plans had to be hastily brought forward. In the West Country and in Leicestershire the risings were chaotic and they misfired. But in Kent Sir Thomas Wyatt led an armed revolt which caused the government serious concern. Mary's regime was still finding its feet. It could not call upon significant armed resources, or rely on the loyalty of most of the political class. The Queen herself, along with her advisers, was anxious and indecisive – until she rallied support with a brave speech at the city Guildhall.[8]

When Wyatt's army entered Southwark, expecting to cross London Bridge into the city, it was kept outside. Boats were ordered to remain moored and did so, and when the hostile army crossed to the north bank at Kingston it found that resistance in the capital remained firm. Early in February Wyatt gave himself up, realising that defeat was at hand. This time Mary had little choice but to be firm.

Wyatt was executed, along with Jane's father, and a hundred or so other men who had been directly involved. 'At present,' the Imperial ambassador reported approvingly in mid-February, 'there is no other occupation than the cutting off of heads and inflicting exemplary punishment.'[9]

By the time he wrote, furthermore, it was not just leading rebels who had died. Jane Grey herself, quite innocent of any knowledge or involvement, had had her sentence revived, along with her husband Guildford, Dudley's son. The plotters had hoped to put Mary's half-sister Elizabeth on the throne in her place, not Jane; but to a regime which was reeling and panicky, Jane still seemed a threat.

Willoughby's young kinswoman brushed aside a final attempt to convert her. She watched from her cell window as a cart was towed past bearing the decapitated body of her husband. Then she walked, with resolution, to place her own neck upon the block.[10]

Forty-Four

Over the course of the subsequent weeks – thirteen or fourteen in all – Chancellor and his men were hampered in their ability to move freely around Moscow by the minders, or 'pristavs', who 'assisted', and watched their every move.

The English certainly spent their time, as Cabot would have wished, accumulating information. Chancellor himself wrote a survey of Russia on his return, which Clement Adams worked up into a slightly longer, more stylised account. Another member of the party, the merchant John Hasse, took careful records specifically for the benefit of the company that concentrated on mercantile matters: on the coins, weights and measures used in Russia, on the customs and tolls paid by other merchants, on the commodities produced in Russia which might be purchased by the English and on the English products which would find a ready market.[1]

Fish, salt, flax, oils, hemp, wax, feathers, hides and furs could all, Hasse thought, be purchased cheaply and resold at a profit in England. Meanwhile English cloth – the nation's primary product – would find a ready market in Russia, he believed, since English merchants could undercut the prices of the Hanseatic traders currently shipping cloth to Russia through ports on the Baltic. He thought the English would be able to do so in spite of the privileges enjoyed by the Hanse, who were exempt from paying certain duties.

While they were in Moscow, Hasse wrote, a 'great ambassador' had come to Ivan's court from 'Liffeland' (as Livonia, the region to the east of the Baltic occupied by modern Latvia, was then known), to confirm the privileges enjoyed by these Hanseatic traders.[2] The Englishmen were aware of accusations being made against them by merchants who disliked the idea of competitors employing a new route. 'Hearing of the arrival of our men', Chancellor told Adams, these 'Flemings', as he called them, wrote letters to the Tsar, accusing the English of being 'pirates and rovers' and urging him to imprison them. The thought that Ivan might do so made Chancellor and his men afraid that they might not see home again.

The English were struck by the magnificence displayed whenever men were 'sent into far or strange countries, or that strangers come to them'. They also witnessed an embassy departing from Moscow: ambassadors sent by Ivan to visit the cultured and capable King of Poland, Sigismund II – who was competing with Ivan for control over the same Baltic region.[3] Chancellor watched the great train depart through the Moscow snow and was hugely impressed.

There were at least, he reckoned, 500 horses, and not only the men who rode them but the horses themselves were dressed with astonishing richness, in velvet, cloth of gold and cloth of silver set lavishly with pearls. 'What shall I further say?' he asked rhetorically, 'I never heard of nor saw men so sumptuous.' All, Chancellor thought, was for the love of ceremony and show, and the belief he found in Moscow in their importance. In their daily lives, he noted, even important men in Russia, from the Tsar downwards, did not bother to dress up.

The English party had other opportunities to witness the love held by Russians, and by Ivan in particular, for theatrical ceremonies. They watched military displays while in Moscow, and the lavishness Chancellor saw for himself quashed any doubts that this normally sceptical man might have had about reports of Russia's capability. He had heard tell, he said, of the expensive finery worn by nobles and gentlemen, of their desire 'to be sumptuous in the field', which he would not have believed had he not been a witness to exercises if not to actual campaigns.

The Englishmen probably saw a display of the Tsar's artillery, held every year in mid-December, in the thick snow of the open fields outside the suburbs of Moscow. Ivan was particularly proud of the royal guns, just as Edward VI had been in England. Chancellor does not mention the occasion specifically – he says only that he had seen the finery of the Tsar and his nobles during what was clearly a military display – but an English visitor four years later records the event as one which took place 'every year in the month of December'.[4]

The Tsar and his nobles rode into the field on their best Turkish and 'Jennet' horses, the latter a small, powerful breed used by riders, like the Russians and their Tartar rivals in the open steppe, who preferred to ride with their legs tucked up in short stirrups.[5] The animals were adorned with ornate gold and silver gear, while Ivan himself, in 1557, wore a rich gown of tissue with a scarlet cap set with countless pearls and precious stones. As he sat stationary on his horse, his nobility rode in front of him in gowns of cloth of gold, and they were followed by some 5,000 'harquebusiers' – each with his long gun resting on his left shoulder, while the match to ignite it was carried in the right hand.

After their ceremonial ride past the gunners took up position on a long stage built from wooden poles. They aimed towards large slabs of ice, two feet thick and six feet high, which had been positioned as targets about sixty yards from the stage. Then, when the Tsar himself was seated and ready, a command was given and the men discharged their weapons, not ceasing 'until they had beaten all the ice flat on the ground'.[6] They celebrated by firing their guns into the air, 'a goodly sight to behold', before turning to the larger artillery pieces which had been brought into position, beginning with the smallest and working upwards, firing each three times.

Two wooden houses had been set up and filled with earth as targets for the ordnance, all kinds of which were brought into action – bases, falcons, minions, sakers, culverins, basilisks and 'great pieces' which fired shot a yard high. By the time they had finished firing, the houses, despite being stoutly built, at least thirty feet thick and packed with earth, 'were beaten in pieces', at which triumph the Tsar rode ceremoniously home as he had come. It was on this or a similar occasion that Chancellor marvelled at the extraordinary luxury of the Tsar's pavilion, set up in the snow-filled field, 'covered either with cloth of gold or silver, and so set with stones that it is wonderful to see it'. 'I have seen', he wrote, 'the King Majesty of England's and the French King's pavilions.' They were 'fair, yet not like unto his'.

Chancellor clearly spoke with Russians about the armies the Tsar could put into the field; he made exaggerated claims for the forces at Ivan's disposal which must have come from a source he trusted. Ivan never went on campaign, Chancellor wrote, without 200,000 men and could muster 300,000 if necessary, while he left his borders guarded by further tens of thousands, in spite of the fact that he never expected farmers or merchants to serve as soldiers.[7] He also marvelled at the hardiness of the Russian soldier, who was expected to cope on campaign, in the most inhospitable conditions, surviving on a meagre diet of oatmeal mixed with cold water:

> ... and though they lie in the field two months, at such time as it shall freeze more than a yard thick, the common soldier hath neither tent nor anything else over his head: the most defences they have against the weather is a felt, which is set against the wind and weather, and when Snow cometh he doth cast it off, and maketh him a fire, and layeth him down thereby ...

'I believe', Chancellor wrote, 'they be such men for hard living as are not under the sun.' English soldiers could certainly learn a lesson from them: 'I pray you amongst our boasting warriors how many should we find to endure the field with them but one month.' But the Russians were ill trained, fighting 'without all order in the field'. Chancellor could only wonder what an exceptional fighting force might be at the Tsar's disposal if men of this toughness were to be exploited in a disciplined fashion.

'I do believe', Chancellor declared, 'that two of the best or greatest princes in Christendom were not well able to match with him.'

Chancellor and his men were in Moscow over the Christmas period. Christmas itself must have followed a few days after their first reception and dinner with Ivan at the Kremlin. No mention was made of particular activities at court associated with the Nativity, but the Englishmen probably witnessed an annual ceremony which took place on the twelfth day, during which the River Moskva, beneath the high walls of the Kremlin, was ritually blessed.

The men of Anthony Jenkinson's embassy a few years later described the procession from the Kremlin church, which moved, at nine o'clock in the morning, in the half-light of dawn, through the snow towards the frozen river. It was headed by a group of young men, one of whom carried a large lantern while the others bore long tapers of burning wax.

Behind them a great Cross was held aloft, while further back men carried on their shoulders images of the Virgin Mary, of St Nicholas and of other venerated saints. Then came a hundred or more priests, followed by the Metropolitan, who walked slowly ahead of the Tsar.[8] Ivan himself was 'richly apparelled with gold, pearls, precious stones, and costly furs', a crown on his head 'of the Tartarian fashion', which may have been the famed cap of Monomakh. His nobility, in orderly rows, brought up the rear.

The procession came to a halt around a large square hole, six yards long by six yards wide, that had been cut in the ice of the river and edged with white wooden boards. On one side a platform had been built upon which stood a fine throne, not on this occasion for the Tsar but for the Metropolitan, the man whom the Tsar himself considered his superior in spiritual matters. Some of the priests moved around the hole, censing – that is, swinging censers in which incense burned and ascended, like the prayers it was intended to represent, in scented clouds.

The other priests stood in orderly lines, incanting the words of Psalm 141, with its invocation for the prayers of the gathered faithful to rise like incense to the Lord. 'With great solemnity and service', Jenkinson wrote, the Metropolitan hallowed the water. He reached down and cupped a little of it in his hands, then threw the droplets over the Tsar, who stood bare-headed as a mark of respect, as well as over some of his senior nobility.

The formal procession – the Tsar, the Metropolitan, the priests and nobility – then filed back towards the Kremlin, leaving imperial officials and ordinary Muscovites to throng around the hole in the ice, pressing forward in great crowds, anxious to gain access to what was now holy water. Thousands of pots were dipped in the river, people being anxious to return home with their personal supply. Men, women and children plunged naked into the freezing river before immediately clambering out, flushed and shivering, while the sick were lowered in and quickly removed. Muslim Tartars who wished to be christened had the service performed. Men even brought their horses to the edge to drink, and the animals of the Tsar's own stable were led to the water in a long line, steam rising from their flanks.[9]

*

Finally, in the middle of March, Chancellor received a visit from a Kremlin official, summoning him to another reception with Ivan. Again he attended as requested and paid his formal respects before the Tsar, who as before was richly dressed and enthroned, though wearing a different crown and robe, and accompanied once more by his privy councillors and other nobles.

Announced by the master of ceremonies, Chancellor was presented with a formal response to the letter from King Edward that he had delivered to Ivan at the first audience. When the ceremony was over, Chancellor took his official leave from Ivan's court. Then, with Hasse and his other colleagues, he made his way back north, on post sledges provided once more at the Tsar's expense, to rejoin his shipmates on the shore of the White Sea.

It was 15 March when he left the Kremlin. By the end of the month the Englishmen were probably back at Kholmogory, the river by which the town was built still frozen solid. From there they continued by sled immediately north to the coast, to reunite with their brethren on the *Edward*.

They arrived back at the White Sea in time to depart promptly when the melting ice made travel in these northern waters possible once more.

The letter given by Ivan to Chancellor was written in the Russian language, in script, as Richard Hakluyt later noted, 'much like to the Greek letters'. A copy was attached in which it was translated into Dutch, a west European tongue with which the Muscovite government was familiar and in which both nations had a common understanding.

It was elegantly produced, as official letters from the Russian Tsar invariably were. Penned by trained scribes, it was 'very fair written on paper with a broad seal hanging at the same, sealed in paper upon wax'.[10] On the seal, which struck those who saw it as similar to England's broad seal, there was a familiar image, of 'a man on horseback in complete harness fighting with a dragon'.[11]

Ivan's titles were proclaimed, as he liked them to be, at length: his dukedom over Vladimir, Moscow, Novgorod and numerous Russian cities, the fact that he was 'lord over all the north coast' along which the English had sailed, the inclusion of 'Kazan' among his patrimonies and, most importantly, the fact that he was 'by the grace of God Emperor of all Russia'. He offered his greeting and respects to Edward, King of England, though unbeknownst to the English or to Ivan, the boy King had died the previous summer.

The Tsar confirmed what Chancellor himself would tell the English government: in 1553, the twentieth year of Ivan's governance – 7059 by Russian reckoning – Edward's servant, Richard Chancellor, had arrived on Ivan's coast, expressing a wish to enter his dominions.[12] He had been permitted to do so and, according to his own request, had 'seen our Majesty and our eyes', as the traditional Russian formula had it. He had, Ivan wrote, passed on Edward's request that his English subjects be granted the freedom to trade unhindered in his lands, along with the letters in which Edward had made the same request.

Ivan was happy to accede. With 'Christian belief and faithfulness', he wrote, he would 'not leave it undone'. The English could send ships to Russia 'as often as they may have passage', with the Tsar's assurance that they would not be harmed. Ivan was aware, of course, that Chancellor was not an officially accredited ambassador, and with all his anxiety about status was keen to suggest that Edward send 'one of your Majesty's council to treat with us', who might forge a formal agreement as to where English merchants might set up a market in Russia. Ivan would be willing, he said, to make extensive concessions. English traders 'shall have their free mart with all free liberties through my whole dominions with all kinds of wares, to come and go at their pleasure, without any let, damage, or impediment, according to this our letter, our word, and our seal'.

No doubt it had occurred to Ivan that with a member of Edward's Council he would also be able to discuss other, princely matters, which would form an important motivation in his dealings with English representatives over the coming decades. For his coming campaigns with the Tartars of Astrakhan, and also the prolonged struggles with the European powers to Russia's north-west, Ivan was anxious to obtain the best possible military supplies. He needed both munitions for his artillery and additional expertise to service and manufacture them, requirements which were deliberately frustrated by hostile powers on his border.

A friendly trading relationship with England by a new northern route would provide, he quickly realised, the opportunity to bypass the traditional trade routes with Europe which were controlled by his enemies.[13]

There was also, of course, the unknown fate of the other English ships.

Chancellor had told the Russian court that his expedition had been led by another man, that his own ship, the *Edward Bonaventure*, left now with its crew in the White Sea, had been one of three English ships which had become separated in a terrible storm while sailing towards the northern cape. Ivan could only promise that if the other Englishmen did in due course appear in his realm, they would be well treated. 'Hereupon', he wrote to Edward, 'we have given order, that wheresoever your faithful servant Hugh Willoughby land or touch in our dominions', he would be 'well entertained'. But as yet, he assured the English government, Willoughby had not arrived, 'as your servant Richard can declare'.

His letter was dated February 1554.

Forty-Five

It was late in the spring that a party of Russian fishermen spotted the two ships in the Varzina estuary, and, clambering on board, discovered the tragic fate of their crew. What exactly, though, had happened to them?

The assumption has long been that Willoughby and his men froze to death on these barren Arctic shores: martyrs at the outset of English commercial expansion. In the history of his country's navigation that he wrote soon afterwards, Richard Hakluyt commented that the crews had 'perished for cold'.[1] An Englishman who was sent out to retrieve the bodies and the company's goods recorded that they had died – apparently, he thought, of exposure – 'for want of experience to have made caves and stoves'.[2] But this conclusion has recently, and rightly, been called into question.

Over the subsequent years surprisingly few sailors, ice-bound in northern extremities, died of the cold alone. The location where the men of the *Bona Esperanza* and the *Bona Confidentia* were anchored was not so bitter that they would not have been expected to survive. Although it was cold, perhaps ten degrees below zero, temperatures for the latitude were actually quite warm here on the north-west Russian coast which, like the western fringe of Scandinavia, was washed by the Gulf Stream. The men had thick clothes of their own, provided by the company, and they had access to more. Among their cargo was a supply of rich woollen garments with which they had intended to tempt foreign merchants and rulers, and which they could certainly have plundered in an emergency. In fact Sebastian Cabot had decreed in his instructions to the expedition that the merchants on board should provide any clothing required by a mariner for the 'conservation of his health' at no more than cost price, which could be deducted from the man's wages.[3]

Supplies of food, as we have seen, were plentiful, and indeed they were not exhausted, for men sent to collect the crews' goods and effects recovered some of their provisions. According to the Venetian ambassador's letter, there had still been dogs on board – frozen into the same bizarre and lifelike poses as the men. Sailors who were starving would scarcely have hesitated to eat their dogs.

The nature of ship supplies has led some to assume that the men died of scurvy, a disease which claimed the lives of many more sailors on long voyages than did the elements. Its origin in a dietary deficiency of vitamin C was not understood, and the foodstuffs supplied on ships – the 'flesh, fish, biscuit, meat, or bread' – were not only monotonous but also devoid of fruit or vegetable content.[4]

Here again, though, there are problems. On the one hand the crews should have been able in the autumn, as they explored the land around the ship, to find berries and mushrooms which would have acted as a prophylactic. On the other hand, men sickening of scurvy would not have become ill and died all at the same time. Those naturally weaker, or already ill, would have fallen victim first. Those remaining alive, meanwhile, would surely have tried to remove, if not to bury, the bodies of their dead brethren. But all, apparently, were found on board. Nor (if we accept the Venetian ambassador's account, and it surely had an element of truth) would the men have died suddenly, in the act of performing what sound like mundane acts of everyday life: opening lockers, writing or eating. They would have sickened, taken to their beds, and died in a recumbent position.

These reasons for doubt have led to another and more persuasive explanation.

For as long as their supplies of wood lasted, the crews were able to burn it on their stoves below deck, and so to remain warm enough, huddled together, wrapped in thick clothes and sheltered from the wind. It must have been obvious, however, that it wasn't going to see them through the long winter. And this far north they were beyond the tree line. There was no wood to gather, and little driftwood to be found. What the crews might have been able to collect along the shores of the estuary, however, were lumps of clean, black coal that had washed up from seams exposed along cliffs or on the seabed.[5] This so-called 'sea coal' had been used since ancient times as a readily available and convenient form of fuel.

Usually, smoke from the cook-room fire was able to escape through a chimney and an open hatch. But as the cold northern winter gripped, the hatch had been closed to retain any warmth. All of the ship's openings had been sealed to keep out the freezing wind. And, unlike wood, sea coal releases carbon monoxide when burned. In an unventilated space this gas, unseen and unsmelt, might have quickly accumulated and killed an entire crew where they sat.

As the fire went out and the temperature in the cabin fell, the bodies would have frozen solid – not, of course, in quite the active positions the embellished Venetian account described, for those affected would certainly have first collapsed as they passed out – but in quite random and varied postures nevertheless, their unfortunate fate unknown by those who had left the Thames with them until many months had passed.[6]

The truth is unknowable, but it is a convincing explanation. Perhaps these Englishmen, keeping warm upon the frozen Varzina River in northern Russia, slipped painlessly and unknowingly into oblivion sometime in the early part of 1554. Perhaps, if so, they might otherwise have survived the Arctic winter, and watched the ice on the river thin and break up. Perhaps they might have continued on their way in the spring, and encountered fishermen or others along the northern shores who could point them towards the gulf of the White Sea, where they would have met again the companions from whom they had been separated.

This, though, is not what happened, and the fate of Sir Hugh Willoughby and his men took a central position in the canon of early English exploration. In any case, the tide was moving away from men like him, unschooled in the naval arts, as captains of significant expeditions.

Years later a copy of Willoughby's ship's log was acquired by a man called Robert Cotton, who went to Westminster School in the late sixteenth century, like Richard Hakluyt, and who began collecting manuscripts at the age of eighteen. He received material from men who had been associated from the beginning with the Muscovy Company, like John Dee and William Cecil, among many others. He amassed a valuable collection which was kept together after his death. Then, in October

1731, a fire broke out in the building where the documents were being stored. As a result the log is singed around the edges, though fortunately, unlike some of the other documents in the collection, it did survive, and is a remarkable witness to the voyage and fate of Willoughby and his men.

In the margin of his log an annotation has been made, later, in another hand. In a phrase of four words are poignantly encapsulated months of fear, though there was perhaps not the gathering anguish that this writer assumed. It reads simply: 'the Haven of Death'. And so, for many men, it was.

Part III

'MERCHANT ADVENTURERS OF ENGLAND'

And surely if ever since the beginning of the world any enterprise have deserved great praise as a thing achieved by men of
heroical virtue, doubtless there was never any more worthy
commendation and admiration than is that which our nation
have attempted by the north seas to discover the mighty and
rich empire of Cathay ...

RICHARD EDEN, *The Decades of the New World* [1]

Forty-Six

On the voyage home made by Richard Chancellor and his men there was not, at least, the anxious uncertainty about their destination which had weighed on each individual during the outward trip. There was only the desperate hope that they would reach it, to see family and friends again, and to tell remarkable tales – not of Oriental spices, silks and gems, but of a cold, northern kingdom, and of a great emperor, of Russia, not of Tartary, holding court amid the snow.

No record was kept, or has survived, of the return journey to match those of the outgoing voyage which took the *Edward* to Russia. Whatever struggles they had, with wind and weather, did not prevent them from reaching home and left no trace in the historical record. Anxious to depart once the ice cleared, it took them perhaps a couple of months and it was midsummer – late July or early August – when they reached England.[2]

One thing is known. Many years later, in the mid-1580s, an old merchant named Henry Lane wrote a letter from his home in Kent to a prominent city man called William Sanderson. Lane had worked from an early date for the company set up under Sebastian Cabot. Although he did not take part in the initial exploration of 1553, he did sail on the second voyage, to work in Russia as an agent, and he came to know Richard Chancellor well. In his letter Lane responded to a request for a summary of the main events of England's north-eastern discovery, and he went to some trouble over it.

Evidently Sanderson had told him that he was planning to publish a more general account, and Lane thought the cause worthwhile. He was apologetic. Some of his paperwork, he said, he had lent out, and he was unable to retrieve it. But he had sat and reread his old letters, he told

Sanderson, 'to content one that meaneth to pleasure many'.

Lane told Sanderson how the *Edward Bonaventure* had safely wintered at St Nicholas while their erstwhile companions confronted the 'extreme cold' and tried, unsuccessfully, to see the season out in a river estuary that they had discovered on 'a desert coast in Lappia'. The following year, he noted, the *Edward* had returned to London, and it was then that the ship had been 'robbed homewards by Flemings'.[3]

Somewhere in the North Sea, the *Edward* was attacked by pirates.

Piracy was one of the perennial hazards of seagoing life in sixteenth-century Europe, as familiar and unremarkable as the storms and foul weather with which the crew were already acquainted. Some years later the company lamented 'their great losses sustained at the seas by pirates and otherwise'.[4] This incident was little enough thought of that it attracted no comment that has survived prior to the throwaway remark in Henry Lane's letter more than thirty years later.[5]

The ships of the expedition had evaded any confrontation with pirates thus far. On the outward journey they had sailed as far as the northern Norwegian coast, until they were out of range of most other European vessels, as a group of three ships, which made them a much less vulnerable target. When she returned, however, the *Edward* was alone. She sailed back into the busy trading waters of northern Europe as a tempting prey for the numerous pirate vessels which concealed themselves in coves, or sailed from foreign ports with the tacit support of local and even central government officials.

Lane wrote that the pirates were Flemings, and Flanders (the coastal region of modern Belgium) was probably where the ship and perhaps many of its crew originated. But pirate vessels were like most merchantmen: they employed any crew that they could, and there was a great deal of 'wandering abroad' among those who manned ships.[6] In 1551 the Imperial ambassador in England reported home that the English had 'seized three vessels from Scottish pirates'. As well, presumably, as Scots, he noted that they had found on board 'Englishmen, Flemings and Frenchmen' – a sign that the make-up of merchant or pirate crews was governed by self-interest and by no means necessarily followed the contours of patriotism or of international war and diplomacy.[7] In any case, the flag under which the ship flew was no certain guide to origin. Flags were switched often enough for tactical reasons to disguise identity.

In general the boundaries between merchant, privateer and pirate were flexible and vague. A ship carrying goods might seize those of a smaller, ill-protected vessel if the opportunity arose and its captain was so minded. The weapons with which any cautious merchantman was defended were a standing invitation to aggression, and neither captains nor their crew were coy about increasing their profit margins in this way – the general economic level of seafaring men as a class was too low; they were, as the famous pirate turned naval captain Sir Henry Mainwaring later put it, 'so generally necessitous and discontented'.[8] In time of war – common enough between European states, which grappled incessantly for supremacy – pirates were of great value to central governments, adopting the flag with a patriotism that was not entirely bogus to plunder the vessels of enemy ships and neutrals alike.

This, indeed, was the central conundrum for naval officials. On the one hand they wanted to rid the seas of pirates, and Acts were passed and treaties signed to clamp down upon the problem. But on the other hand pirate captains were often the very men – brave, determined and remorseless – that the country needed if they were to fight a war at sea.[9] 'Letters of marque', as official permissions were known, were issued willingly to captains who had access to vessels and who were prepared to direct their aggression at the ships of an enemy country.

During the wars with France and Scotland during the 1540s, English naval ships and privateers were barely distinguished. Sir Hugh Willoughby himself had taken charge of one of the ships loitering off the Scottish coast looking for victims. During the later struggles with Spain during Elizabeth's time, such privateers flourished and were openly encouraged.[10] Outright piracy, moreover, was fostered by the willingness both of local and central officials to take bribes for turning a blind eye.

Thomas Seymour, the Lord Admiral when Cabot arrived back in England, was accused of just such corruption. He had, it was alleged, 'maintained, aided, and comforted sundry pirates, and taken to his own use the goods piratously taken against the laws'.[11]

*

The *Edward*, while she now sailed alone, was unusually well defended. The expedition had enjoyed widespread support from merchants and government alike and as such was much better equipped with artillery and weapons than most merchant vessels would have been.

Once the hostile advance was spotted it was first Chancellor, the captain, but then the master gunner, Robert Stanton, along with his mate and the two other gunners, who led the ship's defences. Other crew members rushed to follow their instructions.

Simple numbers of men, of course, were a significant protection, not only in terms of the use of guns but also in terms of fighting at close quarters in the event that pirates attempted to board. Under-manning of merchant vessels by ship-owners anxious to cut their costs and so maximise their profits often presented pirates with easy pickings. 'Overslack manning', as it was later put, was a 'perilous and foolish thrift'.[12] But on this occasion the Flemish pirates must have been confronted by a more resilient and determined defence than they bargained for.

No doubt Chancellor's first response was to try to escape unwanted attention. Frantic efforts would have been made to remain upwind of the pursuing vessel, so that the gap could only be closed by tacking laboriously.[13] But the attacking ship was probably smaller, nimbler and faster through the water, with large numbers of men on board motivated by the fact that payment would only come from a division of spoils. Clearly the pirates did manage to board. Grappling hooks were hurled across into the *Edward*'s rigging to pull and hold it at close quarters, while men scrambled across onto its deck and the defenders used long pikes to try to prevent them. Gradually, over subsequent decades, as the artillery power of naval vessels increased, the importance of boarding as a means of seizing control of an enemy ship declined. Fighting ships preferred to remain clear and to destroy their opponents by bombardment, as Drake's English ships did when confronted by the larger fleet of the Spanish Armada. But for pirates, of course, boarding remained fundamental: there was no other way for the goods and wealth of a merchant vessel to be seized.

Since substantial losses of goods or men are not mentioned in the records that survive, it seems probable that a deal was done. The most valuable commodities that the *Edward* was conveying on its route home in 1554, of course, were the knowledge acquired of the northern route and of the potential trade with Moscow, as well as the hard-learned expertise in oceanic navigation which Richard Chancellor, almost alone among his countrymen, possessed. All the time that he sailed with them, Chancellor was passing on his enthusiasm and knowledge to those who went with him. It was not worth putting all this in jeopardy, and to avoid large-scale loss of life or injury on either side some merchandise was handed over. The *Edward* probably still had on board some of the fine English cloths with which the company had packed the ship, and with these they would have been willing to part.

Attitudes were altered by the fact that, unusually for an English vessel of the time, the merchants were sailing not with goods that they owned but as representatives of a company. This wider organisation was willing enough at this stage to shoulder minor losses in return for information which could prove lucrative in the future.

Forty-Seven

For the men of the *Edward*, their first sighting of the coastline of the land of their birth was an emotional moment – no less so than the moment of leaving it behind had been almost exactly a year before. From the southern bulge of the Scandinavian peninsula the *Edward* set a course south-south-west, leaving the Norwegian shore before she passed too close to Bergen, where the rival Hanseatic traders had their northern base. But, as ever, the crew were at the mercy of the wind.

Perhaps they saw Shetland, or the coast of Scotland, and followed the land south, or perhaps they headed directly for the eastern flank of England. The temptation to pause at one of their country's eastern ports may have been too much to resist; one assumes that this was the case given that the expedition organised by the same backers the following year was explicitly ordered not to do so, lest an opportunity for private trading arise, but to make directly on its return for the Thames estuary and the port of London.[1]

If they did drop anchor in eastern England, word of the *Edward*'s safe return from its great voyage of exploration, and of its discovery of a new route to the empire of the Russian Tsar, may have reached the capital before the ship itself. The news could have been sent overland deliberately, as Cabot had requested, in the hands of a crew member or of another messenger from the port who could ride alone and unladen on horseback on roads which, unlike in Russia, improved in summer, and without the need to confront winds which might be unfavourable. Even if not, Chancellor's vessel would have been sighted in the estuary of the Thames, and word would then have been carried quickly to Cabot and the leading men of the company before the *Edward* itself could drop anchor in its home waters east of London.

Was there definitely only one ship? What, if anything, had Chancellor and his men said about the fate of the other two? Anticipation at the prospect of hearing the men's news must have mingled with trepidation at learning the fate of their fellow sailors.

On its return to the Thames, the *Edward* floated towards London on the incoming tide, exploiting any favourable wind with a small expanse of sail. As it neared the capital smaller craft approached, and excited exchanges were shouted across the water. Each day, as the tide turned, anchor was weighed, and the men came ashore to pass on their news to the inhabitants of Thames-side communities. Londoners were fore-warned, and thronged to the bank to watch the ship heave into view on Limehouse Reach.

Reaction in the capital to the return of Chancellor and his crew was effusive. The men naturally relished their hero status, recounting stories of their journey and of their experiences in Russia – of the plunging temperatures and unremitting darkness, and of life among the people of the far north. There were countless questions about the terrible storm which had separated the expedition ships, and of the men's last sighting of Sir Hugh Willoughby, Cornelius Durforth and the men of the *Bona Esperanza* and the *Bona Confidentia*.

There was no need to embellish. The truth was gripping enough. In huddled groups Londoners joined in speculation about their fate. These crews too, of course, had friends and expectant families in London, hungry for news and watching on painfully as the men of the *Edward* milked the acclaim and showed off the goods they had brought back.[2]

Richard Chancellor had returned to England now after a year's absence. Any sea voyage at the time was dangerous, but this one – con-fronting unknown hazards from both people and climate in the far north – was certainly more so than most. He knew that he could easily not have returned, and indeed his was the only one of three ships yet to have done so.

For all the guesswork, in truth no one in England yet knew the fate of the other two.

There were many people whom Chancellor was relieved and emotion-al to see again, but none more so, surely, than the two sons he had had to leave behind and who were already without their mother. It had been their future, as well as his own and that of his crew, that had played on his mind at difficult moments.

From what we can gather he was a caring and conscientious man weighed down, at times, by anxiety. No record of their reunion survives, but little imagination is required.

Forty-Eight

As the *Edward* had swept up the Thames with the tide on the last stretch of its passage back to London, one old man waited anxiously among the excited crowd of family, friends and general onlookers.

Sebastian Cabot watched the leading members of the crew climb first into the ship's boat, recognising and then greeting each man as he stepped ashore. His most enthusiastic welcome, though, was reserved for the ship's captain, Richard Chancellor. This was the young man he had taken under his wing, talked to for hours about his own experiences sailing to the Americas, and to whom he had imparted all the wisdom accrued through a long lifetime of organising and taking part in voyages on the open ocean. This was the man who had impressed him so much that in spite of quite limited experience he had made him the Pilot Major of his new northern exploration. Both were relieved to see the other man again, still alive: Chancellor in spite of the long and dangerous journey he had undertaken, Cabot in spite of his age, both men in spite of the shadow of death which hovered, ever present, in sixteenth-century England.

They talked a little, amid the general noise and commotion, then met later and spoke again, at length and in private. Cabot's interest was intense as Chancellor described the terrible storm which had made it impossible, in spite of their efforts, to remain together as a fleet of three ships. He listened as Chancellor told of his fruitless wait at Wardhouse for Willoughby and the other two ships, of the Scots who had tried to persuade him to abandon the voyage, and of the *Edward*'s descent towards a great inland sea where they anchored by the mouth of a wide river delta, near a monastery that was Christian, though of a heretical persuasion.

Much would have been familiar to Cabot, and reminded him of his own explorations, with his father and then in command, along the north-western coast of America decades previously. But this was very different country – an area of the world of which he had no first-hand experience, and of which the vagueness of his map confessed an almost total ignorance.[1]

The old man was perhaps surprised, as the crew themselves had been surprised, to learn that they had reached Russia and could travel from where they were by sled – many miles, but quickly and smoothly across the snow and ice – to Moscow, its emperor's capital. Existing accounts of the preparations contain no suggestion that Cabot or the other English merchants and organisers involved had expected their crews to reach Russia by travelling this far north. They knew of it, vaguely, as a country that could be reached by travelling east from the European mainland, a great distance through the vast realms of Poland and Lithuania. It was most often referred to as Muscovy and its leader as the Duke, since the imperial status Ivan now claimed had not been acknowledged or accepted.

Cabot must have been disappointed, when he first heard the outcome of the voyage, at the lack of progress towards the ultimate destination he had set – Cathay and the equatorial spice islands, from which boundless wealth was anticipated.

For the English, the rich empires of the East seemed as far away as ever. Plainly, it would not be as easy as some had hoped to reach them by this north-easterly course, or the Russian communities on the White Sea would have known how to do it; but at the same time, the route's existence had not been disproved, and further efforts would need to be made.

At the same time, the voyage did have something to show for it: there was the tantalising possibility of a regular and direct English trade with Russia by this northern route. Cabot, who had explored in unknown waters and encountered unknown civilisations himself, listened, enthralled, as Chancellor described his journey to the Russian court and the several months he had spent in Moscow, in winter, as an honoured guest of the Tsar. There was much that was similar to what he himself had known – the extreme cold and the ice, the unfamiliar people – but much too that was quite different. People wore furs, certainly, to protect against the elements. But they were not, like the tribes of Cabot's experience, dressed in the skins of bears or large cats purely to intimidate strangers. They did not swim out to ships in the sea in a quest for human flesh to eat. Chancellor recognised that what he had experienced was unique, and that it needed to be told and to be recorded in a more permanent way. Since 'it was my chance', as he later wrote, 'to fall with the North parts of Russia before I came towards Moscovia', he would declare his knowledge.[2]

The two men talked at length about the possibility of a trading relationship between England and Russia, which had opened up in Chancellor's discussions with Ivan. A meeting was arranged at which all of the company's leading men could discuss the voyage's outcome, and a decision be made about their next step.

Forty-Nine

There was another man with whom Chancellor's reunion was unusually joyful: Sir Henry Sidney, whose household the young sailor had been a part of, who had feared to lose him, but who had recognised his extraordinary talents and recommended him passionately to the London merchant company when they were choosing men to lead their pioneering expedition.

During the first half of 1554 Sidney had been on an unusual and important voyage of his own. He had landed back on the English coast, at Southampton, on 20 July, and it was a month later before he reached London. There is no way of being certain whether it was he or Chancellor who returned to the capital first. Probably it was Chancellor, but either way it cannot have been long before the two men were reunited.

By then, of course, Chancellor was well aware what a tumultuous series of events had rocked England since his departure: the premature death of the Protestant King Edward, the attempt to follow Edward's will in placing Jane Grey on the throne as his successor, the acceptance of the Catholic Mary as rightful Queen, the repeal by Parliament of Edward's religious reforms and the serious but unsuccessful rebellion against Mary when word spread of her intended Spanish marriage.

Chancellor and his crew must have been almost as interested and inquisitive as those to whom they spoke. They had travelled to a country of which nothing was known, and some of them had been entertained at the court of a great emperor. But they had also returned to a country much changed from the one with which they were familiar.

Whatever Chancellor had gleaned from other Englishmen, there is no doubt that his patron Sidney knew more than most. He had been uncomfortably close to the action.

*

Sidney had been at the heart of King Edward's circle. He had shared the boy King's education and many of his ideas. He had been with him, and was deeply affected, when he died. Long afterwards he still talked of England's misfortune, and of his own 'still felt grief', at Edward's death in his arms.[1]

He had been closely allied to the late John Dudley, his father-in-law, who had supported Cabot and this voyage of discovery, but whose fall had been so sudden and unlamented in the wider political class. Dudley's sons, Sidney's brothers-in-law, had also been implicated in the plot to establish Jane Grey. One of them, indeed – Guildford – had married Jane and accompanied her to the block. Three others remained incarcerated in the Tower, along with their father. They etched their father's name and emblem, along with a short poem, on the wall of the room in which they were held.[2] The eldest, John Dudley junior, had been tutored by John Dee, who later praised him fulsomely. When he was released that autumn he came to stay with his sister at the house that Sir Henry Sidney had recently inherited from his father, Penshurst in Sussex; but he was so weakened and ill that he died only days later.[3]

Sir Henry had been one of the witnesses of Edward's will as the King lay dying. It was his wife, Mary Dudley, who had carried word of Edward's death to her sister-in-law, Jane Grey, and travelled with her to Syon House – the estate, on the grounds of a former abbey, acquired by her father John Dudley, where Jane was offered the crown. When Queen Mary secured the throne in Jane's place Sir Henry must have fretted anxiously about his position. But he had been careful. He had not been directly implicated in the campaign against her, two of his sisters were favoured ladies of Queen Mary, and fortunately the new Queen was not inclined towards wholesale retribution.

While John Dudley and his closest relatives could not escape punishment, Sidney was able to detach himself from the catastrophe now visited upon his wife's family. He was, perhaps, as he later regretted, 'neither liking nor liked as I had been'. But in July Mary granted him a pardon, while his ownership of his father's lands was confirmed. He was granted further properties in addition, as well as the sinecure post of Royal Otter Hunter.[4] In November, Sidney's wife gave birth to a son who would go on to become a revered courtier, soldier and poet.

His parents christened him Philip: a calculated act of homage to the man who had become King of England, and who stood as the child's godfather.

Sidney had been quick to demonstrate his loyalty to Mary. Fluent in French and Italian, he made a useful envoy – just as he had done for King Edward.

Philip's proposed visit to England, in the winter of 1553, had come to nothing, but in March the following year a ceremony of betrothal was held in England attended by a Habsburg representative. Shortly afterwards a mission departed for Spain to secure Philip's signature on a marriage treaty, and to escort him north. It was led by John Russell, the Earl of Bedford – a man who had not only been a stalwart of Edward VI's regime, but who had been actively involved in funding and supporting Cabot's 1553 expedition. With him went Sir Henry Sidney, and the fate of the exploratory voyage must have been a frequent topic of conversation between the two men.[5]

On 13 July the party set sail from Spain with a strong wind at their backs and on a rough sea. Many of them were feeling sick when, only four days later, they spotted the shores of England.[6] Most of the soldiers who accompanied their leader never disembarked. Word quickly reached Philip from his father that the French had seized important Habsburg forts.[7] He personally could remain in England, Philip was instructed, but money and armed men should be sent on. Philip himself landed on 20 July, with a group of English nobles who had rowed out to meet him and with Sidney and other members of the English party who had travelled back with him from Spain.

An elaborate welcome was put on by members of Mary's court. Artillery fired a salute. The insignia of the Order of the Garter was presented to Philip before he came ashore. Royal horse guards, dressed in Spanish livery, paraded in a guard of honour on the jetty. Musicians played, and a splendid white horse was presented to Philip. The weather, meanwhile, provided a typically depressing welcome of its own. For several days the rain poured down and the cloak intended to protect Philip's fine clothes proved insufficient to the task.[8]

From Southampton the party proceeded to Winchester, where Mary was nervously awaiting her husband-to-be. In Wolvesey Castle, the home of Stephen Gardiner, the Bishop of Winchester, they kissed on the lips, the traditional English greeting for persons of equivalent rank, even strangers. Philip kissed not only his fiancée this way, but Mary's ladies in waiting too. Some of his Spanish attendants were surprised and not, in general, impressed. One of Philip's men wrote home that of the women close to Mary there were 'few attractive and many ugly ones'.[9]

On 25 July Mary and Philip were married in Winchester Cathedral, a religious building which, like so many others in the land, bore the scars of recent ideological battles. There were gaps or splintered wood where images had been removed or impulsively broken off.[10] Here, and across the country, craftsmen were suddenly overworked making repairs.

It was 18 August by the time that Queen Mary and her new husband made the formal procession from the south bank into the capital, across London Bridge, where the putrid heads of those executed for their part in Wyatt's rebellion the previous winter had to be removed.[11]

After the evangelical Protestantism of Edward VI, England now had a Catholic King to go with its Catholic Queen – albeit one who, though granted the title of king by Parliament, was never crowned in his own right and whose independent authority was strictly limited. On coins now in circulation the heads of both Philip and Mary appeared, with a single crown suspended between them to indicate that they reigned together.

Men like Sir Henry Sidney, meanwhile, had tactfully ridden out the changes. Whatever his inner beliefs, he adopted the policy of Sebastian Cabot – a man he knew – and affected to support the culture in which he was immersed. By the time that Chancellor returned, Sir Henry had proved himself a loyal supporter of the new regime, for all his proximity to the old. No doubt he encouraged the young and Protestant pilot to follow his example.

Fifty

Strictly speaking the group of traders behind the voyage was not yet a company. A royal licence had authorised the expedition, but the formal document of incorporation, which would unite the men in a legal body, had not arrived. In law they were not yet entitled, as was clearly vital for a trading body, 'to implead and to be impleaded, to answer and to be answered, to defend and to be defended'.[1] Nor, officially, were they permitted to meet.

A charter had been expected from Edward VI before the initial departure, and an assurance that the matter was in hand had been provided. The permission to impress men had referred to the group as a company.[2] The merchants knew that their ambition was looked upon favourably. Important individuals at court had signed up to the venture; John Dudley, the Duke of Northumberland, himself had helped to bring Cabot over from Spain and supported him in England; and the men had always been aware of what was referred to later as the 'gracious encouragement, and right good liking' for the venture of the young King. But the onset of Edward's last illness had intervened.[3]

Edward was still alive when they left, but was clearly very ill, however gladly men leapt to hail every slight improvement. The three ships could not wait. As a later act of incorporation noted, Edward had died 'before the finishing and sealing of his most ample and gracious letters of privileges promised to the said Subjects'.[4] Plainly, however, the merchant group regarded themselves as a company nevertheless.

The support of men in high places had given them reason to do so, and the grant of the charter was merely a formality. When Sebastian Cabot wrote his book of instructions in the spring of 1553 for the 'intended voyage for Cathay', he styled himself 'governor of the mystery and company'. Now, of course, the situation had changed. Edward had died, and John Dudley, the *de facto* ruler of England, had been executed.

Mary's priorities lay in allaying England's fraught religious situation, and why would her new husband Philip, a Spaniard, wish to back a group whose ambition was to further an English challenge to the trades of Spain and Portugal?

Nevertheless, Philip was preoccupied during the second half of 1554: he had just come to England, not speaking the language, and the Habsburg Empire was at war with France. It had been made clear, furthermore, that in his island kingdom he would be allowed only a secondary role: when the royal couple crossed London Bridge into the capital together for the first time, it was Mary who rode on the right, the position of precedence.[5] And she was naturally anxious, after the upheavals to which her rule had already been subjected, to win the support of her leading subjects, many of whom were either enthused by or directly involved in Cabot's scheme.

The occasion when the 'mystery and company' met as a body, after Chancellor's return, is not recorded. Clearly, though, there was much that needed to be discussed, both with the Pilot Major and with the other leading merchants and gentlemen who had sailed on the *Edward*. It was vital for the company board to understand, as far as was possible, the events of the voyage and to come to a decision about their next step.

Probably, the meeting took place before the company was legally incorporated, and so permitted, officially, to meet as a group. But if so, an exception was granted.

The atmosphere among the leading organisers was tense. In general terms, of course, they were aware of the outcome of the voyage. They would have discussed it at some length among themselves.

For all the major events taking place in England that summer, the regime, and Londoners in general, had for a few days talked of little else. The voyage had been a major departure in every sense; and the story of Willoughby's disappearance made it all the more dramatic and intriguing. Now, however, there was an opportunity for organisers and backers to hear directly from the key protagonists, and to settle important matters of company policy.

The 'principal doers' were there: Sebastian Cabot, the old navigator who had inspired the enterprise, as well as leading merchants and governors of the city like Sir George Barne and Sir William Garrard. Some of those eminent men who had lent the venture their backing, and who had survived the change of regime, may have been there too: near-contemporaries, for instance, of Cabot, like William Paulet, the Marquis of Winchester, who found that his religious convictions shifted conveniently to match those of his monarch, or his friend John Russell, the Earl of Bedford, who had led the English embassy to escort King Philip back to England.

Also present were many of those already chosen as consuls and assistants, though they had not yet been officially confirmed in the roles: the former Lord Mayors Sir John Gresham and Sir Andrew Judde, for instance, or Sir John Yorke. Along with Chancellor, furthermore, other leading men who had sailed on the *Edward* must have attended to support their captain and to develop what he said. The board would have wanted to speak, for instance, to the head or 'cape' merchant, George Burton, to his colleague John Hasse (who would write a report on possible English trade with Russia), and the gentleman James Dallaber who had also travelled with Chancellor to Moscow.

Even assuming that some were unable to attend, there must have been upwards of thirty men present. It was a noisy room, full of opinionated people. One important matter was the fate of the leading individuals who were not present: of the expedition's leader, Sir Hugh Willoughby, and all those on two of the three ships that the group had provided. This, perhaps, was dealt with first.

There was little that Chancellor could say, of course, other than to confess his ignorance. He told the story again, for the benefit of any who had not heard it, of the onset of terrible weather as the party lay off Senja island, and of the *Edward*'s desperate but futile attempts to remain in touch with the admiral. He described, too, how his men had sailed on to the Wardhouse as agreed, and waited there anxiously for the space of a week, praying every day that the sails of the *Bona Esperanza* or the *Bona Confidentia* would break the horizon.

The promise of Ivan IV was described and read out. Should Willoughby and his men arrive, at length, on Russian shores, they would be 'well entertained'. To contemplate what had become of them was dispiriting, because there was obviously a good chance that they had fallen on misfortune. But until more was known, there remained some room for optimism. Perhaps they had sailed on, missed the White Sea entrance (as indeed they had) and found a passage as intended to warmer, wealthier lands from whence they had not yet been able to return.

The main matter on the agenda, meanwhile, was to report what Chancellor had discovered, and did know. He had to admit, of course, that in terms of its stated aim the voyage had been an outright failure. Considerable wealth and effort had been expended, and thus far at least only one of the three ships had returned, knowing nothing of any possible access to the wealth of the East. But Cabot had made clear at the outset that there was also a more general motivation for the enterprise: to explore the world and to uncover opportunities which might not have been anticipated.

In any realms they touched at along their route, the crews were to learn what they could, of customs and trading possibilities. Knowledge was always useful, or at least one never knew when it would be. A culture needed to be fostered in which all such encounters and explorations were carefully recorded for posterity, and this was an ethos that Chancellor had absorbed wholeheartedly. He wrote his own account of the voyage, sending it to his 'singular good Uncle', Christopher Frothingham, enjoining him modestly to 'read and correct; for great is the defect'. He expressed his earnest hope to return to Russia and to have a chance to study its society and customs further: with his discussion of its religion, he concluded, 'I make an end, trusting hereafter to know it better'. He also talked at length to Clement Adams, who set down the story of the voyage again, in a more stylised form.

Anyone with a mind to attempt the exploration of strange countries, Chancellor wrote at the start of his narrative, must bear this imperative to record their experiences in mind. Not only should they seek to understand what commodities a region produced, they needed to write their newly acquired knowledge down. Only by doing so, and by creating a culture where this was the norm, would they 'encourage others to the like travail'.[6]

From the White Sea, as Chancellor now told the company members, access had been obtained to Russia by a northerly route previously unknown to the English. Its Tsar had granted permission to the English to return regularly this way to trade, competing with rivals they knew well – like the Hanseatic merchants – but through a different channel and on preferential terms.

In a sense there was only an easy decision to be made. The condition of established English trades in Europe was not good. A new route, offering a new source of commodities to sell in England and Europe, and a new market for English goods, had been opened up. But only one: there was no range of commercial options on the table.

It is true that certain new trades were being explored simultaneously in northern and western Africa, and that often the same merchants were investors. But these were traditional routes into which the English were attempting to muscle. They were well known, and they involved battling, often literally, against the usual European competition. This was different. Here the English might be able to out-compete their commercial rivals and to avoid physical confrontation in doing so. The verdict was clear.

The company should continue to explore further east by this northern route, to see if it was possible, after all, to get through to Cathay as had been hoped. Enquiries should continue to be made about the *Bona Confidentia*, the *Bona Esperanza* and their crews. But in the meantime a trade with Russia should be actively developed and pursued.

In the course of this meeting, the merchant John Hasse, who had sailed with Chancellor and travelled with him to Moscow, was questioned in depth by senior company figures about the opportunities that existed in Russia. As soon as a resolution had been made, perhaps at this formal meeting, he was asked to write down all that he knew in a practical handbook for future traders. Certainly by the time that Hasse duly wrote a short guide that year, a clear decision had been taken. There was no uncertainty: he put his knowledge down, he wrote, so that 'the merchants of that new adventure may the better understand how the wealth of that new frequented trade will arise'.[7]

He listed in detail all of the information he had recorded in notebooks about coins, weights and other measures. This was an age before any international standardisation existed, and it was a perpetual problem

The *Lartique* was a naval ship, comparable in size to the ships of 1553, but much more heavily manned and gunned.

Ships off Dover, by John Thompson. Early sixteenth-century English ships, as seen here, rose high above the waterline in a manner that was better suited to conflict in European waters than to long-distance navigation.

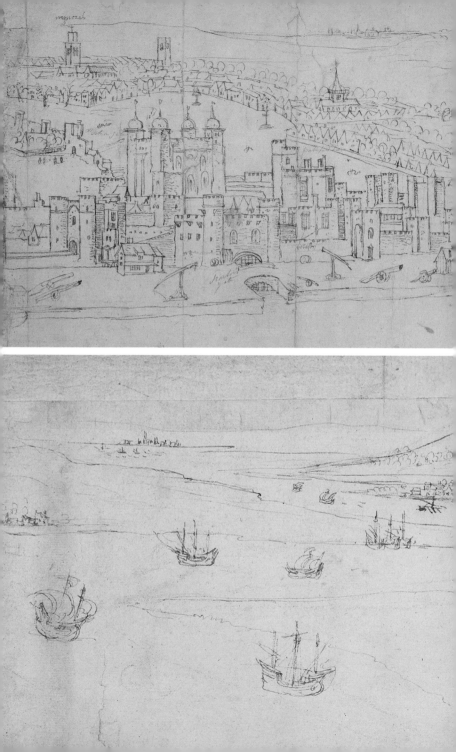

In these contemporary illustrations of London, the small shipbuilding community of Ratcliffe, from which the expedition departed, can be seen downstream of the Tower (*left*), as can the old Greenwich Palace, further downstream on the south bank. It was from here that Edward VI's court watched the ships sail past (*below*) in May 1553.

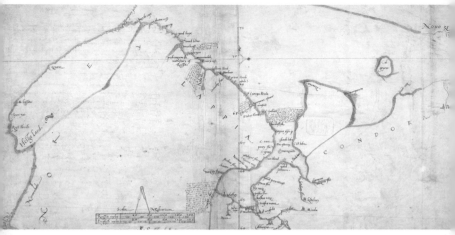

William Borough sailed under Chancellor as a teenager and returned to this northern region repeatedly. He carefully mapped the northern coasts he knew, and marked the river where Willoughby's ship was found.

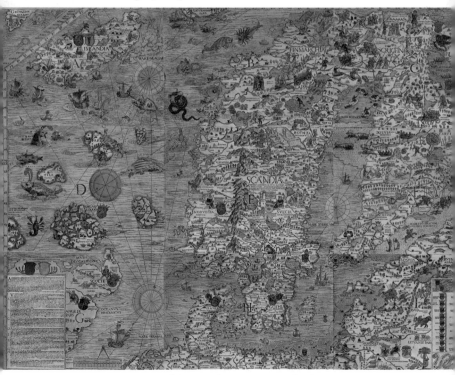

One of the earliest maps of the Scandinavian peninsula, the *Carta Marina* shows many of the dangers, real and imagined, which Willoughby, Chancellor and their crews would fa

first of it,

... we gat the ...
... in w[hi]ch it vntill night, than ...
... shore to do, we gatt vs into the ...
... to have Sea rome,

12[th] of September, we saled to the shore ...
... hauing then Indifferent wynd, and weather ...
being nere vnto the shore, and the Type ...
spent, we came to an Anker in 30 faddomes wat[er]
the 13[th] Day) we ranne along the Cost w[i]th ...
Northwest, and by west and Southeast [&] by East
the 14[th] Day) we came to an Anker w[i]th in 2 ...
... of the shore hauing 60 faddomes, there
went a shore with our Bote, and found ij or ...
... good harborowghes, the land being rocky, and
... But as for people sawe we so none. /
the 15[th] Day) runing still along the Cost vntill
17[th] Day), then the wynde being contrary) to
we thought it best to returne vnto the harborow[gh]
we had found before, and so we bare roomer w[i]th
... same, howbeit, we cold not accomplisshe our ...
... that Day. / The next Day) being the 18[th]
September we entred into the hauen, and the ...
... to an Anker at .6. faddomes / This hauen
... into the mayne about 2. leages, and is in ...
... half a leage, wherin were very many seal [Seale]
...es, and other great fysshes, / And vpon the
... we sawe Beares, greate Deare, foxes,
... divers strange Beastes, as Gulones, & suche ...
..., w[hi]ch were to vs vnknowen, and allso wonde[rful]
... This remayning in this hauen the space of
seuennyght: seing the yere far spent, & allso very ...
... weather: as frost, Snow, and hayle, as ...
... it had bene the depe of winter, we thought ...
best to enter there, wherefore we sent out ...
iij men

...his final page of Willoughby's log has, still just legible in the margin,
...he phrase 'Haven of Death'.

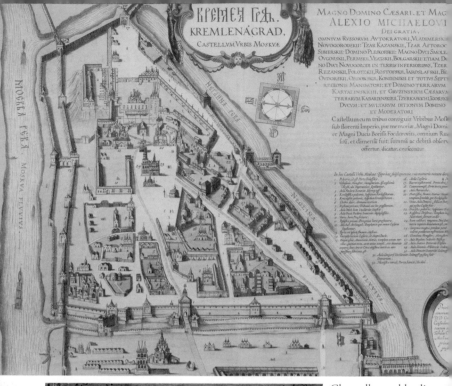

Chancellor and leading merchants paid a visit to Ivan IV (known as 'the Terrible') in the Moscow Kremlin in late 1553 and early 1554. The Englishmen were impressed by the clothing of individuals but not by the buildings.

Ivan the Terrible, seen in an icon from about 1600 portrayed as an older man than when he was visited by Richard Chancellor, after his decline into bloodthirsty madness.

An illustration from a Russian chronicle shows (*from top to bottom*) Ivan bidding farewell to Chancellor and Napea, their shipwreck, and Napea greeting the King and Queen of England, Philip and Mary.

Foreign ambassadors being received at the court of Ivan the Terrible in 1578. Like the English before them, they were treated to dinner and (many) drinks at the Kremlin.

Giles Fletcher was a vicar's son and MP who travelled to Moscow in the late 1580s to meet a later Tsar. His *History of Russia* was the best stud[?] yet made of government and customs in Russia[?]

A stamp or 'seal die' used by the Muscovy Company to fix its seal in wax to documents, and showing the date of its charter.

Anthony Jenkinson's 'Description of Russia, Muscovy and Tartary' was printed in the first modern atlas, published by Abraham Ortelius.

for merchants to be sure how much of a commodity they were buying. 'You must consider', Hasse cautioned, 'that their great weight is not full with ours; for I take not their great pound to be full thirteen ounces, but above twelve I think it be.' At Wardhouse, he noted, dry fish was sold according to the 'basemere' as used in Russia, but that this quantity was further broken up into four different measures – the mark pound, the great pound, the wee pound and the ship pound – which were all distinct. The same complexity applied equally to other dimensions:

As [the Russians] have two sorts of weights, so they have also two sorts of measures, wherewith they measure cloth, both linen and woollen. They call the one an areshine, and the other a locut. The areshine I take to be as much as the Flanders ell, and their locut half an English yard ... They have also a measure wherewith they do mete their corn, which they call a set-forth, and the half of that an osmine. This set-forth I take to be three bushels of London measure. And as for their drink measure, they call it a spanne, which is much like a bucket; and of that I never saw any true rate, but that some was greater than other some.[8]

It was confusing stuff, but vitally important. Without this sort of knowledge a merchant, or a merchant company, could not calculate the profits to be made on any given transaction.

Other factors would affect this too: not least the tolls or customs applied to English merchants. These were never consistent. States treated them as tools of foreign policy, to be bargained with and lobbied for. Merchants of different nationality paid different rates, and in Russia, as Hasse noted, they were higher for Turks and Armenians than they were for the Dutch (that is, the Germans of the Hanse towns) who had recently negotiated, and paid for, an exemption.

The English had not yet signed a formal treaty, but Ivan IV had held out to Chancellor, for his own reasons, the possibility of toll-free trade – and this was a subject of intense scrutiny when the company met. Ivan's written response to Edward VI was studied and discussed. In return for negotiation with one of His Majesty's Council, English merchants, Ivan promised, could have 'free mart with all free liberties through my whole dominions with all kinds of wares, to come and go at their pleasure, without any let, damage, or impediment, according to this our letter, our word, and our seal ...'⁹

Hasse then addressed another key question which, again, was significant only on the assumption that trade was to go ahead: the future location of an English 'standing house', or base, in the country. Some men, he said, would insist on Moscow, because that was the capital and the location of the court. While he could understand the logic, his own view was that this would only make it more expensive, and that the disadvantages outweighed the advantages: 'the charge there', he wrote, 'would be so great by cravers and expenses that the moiety [half] of the profit would be wholly consumed'. Other cities offered a preferable location. 'The town of Vologda', Hasse argued, 'is meetest [best] for our merchants.' It was near enough to the capital that merchants could spend the winter there, paying their respects to the Tsar and his court. It was also conveniently situated, as most large Russian towns were, on a river, and was connected to a regular network of trade with all the country's other major towns.

In any case, this was not a question that needed to be decided immediately. What did was the basic question which had already been resolved of whether to pursue the commercial link with Moscow. No hint survives that any were opposed.

Now it was vital to move fast. The privileges promised by Ivan needed to be formally confirmed. Word quickly spread, inevitably, to other courts, of the route taken by Cabot's men and of the outcome achieved. One Spaniard who was a member of Philip's council in England wrote in 1555 to his lord in Castile, of how the English had discovered 'new Indies':

> A ship went from England to the northern regions with merchandise, under an English captain named Ricardo. Adverse weather drove him to an unknown port, in a large and spacious country, which appeared fertile and very rich, and which had not been discovered till then, and therefore was not in the charts, nor marked in *el mappa mundi*. He found that it was inhabited, and by people who were Christians, and governed by a valorous prince called Ivan, who, learning what they were, gave them very Christian treatment.¹⁰

The Spanish themselves were unlikely to seek to get in on a trade with Russia, but the Netherlands, of course – far more conveniently situated – was a part of the Habsburg dominions. Suspicions were quickly raised about Ivan's motivation for the preferential treatment he was offering to the English. Efforts could be expected to nullify any English advantage and to hinder this new trade.

Another voyage needed to be organised, quickly.

Fifty-One

During the winter of 1554 to 1555 urgent preparations began. With checks and maintenance work the *Edward Bonaventure* could sail again, but in the absence of its two companion vessels, at least one more ship needed to be obtained.

This time, given the need to move quickly, it was probably not commissioned to be newly built, but either had sailed before or was chosen from those already largely complete at the dockyard. More was known, of course, about its immediate destination: to sail to Russia and back through northern waters did not require a hull that was lined to defy a warm-water worm.

If the new ship had a name already, it was tactfully now rechristened: this time the *Edward* would be partnered by the *Philip and Mary*.

The atmosphere in England that winter was tense and uncertain. There was no repeat of the outright rebellion which had broken out a year previously. Mary's legitimacy was accepted, and though the Spanish marriage had inflamed national feeling, Philip's role as King was severely circumscribed. Nevertheless, mutual animosity remained.

Many of the Spaniards in England disliked the English. They found them 'white, pink and quarrelsome' and disdained their tendency to eat, drink and 'think of nothing else'. 'We are in an excellent land,' one wrote, 'but among the worst people in the world.' The Imperial ambassador, meanwhile, lamented the extent to which the English hated foreigners, believing they were going to be 'enslaved'. 'The slightest altercation', he suggested, 'might be enough to bring about a very dangerous situation.' Meanwhile one of Philip's own entourage observed that the English hated the Spaniards 'worse than they hate the Devil'. 'They rob us', he wrote, 'in town and on the road.' It was not for nothing that the Spanish walked the streets of Westminster and London in fear of abuse and violence.[1]

If Spanish influence was not bad enough for the xenophobic English, it was while Chancellor and his crew were in England, at the end of November 1554, that Parliament approved Mary's dearest desire: a formal reconciliation with Rome. It was a prominent investor in Sebastian Cabot's company, Henry Fitzalan, the Earl of Arundel, who escorted the Pope's English legate, Cardinal Pole, to the Palace of Westminster. There, by the 'apostolic authority' accorded him by Pope Julius III, Pole told the assembled monarchs, Lords and Commons:

> We ... do absolve & deliver you, and every of you with the whole Realm and the Dominions thereof, from all Heresy and Schism ... & also we do restore you again, unto the unity of our Mother the holy Church: as in our Letters more plainly it shall appear: In the name of the father, of the son, and of the holy Ghost.[2]

This renewed allegiance to a foreign authority, more than the revival of Catholic ritual, aroused bitter resentment among the English.

In addition, outstanding questions remained which contributed to lasting tension. One such concerned the swathes of property which had formerly belonged to the Church but which had passed, under Henry VIII and his son Edward, into private hands.

Much of the wealth seized by the state, of course, had simply been spent – on warfare in particular. Private owners now claimed rightful possession. Many of them were prominent men, like the Earl of Arundel himself. They had transferred their allegiance, without fuss, from Edward to Mary. They had supported most of her religious goals. But they had accumulated substantial ex-monastic estates, and these, so far as Cardinal Pole was concerned, were 'God's property' which had been 'grabbed'.[3]

At the same time Catholics like Mary worried about the lasting impact of heretical belief and practice. Churches which had hosted heretical services, as all those must be deemed which were conducted using Cranmer's 1552 Prayer Book, were tainted. Until they were ritually purified, they could not be used for righteous, godly worship.

Worse still was the presence beneath churchyards and churches themselves of the buried bodies of men and women who had followed Edwardian practice. These were heretics, who polluted the entire fabric of the Church. Canon law decreed that their remains must be dug up, removed and burned. But this, as can be imagined, was a sensitive matter.

The world in which Chancellor and his companions had grown up had turned on its head.

Under Henry VIII, and particularly under Edward, traditional Christian worship had been violently condemned. As Archbishop, Thomas Cranmer had reminded Englishmen of God's commandment against 'that most detestable sin of idolatry', and decried what he called the 'fantasy of ceremonies, pilgrimage, purgatory, saints, images, works and such like, as hath these three or four hundred years been corruptly taught'.[4]

The walls of churches were whitewashed, to expunge the colourful paintings of saints and biblical figures which had long adorned them. At ceremonies in London and elsewhere images of long-revered saints were publicly demeaned and burned.[5] This was the England the men of the *Edward* had sailed away from in 1553, and its imprint on their way of thinking is evident in their horrified reaction to the veneration of saints that they encountered in Russia.

The country to which they returned had undergone a volte-face and in public, at least, men who valued their liberty turned with it. Under Mary's ultimate authority, evangelicals were no longer free to denounce the practices of traditional religion. Protestant intellectuals, like King Edward's former tutor, Sir John Cheke, fled to the Continent. With another he was betrayed and arrested in May 1556, 'clapped into a cart, their legs, arms and bodies tied with halters to the body of the cart, and so carried to the seaside'. He escaped burning only by making a humiliating recantation.[6]

Craftsmen were overworked restoring the very statues, shrines and other church ornaments which during Edward's reign had been desecrated and destroyed. Attempts were made to revive the cults of numerous saints, whose followings varied from the near-universal to the narrowly local, and who had stood, or knelt, in niches in church walls, shrouded by curtains and honoured with candles ('lights', as they were known), much as in Orthodox Russia.[7] But it was now seventeen or eighteen years since the Protestant assault on such idolatry had begun and it was not easy to return England to the way it had been.

Another piece of the fabric of traditional Christianity consisted of those distinctively dressed men and women who had taken a vow to dedicate their lives to the contemplation of Christ. In pre-Reformation England, just as in Spain and in Orthodox Russia, the religious orders were a part of the landscape. During the later years of Henry VIII's reign, in the second half of the 1530s, monasteries, friaries and nunneries had come under a sudden and devastating assault, which then widened, a decade later, under his son. Like images of saints, men and women in habits had disappeared from the English landscape in which Chancellor and his crew grew up, and their prevalence in Russia seemed symptomatic, now, of an alien culture.

Attempts to re-establish religious houses in England were deeply problematic. After all, the buildings, along with their land and wealth, had been seized and sold off – often to powerful individuals. Many monks, friars or nuns had accepted Crown pensions and would need to be absolved before they could revive their former vows. The English had grown unused to the sight of men and women dressed in the distinctive habits of monastic devotion. Spanish monks who came to England as part of Philip's entourage felt nervous about wearing them in public. Some did return, though, to their former communal life, particularly exiles who did not require absolution for an acceptance of the dissolution. The London diarist Henry Machyn watched a procession through the capital 'after the old fashion', which included monks in their habits.[8]

In general London remained marked by the enforced disappearance of a significant element of its population. The Venetian ambassador lamented in Mary's time that 'the city is much disfigured by the ruins of a multitude of churches and monasteries belonging heretofore to friars and nuns'.[9] Nevertheless, the Observant Franciscans re-established the friary they had maintained adjacent to Greenwich Palace, on level ground 'where the game of ball used to be played'.[10] Twenty-five friars were reinstalled there in the spring of 1555, and their number grew over the coming months. The house had strong emotional resonance for

Mary. It was in this Franciscan church that her parents had married, in which she herself had been christened, and in which her mother, Catherine of Aragon, had risen in the small hours to attend services by candlelight. That autumn the Venetian ambassador wrote of Mary's impatience to return to her monastery at Greenwich, 'in which she delights marvellously'.[11]

At St Bartholomew's in Smithfield on the city's north-western periphery, the Dominicans were quick to re-establish a community.[12] And it was here, adjacent to this site, that burnings of those who refused to conform to the renewed Catholic order in England began in London. In January 1555 the medieval heresy laws were re-enacted by Parliament.[13] Once again heretics were to pay the ultimate penalty: death and, as was assumed, a limitless suffering in hell.

On 4 February John Rogers, a man who had been chaplain to English merchants in Antwerp and who persisted in denying the Christian character of the Church of Rome, became the first of more than one hundred people in London alone to be burned at the stake. He was comforted and acclaimed by the common people of the capital, who demonstrated a residual attachment to holy relics by collecting pieces of his charred and still-smoking remains in parcels of paper.[14]

Four days later a second Protestant, Laurence Saunders, was burned for his beliefs and over subsequent months the fires were continually replenished.

Fifty-Two

In February 1555 the formal approval finally arrived for which those involved in Cabot's venture had been waiting. A charter of incorporation from King Philip and Queen Mary made them officially a company.

The monarchs were keen, the charter read, 'to animate, advance, further and nourish them in their said godly, honest, and good purpose, and, as we hope, profitable adventure'. From henceforth, the group would be 'one body and perpetual fellowship and communality of themselves, both in deed and in name' – permitted, legally, to meet, to hold property and to make charges or answer for itself in court.[1]

Had Edward VI not sickened and died unexpectedly, this official authorisation would have been granted without any knowledge of how the initial venture to the north-east would fare. Would it sail, as hoped, to Cathay and the rich islands of the East, or would it be frustrated entirely by frozen seas in the north? Now, of course, a major exploration had been conducted. While a passage to the East remained elusive, a route to a fascinating new civilisation had been established. Much had already been achieved, and much more, with God's help, was to come.

The charter provided a full list of members of the company. There were just over two hundred of them, a slight decrease on the original subscription of 240, partly due to mortality, and partly perhaps due to the failure to discover an instantly lucrative passage to the Orient. John Dudley, of course, was at least one example of a leading backer who had died in the interim – victim of the political instability which immediately followed King Edward's demise.

The majority of the members were London merchants, though one at least was based in Bristol. There were government officials connected with the financial markets, customs or foreign trade.[2] And there were also senior peers and members of the Council – men of a pedigree that had never invested in comparable trading ventures in the past. The charter alluded to the involvement in 1553 of 'our right trusty, right faithful, and well-beloved Councillors, William Marquis of Winchester Lord high Treasurer of this our Realm of England, Henry Earl of Arundel, Lord Steward of our household, John Earl of Bedford Lord keeper of our privy Seal, William Earl of Pembroke, William Lord Howard of Effingham, Lord high Admiral of our said Realm of England, &c'. They had acted in a private capacity, providing ships, rigging and furnishing them at 'their own adventure, costs and charges'.

All were among the charter members two years later, and with this sort of lobbying power it was scarcely surprising that the joint monarchs, as they put it, 'inclined to the petition', or that pressure was applied to ensure the application was processed quickly. Names were listed in order of precedence. After twenty-seven, which constituted the court interest, there were thirteen city aldermen, then eleven 'Esquires', headed by Sebastian Cabot, eight gentlemen, and lastly all other members.[3]

Among them were at least two women.[4] Elizabeth Wilford, née Gale, was the daughter of a merchant who was linked to Sir George Barne and she had married another, Nicholas Wilford, who had traded in Spain, became a significant exporter of cloth, an MP and a governor of St Bartholomew's Hospital, which had survived the dissolution and whose ownership had passed to the city of London.[5] They were Londoners. Her father-in-law had been a city alderman and they lived in the house she inherited close to the Thames in Billingsgate. When an epidemic of the sweating sickness swept the capital in 1551, her husband became ill and quickly died (one of 800 left dead, according to Henry Machyn, by a disease which struck the young, the old, the poor and 'great rich men and women' alike).[6] As well as being the mother of eleven children, Elizabeth maintained her late husband's commercial interests, and she was the only woman to invest in her own right when Cabot's voyage was organised. Katherine Lomnour, meanwhile, had been married to Richard Wigmour, a subscriber to the voyage of 1553 who died later that summer. She married again, to Edmund Lomnour, and together they maintained her first husband's investment.[7]

The constitution of the company was formally recognised. Sebastian

Cabot, 'the chiefest setter forth of this journey or voyage', was proclaimed governor for life. After his death which, given his age, could not lie far in the future, an election could be held annually, for one or two men to fill the role on a rotational basis. Elections would also be held in conjunction every year for four 'consuls' and twenty-four 'assistants' – 'the most sad, discreet, and honest persons of the said fellowship' – to act as the company's board.

In all these respects, of course, the charter merely formalised an existing situation. Government approval was taken for granted, given the degree of involvement by senior men. Men had already been appointed to these positions, and the first holders of the offices were now named. They included, as consuls, Sir George Barne, Sir William Garrard, Anthony Hussey and John Southcote, who were judged the 'most expert and skilful' of the twenty-eight.

Fifteen of them would constitute a quorum, provided this number included at least two of the consuls, or three if a governor was not present. Together, this board was entitled to meet and to make binding decisions, including judgements regarding 'the good order or rule' of company merchants where disputes or bad behaviour demanded them. They could impose penalties on any employee – 'by fines, forfeitures, & imprisonments' – for offences which concerned the company. They were free to act 'as the quality of the offence requireth, according to their good discretions'. The only proviso was that company rules did not clash with the law of the land, or with treaties, or with other agreements England had entered into with other states.

The discovery of the northern route to Russia was acknowledged. It had pleased Almighty God, the charter declared, to bring one of the three ships to the dominions of 'Lord John [Ivan] Basilivich, Emperor of all Russia' – who had not only received the men graciously but had permitted them to trade freely in his lands. At the same time, however, the company's continued interest in exploring and trading more widely was recognised. It was entitled, the charter affirmed, to discover, and trade with, 'whatsoever Isle, Islands, countries, regions, provinces, creeks, arms of the sea, rivers & streams, as well of Gentiles, as of any other Emperor, king, prince, governor or Lord whatsoever ... and in whatsoever part of the world they be situated'. The only proviso was that any such lands should have been unknown, to Englishmen, prior to the recent expedition.

If any part of these newly discovered lands should lie 'Northwards, North-eastwards, or North-westwards', moreover, so that a plausible claim could be advanced that they did not come under the existing division of the world between the Spanish and Portuguese, then a right could be claimed not only over fellow Englishmen but over all other newcomers. In this case, the company was licensed to resist any encroachment into their trades, and 'to do their best in their defence'.[8]

The company could represent the country. It could, the royal charter decreed, 'rear, plant, erect, and fasten our banners, standards, flags, and Ensigns in whatsoever city, town, village, castle, Isle, or mainland, which shall be by them newly found'. Where Cabot had been careful in his instructions to inculcate the respect and tactful conduct towards other cultures which might foster trade, a way was here left open to the more violent and assertive approach which would also come to characterise English (or British) imperialism.

Where the Spanish or Portuguese states, however, did their own dirty work, the company could carry it out as a proxy. Indeed, the government seemed rather to hope that it would. The charter confirmed that the company: 'shall and may subdue, possess, and occupy, all manner [of] cities, towns, Isles, and mainlands of infidelity, which is or shall be by them, or any of them newly found or descried, as our vassals and subjects ...'

Just as importantly, as far as the merchants were concerned, they could not only claim a right for the English but could also assert a monopoly over their co-nationals. In an era when to forge new trades in previously unknown regions of the world was a dangerous and expensive exercise, a monopoly, rather like a modern patent, was the expected reward.

Any such new discoveries, the charter affirmed, 'shall not be visited, frequented, nor [haunted] by any our subjects, other than of the said company and fellowship, and their successors without express licence, agreement and consent', upon pain of forfeiture of both the ships and all they contained, the proceeds to be split between the company and the Crown.

Along with the charter came use, for the company, of an official seal. A three-masted ship, conspicuously armed, breasted the waves under full sail, below the Tudor rose and the lion of England. It was surrounded by the company's motto: *refugium nostrum in deo est* – God is our refuge.[9]

Fifty-Three

As arrangements were quickly made by the board for a second voyage, there was no disagreement about its command. Richard Chancellor, deputy to Willoughby last time, was rewarded for his success. There was no coincidence, it was recognised, that the ship captained by the man with by far the greatest skills in terms of the science of navigation had reached the safety of a Russian port, and returned. Chancellor was nominated to lead the second expedition, as its 'grand pilot'.

This time a sailor, rather than a gentleman, would take charge. John Buckland and John Howlet would be masters of the two ships, Buckland having been mate to Stephen Borough in 1553, while John Robbins would act as pilot on the *Philip and Mary*.[1]

On 1 May 1555, the 'governor, consuls, assistants, and whole company' met together once more in London – legally, this time – to agree on the instructions that would be issued to the men. No doubt Cabot, as governor, in conjunction with the consuls and assistants, had already drawn up a new draft to be put to the wider membership, discussed and approved. The previous ordinances remained in effect, however, 'to be in all respects observed'.[2] This time, now that an initial exploration had been made and the radical organisation of the company established, the role of the leading merchants was evidently uppermost, and the instructions bear their stamp.

The appointment was confirmed at the meeting of two men who would act as the company's resident agents in Russia. Richard Gray and George Killingworth were not charter members who had made an investment, but were employees of the company. They were given authority to sell or to barter English goods, and to buy Russian ones, according to their judgement, 'as occasion and benefit of the company shall require'. They could buy on credit, 'as good opportunity and occasion shall serve', with authority to commit the company to future payment. And they, together with Chancellor, were tasked to travel once more to the court of Tsar Ivan in Moscow, where they were to hand over letters from King Philip and Queen Mary 'written in Greek, Polish, and Italian', as well as presents from the company, prior to seeking the grant of further privileges.

Gray, Killingworth and those others who worked with them were to keep always in mind how important this voyage was. They would be the first men to set up a regular trade between England and Russia. Precedents would be set which it would be impossible to revoke or revise: 'the first precedent shall be a perpetual precedent for ever', the company's new instructions for this first deliberate trading mission to Moscow reminded them, 'and therefore all circumspection is to be used'. Many in England, from the Queen and the Lords of the Council downwards, had high expectations, and these were 'not to be frustrated'.

It was vital, both that no offence was given, by bad behaviour or by ignorance of local custom, and that poor bargains were not struck which it would be difficult later to renegotiate. Agents employed by the company were urged to read and reread the information which now existed, written down by men like Chancellor and John Hasse, to ensure that no law – religious or otherwise – was infringed. Diligent study should be made of the subtleties with which the Russians did business, so that the best possible deals were struck. Familiarity was expected with Russian 'dispositions, laws, manners, customs, uses, tolls, carriages, coins, weights, numbers, measures, wares, merchandises, commodities and incommodities, the one to be accepted and embraced, the other to be rejected and utterly abandoned'.

With the knowledge that had now been acquired, ignorance was no excuse.

For the first time in an English trading organisation, employees needed to bear in mind the profitability not just of personal transactions but of the company as a whole.

They needed to account, when they were calculating potential gains, for 'the notable charges that the company have defrayed in advancing this voyage; and the great charges that they sustain daily in wages, victuals, and other things, all which must be requited by the wise handling of this voyage'. In everything they did, moreover, careful accounts should be kept and daily decisions recorded. At the end of every month all transactions should be 'brought into perfect order into the ledger or memorial'.

Meanwhile a third merchant, John Brooke, was appointed as the company resident on the northern tip of Scandinavia, at the Wardhouse, where it was hoped also to operate a profitable trade by bartering cloth, meal, salt or beer for fish or train oil. Brooke would not travel to Russia, but would be deposited en route, while one of the two ships, the *Philip and Mary*, either waited there with him until the *Edward* returned, or sailed directly back to England after completing its commerce.

Chancellor and the other leading men could take such decisions on their arrival, after conferring with the governor of the castle and the local inhabitants. Brooke was to spend his time there fruitfully, as other agents of the company would be only too pleased to advise. He was to discover all he could about the wares of the region, establishing, for instance, which varieties of fish were available when, and how it would be best to transport them back to England: piled in bulk in the hold, or preserved in casks.

He was to be cautious about what he believed: quicker to 'be trusted', as his instruction ran, 'than to trust'. And again the company was anxious to ensure that none of its sailors made trouble or infringed local laws: 'The company to be quiet, void of all quarrelling, fighting, or vexation; abstain from all excess of drinking as much as may be, and in all to use and behave themselves as to quiet merchants doth and ought to appertain.'

The merchants involved were anxious that an active trade be established sooner rather than later. Substantial losses had been sustained last time around: two ships had not come back at all, and the third had been robbed on its return. For all the obvious importance of Chancellor and other leading men travelling to Moscow to discuss matters further with the Tsar, the company specified that both the *Edward* and the *Philip and Mary* were to sail back to England that same year rather than wintering in Russia. They should bring with them what goods from Russia or Wardhouse they could obtain, along with all possible advice about the

English goods to be packed for sale in Russia the following year.

Continued thought and enquiry should be given to the company's wider remit. Their charter had authorised them to trade exclusively in all lands newly discovered which could be reached sailing north, north-west or north-east, and it was imperative that this potential was maximised while the royal licence lasted.

The company's original ambition, with its dream of spices, silks and gold, had not been forgotten. 'It is to be had in mind', the instructions of 1555 advised, 'that you use all ways and means possible to learn how men may pass from Russia, either by land or by sea, to Cathaia.' Further knowledge should be garnered wherever it was possible to do so, 'by conferring with the learned or well-travelled persons, either natural or foreign, such as have travelled from the north to the south'. Perhaps an English path to the East could still be discovered.

Enquiry should also be made, of course, regarding the fate of the two ships of the first expedition, of which nothing had since been heard. There was a sound business reason for doing so: these were expensive ships, packed with valuable goods (in the days before any kind of insurance policy) and it was possible of course that they had landed at other and perhaps richer lands. But there was also a genuine human bond, and a regret that men they had known well had been lost, like numerous others before them, to the hazards of seaborne adventure. If the agents learned of the ships' arrival in any place employees could get to, the company instructed, then men should be despatched to find out how the crew were, to take care of any material requirements:

> ... and to embrace, accept, and entreat them as our dear and well-beloved brethren of this our society to their rejoicing and comfort, advertising Sir Hugh Willoughby and others of our carefulness of them and their long absence, with our desire to hear of them, with all other things done in their absence for their commodity, no less than if they had been present.[3]

Finally, all the 'servants of the fellowship' who were to travel on the second voyage were required to swear an oath. A Bible was solemnly produced, and the room hushed to hear each man repeat the text read out to him. Again, the company's primary concern was to prevent the private trade which had long preoccupied merchants unused to working for others. Each man promised not to indulge in any activity for his own benefit, and not to know, without reporting it, of any such trade being conducted by his colleagues.

'You shall prosecute and do', the words were gravely recited, 'all that which in you lieth for the good renown, commodity, benefit, and profit of the said fellowship.'

As the meeting proceeded, and particularly as the men grew quiet to hear one man speak, the sound of celebrations could be heard in the city outside. Church bells rang, while noisy processions wove their way through the city streets. It was May Day, a traditional holiday in England – but in 1555 the festivities in London were swelled by a further, impromptu outpouring of relief.

Since the previous October, word had spread that Queen Mary was pregnant. Those who had doubted that Mary could produce an heir at her advanced age, including many Spaniards who had strongly disapproved of the match for Philip, had been proved wrong. Mary might recently have turned thirty-nine, but, God willing, the offspring who could provide the dynasty and the country with the stability it craved was at last to be born. 'There is no doubt that the Queen is with child,' the Imperial ambassador had reported, 'for her stomach clearly shows it.'[4]

By the terms of the marriage, an heir would not inherit Spain, which was reserved for Philip's existing son, Don Carlos. Nevertheless he (preferably) or she would unite England with the Habsburg dominion in the Low Countries, creating a more powerful European state. For the time being, England and Spain did share a ruler, although Philip remained somewhat aloof from English affairs, and much as many in England despised the situation, writers like Richard Eden tripped over themselves to eulogise their Spanish King and Spain's imperialistic endeavours. In their 'merciful wars against these naked people', he affirmed, the Spaniards had 'shown a good example to all Christian nations to follow'.[5]

In April the Queen had travelled downriver to her palace at Hampton Court. There a private chamber, richly decorated and with numerous fireplaces to keep it warm, equipped with the lavish paraphernalia deemed necessary for a royal baby, had been prepared in which she could lie in. Mary's half-sister, Elizabeth, was released from the house arrest under which she had been held since the rebellion of Sir Thomas Wyatt and summoned to court as a witness to the birth.[6]

Then, on the last evening of the month, a rumour reached London and quickly circulated that the hoped-for son had been born. Mary, like her namesake and spiritual guardian, had given birth to a boy who could be a saviour, to his country if not to mankind. The news was eagerly embraced by the city authorities. At their command, bells were rung, processions organised and services of celebration held. Around bonfires and at street parties men and women exchanged accounts, from unimpeachable sources, of the child's great beauty. Sir Henry Sidney had been appointed to sail again, as a formal envoy: to take the happy news of an heir to Philip's uncle, Ferdinand, brother of his father Charles V and the so-called 'King of the Romans'.[7]

Sadly, however, it was not true. No child, Londoners confided to each other late on May Day afternoon, had been born.

At Hampton Court male experts, increasingly, were permitted within the sanctum of Mary's chamber as the Queen sought advice and reassurance about her condition. She yearned for a baby, as the surest sign that God favoured her cause – as, to her at least, He had always seemed to do. Her stomach had swollen, her breasts leaked milk and her periods ceased. Those close to Mary continued to reassure her as she clung, anxious and tearful, to her prayer book within her chamber. Within a month or two, they promised, her pregnancy would come to term.

As Chancellor set sail down the Thames once more, this time knowing, at least, his intended destination, none in London was certain what the outcome would be. Everything, the Venetian ambassador wrote, was 'in suspense, and dependent on the result of this delivery'.

But already there were those, and her husband was one of them, who suspected that the English Queen was not pregnant at all, and never had been.[8]

Fifty-Four

As the *Edward* and the *Philip and Mary* rowed and then sailed downriver from London, all on board, and all otherwise connected with the company, were anxious as before to make use of the northern summer while it lasted.

This time the crew knew where they were going. There was not the same fear of the unknown. The Venetian ambassador remarked that the ships departed 'with greater hope of prosperous navigation out and home than the last time'.[1] But the pressure remained. The company's senior merchants had issued instructions to the ship's captains to make it to Russia and back in a single season.

The outward voyage was an easier one, without the dramatic weather which struck the first expedition as it sailed along the northern Norwegian coast. The men had the benefit of experience; and the *Philip and Mary* sailed only as far as Wardhouse, rounding the North Cape and dropping anchor to unload its goods and to take on others before it returned to England. The *Edward* paused there too, to allow Richard Chancellor to discuss plans with John Brooke and the other senior English merchants. Then, with the coming of a favourable wind, she sailed on alone, south-east towards the White Sea.

As they traced the bleak coast of Lapland at a safe distance they passed the gulf of the River Varzina, where Willoughby and his crew – though Chancellor did not yet know it – had arrived, and died, some eighteen months previously.

It was shortly after their arrival in the mouth of the Dvina that the painful news of the discovery, late the previous spring, of the *Bona*

Esperanza and the *Bona Confidentia*, was passed to Richard Chancellor and his men.[2] News of the grim discovery travelled back to England with the crew of the *Edward* when the ship returned from Russia for the second time.

Soon after they arrived, in the autumn, the fate of Willoughby and his men dominated the conversation on the streets of London, as the sailors milked the limelight by relating the tales they had been told. In November that year the Venetian ambassador in England, Giovanni Michiel, reported back to his government that the mariners who had recently returned from the second voyage to Russia were telling graphic stories about the discovery of the corpses on board two of the first three ships.[3] Any hopes still harboured by the company merchants, or by the friends and families of Willoughby, Durforth and those who had journeyed with them, that they had sailed on beyond Russia and discovered a passage to rich lands beyond, were suddenly and tragically shattered.

In Russia, word of the discovery had travelled quickly to Ivan's court in Moscow. The Tsar himself was loyal to the promise he had made to Richard Chancellor. He treated Willoughby and his men well in death, as he had never had the chance to do in life. Orders were immediately sent to his appointed governor in the Dvina province, Prince Semen Ivanovich Mikulinsky-Punkov, as well as to elected officials in the region like Feofan Makarov, to have the two English ships sailed to Kholmogory where they could be kept secure until Chancellor returned from Moscow.[4] Henry Lane wrote years later that George Killingworth, the merchant chosen to be the company's first agent in the Russian capital, had sent a man to inspect the ships, 'with the dead bodies of Sir Hugh Willoughby, and his people'.

A large part of the food supplies and the goods which the ships had contained, Lane wrote, 'were recovered and saved'.[5] The 'effects and merchandise', Michiel likewise reported at the time, had been found 'all intact in the hands of the natives', by which he presumably meant the Lapps. Mistakenly, he thought that the two ships had been sailed back to England with their goods that year, in 1555, though in reality there were not enough crew members on the *Edward* to sail two additional ships on the difficult voyage home. They had to wait until additional men could be brought the following year. Perhaps, though, some valuable goods were retrieved which were not considered saleable commodities in Russia, and these were shipped back to London that year.

Fifty-Five

Some months later, in November 1555, one of the men who was to work for the company as an agent in Russia sent a long letter back to England from the Russian capital.

At that time of year, any communication via the northern route had been closed off by the advance of the winter ice. Instead the letter was carried overland to the Baltic, for conveyance to England, by a merchant from Poland. The trader in question, whether Polish or a Baltic Hanseatic merchant, would not have looked favourably on the arrival of the English company. It is unlikely that he made a willing courier. But, as George Killingworth noted, he carried the letter at the commandment of the Tsar's secretary and probably felt that he had no option.

The English were anxious to establish regular communication with Moscow through the Baltic so as to be able to send messages to their representatives in Russia at all times of the year, and Killingworth reported that he had sent word to contacts in Danzig. Letters from London sent this way, he had instructed, should be attached to anything for the Tsar's secretary, who seemed well disposed to the English and could be relied upon to pass on correspondence.

Killingworth's letter provides information about what happened after the *Edward* arrived back at the mouth of the Dvina.

Without the delays that had affected Chancellor and his men in the autumn of 1553, as they waited for permission to travel to the capital, the English merchants were able to make quick progress from the northern town of Kholmogory towards Moscow. As a result it was significantly earlier in the year when they did so, and the River Dvina, a 'great inland highway', remained unfrozen and open for water transport.[1] The English merchandise – a variety of goods that the merchants planned to try selling in Moscow and elsewhere – was loaded into the long, narrow boats which were used in Russia for river transport.

Years later Stephen Borough's son described how goods were 'discharged & laden into *doshniks*, that is, barks of the country', before by 'continual sailing, rowing, setting with poles, or drawing of men', depending on the conditions of the wind and the river, they travelled south. The river from Kholmogory ran, as an English ambassador later wrote, 'pleasant between high hills of either side'. For long stretches there was nothing but 'a wilderness of high fir trees, and other wood', but interspersed within were 'pretty villages' which, before winter smothered the landscape, seemed 'well-situated for pasture, arable land, wood, and water'.

First they travelled to the mouth of the Sukhona, a tributary of the Dvina, and then up this waterway as far as the city of Vologda, a journey of about 600 miles in total.[2] All who had travelled onward from St Nicholas remained in good health, Killingworth reported, 'save only William, our cook, [who] as we came from [Kholmogory] fell into the river out of the boat and was drowned'.

Without something to grab onto immediately, his chances of recovery were poor. Though not unknown, the ability to swim was little valued in Tudor England. Contact with the New World had meant increased awareness of others who could; but it remained sufficiently unusual for Cabot, who had spent much time in America, to have felt the need in his original instructions to warn of attacks by people that could swim. Even those who made a living on ships rarely learned the skill. Sometimes they were even superstitiously determined not to do so. Falling into the water, as a result, was all too frequently fatal.[3]

On 11 September the party reached Vologda, the city which had struck the English favourably during their first visit, as John Hasse, who does not seem to have been among the merchant contingent in 1555, had written in his report.

Hasse, no doubt, had formed his opinion in discussion with Chancellor among others, and certainly his advice was taken to heart, for at Vologda, as he had recommended, the English company planned to establish a trading station. Initial attempts to market their goods were not particularly successful. 'We laid all our wares up', Killingworth reported, but 'sold very little', though they did decline some offers on the grounds that they did not yet know their market and that most of the Russian merchants had not yet arrived.

There, at the end of September, the party planned to divide. Seven would remain. These included Richard Gray, who was to be the company agent in Vologda, along with Arthur Edwards, John Sedgewicke and Richard Johnson, all of whom had sailed on the *Edward* in 1553, as well as three others: Thomas Hattery, Christopher Hudson and Richard Good.[4] Five, meanwhile, would continue their journey overland to Moscow.

There was Chancellor, of course, as overall Captain of the expedition, Killingworth himself who was to act as the company agent in the Russian capital, as well as Henry Lane, Edward Price and Robert Best. Of these five, only Richard Chancellor had certainly been to Moscow, and to the Kremlin, before. Edward Price may have sailed to Russia on the *Edward Bonaventure* in 1553 if, as some have assumed, the Edward Pacie listed among the ship's crew was actually also Edward Price; but if so he was probably a teenager beginning his naval career and would have been unlikely to have travelled to Moscow. Henry Lane had not, but was already a reliable company servant and was promoted, within a couple of years, to be one of its agents in Russia. Robert Best had not either, but he too was a useful man to have in the party. He was physically imposing, described afterwards as a 'strong willing Englishman'.[5] When he was later put forward as the merchants' champion for a trial by combat, his potential Russian opponent declined the opportunity to fight. And there was more to him than brawn, because he was also gifted at languages. He had already begun to pick up the Russian tongue. Within months, remarkably, he was sufficiently fluent to be employed by the company as an interpreter – albeit there was not an abundance of alternative candidates.[6]

The weather may have been unusually warm. Certainly Killingworth wrote that this was the case two months later: 'men say', he reported, 'that these three hundred years was never so warm weather in this country at this time of the year'. Either way, it was too early to travel on to Moscow by sled, and they had not yet had the painful experience of attempting to travel long distances in Russia overland before the ground had frozen hard. Heedless, they loaded a portion of their wares into wagons, including the gifts that they had brought with them to present to Ivan.

Among these gifts were bags of sugar, still a great luxury in sixteenth-century Europe, particularly away from the Mediterranean and Atlantic coasts, though production in the New World was increasing supply. They also had fine Spanish sweet wine. But the wheels, weighed down, sank into the mud and they made little progress before abandoning the attempt in frustration. 'The way', Killingworth wrote, 'was so deep that we were fain to turn back and leave [the goods] still at Vologda till the frost.'

Instead the five Englishmen hired post horses, along with guides, and they rode ahead until on 4 October they reached Moscow. Initially they were lodged in what they described as a 'simple house', small, wooden and bare of comforts. After Ivan's secretary had sent for them, however, greeted them warmly at the Kremlin and taken from them the letter for Ivan they had brought from Queen Mary and King Philip, the Englishmen's accommodation was upgraded. The Tsar, they were told, had commanded that they be well looked after.

Soon afterwards an imperial official arrived with two different types of mead, a pair of chickens and an assurance that no payment would be required for their more comfortable house. From then on a delivery arrived every two days: eight more chickens, additional supplies of mead and some Russian currency to cover any expenses. There was also a 'poor fellow' who was ordered to clean their house and to perform any tasks that they might require.

On the 9th a messenger called at their house. He told the men to be ready to meet the Tsar on the following day. He also returned the royal letter from Philip and Mary, which had been carefully studied and translated, so that they could deliver it to Ivan themselves.

Fifty-Six

On 10 November the five Englishmen were given a formal welcome at the Tsar's court. They were brought to the Kremlin and, like the leading men of 1553, were led through a great chamber filled with cupboards of silverware to another in which around a hundred men, richly dressed, were seated on benches. They were 'ancient grave personages', as Henry Lane wrote later, dressed 'all in long garments of sundry colours, gold, tissue, baldakin, and violet ... with caps, jewels, and chains'. The Englishmen again assumed them to be courtiers, but as Lane recalled, they later learned that they were actually ordinary inhabitants of Moscow, dressed by the royal wardrobe, 'waiting and wearing this apparel for the time, and so to restore it'.[1]

They came then to the audience chamber of the Tsar. In 'a large room floored with carpets' sat another hundred men, genuine courtiers this time, and more elaborately dressed still. As Chancellor and his four companions entered all rose to their feet, with the sole exception of Ivan himself, who remained seated on his throne.

In turn the Englishmen paid the Tsar their respects, bowing and kissing his hand. As Chancellor stepped forward he presented to the Tsar's secretary the letter he had brought from his monarchs. King Edward, he informed the Russians regretfully, had, though young, died in the interim. The secretary and Ivan himself affected to read the letter.

In it, Philip and Mary – though primarily Mary – gave thanks to the Tsar for his initial generous reception of Richard Chancellor, 'governor and great Captain' of the *Edward Bonaventure*, which by the grace of God and 'the good conduct of the said Chancellor' had managed to arrive in the northern parts of his 'Empire of Russia'. She had heard, she said, how Ivan had 'entertained and banqueted them with all humanity

271

and gentleness', and she gratefully acknowledged his promise to permit English merchants and ambassadors free access to his realm. 'We cannot', she wrote, 'but much commend your princely favour and goodness', and she begged him to 'continue the same benevolence toward them'.

Mary urged Ivan to appoint commissaries to negotiate with Chancellor, Killingworth and Gray (though Gray, of course, had remained in Vologda), and to confirm the 'liberties and privileges' required by the English merchants. The same rights and freedoms, she promised him, would be extended to any Russian merchants who wished to travel to England.[2]

Ivan could not have missed the letter's implication of major religious change in England. When Mary spoke of her 'most dear and entirely beloved late brother', it was with the added entreaty: 'whose soul God pardon'. Russians were well aware of the fierce disputes which for decades had burned, often literally, in the lands of central and western Europe – though to them the beliefs of Protestants and Roman Catholics were equally heretical. Where Edward had thought best to mention God alone, since he did not know for whom he was writing, Mary concluded with an invocation of the Trinity: 'thus right high, right Excellent, and right mighty, Almighty God the Father, the Son and the holy Ghost have you in his blessed keeping'.

This was a formulation which Orthodox, Protestant and Roman Catholic could accept, since all three major Christian communities affirmed the Trinity. Nevertheless, it called to mind the major rift between Orthodox and Western Christians which, as Mary well knew, occurred over the procession of the Holy Spirit from either the Father alone, as the Orthodox had it, or from the Father and the Son, as Christians in the West insisted.[3]

If a deliberate dig was understood by Ivan and his councillors, no reference, certainly, was made. Speeches and responses were made through interpreters, at which Ivan, as was customary, asked after the health of the English Queen, whom he called his cousin. Having remained seated on his throne up to this point, the Tsar rose to his feet as a mark of respect, Lane remembered, whenever the King and Queen of England were mentioned. He then concluded the formal conversation, in the usual way, by inviting the men to dinner.

After a short wait, the five Englishmen dined in Ivan's presence from gold platters. Again, cupboards displayed the fine royal collection of plate – some of the vessels as big as washbowls or 'kilderkins' (small barrels). The Tsar 'was [sat] bare headed, his crown and rich cap standing upon a pinnacle [close] by'. Ivan's metropolitan was next to him, as were members of his family and chief Tartar nobles, though none were close enough to invade his royal space.

The Englishmen were led to a table of honour in the middle of the room, not far from the Tsar himself. The Russians referred to them as 'Ghosti Carabelski' – that is, the strangers or merchants who came by ship. At periodic intervals, Killingworth and Lane agreed, 'his grace sent us meat and drink from his own table', including 'sundry drinks of purified mead, made of fine white and clarified honey'. As they delivered these offerings, the 'Lords and Gentlemen' serving pronounced the Englishmen's Christian names: 'viz. Richard, George, Henry, Arthur'.[4]

At the end of the meal each went individually to receive a cup of drink from Ivan directly. As Killingworth went up, Lane remembered, Ivan 'took into his hand Master George Killingworth's beard, which reached over the table'. The Tsar let it run through his hand in evident admiration, as well he might. The relevant statistics were well imprinted on the memory of Henry Lane. The growth, he attested years later, was 'not only thick, broad, and yellow coloured, but in length five foot and two inches of assize'.

Shaving, in Russia, was frowned upon for mature men, and while the relatively young are sometimes portrayed with hairless faces, clerics and senior councillors are invariably not.

Among clerics, moreover, the practice was fiercely condemned for its purported association with wealth, spiritual and moral laxness and even with sodomy. For a man to have smooth cheeks, like a woman's, was regarded as a dangerous incentive, and this was a crime for which it was feared that the whole community would pay the penalty, just as Sodom had done in biblical times.

Four years earlier, in fact, the matter had been one of those gravely discussed at a great Church council which Ivan had attended, and it was with a smile and a knowing wink, therefore, that the Tsar passed the end of Killingworth's beard to the metropolitan sitting close to him. For the cleric it was no laughing matter. He remained deeply serious, and was duly impressed. He seemed, Lane thought, to bless the beard. And he uttered a simple Russian phrase which the Englishmen could understand. 'This', he said, 'is God's gift.'⁵

Later that night, lest they feel empty, or dry, high-ranking men arrived at their house with additional supplies of dressed meat, wine and mead.

Fifty-Seven

While in Moscow, the English met some Italian merchants, Italians being among those Europeans who had maintained regular contact with Moscow since the days when their architects had been summoned by Ivan's grandfather to design important buildings in the Kremlin. These men warned the English to be on their guard. Be careful, they were told, that the detailed trading privileges they expected were not distorted when they were translated into the Russian language. Perhaps they were motivated by bad experience, perhaps purely by an anxiety to sow distrust.

Chancellor made this concern known to his hosts. In response, Ivan urged the Englishmen to write down what they expected, for him to see. He also asked them to note what type of goods they anticipated bringing to Russia. For Ivan, the terms on which the English merchants traded were not now his primary concern, and probably he was ingenuous enough.

We can't be certain what was on the list the Englishmen provided, though a wide range of cloth goods no doubt was foremost.[1] In the ships the company sent less than two years later, there were carefully wrapped and protected packages of cloths – cottons, kerseys, watchets, in all manner of colours: scarlet, violet, blue, red, green, ginger and yellow, though the interest of English merchants in the techniques and materials that foreigners used for dying remained strong. 'Send us for proof', the governors wrote, 'a quantity of such earth, herbs, or what thing soever it be, that the Russians do [use to] dye and colour any kind of cloth linen or woollen, Leather or any other thing withal: and also part of that which the Tartars and Turks do bring thither, and how it must be used in dying and colouring.' There were also nine barrels of pewter goods, made by a man called Thomas Hasel.[2] This wasn't a complete list, though; the four ships sent that year would have carried much more.

Some years later Richard Hakluyt produced a detailed catalogue for another man who had sailed as a boy with Chancellor in 1553, and who also went on to trade and explore in Russia. By this time English manufactures had diversified, but the list remains relevant and interesting. Among those 'things to be carried with you', to show off English commodities, Hakluyt included a wide variety of goods with names which recorded places of early manufacture as well as dyes, fabrics and styles of cloth.

There were kerseys 'of all orient colours': coarse cloths which were an English export staple, made originally in the Suffolk village of Kersey. There were red woollen cloths called Frizadoes. There were Says, Bristol Friezes, Spanish blankets and Rashes – all styles and types of cloth. There were Worsteds made from yarn whose name derived from the Norfolk village of Worstead. There were silk garters and taffeta hats, as well as a wide variety of goods made of leather or pewter.[3]

The samples the English crew had brought with them were sent to Ivan, on his request, so that he could inspect them. After an anxious wait he sent a favourable response, and concurred with Queen Mary's suggestion that the English merchants should meet with their Moscow counterparts. With the Tsar's encouragement a conference was duly arranged, and took place in the office of Ivan's secretary.

A larger range of samples, Chancellor and his merchants assured their Russian counterparts, would have to wait until the first sleds arrived from Vologda.

Guarantees regarding prices would also need to wait: both until the goods themselves could be displayed, and until assurances were obtained regarding Russian weights and measures, which seemed to vary so much from place to place. The sleds bearing the English goods did presumably arrive soon afterwards, though the unseasonably warm weather delayed them longer than might have been expected.

At the time of writing, Killingworth noted, he had just received a letter from his colleague Christopher Hudson, who was bringing some

of them, and who had made it as far as the city of Yaroslavl' in the for-
ested and gently rolling plain between Vologda and Moscow. Winter,
however, had not set in as hard as Hudson had thought and he had
been forced to wait. Nor was he the only one struggling in the slushy
conditions. Hudson wrote in his letter that he had earlier entrusted part
of the Tsar's present with a gentleman at Vologda, who had agreed to
take it to the capital. Unfortunately the runners of this man's sled had
become stuck, causing the whole contraption to capsize. In the crash, he
reported, 'the butt of Hollock [that is, the Spanish wine] was lost, which
made us all very sorry'.

The English and Russian merchants also discussed, along with Ivan's
officials, where the English should base their trading operation. The
matter was left open, though both Kholmogory and Vologda were
thought likely possibilities: probably, Killingworth thought, 'we shall
have need of one house at [Kholmogory] and another at Vologda'. This
at least would give the English a chance to test the water. 'And thus', he
wrote, 'may we continue three or four years, and in this space we shall
know the country and the merchants, and which way to save ourselves
best, and where to plant our houses, and where to seek for wares.' He
was optimistic that they would soon obtain the written privileges they
hoped for – but did not go into detail regarding company plans in what
was an insecure communication sent via a rival merchant. In any case,
he did not need to: 'you know', he wrote, 'what I mean'.

In the meantime, Killingworth assured the directors in London that
he would continue to explore the country. As soon as his companions
had departed to sail back to England, he told them, 'I do intend to go to
Novgorod and Plesco ... and such wares as are there I trust to buy part'.[4]
The company, he said, should have another ship ready to depart in April
from the coast of England. 'Fear you not,' he reassured his employers,
'we will do that may be done, if God send us health.' He concluded his
letter with a send-off which then, as now, justified any gaps or imperfec-
tions and testified to his dedication on the company's behalf: 'Written in
haste, by yours to command, George Killingworth, Draper.'

Negotiation was slower than it might have been because of Ivan's personal authority. 'All matters pass his judgement,' Anthony Jenkinson

observed soon afterwards, 'be they never so small.'⁵ His attention was also, that winter, elsewhere.

Although he invested in trade himself, Ivan always considered purely commercial matters as inferior to the business of war and government. 'We know that Merchants' matters are to be heard,' he later told Jenkinson, 'for that they are the stay of our Princely treasures: But first Princes' affairs are to be established, and then Merchants'.'⁶ In the autumn of 1555 he was particularly distracted, and this delayed any response to the English requests. 'His grace is so troubled with preparations to wars', Killingworth reported, 'that as yet we have no answer.'

The year before Chancellor's first visit, after years of unrest on his south-eastern border, Ivan's forces had conquered the khanate of Kazan – which obstructed possible trade flowing from Russia to the Middle East via the Caspian Sea. (In the market square outside the Kremlin, building work continued on the Cathedral of the Holy Veil – St Basil's, as it would become known – which was created to celebrate this victory.) Since then, major revolts had had to be suppressed. Muslims were evicted from the city of Kazan itself, and Russian Orthodox colonists moved in to take their place. That year, furthermore, in 1555 an army under the Khan of the Crimea had invaded Russia and come close to winning a significant victory.⁷

Now Derbysh-Ali, the man installed with Russian help as Khan of Astrakhan – another successor state of the Mongol horde near the southern outflow of the River Volga into the Caspian – had turned against his backers.⁸ With the help of the Turks, who had a strong interest in preventing Russia emerging as a major power in Central Asia and the Middle East, he had attacked Russian troops in the region where the Don and Volga rivers drew close to one another before parting once more. Here too outright conquest seemed the only course of action.

The decisive campaign which would make Ivan the direct ruler over Astrakhan as well as Kazan, reinforcing his claim to imperial status (and furthering the development of Russia as a multicultural, multi-ethnic state, in spite of Ivan's religiosity) would take place the following year, and preparations were already under way. In the snow-covered fields outside Moscow the new *streltsy* musketeer units, which had made an impact in Kazan, were mustered for action once more, as were the Russian cavalry, steam rising in the cold air from the flanks and mouths of many thousands of horses.

Ivan himself prepared to travel south with his army in the early spring, as Richard Chancellor and those members of the English party who were not remaining in Russia made their way back to the White Sea to meet the returning English ships.

When Chancellor took his leave and departed Moscow, he took with him the formal charter of privileges for which their company had hoped. Hakluyt records what he claims to be a translation of the document. Some historians have felt that the rights it enshrines are too good to be true, and that what it actually represents are the rights requested by the company from the Tsar (which he had urged the Englishmen to write down).

Given Ivan's delight at the English arrival for non-mercantile reasons, and the great favour he showed the Muscovy Company for some while afterwards, this alone may not be a cause for doubt. Subsequent privileges, certainly authentic, are scarcely less favourable. Elements like the hymn to trade and its promotion of amity between nations do certainly echo the text of Edward's original letter. Other phrases sound less like an English draft, though they could have been. 'Upon the contemplation', the document declares, 'of the gracious letters, directed from the right high, right excellent, and right mighty Queen Mary.'

In the first half of the nineteenth century, a Russian historian who worked in the English archives professed to have found an English translation of the original document, and published these terms in Russian, though the manuscript he found has never subsequently been traced.[9] There are significant differences between the two versions. Only the one provided by Hakluyt offers the company's chief agent authority over all Englishmen in Russia. The alternative version, meanwhile, is alone in specifying that a house in Moscow, 'not far from the market place', is to be provided to the company tax-free, and that the English merchants should also have the right to buy houses in Vologda and Kholmogory and to build a warehouse 'where they find a suitable wharf for their goods'.

Fundamentally, though, both versions of the document show that the company obtained what it most wanted. It could trade freely throughout Russia, not just in Moscow or on the White Sea coast, entirely free of tolls and duties. It would have an effective monopoly of English trade in the country, while full legal protection of property and person would be guaranteed by the Tsar.[10]

While Chancellor and his compatriots had been in Moscow this time, the *Edward* had not waited in the White Sea but sailed back to London. In the early summer of 1556 she returned, with the *Philip and Mary*, bringing both further English goods for the company agents to sell and also a large number of additional sailors.

These men were on board in order to bring the *Bona Esperanza* and the *Bona Confidentia* back to England. The two ill-fated ships were due now to return to London, three years after their initial departure. Among the cargo the small fleet was to take home was the dead body of Sir Hugh Willoughby.[11]

With the crew of the *Edward* was the elder of Richard Chancellor's two sons, who had reached his early teens. His father had taken care that he was well educated, and he was old enough now to be apprenticed as a junior sailor – the first step in any career at sea. He hoped to follow in his father's illustrious footsteps.[12]

Further instructions had been provided by the company board. Primarily, though, these were practical guidelines, intended as a permanent rule book, for pursers in particular, who were in charge of the goods transported on company voyages. Once again they demonstrate the self-interested behaviour that was expected of sailors and merchants not used to company employment.

Repeatedly the purser was urged to take measures against the private conveyance of goods or people on board company ships. A register should be taken to ensure that no stranger passed 'under the cloak and colour of some mariner'. Careful inventories should be kept of company equipment on board ship, and company goods. Goods should be registered as they were loaded and unloaded. The purser was to keep a diligent watch over all his colleagues, no matter what their status, and was not, evidently, to think much of making friends:

... ashore, and likewise aboard, you shall spy, and search as secretly as you may, to learn and know what bargaining, buying, and selling there is with the master and mariners of the ship, and the Russians, or with the company's servants there; and that which you shall perceive and learn you shall keep a note thereof in your book, secretly to yourself, which you shall open and disclose at your coming home, to the governors and the assistants ... You shall need always to have Argus' eyes, to spy their secret packing and conveyance, as well on land as aboard the ship ...

Along with that of the company hierarchy in London, the only good opinion he should seek was that of God, whose approval would work to everyone's advantage.

'See that you forget not daily in all the voyage, both morning and evening, to call the company within board to prayer,' he was reminded. By doing so, 'you shall please God, and the voyage will have the better success thereby and the company prosper the better'.

Fifty-Eight

On 20 July 1556, the four ships departed from St Nicholas.[1] There was the *Philip and Mary*, and with it sailed all of the ships from the original expedition organised by Cabot three years earlier: the *Edward Bonaventure*, the *Bona Esperanza* and the *Bona Confidentia*. It was a strange experience for the officers and crew who were given the task of manning the last two, knowing the fate of the Englishmen who had sailed in them, and died in them, just over two years previously.

On one of the ships, it has been claimed, the body of Sir Hugh Willoughby was loaded. Even in a coffin the smell of decomposition would have been strong, now that the temperature had lifted above freezing for a second summer. If he was to be returned to England for a proper Christian burial, the rite would now have been Catholic, not Protestant as he might have expected.

Also packed into the holds of the ships were quantities of merchandise bought in Russia for the company to sell in England: wax, train oil, tallow, furs, felts, yarn 'and such-like'. On board the *Edward* alone there were goods worth £20,000 (worth around £5 million today), some of which were owned not by the company but by a party of Russians who joined the English merchants and crew and who were anxious to take the opportunity to make a profit. On the *Bona Esperanza* £6,000 worth of goods were carried, while it is known that the *Philip and Mary* shipped over £4,000 worth of wax, entered in the London customs accounts on arrival in the name of Sebastian Cabot.[2]

Embarking with Chancellor and his crew was a Russian aristocrat named Osip (or Joseph, as the English called him) Napea: an important man who was governor of the city of Vologda and its surrounding

282

region, and who had been charged by Ivan with leading an embassy to the English court.

With him, and carefully packed into the hold, he brought gifts for King Philip and Queen Mary. There were fine skins and furs, including 'twenty entire sables exceeding beautiful with teeth, ears, and claws', and skins so rich and rare they were 'worn only by the Emperor'. He also brought four live sables, each with its own collar and chain, and a white gyrfalcon – a bird which was rare and difficult to catch and which had, in consequence, often been considered exclusively royal and a suitable gift for one monarch to bestow upon another. It was the greatest of the falcon family, used to catch large wild birds such as geese, swans or herons. It travelled now with 'a drum of silver, the hoops gilt, used for a lure to call the said hawk'.

Travelling with Napea on the *Edward*, with Chancellor as grand pilot and John Buckland as master, were sixteen other Russians. Nine of them, whose names Hakluyt provides, went purely to attend upon the ambassador and to provide him with an entourage appropriate to his standing. The Englishman Robert Best had travelled with this party from Vologda as their interpreter.[3] The other Russians on the *Edward* were presumably merchants.

Ten more, meanwhile, were among the twenty-four men who embarked from St Nicholas on the *Bona Esperanza*. Among them was Feofan Makarov, the 'elected' chief magistrate of Kholmogory, who had dealt with the English since their first arrival in 1553.

Many, if not all, of the Russians who boarded the English ships had never sailed on the open sea before.

Initially the voyage proceeded according to plan. 'God sending you a fair wind', the instructions of 1556 had predicted optimistically, 'to make speed and away.' And so, at first, He did. The ships, the company clerk John Incent later reported, came 'in good order into the seas'.

After rounding the North Cape safely the flotilla passed the Lofoten island chain, and sailed down much of the western coast of Norway. Then – suddenly – the weather deteriorated. The skies darkened. The wind picked up. In Sebastian Cabot's first book of instructions an understandable emphasis had been placed upon the ships of the company remaining together, but since the events of the first voyage, this was even more the case. Such good intentions, though, counted for little against the vagaries of the elements. Once again conditions became impossible. 'By contrary winds and extreme tempest of weather', Incent wrote, the ships were 'severed the one from the other'.

Again Chancellor's remarkable seamanship was apparent, as the *Edward* alone escaped being driven helplessly by the wind towards the Norwegian coast. The other three ships, the *Philip and Mary*, the *Bona Confidentia* and the *Bona Esperanza*, disappeared from view into a large gulf known to the English as 'Drenton Water', near the city of Trondheim (Drontheim, or Drenton), where shelter might be sought from the strong winds which now, as often, battered the western Scandinavian seaboard.

Once again Chancellor had the experience of watching his fellow ships vanish into the mist as the waves thundered across his decks, off this fragmented coast. He and the mariners on the *Edward* looked on aghast as, before they passed entirely from view, the ill-fated *Confidentia* was hurled headlong into rocks which reared up from the water. There was nothing anyone could do to help. The ship immediately foundered, and all on board were thrown or dragged down to their deaths.

The *Bona Esperanza*, with its deputation of Russian merchants, was assumed to have sought shelter within the gulf and to have wintered there on the Norwegian coast. It too, however, was damaged and sunk by the weather before it reached safety. What exactly became of it was never discovered. The ship on which Sir Hugh Willoughby and all his men had died in the early months of 1554 disappeared without trace, claiming further lives – including that of Feofan Makarov, the senior official in Kholmogory, who had little thought to meet his end in a shipwreck off southern Norway. 'Of the Bona [Esperanza]', Incent wrote in May 1557, 'no word nor knowledge was had at this present day'. 'As yet we have no news of her', the company informed their agents in Russia in the same month. But they were not hopeful. 'We fear', they wrote, that 'it is wrong with her'.[4]

Neither the *Bona Esperanza* nor the *Bona Confidentia*, feared lost in 1554, then rediscovered the following year, was ever to make it back to London. After two years spent wintering on the coast of Lapland they may not have been in a seaworthy condition. They were not designed, as were the smaller boats of the Russian north, to be pushed upwards by a freezing sea and so to avoid the intense pressure that ice could impart. Becoming 'as is supposed, unstaunch', as Henry Lane later wrote, they sunk 'in foul weather, and wrought seas'. As well as their English crews, they took with them into the waves those Russian merchants and servants of the ambassador who had been chosen to sail in them.'

The *Philip and Mary*, at least, did manage to reach a safe harbour within the gulf. No word of her reached London for some months, and she too had been given up for lost when, in mid-April the following year, she appeared suddenly in the Thames estuary. 'The *Philip and Mary* arrived here ten days past,' the company wrote in relief to its agents; 'she wintered in Norway.'

Under the captaincy of Chancellor and Buckland, the *Edward* did manage to remain at sea even as the waves and the gales threw and pummelled her. But she was blown badly off-course, and even after the storm had abated, unfavourable winds continued to defy her attempts to make progress back towards England. For months, Incent wrote, she traversed the sea before eventually finding her way onto a remote strip of coastal Aberdeenshire.

Here, on 10 November, she dropped anchor in a harbour at Pitsligo, on the south-eastern corner of the Moray Firth. To the English, of course, Scotland was a foreign country; and this, though not the Highlands, where the authority even of the Scottish government barely ran, was a long way from its capital in Edinburgh.

Chancellor and his men had reached, even so, the island mass that they called home and they must have felt that they were now close at last.

The danger from the elements and from the seasons was not over. Winter was quickly setting in. The Englishmen had descended from higher latitudes, but the weather in northern Scotland was bad enough. Pitsligo Bay, where they lay at anchor, was only a shallow inlet on a flat, rocky coastline which lay exposed to the North Sea.

As the sky grew black again and another storm swept in, the men were forced once more to lie prone below deck, praying that the anchor lines would hold, as their ship was violently thrown by the water. In their darkened cages the martens ran and fell frantically and the hawk flapped its wings in terror, unable to find a perch that did not reel and plunge. Above the noise of the wind the sharp crack could barely be heard as the rope which secured the ship's anchor snapped or broke loose under the strain.

There were shouts of panic from on deck as crewmen on watch realised what had happened, but there was little that could be done. The wind blew hard towards the shore and high, foaming waves crashed in the same direction, beating the ship before them. Chancellor and Buckland yelled instructions through the noise of the storm as the crew tried desperately to steer the *Edward* towards the safety of the open sea, but they could not manage it. A sudden jolt hurled men to the deck, immediately followed by a hideous, tearing crash as they hit the rocks close to the shore. A hole was ripped in the wooden ship's flank and water rushed in, causing the *Edward* to lean dangerously.

Unable to save his ship, Chancellor ordered that its small boat be launched on which he could try to protect the ambassador by getting him, along with some of his train, to shore. Their faces wet with spray and riven with fear, Napea himself and seven other Russian attendants managed to climb, or fall, into the boat alongside Chancellor, Buckland and a few other Englishmen. As they cast off, the *Edward* was dashed once more into the rocks, 'where she broke and split in pieces'.

With oars and poles the men tried frantically to drive their boat towards a beach where they could land, but their light craft was thrown more easily still by the water and there was little they could do to guide it. Like driftwood they rode and plunged through the foam, as the dreadful noise of the wind and the sea screamed in their ears. Already, by early afternoon, the sky was blackening further as night fell, and the men struggled to make out the shoreline.

Suddenly, just as they began to get near, a great wave flipped their boat over and they were plunged into the water, flailing and gasping desperately for breath. Napea himself was lucky. He was thrown by the waves onto a sandy stretch of shore where he was able, perhaps with help, to scramble to safety.

A few more occupants of the boat, 'by God's preservation and special favour', were spared. Among them were the captain, John Buckland, and Robert Best, the rugged Englishman who had remained with the ambassador to act as his interpreter. Cold, bruised and shaken, they were 'with much difficulty saved'. In their different ways, they gave thanks to a God they believed had chosen them, for His own inscrutable purposes, to survive.

Others were less fortunate. A number of the Russians who were sailing at sea for the first time died. The majority of the English officers and crew who had remained on the *Edward* as it splintered and broke up were dragged beneath the water and also drowned, if they were not first dashed against the rocks. Richard Chancellor, the grand pilot who had led his country's first great exploratory trading venture, who had embraced a scientific mode of thought and study which still seems startlingly modern, and who combined this intellectual leaning with practical seamanship and with loyalty and bravery towards those who sailed with him, was also drowned.

Among the crew who died with him was a young boy who was sailing for the first time as an apprentice on a long-distance voyage: Chancellor's son, the elder of the two boys their father had worried to leave behind in 1553. Like other young men on board, and like so many in a dangerous profession, he was killed before he had a chance to learn his family trade. We do not even know his name.

A letter written by the company to its agents still in Russia lamented the 'heavy news of the loss of the said good ship and goods at [Pitsligo] in Scotland, with the death of Richard Chancellor and his Boy'.[6] Nicholas, Richard's younger son who had stayed behind, had already lost his mother. He was now bereaved too of the father who had been such an influence in his life, as well as his elder brother, and was left alone.

Fifty-Nine

O n 6 December 1556, nearly a month after it happened, news of the wreck of the *Edward* on the Scottish coast arrived by urgent letter in London, along with letters and papers that had been saved and which were of little interest to the local Scots. Leading members of the company read and reread the information with dismay. It was then that they certainly knew, Incent wrote, 'of the loss of their pilot, men, goods, and ship'.

In most such incidents, the attentions of the local community were barely less to be feared than the actions of wind and waves. Wrecking is a myth, but a small society living on the edge of subsistence was quick to seize on what seemed a providential opportunity, and a ship packed with valuable commodities, beached or broken open on a rocky coast, was certainly this. Surviving goods belonging to the company, and to the Russian ambassadorial party, were taken, and so too was anything else of value – the artillery, weapons, ammunition, food supplies, chains, ropes, sails, or any part of the furniture and equipment of the ship. No official response could arrive fast enough to intervene. 'All [the Ambassador's] goods and ours . . .', the company lamented to its agents in Russia, 'were lost and pilfered away by the Scots.'[1]

Efforts to decipher the trading records and letters rescued from the *Edward* proved unavailing. To the governors' regret, they were 'so sore spoiled and broken with water' that 'we cannot make our reckoning by them'.[2] Richard Chancellor's own account of his further time in Russia, and the logbook he must have kept of the voyages, were lost, along with the man himself who, more than any other individual, represented the company's hope for establishing a lucrative English commerce beyond the traditional channels.

About such vagaries of fate nothing could be done. No insurance policy existed. There was 'no remedy but patience', the company wrote, 'and to pray to God to send us better fortune hereafter'.

The leading men in London knew, all the same, that there were a few survivors, including the ambassador from Russia himself, and that their transport to London needed to be arranged. Relations between the English and Scottish governments were tense and unfriendly, but not (for now) actively belligerent. In December 1556 letters from Queen Mary were carried north by representatives of the company to her counterpart, the widowed Regent of Scotland, Mary of Guise.

In Edinburgh the Englishmen were favourably received, and there they met Napea and those others, like the captain John Buckland and the interpreter Robert Best, who had escaped the wreck. Efforts to retrieve goods and furniture from the Scottish population in Pitsligo proved largely unavailing. Even an order from the government in Edinburgh to return stolen material met only sullen silence and denial.

Gradually, 'after a long time' and after 'great labours, pains, and charges', insignificant offerings began to appear. 'Diverse small parcels of wax, and other small trifling things of no value' were handed in 'by the poorer sort of the Scots.' But the more substantial, expensive items remained elusive: the 'jewels, rich apparel, presents, gold, silver, costly furs, and such-like, were conveyed away, concealed, and utterly embezzled'.

In frustration, the ambassador complained to the Scottish government, surprised at the difficulty a monarch could have in making her will felt in a small country. At his request, numerous inhabitants of Pitsligo were summoned to the court at Edinburgh. Some further items did slowly appear as a result, but Napea grew exasperated, disillusioned and anxious to leave. Representatives of the English company were left to pursue the return of the goods, though largely for form's sake; the quantity saved, as leading members later admitted, would 'scant pay the charges for the recovering of it'.

Napea himself, meanwhile, was escorted across the border into England and then along the Old North Road to London. Outside the capital the party was met by a large delegation of merchants, formally dressed 'in coats of fine cloth bordered with velvet and with fringe of silk and chains of gold'.[3] Entertainments were arranged and sports laid on for the ambassador's interest, including men on horseback, with large packs of dogs, hunting a fox in the traditional, aristocratic manner.

The party continued to swell, with lavishly dressed groups arriving to meet them on behalf of both the civic government and the English Queen.

Sixty

At the city gates Napea was welcomed by the Lord Mayor, accompanied by all his aldermen in their ceremonial scarlet clothing, and together the unwieldy group pressed through the narrow city streets – cobbled but smelling richly of the human and animal waste piled and smeared across the stones in every corner.

Everywhere the noise was so great that men in the party found it hard to converse, though the Russians were naturally intrigued. Above the general tumult of the city – the yells and cries, the coach wheels on hard stone, the whinnies, grunts and squawks of animals – inquisitive men, women and children cheered and shouted as they glimpsed the man they called the 'Duke of Muscovy'. Increasingly, the streets were densely packed, as migrants pressed into the city in search of work. Down side streets and alleys buildings leaned across, high over the road, almost touching the building opposite. Vastly more people – perhaps 90,000 – were congregated here than in other settlements in the land. And for many this ceremonial procession was the centre of attention. With Londoners 'running plentifully on all sides', it was hard for the embassy to progress.

Napea himself, in his 'garment of tissue embroidered with pearls and stones', was sandwiched by the Lord Mayor on one side and by the young but conservative Viscount Montagu (in favour with the Catholic Mary) on the other. Pushing forward in front of them, making a path through the crowd, were 'a great number of merchants and notable personages', while they were followed by 'a large troop of servants and apprentices', along with the hundreds of others who already made up the party. Among them were the nine Russian attendants who had survived the shipwreck of the *Edward* with Napea, wearing the splendid clothes they had been given since their own possessions had been lost: 'coarse cloth of gold down to the calf of the leg (like gowns) and high coping capes'.[1]

Napea was escorted to a fine house in Fenchurch Street, in the east of the city, which belonged to John Dymocke, a leading member of the company. Two rooms were done up for the ambassador's use, 'richly hung and decked over and above the gallant furniture of the whole house'. At the order of the Privy Council, a lavish 'bed of estate' was delivered for Napea to use, along with other furniture and hangings. The government also sent to the royal jewel house, requesting the loan of two pairs of 'great silver pots', to adorn an 'ample and rich cupboard of plate of all sorts'.[2] Presents awaited him from Queen Mary: samples of the finest cloths, of gold, velvet and damask, with which Napea declared himself well pleased. Even the nightcap provided for him was 'set with pearls and stones'.[3]

There was no denying the unusual enthusiasm of the welcome Napea received in the capital. The like of it, the company later assured its agents, 'have not been seen nor shown here of a long time to any Ambassador'.[4] The London merchants, the Venetian envoy reported, 'greatly favour the Muscovite, because they expect through his medium to enrich themselves, by commencing a trade in those parts'. Greater honour, he commented, 'could not be done to the greatest sovereign'.[5]

From the outset Napea was kept busy by frequent visits, from city aldermen and senior merchants of the company, though he was not immediately able to visit the court.

The public backing Mary had received at the time of her coronation had collapsed. Numerous heretics had remained steadfast to the end, refusing to recant their views, and were often acclaimed rather than vilified by the crowds who gathered to watch them burn. In 1556 the Venetian ambassador had written of 'the ill-will of the majority of the population here' on account of religion. One conspiracy was quashed in the spring of 1556, but fears of another remained.

The Queen herself was depressed and anxious. Looking wan and old beyond her years, she waited, at times rather desperately, for the return of her husband, King Philip, who was campaigning in Flanders – though Parliament refused to contemplate her dream that he should be crowned in his own right.[6] In his 'beautiful lodging' Napea waited and entertained civic dignitaries, until word arrived that in the late afternoon of 20 March King Philip had returned. On the 23rd there was a great celebration in London as Mary and her husband, with a column of their nobles and retainers, rode through the capital.

Then finally, two days later, the Russian ambassador was rowed upriver with a party of great merchants to pay his formal respects to the joint monarchs at Westminster Palace.[7] Here Napea was on more familiar terrain. He was led into a richly decorated chamber where Philip and Mary waited, seated on twin thrones, beneath cloths of estate. He delivered Ivan's greeting, his speech in Russian being translated into both English and Spanish, since King Philip had not learned English.

This audience was purely formal. Two days later, Napea was paid a secret visit at his lodging by two royal Councillors – the diplomat (and Bishop of Ely) Thomas Thirlby, and the suave and adroitly non-committal Sir William Petre, an investor in the Muscovy Company, who managed to serve Henry, Edward, Mary and then Elizabeth, with an intervening declaration of loyalty to Jane Grey, without ever suffering imprisonment or disgrace.

This was the negotiation which Ivan IV had been angling for ever since the English had first arrived at his northern shore. To his frustration, his early suggestion to Richard Chancellor that King Edward send a member of his Privy Council to talk with him had not been taken up. But by sending Napea to England, a high-level diplomatic discussion was made possible. Now, finally, Napea could raise Ivan's particular interest regarding the new northern sea route to England: not the exchange of trade goods, but the supply of materials and skilled individuals to assist in his conflicts both with the Muslim khans to his south and with the European states to his west and north-west.

This, certainly, is what agitated certain European courts, as their diplomats and spies sent back anxious letters about the visit of the Russian ambassador. Few worried that England had discovered a bountiful new source of wealth. Russia was not Cathay, and few believed it was. The fear was rather the other way around: that Russia might thereby have discovered a means of obtaining financial, commercial and military support that she had hitherto been denied.

In Moscow, from the start, Polish and other merchants were ordered to disrupt relations between the Tsar and the English. In July 1555, almost three months after the company's second voyage had left London, the Venetian ambassador in England reported an attempt by his Polish counterpart to influence the English government – who received, or thought he had, the assurance for which he asked:

> ... it having been promised him that for the future not only should this new Muscovite navigation not be permitted, but be forbidden under heavy penalties, the exportation hence to those parts of any sort of arms or military engine, in order that the Duke of Muscovy, who is always at war with his King, may not be able to avail himself of such instruments against him, which would have been much to his detriment.[8]

This promise, plainly, was disingenuous. Only a few months earlier Queen Mary had issued the charter of incorporation for which the company had been waiting, explicitly permitting trade with Muscovy as with other realms, and making no conditions about the nature of goods which could be exported.

With Napea's visit to London, concern grew among foreign observers who never doubted the Russian's intentions. 'There is now here an ambassador from the Muscovites', reported the new Venetian ambassador on 3 April, 'who demands a loan of ammunition and artillery, his lord being at war.' Immediately, he reported, a response had been provoked: 'another ambassador arrived from the King of Sweden, to prevent the grant of this demand, protesting that it would cause a rupture between his King and this Crown'.[9]

Whatever assurances were given to the representatives of other nations, the noises made to Napea himself, in his conversation with Thirlby and Petre, seem to have been wholly positive. In the formal letter to Ivan which the ambassador took back with him from Philip and Mary, no explicit reference was made to the supply of munitions. But it did state that all of Ivan's requests had been granted, and assured him that English 'artificers' – those skilled, for instance, in the manufacture of ships or guns – would be free to travel to Russia.[10]

From those states on the Baltic which feared that England might support Russia, a serious pre-emptive threat to English ships was anticipated, and one, evidently, had been promised. The instructions issued to the ships which took Napea back to Russia in the spring of 1557 cautioned against stopping at the Wardhouse, lest any:

> ... treachery, invasion, or other peril of molestation be done or procured to be attempted to our ships by any kings, princes, or companies, that do dislike this new found trade by seas to Russia, or would let & hinder the same: whereof no small boast hath been made: which giveth occasion of more circumspection and diligence.[11]

The following spring a company employee named Thomas Alcock was imprisoned in Poland en route home by land from Russia. His possessions were seized and searched, his money taken, and he was questioned at length about the goods his company had supplied to Russia. 'Thousands of ordnance', it was charged, had been shipped, 'as also of harnesses, swords, with other munitions of war, artificers, copper, with many other things'. Alcock denied it, but his claim that the only thing of military value provided was some outmoded chain mail was given little credence. Ambassadors from Danzig, Lübeck, Hamburg and Liefland (Livonia) united to persuade the Polish King to lead a naval expedition to prevent company ships sailing from England in future.[12]

Under Queen Mary, however, as well as under her successor Elizabeth, Tsar Ivan had found in England a willing source of military goods and expertise. Further entreaties from the Emperor (now Charles V's brother, Ferdinand) soon afterwards about the 'calamity' of allowing Russia to conquer the Livonian Confederation, dominated by a branch of the German 'Teutonic Knights', and which formed 'a sort of bulwark' for European states, were ignored.[13]

When Livonia did duly fall to Ivan soon afterwards, the English ambassador in Antwerp reported the word among the princes of Germany. They put it down entirely, he wrote, to 'the furniture of ammunition which the English sent to the Russians'.[14]

*

What general picture of England did Napea take back to the Russian court?

Perhaps the climate struck him as preferable. The winter in England (or in Scotland for that matter) was certainly nothing like it was in Russia, and he stayed long enough for early spring to bring a moderate temperature. In a report written the same month that Napea departed, the retiring ambassador from Venice, Giovanni Michiel, acclaimed the country's 'very temperate climate'. But this was no Eden, and Napea certainly had the chance to see as much.

Persistent wet weather – 'the greatest rain and floods that ever was seen in England' – had led to crop failures for the two preceding years, and with them came starvation and disease, a sign, for later writers, that God disapproved of the government's Catholic policies.[15] Widespread 'spotted' or 'great burning fevers', caused by famine or typhus, weakened immunity, and later that summer, and again the following year, an influenza epidemic took a terrible toll. Across the country from 1556 the rising death rate is reflected in a vast increase in the proving of wills.[16]

In England, Napea found a society scarcely less governed and shaped than was Russia by the Christian religion. It was practised here in a slightly different form, but the Russian attended numerous services and diplomatically declared his approval. He visited the revived monastery at Westminster Abbey to hear Mass, to dine with the abbot and to visit the tomb there of Edward the Confessor.[17] He took part in the celebrations and religious services for St George's Day (a saint whom, as a Russian, he revered no less than the English). He was in London over the Easter period, at a time when a return to old-fashioned devotional practices was encouraged, while other traditions continued, such as the series of public sermons given in the capital. On Easter Monday, some 20,000 people, including the Lord Mayor and the city aldermen, were said to have attended the 'sermon of old custom' at St Mary Spital, and Napea, very likely, was an honoured guest.

His impression could scarcely have been of a much less violent society. While he was resident in London not only were five heretics burned to death outside the city walls, watched by a great (and largely sympathetic) crowd, but eight 'felons' were hanged at Tyburn on 6 April, while on the same day seven men suffered the traditional penalty for piracy, hanged 'at the low watermark at Wapping ... for robbing on the sea', their corpses left suspended to be washed over by the incoming tide. Richard Chancellor, it should be remembered, had been struck by the relative clemency of the penal system in Russia. During Napea's final weeks in London a man named Thomas Stafford landed in the north, seized Scarborough Castle and proclaimed a rebellion against Mary's rule. On 30 April his capture was announced in London, and men of the city talked, no doubt, of little else. It was a few weeks after Napea left that he was beheaded on Tower Hill, quartered and hanged from a cart, 'and so', the diarist Henry Machyn jotted routinely, 'to Newgate to boil'.[18]

Preparations for war, moreover, were in evidence for Napea to see, just as they had been for Chancellor in Moscow a year earlier. For some time rumours of a new conflict with France had been gaining ground. Back in November 1555 the Venetian ambassador had reported that noblemen were cautiously stockpiling 'tents, pavilions, and similar military requisites'.[19] As the struggle between France and the Habsburg territories of Mary's husband Philip escalated, the royal couple exerted pressure on a reluctant English Council to get involved. In the early months of 1557 ships were refitted, and troops were mustered, under standards which combined the symbols of England and Castile.[20] While Napea was in London furious exchanges were taking place between Mary and her obstinate Councillors, who insisted that England was in no fit state to embark on a land war.

It was a month after Napea left when the war was finally declared which would lead to the demoralising loss of the last of England's territories on the European mainland: Calais.[21]

There was much about England, then, that was familiar, or at least readily comprehensible, to the visiting Russian. Among significant differences, though, was the nature of the city in which he temporarily resided. He might not have told Ivan as much, but the English capital plainly cherished its independence far more than Moscow did, and life there revolved much less around the monarch. The Venetian ambassador's report in May 1557 noted the way in which elected city aldermen ruled London 'almost like a Republic, neither the King nor his ministers interfering in any way', while the nobility 'all live in the country remote from the city'.[22]

The Russian ambassador was treated to a great deal of hospitality in the city which involved neither the monarchs nor the court. Merchants and aldermen came to call on him, and he was invited to dine with the Mayor and at 'diverse worshipful men's houses'. They showed him the sights of London. Some of them – 'the King's Palace and house, the Churches of Westminster and Paul's, the Tower' – would have seemed familiar enough in their basic purpose, while others, like the Guild Hall, or the Drapers' Hall, spoke of a civic, independent life which barely existed in Moscow.[23]

Merchants of the Muscovy Company continued to treat Napea lavishly throughout his stay. When he left, it was at Draper's Hall – home, prior to his fall from grace, of Thomas Cromwell – that they laid on a parting dinner for him. By the flickering light of countless candles, a cup of wine was raised and drunk to him on behalf of the company. An offer was made to cover all the expenses he had incurred since his ship was wrecked on the Scottish coast: 'a testimony and witness of their good hearts, zeal, and tenderness towards him and his country'.

In private, though, the merchants of the Muscovy Company had grown less than enamoured of their guest. Having liked him at first, they came to find him secretive and untrustworthy. A letter sent by the company's leading men to their agents in Russia declared that they did 'not find the Ambassador now at the last so conformable to reason as we had thought we should'. He is, they wrote, 'very mistrustful, and thinks every man will beguile him'. Assumptions were made about Russians in general, and instructions were modified accordingly:

> ... you had need to take heed how you have to do with him or with any such, and to make your bargains plain, and to set them down in writing. For they be subtle people, and do not always speak the truth, and think other men to be like themselves. Therefore we would have none of them to send any goods in our ships at any time, nor none to come as passengers, unless the Emperor do make a bargain with you ... for his own person.[24]

Sixty-One

On 1 May, as the city reeled and drank to mark the traditional May Day celebration, Thomas Thirlby and Sir William Petre, the Councillors who had visited Napea before, called again at his Fenchurch Street lodging. A week earlier Napea had taken his formal leave of Philip and Mary, but Thirlby and Petre brought with them formal letters from the King and Queen addressed to Tsar Ivan, 'very tenderly and friendly written', with the Great Seal of England attached. They also brought gifts, both for Napea personally and for his Tsar. Attendants conveyed them in a cart, exciting curious looks and shouts as it wheeled through the city streets.

To Napea was presented a heavy golden chain, a silver basin and ewer and some gilt flagons and pots. For Ivan, meanwhile, were brought fine samples of cloth, an ornate breastplate 'covered with crimson velvet and gilt nails', and a pair of lions.

With Richard Chancellor's death, it was Anthony Jenkinson who this time took charge of a fleet of four different ships. Again, rather desperately, the company urged them to remain together. If mist or bad weather made it hard to see, the admiral should 'make sound and noise by drum, trumpet, horn, gun or otherwise or means, that the ships may come as nigh together, as by safety and good order they may'.

Instructions were issued on 3 May 1557, witnessed and signed at a meeting of the company hierarchy on the same day. Most of the prominent men were there. But, for perhaps the first time, one central figure in the company was not present. Sebastian Cabot had still been actively involved – even joining in the dancing, and declaring his wish to travel too – when ships departed from London in 1556. By February 1557, however, when Anthony Hussey had succeeded him as governor, Cabot was clearly too ill or frail to fulfil his duties. No mention of him is made in the accounts of official celebrations during the time of Osip Napea coming to London.

We don't know where Cabot was living during his final months, but the scientist and translator Richard Eden, who had helped to promote the cause of commercial exploration in which Cabot had played such a prominent part, travelled to visit him as he lay mortally ill.

To the last, it seems, the old man was claiming mysterious knowledge that was uniquely his own. Drawing Eden close, he whispered that God had granted him a revelation. Now, he said, he understood the secret to a problem which had perplexed the finest minds of the time: that of measuring longitude at sea. Like others, Cabot had long thought it might be solved using the phenomenon of the variation of the compass. He was determined not to be foiled by old age – and dreamed, still, increasingly divorced from reality, of the ground-breaking discovery which would enshrine his name.[1]

Eden, no doubt, expressed appropriate interest and amazement. After the years that they had worked together, though, he knew Cabot well. He understood that this was just the fabrication of someone disposed to make himself the centre of attention. Cabot had done it for so long that by now he probably deceived himself. Even so, Eden plainly admired and liked the old man enormously, or he would scarcely have travelled now to pay his respects.

The encounter stayed with him. Many years later, he remembered it in the preface of one of his translations:

> Sebastian Cabot on his death-bed told me that he had the knowledge thereof [of longitude by variation] by divine revelation, yet so that he might not teach any man. But I think that the good old man in that extreme age somewhat doted, and had not, yet even in the article of death, utterly shaken off all worldly vainglory.[2]

In March that year Cabot drew his quarterly pension in person, but by May this had been re-granted jointly to him and another man, suggesting that, though alive, he was no longer well enough to do so.

In June and September it was drawn on his behalf, but by December, when it was not, the man who founded and inspired the venture from which the company trading with Russia had sprung must have died.[3]

Sixty-Two

After the fêting of Ivan IV's ambassador in London, the merchants of the Muscovy Company had managed to establish a new and regular trade through the seas of the north-east. But they had not achieved their original aim: to reach Cathay. For many, for some time, this motivation remained.

In 1555 the new company agents had been instructed to 'use all ways and means possible to learn how men may pass from Russia, either by land or by sea to Cathay'. And men who travelled further in search of it reported talk of a country 'civil & unspeakably rich'.[1]

In 1556, the year before Napea visited London and while Cabot still lived, Stephen Borough had embarked on a smaller boat, a 'pinnace', tasked with sailing north-east once more before pushing further beyond the White Sea in search of the fabled passage – along a coast which would begin to descend, as Robert Thorne and John Dee had confidently asserted, towards the warmth and wealth of the East. Failing that, the River Ob, emptying into the northern seas, might provide access to the inland regions of the Khan's great empire.

Borough, who had sailed in 1553 as Richard Chancellor's second-in-command, had departed from London on board the *Serchthrift* in the late spring. With the two larger ships of that year's voyage, carrying additional men to bring home the ill-fated vessels of Willoughby and Durforth, he had cast anchor at Gravesend. There, on 27 April 1556, Cabot, the venerable head of the company, had come on board the pinnace with a party of gentlemen and women. The old man had lost none of his passionate enthusiasm for further exploration and discovery: it was this, after all, rather than regular commercial activity, which had been his life and which was in his blood.

Having 'viewed our Pinnace', Borough wrote, 'and tasted of such cheer as we could make them aboard', the party had disembarked, handing the sailors generous tips as they did so. Poor men and women of the local community, meanwhile, had gathered at the water's edge to watch, and to these, as they clambered back onto dry land, 'the good old Gentleman Master Cabot' had given generous alms. As he did so he had asked them to pray, 'for the good fortune, and prosperous success of the Serchthrift'.

Later the company had gathered at a nearby inn, the 'Sign of the Christopher', named in honour of a saint revered by travellers for his assistance to those who attempted to cross hazardous waters. There they had banqueted and had drunk toasts to Borough and his companions. They 'made me, and them that were in the company', Borough recalled, 'great cheer'. Musicians had been summoned and dancing had begun, and before long younger men were gesturing to Cabot himself, seated, half-dreaming at the table, to join in.

In the headiness of the moment, the old man had been overcome. 'For very joy that he had to see the towardness of our intended discovery,' Borough recalled, 'he entered into the dance himself, amongst the rest of the young and lusty company.' Then, as night drew on, he and his friends had taken their leave, wishing the explorers good fortune and 'commending us to the governance of almighty God'.

Borough must have known then that, one way or another, he was unlikely to see Cabot again.

With his small crew of ten men, which included himself and his younger brother William, Borough crossed the North Sea on the *Edward Bonaventure*, their pinnace roped behind. After passing the North Cape they transferred to the *Serchthrift*, inching their way through thick mists, until a muffled blast of ordinance from the *Edward* signalled farewell.

Along the coast of Lapland they encountered fleets of Russian fishing boats, some of whose men they befriended – obtaining bread, oatmeal and dried fish in return for simple manufactured goods. One captain, named Gabriel, showed them 'very much friendship'. He was heading east in search of walrus and salmon and kept the Englishmen company, providing invaluable help. He struck the sails of his faster boat to wait for them, warned them of dangerous shallows, and guided them to shelter when a storm threatened. He also brought a young Samoyed man aboard, with an offering of four geese, whose clothing, as Borough noted, was 'strange unto us'. Later, with another Russian, he went on-shore to be shown a pile of Samoyed idols which appalled him: bloodied with sacrifice, and 'the worst ... work that ever I saw'.

Over subsequent weeks Borough sailed north-east, through the same Arctic waters that Sir Hugh Willoughby and his men had traversed three years earlier, but keeping careful track, this time, of their location. In the pinnace they were able to pass through shallows that would have been impossible in larger ships, causing the Englishmen to 'thank God that our ship did draw so little water'. Even so, they soon found that their way was hampered by 'great and terrible abundance of ice'. Huge sheets and blocks floated menacingly, accumulating, often, into a 'monstrous heap' that the sailors mistook at first for land.

Day after day strong winds blew, freezing rain and snow fell or thick enveloping mists descended, so that 'we were not able to see a cable's length about us'. Ropes encrusted and glistening with ice were fed through frozen hands. The mariners, Henry Lane later recalled, had to shovel snow from the pinnace in August.[2] One night a dreadful storm developed, worse than any they had encountered, though (as Borough wrote) they 'had endured many storms since we came out of England'. It seemed 'wonderful', he noted, 'that our bark was able to brook such monstrous & terrible seas'. On one occasion a great whale emerged suddenly from the water so close to the boat that they could have cut him with their swords: 'There was as much above water of his back as the breadth of our pinnace, and at his falling down, he made such a terrible noise in the water, that a man would greatly have marvelled except he had known the cause of it ...'. Knowing nothing of whales, the sailors shrank back in terror, not daring to assault this monster 'for fear he should have overthrown our ship'. Borough got his men to yell in unison from the side of the boat, until 'with the cry that we made he departed from us'. 'God be thanked,' Borough wrote, 'we were quietly delivered of him.'[3]

*

Borough was fastidious about recording his location and surroundings. His journal shows that he was a man in the mould of his former captain, Richard Chancellor, and that he had imbibed the strictures of their patron, Sebastian Cabot, about the importance of written records.

From the position of the sun, he took numerous measurements of their latitude, taking a small skiff ashore for this purpose whenever he could. He gave regular readings of the water depth, and used the wax-covered weight on his lead and line to take samples of the seabed, detailing the 'sand', 'broken winkle shells', 'soft black ooze' or 'tough ooze-like clay' that he brought to the surface. He carefully described the tides in relation to the position of the moon in the sky, or the 'sandy hills' of the shore when they were visible. And he recorded the curious phenomenon of 'the variation of the Compass'. All of it was information which would be of great help to subsequent sailors, and Borough's brother, William, with Stephen on the voyage now, would use it later to create a chart of these northern waters.

Eventually, though, by late August, signs of the advancing year became evident. 'The nights waxed dark,' Borough wrote, 'and the winter began to draw on with his storms.' He decided to return, with 'the first best wind that God should send', back to the shelter of St Nicholas. The following spring, he resolved, they could push further on towards the mouth of the Ob which might take them, if the coastal route would not, to the fabled realm of Cathay. But urgent word from London ordered him instead to search westwards, for the ships which, unbeknownst to Borough, had gone missing on their return to England the previous autumn.

He did not find them. From a 'Dutch-man' who had been at Trondheim, however, he heard that the *Philip and Mary* had wintered there, while the *Confidentia* was lost. He had, the Dutchman confessed, 'bought her sails for his ship'.[4] In the meantime, various factors deprived the search north-eastward of its immediate urgency.

For one thing, Borough had seen enough on his first expedition in the *Serchthrift* to be sure that it would not prove easy. For another, the death of Cabot in 1557 had removed one of the exploration's most influential advocates. Word had now reached the company in London, meanwhile, of the Tsar's successful conquest of the khanates on his southern borders, giving Russia secure access for the first time overland to the Caspian Sea.

A safe and preferable land route, it now seemed, might exist. Company merchants could use this to intercept the trade with Cathay and the East, before it was either interrupted by the Turks or claimed by southern Europeans who had dominated the western end of the 'silk road' at England's expense.

Anthony Jenkinson, like Chancellor, was not only a skilled navigator but possessed the character and self-possession to deal with kings and emperors. In his bearing, Eden commented, he seemed 'more like an Ambassador sent from any Prince or Emperor, than from a company of merchant men'.[5]

He did not find the overland route easy. The southern khanates were devastated by warfare, famine and plague. Unburied bodies lay in heaps. Access to China was difficult and would, he was told, take another nine months. 'Incessant and continual wars' in these 'brutal and wild countries', he was sorry to report, made it impossible at present to get through.[6]

He tried instead to develop a lasting trade in Persia, by a route which seemed to offer great promise for the English merchants. But Persia's on-and-off warfare with the Turks obstructed the route, and for the company hopes were continually raised and then frustrated.[7]

Sixty-Three

A ll the time, though, in Russia itself commerce was actively developed. Between 1555 and at least 1560 voyages were organised
annually, and they remained frequent for decades thereafter. The company felt its way, always anxious for information, discovering which
Russian products would sell at a profit in England, and vice versa.

In 1558 Russia conquered the Baltic port of Narva, providing another potential entry point for English merchants, though the company's
claim that its monopoly applied here too was disputed.

The letter sent back to Russia in 1557 referred to wax, tallow, train
oil, hemp and flax as the Russian wares which in England were 'most
vendible'.

Wax in particular was an early focus: much in demand in England,
not least by the government, which used it to seal letters and documents.
Chancellor had spoken after his first voyage of the 'cakes of wax' to be
found at Novgorod, Vologda, Plesco and elsewhere. Word of Russia's
abundance had been further spread by the translations of Richard Eden.
Russia's 'chief harvest', he wrote, 'consists of honey and wax', which were
'of small price' in Russia.[1] The region was so 'replenished with fruitful
bees' that great swarms were seen in the wild, 'hanging on the boughs
of trees'. 'We would you bought as much Wax principally as you may
get,' the agents were instructed: 'for if there be in that country so great
quantity, as we be informed there is, it will be the best commodity we
may have.'

Tallow – made from animal fat, and used, like wax, for candles – was
even more profitable, provided it was 'well purified' and so did not go
off.[2] (Some of it, the board complained early on, had arrived 'very evil,

black, soft and putrefied'.)[3] In 1560 the governors urged that they could sell a great deal more in England than was sent, and suggested their agents be willing to pay more: 'for we do most good in it'.[4] Train oil, too, made by the White Sea 'where our ships came in', was readily marketable for lamps and candles. Fill 'all such Butts and Hogsheads as may be found to serve', the governors instructed in 1557. But its resale value fluctuated. Three years later the company was lukewarm: 'the price', they noted, 'is not here so good as it was'. The oil was also prone to leaking if the casks were ill made, and caused terrible damage to other goods when it did, not least to the furs for which a cold region like Muscovy was also renowned.

'The north parts of Russia', Chancellor had confirmed to the company board, 'yield very rare and precious skins.' Animals, as Eden wrote, were hunted in winter, when 'their hair is then thicker'.[5] A skinner was sent from England to cast an eye over what was available and to judge what would sell well, and profitably. Chancellor had noted that the sables available in Russia were 'worn about the necks of our noblewomen and ladies'. But the experienced merchants on the company board urged that unless such expensive furs were of very good quality, they should be rejected in favour of others like marten or mink, which could be bought at a reasonable price and sold to a large market.[6]

There was certainly, in some quarters, a moral hostility to the importation of luxury goods, which led to what seemed a damaging loss of bullion, and to the distribution of such wares beyond the echelons who traditionally sported them. Many feared that the 'excess of apparel and the superfluity of unnecessary foreign wares' would promote 'the manifest decay of the whole realm'. So-called 'sumptuary' laws placed strict and increasing limits on the goods (and clothes in particular) permitted to certain classes of people, so that 'there may be a difference of estates known by their apparel after the commendable custom in times past'.

The company noted a 1559 proclamation which limited the wearing of sables to earls and those 'of superior degrees', along with viscounts and barons in their doublets and sleeveless coats. Unlawful garments were to be handed in.[7] There should not, the company sent word the following year, be 'great provision of any rich Furs'. A proclamation in England meant 'they will not be so commonly worn here as they have been with noble men'.[8] But this was testimony too to the appearance of a commercial mindset that was strikingly modern: the view that it was more profitable to ship cheaper goods which would appeal to a large market than luxuries which could interest only a narrow upper class. Rich furs were desired in 'no great plenty'. They were 'not every man's money'.

Tar and hemp were also good products in Russia, as were masts – cut from the vast, thick Russian forests – but it was quickly decided that the profits they would yield if brought to England in their raw form would not justify the expense of shipping. Instead, rope-makers were sent out to Russia. A rope-walk was constructed in Kholmogory, and native Russians were employed for the less skilled tasks.[9] Already, the advantages of manufacturing in a less developed economy (cheaper labour and a closer proximity to raw materials) were apparent. Five Russians, the company agent Richard Gray reckoned, would not cost as much as one Englishman sent to Russia, and they could certainly do the work of three.[10]

The first ropes were made not from hemp but from flax, which was also widely available, but they were quickly deemed inferior. As soon as they became wet, the governors complained, 'they will rot and moulder away like moss'. Good, well-tarred, hempen ropes, however, could be provided to both the English and European markets at prices which undercut the supply from the Baltic. Before long, the English navy was a substantial customer. In the 1580s over a quarter of its total expenses were for rope bought from the Muscovy Company.[11]

Needless to say, not all attempts to market Russian goods in England, or English goods in Russia, proved a success. In London the company could barely suppress its annoyance at the repeated shipping of seal skins. What, it demanded to know, were the agents playing at? 'We much marvel what you mean to buy Seal skins and tan them. All that you have sent in times past lie here unsold, and will yield no money.'[12]

Like other organisations of the time, the company prepared for the future by taking on apprentices. Ten young men who had worked for them in London were quickly sent out to Russia, to learn the language and become familiar with Russian culture and commerce. The agents were told to appoint them to whatever work seemed best suited, and to keep a vigilant eye on their progress and conduct.[13]

Younger boys, meanwhile, were taken on and given work experience in London. One, too young to be sent abroad among the first wave, was educated and looked after with more attention than most. He was an orphan, deprived of all his immediate family. His mother had died early. Both his brother and his father had drowned at sea. When, some years later, he was sent out to Russia, a letter to the agents mentioned that he had for years been an apprentice to the company in London. 'Our mind', the board declared, 'is he should be set about such business as he is most fit for: he has been kept at writing school long: he hath his Algorithm, and has understanding of keeping of books of reckonings.'[14]

The boy was called Nicholas, and he was Richard Chancellor's only surviving son. He had been particularly well nurtured and educated under the company's supervision in part, no doubt, because they hoped that he would follow in his father's illustrious footsteps. It was felt, too, that this was the least they should do for the orphan of the company servant and member to whom they all owed so much.

For many years afterwards Nicholas served the company as a merchant and purser, as well as sailing on other long-distance voyages (like those made by Sir Martin Frobisher to the north-west). He was never, perhaps inevitably, the outstanding man his father had been – but he took part in a subsequent attempt to find a north-east passage in 1580. Using sails, and oars when necessary, he battled with his companions against the 'extremity of ice' which hampered their progress and threatened, more than once, to trap them entirely. Like others before they were deceived into thinking that layers of arctic fog to their north were islands.[15] In spite of largely favourable winds, Chancellor wrote, which should have taken them beyond the northernmost land 'according to the estimate of those that gave us instructions of this said voyage', their difficulties only increased. The further they progressed towards what they assumed must be the open ocean, leading southward to Cathay, 'the thicker we find the ice, and small hope of a clear sea.'[16]

Nicholas Chancellor was lucky, at least, as his father, in 1556, had not been. He was on board the one ship (of two) which returned from the attempt safely, though winter was well set in by the time that they did so, and it was Christmas Day when his ship reached the mouth of the Thames.

*

The geography of the route, of course, was – as Stephen Borough, Nicholas Chancellor and others learned by experience – much less favourable in reality than men like John Dee had speculated.

Hopes remained, and were not abandoned until the early seventeenth century. Not until the nineteenth century did anyone succeed in navigating a 'passage', which was never viable commercially.[17] Nor did the River Ob allow access to sixteenth-century Ming dynasty China, though its major tributary the Irtysh does just cross the north-western border of modern China. Men had simply not appreciated the distances involved.

In Russia, though, in its first decade of operation, the English company established a substantial operation. It sold English goods, and bought Russian, all year round, with the focus being the annual arrival of ships from England at the White Sea. The substantial losses the company sustained in its very early years, caused by the wreck of ships with their goods, entailed calls for further investment by shareholders. Important members like Sir William Cecil made a careful note of each payment as it was made. But in the longer term there was reason for optimism that the company's 'business and traffic may take good success'.[18]

'Of an hard beginning', the company wrote, 'we trust God will send us a good ending.'[19] They were referring to teething problems for the rope-makers in Kholmogory, but the sentiment applied equally to the business in general.

Sixty-Four

For a time things only got harder. In England, 1558 was yet another year of change and unrest.

It began badly, when a large French army besieged and quickly took Calais, the final English territory in Continental Europe, whose loss was a grave blow to English pride. Henry Machyn jotted in his diary that it was 'the heaviest tidings to London and to England that ever was heard of'.[1] It reverberated also, for more pragmatic reasons, in the city's merchant community. Wool exports had been superseded by cloth as the country's economic mainstay, but nevertheless the loss of the 'Staple', as the old wool exchange in Calais was called, was very damaging. Queen Mary's already profound unpopularity with the political class deepened further.

At the end of January, Mary was sure once again that she was pregnant with an heir. She wrote in a letter to her husband that this consoled her for the loss of Calais, and he replied in accord. In March, as was customary for a noblewoman anticipating childbirth, she made her will, which included legacies for the restored religious houses (including her beloved Observant Franciscans at Greenwich). Few this time, however, shared her conviction, and the matter was kept quiet. Her own husband was doubtful. Embroiled in conflict on the European mainland, he sent a close ally to report back. By the late spring it was clear that she was again sadly deluded.

In the country at large the summer brought only further suffering. The harvest was bad once more. Mary's religious policy continued to be severe. Eleven were burned at Smithfield in June and some twenty more suffered the same fate before the year was out. The sickness which had tormented England in recent years returned and this time inflicted more devastation than ever. A new form of influenza affected almost half the country and caused the worst death rates of the sixteenth century, hitting the upper classes with particular venom, starting from the top.[2]

Mary's health was already bad. She suffered from chronic headaches and fevers. When she caught this virus in August, it sent her into a further decline. By the late autumn it was feared that she would not survive, and by mid-November she was accorded the last rites. On 17 November, early in the morning, she heard Mass in her privy chamber and soon afterwards she died.

England's first Queen Regnant had reigned for only a little over five years, to be followed by its second.

After accepting that she would not, in spite of all her fervent prayers and hopes, bear a child, Mary had been obliged to acknowledge that her successor would be the half-sister she bitterly resented. But it hurt.

In the presence of Elizabeth, this 'illegitimate child of a criminal', the retiring Venetian ambassador had written the previous year, 'it was as if [Mary] were in the presence of the affronts and ignominious treatment which she was subjected to on account of [Elizabeth's] mother [Anne Boleyn]'. With her own failure to produce an heir, moreover, she felt 'the eyes and hearts of the nation already fixed on this lady as successor to the Crown'. In public, the same ambassador wrote, Mary 'dissembles her hatred and anger as much as she can', but there was no hiding her feelings towards this half-sister who, if not beautiful, was tall and elegant where she was short, and who was proud, with fine eyes and a fine mind.[3]

In desperation, Mary had asked her sister not to alter the re-established Catholic religion, but she knew the request was in vain. If Elizabeth adopted the outward show of a Catholic, Mary realised that this was a front. In her will she could not bring herself to name Elizabeth, referring to her simply as 'my next heir and Successor'. When Mary's coffin was lowered into a vault at Westminster Abbey, the senior officers of her household snapped their white staves of office and threw them on top. The royal heralds then proclaimed Elizabeth as Queen.[4]

Two-thirds of Mary's Council were promptly removed, including all of the prominent Catholics. 'That Woman', as a Spaniard in England described Elizabeth to Mary's bereaved husband, ordered immediate changes in a Protestant direction. Once again the Lord's Prayer was said in English not in Latin. Her half-brother Edward VI's Book of Common Prayer was revived, albeit in a slightly modified and more conservative form. The lesser clergy were substantially untouched, but bishops were purged and replaced. Most of the ardent Protestants who had fled to mainland Europe on Mary's accession, and who had absorbed further radical ideas from reformers there, now returned.

In London church bells rang, while bonfires and street parties welcomed a new Queen, and a new direction.[5] Elizabeth herself might not have been dogmatic. There was, she said, only one Jesus Christ and the rest was a dispute over trifles. But she was an affirmed Protestant, and in the course of the next few decades it was this faith which finally established itself at the core of the English make-up.

One returning exile, John Foxe, condemned Mary vehemently and helped to establish the black reputation which has survived, only somewhat lightened, to this day. Her zealotry does not appeal to the modern mind, for all that she could also be loving and courageous, and though many of her enemies were equally zealous in another direction. Foxe wrote that he doubted any reign either in England or elsewhere had provided such good evidence of 'God's wrath and displeasure'.

A few years later, with any knowledge of events in Russia, he might have altered his opinion. If Mary was bloody, Ivan, truly, became terrible.

Sixty-Five

The terms that the company secured from Ivan IV were very favourable. To be granted a complete exemption from tariffs both into and within Russia, and a monopoly of the new northern trade route via the White Sea, gave them a significant competitive advantage. Ivan, however, had his own reasons for this beneficent treatment. Increasingly, he felt besieged by enemies, both on his borders and within his state. Everywhere he sniffed betrayal.

Over the winter which bridged the latter end of 1564 and the beginning of 1565, his dread of conspiracy and treason led Ivan to launch a prolonged campaign of terror which has appalled and puzzled historians ever since.

From a newly fortified monastery distant from Moscow, Ivan declared his absolute and divinely inspired authority both to distribute mercy and to inflict punishment. 'He who resists power', he declared, 'resists God.'

His justice was wielded, he said, with the sanction of heaven. Those he judged to have evil intentions should expect only 'fierceness and torment'.[1] When he returned to his capital in February his eyes were dim and haunted, while his thick hair and long beard had fallen out. Most historians attribute his intense paranoia to mental illness. He rejected his entire existing government and carved out an alternate, parallel state for 'his chosen side of his people', as the baffling development was described by English company men.[2] From this territory all those of high rank considered suspect were expelled, and a new and militant cadre was installed in their place.

The rule of these *oprichniki* – 'children of darkness', as some called them – was arbitrary and cruel. They carried long brooms to symbolise the sweeping of 'everything superfluous out of the land'. They wore black cloaks and rode black horses with the severed head of a dog dangling at their bridles.[3] They carried out the arrests and cruel executions not only of eminent men but of their entire families, including babies and young children, responding to anonymous denunciations which Ivan encouraged with the installation of a special letter box, 'box 200', at his court. In a pattern which would be repeated in subsequent terrors down the ages, men were denounced, and savagely and sadistically killed, in turn.[4]

In vain did nobles and princes protest that 'no Christian ruler had the right to treat human beings like animals'. Thousands died, while many more were stripped, often literally, and cast into exile.[5] Throughout the late 1560s the executions continued. When the English diplomat Thomas Randolph arrived in Russia in the autumn of 1568, he reported that Ivan had recently 'beheaded no small number of his nobility'. In his official report he was reserved, but in private letters he confessed he could not wait to fulfil his mission and to depart, 'the sooner to be out of his country where heads go so fast to the pot'.[6]

As if the 'miserable state of the country' caused by Ivan's policies was not enough, in 1571 a Tartar army took advantage of the absence of most Russian troops on campaign in the Baltic to descend on Moscow. When they set fire to the capital, high winds fanned the flames to a fury and the wooden city was devastated. Not one house, Anthony Jenkinson reported, was left standing. The residence occupied by the English merchants in Moscow was burned to the ground and most of the men who sought refuge in its cellar died.

In the city at large, few inhabitants escaped. Some were incinerated to powder. The bodies of countless others, as well as of horses, filled the streets. Two months would not be enough, wrote one English survivor, to clear the corpses. It was, Jenkinson could only conclude, 'a just punishment of God for such a wicked nation'. Sodom and Gomorrah, a fellow Englishman agreed, had not disappeared so quickly.[7]

'I pray God', wrote another, less righteously, 'I never see the like again.'

*

For the English merchants, not surprisingly, this whole period was dreadfully unstable. The northern region in which they traded was brought within Ivan's alternate, personal state. Vologda, with its company station, was taken over, while all its well-born men and their families were expelled. On the road from Vologda to Kholmogory Ivan built a new fortress: a remote refuge in the north which increasingly became his base. English artisans were employed to strengthen its fortifications and to build the ships on which Ivan could escape, if necessary, via the White Sea. The Tsar protected the houses and activities of the English company, but the country was in turmoil. Men who accompanied Randolph found 'the estate of the Company to stand very evil'.[8]

Added to the chaos in Russia was a violently changeable attitude on Ivan's part towards the company itself. He had always hoped that a close political relationship with England would follow on from the mercantile one, and indeed it was unrealistic of the English merchants to expect a monopoly and favourable privileges without there being a political price. In his increasingly paranoid state, Ivan became desperate for allies. Through Englishmen like Jenkinson and Randolph who came to Moscow, and Russian ambassadors who were sent to England, he sought a formal alliance, by which enemies of Russia would automatically become enemies of England and vice versa. He even made a secret, bewildering request for asylum in England should he need to flee his realm, which was granted, and he offered similar sanctuary for Elizabeth, though she insisted she would not require it.

Elizabeth was careful to avoid the tight military alliance that Ivan wanted. Too many enemies or potential enemies of Russia were rulers with whom she wished to be on good terms. She would support, he was told, his 'just causes', while she retained the right to judge the justness of any particular cause. English ambassadors were told to focus on securing privileges for the company while they skirted around his desire for political terms.

Ivan flew into a rage. These men, he complained, were sent only to deal with 'merchant's affairs', rather than with 'our highness' affairs'. All countries acknowledged, he insisted, that 'princes' affaires should be first ended, and only after that to seek a gain'.[9] The means of retaliation was at hand: he could cancel the privileges granted to the English company, and did so. More than once English ambassadors succeeded in having favourable terms reinstated, but Ivan expected a political alliance to follow, and when it did not he revoked them again, lambasting Elizabeth for governing 'like a maid', while really it was 'boorish merchants' who were in charge.

Anxious to placate Ivan without contracting damaging obligations, company ships evidently did deliver arms to Russia, as the Tsar's enemies in central and eastern Europe feared and alleged. Categorical evidence has not survived. But English letters to Ivan referred pointedly to the fact that he had been supplied with goods that 'her Majesty does not suffer to be transported forth of her realm to no other prince of the world'.[10] This statement did not refer to cloth.

Through all of these difficulties, trade continued, and it was profitable enough, or at least potentially profitable enough, to be worth the perseverance.

Already, by the mid-1560s, the company, or 'fellowship', was expanding its pool of investors: with some exaggeration perhaps, it then claimed to have 'above 400 persons' as shareholders.[11] Ten years later, one enthusiastic company merchant declared that with more stability and 'an assured amity' between the two nations, England and Russia, there would be 'a trade of merchandise of such importance for the benefit of England as never has been by any one trade'.

Certainly the new commerce opened up by the exploratory voyage of 1553 did not reap the kind of vast profits Cabot and his consortium of London merchants had dreamed about. For all the perennial promise of the Persian trade, accessed via Russia from the north, the company did not find a new and safe sea route to tropical islands, where the sun baked precious metals and stones in the soil while markets were stacked high with valuable silks and spices.

Richard Chancellor and his men did dine with a great emperor, from goblets and plates of gold, just as they had hoped they would do in Cathay. But the ground outside was thick with snow and most of the country was poor. The commodities they shipped home were more mundane: hemp or flax, oils from animals, or wax from bees.

The trade could make money, when ships with their goods were not lost. But it did not create instant fortunes, as had some of the Spanish or Portuguese voyages to the Americas or the East. Even so, its impact on English history is difficult to overstate.

Sixty-Six

In practical terms, the voyage of 1553 had opened up an important new route at a difficult time, when trade, as Thomas Edge later wrote, was 'waxing cold and in decay'.[1]

English commerce with Russia didn't rival the traditional routes to mainland Europe in terms of the quantities shipped. Most of those who invested in the Muscovy Company had other, more important commercial interests elsewhere. Substantial early losses cost them ships (initially often built by the company at great expense), goods and important individuals with skills and experience which were rare and hard to replace.

All the same, England entered into a significant trading relationship with a state that was less advanced, economically, than itself: the sort of relationship on which an empire would later be built.

Where cloth sold to the traditional markets of mainland Europe still went in a crude, undyed form, ready to be coloured and finished by skilled artisans on the Continent, to the more primitive Russian market it could be sold fully dressed – a significant spur to England's young manufacturing sector. This prompted the company to research products and techniques used elsewhere for dyeing. How did they do it in Persia? How in Russia? How elsewhere? Gradually, in response to this demand, a sophisticated finishing industry was developed.

By building up a significant rope-making business in Russia, moreover, near an abundant supply of the necessary raw materials, the company was able to take advantage of lower costs and to undercut other supplies. These, being in foreign hands, were of less economic benefit to England, and were dangerously unreliable in a time of conflict.

The novel way in which the Muscovy Company was set up led not only career merchants but other, more rarefied elements of society to participate. The joint stock nature of the business allowed men to invest without playing any active role – behaviour that had not been possible for members of earlier, regulated companies. It also capitalised, literally, on major changes in Tudor England which had left disposable income in the hands of a wider middle class, who flaunted their wealth, at times, and frittered it on luxuries, but who were also prepared to invest it.

The Muscovy Company was pioneering. Regardless of its profits, it was successful in that it inspired others to emulate its example – eating, often, into its business as they did so. Suddenly joint stock enterprises became relatively commonplace. The company's constitution was imitated by the so-called Company of Cathay which was set up (in the teeth of opposition from the Muscovy Company, which believed its own right was infringed) to look for a north-west passage, and under whose aegis Martin Frobisher launched his ultimately fatal attempts to find an alternative route to Asia. It was imitated too by the Eastland Company, which was established in 1579 to develop trade with Scandinavia and the Baltic. Two years later the Levant Company established a trade, on similar lines, with the eastern Mediterranean, forging a route to Turkey, Syria and Persia which supplanted the vulnerable commerce attempted for so long by the traders to Russia. At the end of December 1600, as Queen Elizabeth's long reign drew towards its end, a charter was granted to another, similar joint stock operation. Over time it grew and became particularly successful. Popularly, it soon became known as the East India Company.

In the trade of these chartered companies – granted monopolies by a crown which took an interest but was happy to leave such work to its private citizens – lay the practical and intellectual origins of the English and then the British Empire.

In the latter half of the sixteenth century ideas emerged, in embryonic form, which developed and established themselves at the heart of the imperial agenda. They were various and influenced by differing regional circumstances as well as by the political and cultural climate in England. Some seem now more admirable than others.

Sir Walter Raleigh believed in the importance of trade as the means by which England could become rich and powerful. But he was schooled in the Atlantic struggle with Spain, in particular, and favoured what he called 'forcible trade', backed by an aggressive navy and the acquisition of colonies and imperial territory: the sort of domination of primitive but resource-rich lands on which the Spanish Empire had been built. Countless others shared his approach, just as Sir Hugh Willoughby had done, after his battles with the French. This buccaneering spirit burgeoned in the reign of Elizabeth, and it reverberated down the ages. Many supported the establishment of an empire of settlement as well as trade. Even a writer like Richard Hakluyt, who generally favoured peaceful enterprise, hoped exploratory expeditions would use suitable regions in the north of Asia or America as dumping grounds for what he called 'the offals of our people'.[2]

The geographer and polymath John Dee, on the other hand, who advised the Muscovy Company on their explorations to the north-east, developed a vision of England at the centre of a peaceful web of trade, not looking to impose itself by force. It would make for the 'Honourable Renown of this Island Empire'. And over it a navy would police the seas 'in the most decent, peaceable, and friendly manner'.[3] Dee was certainly atypical. Some of his ideas were perplexing for most people, both at the time and later. But there is no doubt that trade to the East, which eschewed the undeveloped lands and relatively primitive civilisations of the American continent in favour of societies in Asia that were often rich and sophisticated, did foster a different, less confrontational approach. Sailing north-east, of course, also meant avoiding direct competition with the Spanish or the Portuguese on established routes. There might have been occasional threats from Swedes or Poles, but by and large there was not the same need to fight. It was not that the men as a group were better or more principled; often enough they were the same people. But the circumstances and the context were different.

Sebastian Cabot, the organiser and inspiration behind the 1553 expedition, plainly leant more towards Dee's view than to Raleigh's. Most of his own exploration had been to the west, to the new lands of the Americas, north and south, and his own career was not unchequered. But in the handbook which he wrote for the voyage that he initiated and oversaw as an old man, we hear a voice which is warm, contemplative and wise. He knew there was a limit to how much he could dictate. He was too old. He would not be there, and could not guess what problems or challenges might arise. 'Of things uncertain', he wrote, 'no certain rules may or can be given.' Misconduct by members of the crew was to some extent inevitable; and when it arose, it was to be 'chastened charitably with brotherly love'. Nevertheless, he had learned lessons from his own long experience which he was anxious to impart.

From other evidence it seems that humility was not always Cabot's strong point, but in this text – almost the only one in which his authentic voice survives – he comes across with dignity and restraint. Richard Hakluyt praised these 'excellent orders and instructions', and to this day they seem sensible and almost unobjectionable.

Cabot put his faith in knowledge which was accrued by first-hand experience of the world and then carefully recorded. He understood, as Francis Bacon would later observe, that knowledge was *power*.

The English could use it to create wealth, through trade, and this wealth in turn would raise England to the front rank of maritime nations. In pursuit of this greater awareness, men should listen, and observe, and not thrust themselves forward. He urged a practice entirely at variance with the Catholic zealotry he had witnessed in Spain: matters of religious faith and ritual should be kept under wraps. Sailors should seem, rather, 'to bear with such laws, and rites, as the place has, where you shall arrive'. In general the inhabitants of every region were to be treated 'with all gentleness, and courtesy', and shown 'no point or sign of rigour and hostility'.

Only his advice to get foreigners drunk as a means of obtaining information might now raise a disapproving eyebrow, though not because it was not sensible enough. In any case, any person who did come on board, voluntarily, was to be 'well entertained, used, and apparelled', and treated 'without violence or force', while women were not to be solicited or mistreated. This wasn't just common humanity. ('Consider you that they also are men', declared the letter signed by Edward VI, but drafted perhaps by Cabot or one who knew him well.) It also made mercantile sense, as the best means of encouraging others to show an interest in, and a lack of hostility towards, the English merchants. The reaction of Russians on the shores of the White Sea, well treated by Richard Chancellor, amply justified Cabot's advice.

Trade, always – a hard-nosed desire for profit – was the venture's predominant aim. It was a search both for new sources of supply and for new markets. Certainly Cabot and the other leading members of the company allowed themselves to imagine the vast returns achieved by the Iberians. They saw, as Clement Adams wrote, 'that the wealth of the Spaniards and Portuguese, by the discovery and search of new trades and countries, was marvellously increased' and they wistfully supposed 'the same to be a course and means for them also to obtain the like'. Cabot, in his instructions, seems to have anticipated the discovery of 'jewel, stone, pearls, precious metals'. People collecting such gold or stones along the seashore should be carefully approached and observed, he advised, in pinnaces from which enchanting music was played and sung.[4]

Unlike these imagined, innocent natives, the men and women encountered on the shores of the White Sea extracted salt, or caught and clubbed seals, rather than panning for gold. But no sense of disappointment survives at what Russia had to offer. Certainly, the hope did not die that a route might be found to Cathay. Still – train oil or wax could be traded for a profit just like cloves or pearls, and the business was energetically pursued.

In the longer term, Spanish Imperial affluence did not endure. Bullion might pay for the adornment of individuals. It might even pay the salary of armies. But it offered no lasting national advance, no impetus to manufacture: the gold and silver fell on Spain like rain and it drained away. Russia, however, was a good market for manufactured English cloth which could be exchanged for raw materials. This secured the industry and encouraged its advance.

In England, organised mercantile exploration began in 1553.

Had all three ships that year been lost, there would probably have been no sequel – not, at least, in the short term. The arguments for a venture to the north-east would have seemed discredited. As it was, a body of opinion among merchants in London had been dubious about putting money into a scheme some experts gave little chance of achieving its goal. Had it failed, such mutterings would have become impossible to dampen.

One ship, though, did make it into the White Sea. It established a new trading relationship with Russia which meant that, even though the expedition had failed in its primary aim, it could overall be deemed a success. And it made, as a result, a huge impact on the course of English history. All of this was owed substantially to one man.

It was Sebastian Cabot who had inspired the voyage and set its parameters. But he was too old now for adventurous travel into the unknown. He needed someone who reminded him of his younger self. It had been made clear to him, moreover, that the English government wanted to foster a genuine culture of trade and exploration, and to reduce the country's dependence on foreign merchants and foreign sailors. On previous long-distance voyages England had employed experts from abroad as pilots and navigators. This time the temptation was reduced, since no Portuguese or Frenchman could claim to know the north-eastern route as they did, say, the sea journeys to west Africa or south America. More importantly, though, if there was to be a shift in the national culture, it needed to be led by an Englishman: a man who could combine, for almost the first time in the country's history, the practical experience of a sailor with the academic gifts of a 'cosmographer' and a mathematician. English sea captains, in days gone by, had often not been literate. Now they wanted a scientist.

For years, Cabot had held a senior post in Spain's transatlantic empire. He had been responsible for examining and granting qualifications to young pilots. He knew what he was looking for. On his return to England he had been heartened to find a number of talented and ambitious young pilots and mariners, the first shoots of a significant shift in the maritime culture. One of them, though, stood head and shoulders above the rest. In the shape of a young man brought up in his old seafaring community of Bristol, inspired as a child – one can guess – by stories and memories of his own famous exploits sailing west into the Atlantic, Cabot found what he wanted.

Richard Chancellor impressed all who knew him: from the nobleman in whose household he had lived, to the great mathematician and geographer who worked with him to prepare charts for the voyage, which listed the positions of the sun and the stars. Richard Eden, who knew him well, hailed the 'excellent young man Richard Chancellor no less learned in all mathematical sciences than an expert pilot'.[5] His talents and reputation created a buzz of excitement among the London merchants who worked with Cabot to organise the venture. On their hands, it seemed, was a man who could make a difference. With the possible exception of Cabot himself – who for most of his career had lived and worked in Spain – Chancellor was the first Englishman to master the techniques of ocean-going navigation, by which the Spanish and the Portuguese had tamed the vast stretches of water separating themselves from the distant Indies.

Chancellor embraced what now seems a modern and scientific way of thinking, which gradually took root in England during the latter half of the sixteenth century. Like his mentor, he believed that assertions should be supported by evidence from the senses: that observation, as Cabot had put it, was the 'most certain Master of all worldly knowledge'. Whether it was the regions of the world where human habitation was possible, or the thickness of the walls of the Kremlin, both men believed that personal experience – not hearsay, or ancient authority, or reason cocooned from the world – was what counted. It was a fundamental mental shift, and was the bedrock on which the modern scientific revolution has been built. As it has been put, 'experiment came to seem preferable to miracle, evidence to belief, change itself to the status quo'.[6]

This general philosophy applied in exploration just as it applied to learning about how the world, or indeed the universe, worked. Commerce, and science, advanced together. It is enough to recall that John Dee, the scholar who stands astride a line dividing the medieval and modern worlds, paid fulsome tribute late in life to a man he still fondly remembered as the 'incomparable Richard Chancellor'.

With the help of Stephen Borough, his second-in-command on the *Edward Bonaventure* – a man in the same mould, who built on Chancellor's achievement – the new route to the north-east was meticulously recorded and mapped. In what was the first great age of English map-making, people in Tudor England had come to understand that accurate knowledge of the world, recorded in maps, would lay the foundations for political and commercial power. For the first time geography was put on a scientific footing, and once again the voyage of 1553 was a decisive turning point. By inspiring further exploration, it helped to inculcate this new empirical mode of thought. A little later it was Francis Bacon, again, who noticed the crucial connection: the 'proficiency in navigation and discoveries' which by then was apparent, he wrote, 'may plant also an expectation of the further proficiency and augmentation of all sciences'.

It was Chancellor who led the way, and who should today be remembered much more than he is. Dee was an admirer and a friend, rather than an impartial witness. He greatly missed the man he called his 'dearly beloved Richard Chancellor'. But he was right, all the same, that this was someone 'worthy of eternal good fame and grateful memory'. Tragically, Chancellor died while still young, attempting, successfully, to save the life of an important passenger with whom he had been entrusted. Francis Godwin, the Bishop of Hereford, spoke truly when he said that the company's loss of a ship and its goods was 'a Trifle, compar'd to that of Richard Chancellor, worthy of Immortal Memory'.[7] Had he not died when he did, he would surely have gone on to greater achievements and to greater renown. Where he led, others, like Sir Martin Frobisher or Sir Francis Drake, more famous and more celebrated, followed.

It was Richard Chancellor, wrote a man who had known him, who was 'the odd [by which he meant outstanding] man of his Time, for matters touching the Sea'.[8] He might perhaps have added that the matters he touched extended further, from the sea onto dry land – to the hearts and minds of many of those who knew him, and to those of many more who did not.

Notes

Introduction

1 Hamel, *England and Russia*, pp. 87–8. Henry Lane records that Willoughby et al. were found by Russian fishermen in the summer of 1554 in his letter to William Sanderson, Hakluyt, *Principal Navigations*, 2, p. 265.

2 Today this is the northern coastal region of China.

3 Taylor, *Tudor Geography*, p. 9.

4 Arber, *First Three English Books*, p. 43.

5 Arber, *First Three English Books*, p. 9.

6 DNB. Taylor, *Original Writings and Correspondence of the two Richard Hakluyts*, 2, p. 369.

7 DNB. Quote in Crone, 'Richard Hakluyt, geographer', in D.B. Quinn (ed.), *The Hakluyt Handbook*, p. 10.

8 Hakluyt, *Principal Navigations*, 1, p. 243.

Chapter One

1 The tide's range here is larger than anywhere else in Europe.

2 On the background to this story see Williamson, *The Cabot Voyages* and Jones, 'Alwyn Ruddock'. There is also a good short summary in the article on Sebastian Cabot by R.A. Skelton in the *Dictionary of Canadian Biography Online*.

3 Precisely what Bristol mariners had discovered before Cabot is hotly debated, and is unlikely, barring new evidence, to be resolved. Perhaps they had already found a mainland, but if so it was kept a closely guarded secret. Why else was such a fuss made of Cabot in London after his return? See Quinn, *England and the Discovery of America*, p. 13 and the short summary in I. Wilson, *John Cabot and the Matthew*, pp. 11–13.

4 The explorer was Sir Humphrey Gilbert. Quinn (ed.), *Voyages and Colonising Enterprises*, p. 134.

5 See Latham, *The Travels of Marco Polo*, p. 130 and pp. 243–4. As Williamson notes, Polo's exaggerated picture of Japan was 'his greatest error' (*The Cabot Voyages*, p. 88). In general, on European dreams of Asia see for instance Abulafia,

The Discovery of Mankind, pp. 24–30.

6 See the map of currents in Johnson and Nurminen, *History of Seafaring*, p. 29.

7 Varied estimates of the size of the earth's circumference were at the heart of the matter. See Quinn, *England and the Discovery of America*, p. 26.

8 Henry VII listened to the pitch made by Columbus' brother, Bartholomew: Quinn, *England and the Discovery of America*, pp. 76–7.

9 Jones, 'Alwyn Ruddock', pp. 231–6.

10 Quotes from Eden, *The Decades of the newe worlde*, in Arber (ed.), *First Three English Books,* p. 288.

11 The ambassador Puebla's letter is known from the surviving reply from Ferdinand and Isabella. Williamson, *The Cabot Voyages*, p. 48.

12 Williamson, *The Cabot Voyages*, pp. 52–3. The original document is in the National Archives, Treaty Roll 178, membr.8. http://www.bris.ac.uk/Depts/History/Maritime/Sources/1496cabotpatent.htm

13 Jones, 'Alwyn Ruddock', p. 242. Williamson, *The Cabot Voyages*, pp. 208–10. Wilson, *John Cabot*, pp. 32, 39.

14 Ruddock may have been dismissive of the sum, but it was perhaps around £5,000, equivalent, Jones points out, to two years' earnings for a common labourer, and Cabot had struggled financially: Jones, 'Alwyn Ruddock', pp. 229–30.

15 Hay (ed.), *The Anglica Historia of Polydore Vergil*, pp. 116–17, this extract of which is printed in Williamson, *The Cabot Voyages*, pp. 224–5. Williamson summarises the evidence in pp. 54–115. Alwyn Ruddock claimed to have found evidence that Cabot had returned, and had died shortly afterwards, but she didn't publish it before her own death and it has not been discovered since. Given that Vergil arrived in England in 1502, only a few years after Cabot's purported return, as a deputy for the same papal tax collector who backed Cabot, and then held an ecclesiastical position in the West Country (albeit largely an absentee one), it would be surprising if he was not aware of this. On Vergil see W.J. Connell, 'Vergil, Polydore' in DNB.

Chapter Two

1 On Sebastian's north-western voyage of 1508–9 see Williamson, *The Cabot Voyages*, pp. 145–72.

2 Deane, 'The Mappemonde of Sebastian Cabot', p. 63.

3 Eden, *The Decades of the newe worlde*, in Arber (ed.), *First Three English Books*, p. 288.

4 See A. Ruddock, 'The Reputation of Sebastian Cabot', p. 97 and generally.

5 The quotation is from a well-informed Venetian account of 1536, quoted in Quinn, *England and the Discovery of America*, p. 142.

6 See Bratchell, 'Alien Merchant Communities in London 1500–1550'.

7 Hakluyt, *Principal Navigations*, Epistle Dedicatorie in the first volume of the second edition: Vol. 1, p. 16. See Parker, *Books to Build an Empire*, chapter 3.

8 Williamson, *Maritime Enterprise*, pp. 19, 37–9.

9 Arber (ed.), *First Three English Books*, p. 288.

10 Quinn, *England and the Discovery of America*, pp. 144–5.

Chapter Three

1 Pike, *Aristocrats and Traders*, p. 23. D. Loades, 'Sebastian Cabot', DNB. Thomas, *Rivers of Gold*, p. 204 and chapter 38, pp. 458–74. Elliott, *Empires of the Atlantic World*, pp. 109–11. The formal organisation of two annual fleets, though, began in the mid-sixteenth century.

2 On the English émigré community in Seville see H. Dalton, 'Negotiating Fortune: English Merchants in Early Sixteenth-Century Seville', and on Bristol trade in general, Harris Sacks, *The Widening Gate* and Lobel and Carus-Wilson, 'Bristol'.

3 'Book of Robert Thorne', Hakluyt, *Principal Navigations*, 1, p. 229. Thorne's father was a leading Bristol merchant who had also crossed the Atlantic. On the Thornes see DNB articles, Williamson, *Maritime Enterprise*, pp. 259–62, and Nicholls, 'The Royal Grammar School of Bristol, and the Thorns, its Founders'.

4 Taylor, *Tudor Geography*, p. 49.

5 On the office see Rubio, *El Piloto Mayor*, Haring, *Trade and Navigation*, pp. 21–45 and Lamb, 'Cosmographers of Seville: Nautical Science and Social Experience'. Cabot's Spanish career is discussed in Sandman and Ash, 'Trading Expertise: Sebastian Cabot between Spain and England'.

Chapter Four

1 See R.C.D. Baldwin, 'Robert Thorne the younger', DNB, and Nicholls, 'The Royal Grammar School of Bristol, and the Thorns, its Founders'. On the history of maps see Shirley, *The Mapping of the World*.

2 Thorne's letter to Lee is in Hakluyt, *Principal Navigations*, 1, pp. 216–31.

3 Barlow, *Brief Summe*, p. 180. Woolley, *The Queen's Conjuror*, p. 102.

4 Hakluyt, *Principal Navigations*, 1, p. 228. Pierre d'Ailly, early in the fifteenth century, wrote that to the north-east of Iceland was 'a region uninhabitable on account of the cold'. Quoted in Quinn, *England and the Discovery of America*, p. 64.

5 On Thorne's map see Skelton, *Explorers' Maps*, pp. 99–100.

6 Taylor, *Tudor Geography*, p. 11.

7 Hakluyt, *Principal Navigations*, 1, pp. 212–16.

8 Connell-Smith, 'English Merchants Trading to the New World in the Early Sixteenth Century', pp. 61–2.

Chapter Five

1 On *The Saviour* see Jones, 'The Bristol Shipping Industry in the Sixteenth Century', pp. 232–5. The ship was later rebuilt not newly built, as R.C.D. Baldwin implies in his DNB article on the Thornes.

2 See Taylor, 'Roger Barlow: A New Chapter in Early Tudor Geography'.

3 Eustace Chapuys to the Queen of Hungary, 26 May 1541: Gairdner and Brodie (eds), *Letters and Papers, Foreign and Domestic, Henry VIII*, Vol. 16 (1540–41), pp. 409–10. It has been suggested, in Bradley, *British Maritime Enterprise*, p. 247, for example, that the foreign pilot from Seville might have been Sebastian Cabot. But this cannot be right. The prolonged absence from his post of Spain's Pilot Major would certainly have provoked comment.

4 On Dudley see Loades, *John Dudley, Duke of Northumberland* and his article in DNB.

5 See the report of Marillac, the French ambassador, in E.T. Hamy, 'Jean Roze, Hydrographe Dieppois', pp. 232–3. Cited in Taylor, *Tudor Geography*, p. 64.

Chapter Six

1 On all of this see Sandman and Ash, 'Trading Expertise: Sebastian Cabot between Spain and England' and Lamb, 'Science by Litigation: A Cosmographic Feud'.

2 Wyatt to Philip Hoby, Add. MS. 5,498, f. 8. Cited in Williamson, *Maritime Enterprise*, p. 308.

3 Skelton, 'Sebastian Cabot'. Beazley, *John and Sebastian Cabot*, p. 166. Williamson, *Maritime Enterprise*, p. 308.

4 François van der Delft to the Emperor, 28 May 1549: Hume and Tyler (eds), *Calendar of Letters, despatches and state papers ... Spain. Vol. 9: 1547–1549*, pp. 372–83.

5 Emperor to van der Delft, 18 January 1550. Van der Delft to the Emperor, 31 January 1550. Quoted in Quinn, *England and the Discovery of America*, p. 153.

6 See the National Archives converter, which produces values for 2005: www. nationalarchives.gov.uk/currency, and at www.measuringworth.com

Chapter Seven

1 It is generally accepted that he was born in or not much before 1484. See Skelton, 'Sebastian Cabot'.

2 Harris Sacks, *The Widening Gate*, p. 30.

3 Harris Sacks, *The Widening Gate*, p. 24.

Chapter Eight

1 Harris Sacks, *The Widening Gate*, p. 29. Stow, *Survey of London*, p. 12.
2 Jordan (ed.), *The Chronicle and Political Papers of King Edward VI*, pp. 12–13.
3 Loades, *Duke of Northumberland*, p. 120 (citing Jordan, *Edward VI*, p. 445).
4 Loades, *Duke of Northumberland*, p. 161.
5 Loades, *Duke of Northumberland*, p. 146.

Chapter Nine

1 Sir William Pickering, quoted in Crane, *Mercator*, p. 164; Deacon, *John Dee*, p. 23; French, *John Dee*, pp. 22–4.
2 Act against Sorcery 1542 repealed 1547. Gibson (ed.), *Witchcraft and Society*, p. 2. K. Thomas, *Religion and the Decline of Magic*, pp. 280, 292. Woolley, *The Queen's Conjuror*, pp. 11–16.
3 Feingold, *The Mathematicians' Apprenticeship*, pp. 35–6. A mathematical examiner was tasked to question pupils for one hour daily on the public lectures of the schools, to discourse with pupils when no public lectures took place, and to deal three times a week with pupils who found the lectures too difficult. See also C. Cross, 'The English Universities, 1553–58', in Duffy and Loades, *The Church of Mary Tudor*, pp. 57–76. Dudley was the university's Chancellor.
4 French, *John Dee*, pp. 29–30.
5 Waters, *Art of Navigation*, pp. 78–9, p. 84 note 1.
6 On this map see Deane et al., 'February Meeting, 1891: Cabot's Mappe-Monde'. Hakluyt, *Principal Navigations*, 7, p. 194 (this reference is to the 12-volume 1903 Maclehose edition). Beazley, *John and Sebastian Cabot*, p. 253.
7 Gilbert, 'A New Passage to Cataia', in Quinn (ed.), *Voyages and Colonising Enterprises*, pp. 139–40, 147. Gilbert's essay exists now in the form in which it was published in 1576, but was written by 1566. See ibid., p. 8. On the world map which was published with it, based on the Ortelius world map of 1564 see Skelton, *Explorers' Maps*, p. 120. On it there is a clear and viable passage north of America.
8 Deane et al., 'February Meeting, 1891: Cabot's Mappe-Monde', p. 339.

Chapter Ten

1 Deane et al., 'February Meeting, 1891: Cabot's Mappe-Monde', p. 309.
2 Hakluyt, *Principal Navigations*, 3, p. 12. Bodenham did also remember the shipwright Matthew Baker.
3 See Skidmore, *Edward VI*, p. 227 on the control over Edward which Dudley exerted via Sidney.
4 Waters, *Art of Navigation*, p. 15.

5 William Borough. Quoted in Taylor, *Tudor Geography*, p. 97.

6 Sandman and Ash, 'Trading Expertise: Sebastian Cabot between Spain and England', p. 821.

7 Taylor, *Tudor Geography*, pp. 89–91.

Chapter Eleven

1 Scheyfve replied to d'Eecke's concern in a letter to the Queen Dowager, dated 24 June 1550. Tyler (ed.), *Calendar of Letters, despatches and state papers ... Spain. Vol. 10: 1550–1552*, pp. 108–18.

2 Incorrectly transliterated 'Ireland', see Taylor, introduction to Barlow, *Brief Summe*, p. lv.

3 Scheyfve to the Queen Dowager, 24 June 1550.

4 Advices of Jean Scheyfve, Jan. 1551.

5 Taylor, introduction to Barlow, *Brief Summe*, p. liii.

6 Taylor, introduction to Barlow, *Brief Summe*, p. lv.

7 Quoted in Taylor, *Tudor Geography*, p. 93.

Chapter Twelve

1 See also, for instance, the map made by Jean Rotz for Henry VIII in 1542, on which northern Asia is completely blank. See H. Wallis (ed.), *The maps and text of the Boke of Idrography presented by Jean Rotz to Henry VIII, now in the British Library*.

2 Willan, *Early History*, p. 2.

3 Andrews, *Trade, Plunder and Settlement*, pp. 7–8.

4 Williamson, *Maritime Enterprise*, chapter 7. Stow, *Survey of London*, p. 32.

5 On the preponderant involvement of merchants with Iberian interests see Andrews, *Trade, Plunder and Settlement*, p. 20.

6 Latham, *The Travels of Marco Polo*, pp. 329–32.

7 Hakluyt, *Principal Navigations*, 'Epistle Dedicatorie to Sir Robert Cecil', 1, p. 44.

8 As there had been, of course, until about 10,000 years ago, and which allowed the first humans to populate America.

9 Crane, *Mercator*, pp. 138, 233.

10 Letter to Richard Hakluyt of 1580. Quoted in Crane, *Mercator*, p. 276.

11 Hakluyt, *Principal Navigations*, 1, p. 267.

Chapter Thirteen

1 Hakluyt, *Principal Navigations*, 1, p. 267. Willan, *Muscovy Merchants*, pp. 28–9.

2 On John Cabot's second voyage, Henry VII provided one of the five ships. The

others were provided by private merchants. Williamson, *The Cabot Voyages*, pp. 95–115.

3 Hakluyt, *Principal Navigations*, I, pp. 267–8.

4 Hakluyt, *Principal Navigations*, I, p. 247. Willan, *Muscovy Merchants*, p. 7. Cabot himself was perhaps more realistic. His ordinances forbade private trading until company business had been completed: Hakluyt, *Principal Navigations*, I, p. 237 (article 21).

5 Willan, *Muscovy Merchants*, pp. 6–7.

6 Willan, *Muscovy Merchants*, p. 22.

7 Over £5,000 in the money of 2005 according to the National Archives converter.

8 Willan, *Muscovy Merchants*, pp. 9–21.

9 Arber (ed.), *First Three English Books*, p. 6.

10 Willan, *Early History*, p. 41.

11 Russell was born around 1485, so was about 68 in 1553. He died early in 1555. It was his son, Francis Russell, the 2nd Earl who is mentioned some years later as having a copy of Cabot's map hung in his manor at Chenies, perhaps inherited from his father. Cecil also recorded his payment (Willan, *Early History*, p. 41).

12 Hakluyt, *Principal Navigations*, I, p. 239.

Chapter Fourteen

1 Scammell, 'European Seamanship in the Great Age of Discovery', p. 358.

2 Loades, *Tudor Navy*, p. 94.

3 Loades, *Tudor Navy*, pp. 94–5.

4 The standard measure of the size of a ship, the 'ton', was one of volume not of weight, and referred originally to a 'tun', the largest standard cask of wine. When used in reference to ships, therefore, the measure indicated initially the number of tun casks it could carry. In fact the derivation was the same, because a tun of wine – 256 gallons – weighed close to a ton.

5 Mayers, *North-East Passage*, pp. 29–31.

6 Loudon, *Arboretum et Fruticetum Britannicum*, Vol. 3, p. 1380.

7 Loades, *Tudor Navy*, p. 87. Morris, 'Naval Cordage Procurement in Early Modern England', p. 90 *passim*.

8 Oppenheim, *Administration*, p. 103, cited in Loades, *Tudor Navy*, p. 154. Morris, 'The Rise of the English Sailcloth Industry 1565–1643'.

9 Scammell, 'European Seamanship in the Great Age of Discovery', p. 360. Block, *To Harness the Wind*, p. 41.

Chapter Fifteen

1 Hakluyt, *Principal Navigations*, I, pp. 266–93.

2 In the will of Sir Hugh's half-brother, Sir John, proved in January 1548–9, mention is made of 'my niece Rose, daughter of my brother Hugh'. In the Wollaton accounts there is also mention of 20*l.* a year paid to Henry, son of Sir Hugh. See the article on Sir Hugh Willoughby by John Knox Laughton in the previous edition of the DNB edited by Sir Leslie Stephen and Sir Sidney Lee.

3 During the recent war with Scotland, John Dudley had regretted that it was impossible to find well-born men to lead all of Henry's many ships. 'As concerning the mean ships,' he wrote, 'I know no other way … but to place them with mean men to be their captains': Loades, *Tudor Navy*, p. 102.

4 Scheyfve to the Emperor, 7 March 1553 (Tyler (ed.), *Calendar of Letters, despatches and state papers … Spain. Volume II: 1553*, p. 14). It has often wrongly been suggested that Willoughby had no naval experience at all, but it is true, as Willan writes, that 'there is no evidence that he knew anything of seamanship' (*Early History*, p. 3). Emphasis to Adams' quotation added.

5 Arber (ed.), *First Three English Books*, p. 288.

Chapter Sixteen

1 Quoted in Ash, *Power, Knowledge and Expertise*, p. 112.

2 Couper and Henbest, *The Story of Astronomy*, pp. 42, 86. Richey, 'Astronomy and Astrology', pp. 49–51.

3 The Latin extract is printed in Taylor, *Tudor Geography*, p. 253 (*scipsisse* being a misprint for *scripsisse*). I am very grateful to Alexander Evans for his help with Latin translation. See also J.C. Warner (ed.), *John Bale's Catalogue of Tudor Authors*, p. 333, which notes that Chancellor is 'said to have written much on *astrologia*'.

4 Crossley (ed.), *Autobiographical Tracts*, p. 5.

5 Dee, *Compendious Rehearsal*, and Thomas Digges, *Alae seu Scalae mathematicae*, the relevant extracts of which are quoted in Taylor, *Tudor Geography*, pp. 253–6. The *Compendious Rehearsal* is in Crossley (ed.), *Autobiographical Tracts of John Dee*. See also R. Julian Roberts, 'John Dee' (DNB). Transversals had been invented earlier by Levi ben Gerson, but Chancellor invented them independently.

6 See Mayers, *North-East Passage*, pp. 100–1 and references.

7 Crossley (ed.), *Autobiographical Tracts of John Dee*, p. 28. See Richey, 'Navigation: Art, Practice and Theory', p. 509.

Chapter Seventeen

1 For Adams' account of the meeting see Hakluyt, *Principal Navigations*, 1, pp. 269–70.

2 Adams was mistaken about the date. As Willoughby's log records, the ships left on 10 May, and no doubt this was the deadline set.

Chapter Eighteen

1 He is also listed as Richard Stafford. One name, clearly, was a mistake.

2 Williamson, *The Cabot Voyages*, p. 47.

3 Willan, *Early History*, pp. 3–4.

4 Fury, 'Health and Health Care at Sea', p. 211.

5 On the Anthony Roll, the *Lartique*, smaller at 100 tons than two of the three expedition vessels, carried fifty-two mariners, eight gunners and eighty soldiers, making a complement of 140 men.

6 Scammell, 'Manning the English Merchant Service', pp. 131–2.

7 Morison, *European Discovery*, p. 134.

8 Scammell, 'Manning the English Merchant Service', p. 134.

9 Sir Henry Sidney, in Clement Adams' account of his speech: Hakluyt, *Principal Navigations*, 1, p. 269.

10 At a high level, gunnery, like navigation, was increasingly scientific. As well as the chemistry and physics which went into the design of powder and of cannon, ability at maths helped the artilleryman aiming the piece. In general, though, a more haphazard, trial and error approach to shooting prevailed. See Scammell, 'Manning the English Merchant Service', p. 151.

11 Hakluyt, *Principal Navigations*, 1, pp. 248 and 268.

12 Richard Morgan was the cook on the *Esperanza*, Thomas Hante on the *Confidentia*.

13 Burwash, *English Merchant Shipping*, p. 36.

14 James Watt, 'Some forgotten contributions of naval surgeons', p. 753.

15 Fury, 'Health and Health Care at Sea', *passim*.

Chapter Nineteen

1 The ordinances are to be found in Hakluyt, *Principal Navigations*, 1, pp. 232–41.

2 Roger Barlow, who accompanied Cabot to the Plata estuary, had written of the 'very ill people' called the Guaranies who 'continually make war upon their borders and one eat another': *Brief Summe*, p. 157.

3 Deane et al., 'February Meeting, 1891: Cabot's Mappe-Monde', p. 334.

4 Johnson and Nurminen, *History of Seafaring*, p. 239.

5 See Quinn, 'Sailors and the Sea', p. 30.

6 Barlow, *Brief Summe*, p. 64.

7 Deane et al., 'February Meeting, 1891: Cabot's Mappe-Monde', p. 334.

Chapter Twenty

1 Adams suggests the deadline was 20 May, but Willoughby's log gives 10 May as the departure date and this is confirmed by other sources.

2 Arber (ed.), *First Three English Books*, p. 288.

3 Stow, *Survey of London*, p. 12.

4 Porter (ed.), *Survey of London vols 43 &44: Poplar, Blackwall and the Isle of Dogs*, vol. 43, pp. 375–7. Baker (ed.), *A History of the County of Middlesex volume 11: Stepney, Bethnal Green*, p. 26.

5 Zell (ed.), *Early Modern Kent, 1540–1640*, pp. 128–9.

Chapter Twenty-One

1 See the contemporary illustrations of the palace by Antonis van der Wyngaerde, held by the Ashmolean. Chettle, *The Queen's House, Greenwich*, pp. 16–24, and Jennings, *Greenwich*, p. 35ff.

2 Skidmore, *Edward VI*, p. 246.

3 Nichols (ed.), *Diary of Henry Machyn*, pp. 33–4 (11 April 1553). Their destination, of course, was not the 'new found land' to the west. But gossip was as unreliable then as now.

4 Jehan Scheyfve to the Emperor, 28 April 1553.

5 Jordan (ed.), *The Chronicle and Political Papers of King Edward VI*, p. 55 and p. 80.

6 Scheyfve to the Emperor, 12 May 1553. Skidmore, *Edward VI*, p. 247.

7 Scheyfve to the Bishop of Arras, 5 May 1553; Scheyfve to the Emperor, 12 May 1553. Skidmore, *Edward VI*, p. 247.

8 Hakluyt, *Principal Navigations*, 1, p. 271.

9 Scheyfve to the Emperor, 12 May 1553.

10 Skidmore, *Edward VI*, p. 254.

11 Hakluyt, *Principal Navigations*, 1, pp. 241–3.

Chapter Twenty-Two

1 John Norden 1593, detail. Porter (ed.), *Survey of London vols 43 & 44: Poplar, Blackwall and the Isle of Dogs*, pp. 548–52.

2 The Thames was preferred to the south coast as a dockyard location for its proximity both to London merchants who could supply raw materials and to the forests and foundries of the Kent Weald, the main source for timber and cannon.

3 It is not entirely clear from Willoughby's account whether he means 9 a.m. or 9 p.m. The latter is an educated guess. Willoughby's account of his voyage is in Hakluyt, *Principal Navigations*, 1, pp. 248–54.

4 On this famous ship see L.P. Paine, *Warships of the World to 1900*, pp. 72–3.

5 Jehan Scheyfve to the Emperor, 7 March 1553.

6 Emperor to Prince Philip, Brussels, 2 April 1553.

7 Scheyfve to the Bishop of Arras, 10 April 1553.

8 Scheyfve to the Emperor, 11 May 1553.

Chapter Twenty-Three

1 Square-rigged ships could at best sail at an angle 70 degrees off the wind as opposed to about 40 degrees off for a modern 'fore-and-aft' ship.

2 The word 'lateen' may have derived from 'latin', owing to the technique's early adoption in the Mediterranean. See also Parry, *The Age of Reconnaissance*, pp. 81–4 and Block, *To Harness the Wind*, p. 13ff.

3 Loades, *Tudor Navy*, p. 84.

4 See law 7 of the *Laws of Oléron (The Judgementes of the See)*, with an English translation of the French text extracted from Pierre Garcie, *The Rutter of the See*. It is on p. 60 (taking the title page as p. 1) but the copy consulted had no page numbers. Loades, *Tudor Navy*, p. 100.

5 Carter and Mendis, 'Evolutionary and Historical Aspects of the Burden of Malaria', p. 582.

6 An important maritime court was based there at the time, in the twelfth century, that Eleanor of Aquitaine reissued the laws which derived from the ancient Mediterranean.

7 Fury, *Tides in the Affairs of Men*, p. 66.

Chapter Twenty-Four

1 From a shanty dated to 1548, quoted in Mayers, *North-East Passage*, p. 58.

2 Hakluyt, *Principal Navigations*, 1, pp. 271–2.

3 Waters, *Art of Navigation*, pp. 137–8.

4 William Bourne, *Regiment of the Sea*, quoted in Waters, *Art of Navigation*, p. 36.

5 Dates were ten days adrift in the sixteenth century due to slippage of the Julian calendar; 14 July was equivalent to 24 July today. The beginning of Leo is generally given as 23 July.

Chapter Twenty-Five

1 George Best, son of the interpreter Robert Best, quoted in Mayers, *North-East Passage*, p. 100.

2 This is currently at 66° 33' 44", though it has drifted slightly northward since the sixteenth century, with a slow change in the tilt of the earth on its axis. Currently it is moving northward at about fifteen metres per year – or just under seven kilometres in the 459 years since 1553.

3 Mayers, *North-East Passage*, pp. 59–61.

4 Fury, 'Health and Health Care at Sea', p. 194. William Cloves was the surgeon.

5 Puffins are still caught and eaten in Iceland. On the puffin (and countless other

birds) as part of an earlier English diet see Thomas, *Man and the Natural World*, p. 55.

6 Anthony Jenkinson: Hakluyt, *Principal Navigations*, 1, p. 410.

Chapter Twenty-Six

1 Hakluyt, *Principal Navigations*, 1, p. 336.

2 In fact a nearby point was slightly further north, and technically a neighbouring promontory was the uppermost reach of the mainland, since the 'North Cape' was part of an island that lay slightly offshore, but the psychological force was the same. It is Kinnarodden on the nearby Nordkinn peninsula that actually marks the northernmost point of the European mainland.

3 See the illustration of Wardhouse in 1594 in Mayers, *North-East Passage*, p. 70.

Chapter Twenty-Eight

1 Thomas Randolph embassy 1568, Hakluyt, *Principal Navigations*, 2, p. 81. Hamel, *England and Russia*, p. 97.

2 Embassy of Giles Fletcher, Hakluyt, *Principal Navigations*, 2, pp. 294–5; Berry and Crummey (eds), *Rude & Barbarous Kingdom*, pp. 119–20.

3 We cannot be sure how much of a surprise this was. On the Continent, von Herberstein had recently published an account of Russia which showed access to Moscow from a 'Mare Glaciale' in the north. John Dee may have brought his information to England. See Baron, 'Herberstein and the English "Discovery" of Muscovy'. Adams' account certainly gives no suggestion that an arrival in Russia was anticipated.

4 Planché, *Cyclopedia of Costume*, pp. 216–18.

5 Hakluyt, *Principal Navigations*, 1, p. 275.

6 Berry and Crummey (eds), *Rude and Barbarous Kingdom*, pp. 9–10 (n. 1), 98–9.

Chapter Twenty-Nine

1 Waters, *Art of Navigation*, pp. 18–19.

2 All such observations were made with the naked eye. The idea for a telescope was not new, but the first that were practicable were not developed until the early seventeenth century. Waters, *Art of Navigation*, pp. 52, 296n. Woolley, *The Queen's Conjuror*, p. 150.

Chapter Thirty

1 Quoted in Lamb, 'Science by Litigation: A Cosmographic Feud', p. 45.

2 On the compass see Johnson and Nurminen (eds), *History of Seafaring*, pp. 90–6.

3 R.A. Skelton, 'Sebastian Cabot', *Dictionary of Canadian Biography Online*. Burwash, *English Merchant Shipping*, p. 5.

4 See the article by Prince Kropotkin in the 1902 *Encyclopedia Britannica*. For a recent attempt to plot Willoughby's likely course by a sailor see Mayers, *North-East Passage*, pp. 64–6.

5 An interesting picture of Kolguev island is to be found in the account given by the Victorian naturalist Aubyn Trevor-Battye in *Ice-Bound on Kolguev* (1895).

Chapter Thirty-One

1 Skidmore, *Edward VI*, p. 249.

2 On links between the Willoughbys and the Greys see Ives, *Lady Jane Grey*, pp. 36–7 and on Willoughby's family in general, Hamel, *England and Russia*, pp. 5–15.

3 Stow, *Survey of London*, 1, p. 67.

Chapter Thirty-Two

1 Hakluyt, *Principal Navigations*, 1, p. 292.

2 See, generally, Kudriavtseva, 'Ambassadorial Ceremony at the Tsar's Court'.

3 Hakluyt, *Principal Navigations*, 2, p. 99. George Turberville, with Thomas Randolph, 1568.

4 Hakluyt, *Principal Navigations*, 2, pp. 81–2. Embassy of Thomas Randolph in 1568. Randolph was in fact a diplomat, and was careful in his formal despatch not to make specific allegations. Less cautious was another Englishman, whose charge that buggery was widespread was excised by Hakluyt lest it cause unnecessary offence. See Berry and Crummey (eds), *Rude and Barbarous Kingdom*, p. 76 (and compare Hakluyt, *Principal Navigations*, 2, p. 99 where six lines are omitted).

5 The brief account he later wrote, and the description he gave to Clement Adams, comprised the first attempts in English to analyse Russian society. It was the first of a number of studies by Englishmen, several of which were of high quality, and which are important sources for historians of Russia since Russian primary source material can be sparse. See Berry and Crummey (eds), *Rude and Barbarous Kingdom*.

6 Hakluyt, *Principal Navigations*, 1, pp. 432–3.

7 See E. Duffy, *Stripping of the Altars*, chapter 13 regarding changes in religious practice in England under Edward VI. On the participation of icons in the sanctity of their prototypes see Miller, 'The Viskovatyi Affair', p. 295.

8 Hakluyt, *Principal Navigations*, 1, p. 432.

Chapter Thirty-Three

1 Arthur Edwards, Hakluyt, *Principal Navigations*, 2, p. 55. Alef, 'The Origin and

Early Development of the Muscovite Postal Service', p. 2.

2 Quoted in Kudriavtseva, 'Ambassadorial Ceremony at the Tsar's Court', pp. 47–8.

3 Hakluyt, *Principal Navigations*, 2, p. 82. Thomas Randolph was the ambassador.

4 Hakluyt, *Principal Navigations*, 2, p. 55.

5 Marco Foscarini, quoted in Kudriavtseva, 'Ambassadorial Ceremony at the Tsar's Court', p. 47. Giles Fletcher made the same observation: see Berry and Crummey (eds), *Rude and Barbarous Kingdom*, p. 122.

6 Kudriavtseva, 'Ambassadorial Ceremony at the Tsar's Court', p. 47.

7 Hakluyt, *Principal Navigations*, 2, p. 105. George Turberville, 1568.

8 Stevens, 'Banditry and Provincial Order in Sixteenth-century Russia'. Adams refers to the 'many cutpurses among them' in Hakluyt, *Principal Navigations*, 1, p. 288.

9 Kudriavtseva, 'Ambassadorial Ceremony at the Tsar's Court', p. 47.

Chapter Thirty-Four

1 R. Lemon and M.A.E. Green (eds), *CSP Domestic: Elizabeth 1601–3; with Addenda 1547–65*, pp. 382–96. On the background to this conflict see Sadler, *Border Fury*, chapter 18.

2 Jordan (ed.), *The Chronicle and Political Papers of King Edward VI*, p. 26.

Chapter Thirty-Five

1 Picard and Grundy (eds), *Description of Moscow and Muscovy*, p. 19.

2 He was perhaps too pessimistic, since a short growing season did exist in the summer months. Giles Fletcher later noted that 'a man would marvel to see the great alteration and difference betwixt the winter and summer in Russia', Berry and Crummey (eds), *Rude and Barbarous Kingdom*, p. 114.

3 Robert Best noted, after his voyage of 1557, that 'barks of trees are good meat with them at all times': Hakluyt, *Principal Navigations*, 1, p. 437.

4 Fletcher, 'A Note on Two Words in Milton's *History of Moscovia*', p. 316. There is an illustration on Olaus Magnus's map of this animal involved in a similar procedure, though it appears to be defecating rather than giving birth.

5 Deane et al., 'February Meeting, 1891: Cabot's Mappe-Monde', p. 334.

6 Anderson, *Britain's Discovery of Russia, 1553–1815*, p. 12.

7 Alef, 'The Origin and Early Development of the Muscovite Postal Service', p. 6.

8 Many pursued a discipline which was at least nominally loyal to the instructions of St Benedict, just as many monks did in the Western Catholic Church, and Benedictines were noted for their adoption of black clothing.

9 Crummey, *The Formation of Muscovy, 1304–1613*, p. 2 and chapter 1 *passim*.

10 At the time these were spelt Yeraslav, Rostov and Pereslav: see Jenkinson's ac-

count in Hakluyt, *Principal Navigations*, 1, pp. 413–14. Jenkinson says there were fourteen posts between Vologda and Moscow but he only lists thirteen. See also Robert Best's account, p. 419.

11 See Alef, 'The Origin and Early Development of the Muscovite Postal Service', pp. 1–15.

Chapter Thirty-Six

1 Hakluyt, *Principal Navigations*, 2, p. 257 (A brief discourse on the voyage of Sir Jerome Bowes in 1583).

2 The English still often referred to him as the 'Duke'. They had known, vaguely, of the Duchy of Moscow, and had not taken into account Ivan's self-elevation to emperor or 'tsar'.

3 De Madariaga, *Ivan the Terrible*, pp. 62–3. Ivan himself remembered that 'a fiery flame burned the ruling city of Moscow': Fennell (ed.), *Correspondence*, p. 81.

4 Giles Fletcher was the visitor. Berry and Crummey (eds), *Rude and Barbarous Kingdom*, p. 126. Hakluyt, *Principal Navigations*, 2, p. 301.

5 Hakluyt, *Principal Navigations*, 1, p. 255.

6 De Madariaga, *Ivan the Terrible*, p. 56; Bushkovitch, 'The Moscow Kremlin and its History', p. 226.

7 Bushkovitch, 'The Moscow Kremlin and its History', p. 225.

8 On his lavish building campaign, unlike any that came before it, and epitomised at new palaces like Hampton Court and Nonsuch, see Scarisbrick, *Henry VIII*, pp. 505–6.

9 Hughes, 'The Courts of Moscow and St Petersburg', p. 299.

Chapter Thirty-Seven

1 Filatov et al., *White Sea*, pp. 9–11. Took, *Running with Reindeer*, p. xii.

2 Took, *Running with Reindeer*, p. 169.

3 Hakluyt, *Principal Navigations*, 1, p. 298.

Chapter Thirty-Eight

1 Hakluyt, *Principal Navigations*, 1, pp. 417–18.

2 On one of Ivan's thrones, made in 1551, bas-reliefs depicted the coronation of his ancestor Grand Prince Vladimir Monomakh, alleged to have physically conveyed the crown – and Byzantine imperial authority – to the 'Russians' then centred on Kiev: Bogatyrev, *The Sovereign and his Counsellors*, pp. 75–6.

3 Bogatyrev, *The Sovereign and his Counsellors*, pp. 39–41.

4 Kudriavtseva, 'Ambassadorial Ceremony at the Tsar's Court', p. 55; De Madariaga, *Ivan the Terrible*, p. 32.

5 Hakluyt, *Principal Navigations*, 1, p. 280. De Madariaga and Crummey both assume this was Adashev (*Ivan the Terrible*, pp. 121–2; *Rude and Barbarous Kingdom*, p. 25). On the career of Adashev see De Madariaga, *Ivan the Terrible*, pp. 67–9. Miller 'The Viskovatyi Affair'.

6 Bogatyrev, *The Sovereign and his Counsellors*, p. 148.

7 Fennell (ed.), *Correspondence*, p. 93. Cavendish, 'Kazan falls to Ivan the Terrible'. On the importance of the *streltsy* musketeer units see Paul, 'The Military Revolution in Russia, 1550–1682', pp. 22, 28–9 and Martin, *Medieval Russia*, pp. 353 and 360.

8 In general, on the importance of the Kazan campaign for Russia, see Romaniello, *The Elusive Empire*.

9 Fennell (ed.), *Prince A.M. Kurbsky's History of Ivan IV*, p. 49. This work also contains an account of the fall of Kazan.

10 The full title was given by Ivan in the letter he sent home with Chancellor; see Hakluyt, *Principal Navigations*, 1, p. 293. Place names have not here been modernised. A later English ambassador, Sir Jerome Horsey, referred to the 'great rabblement' of the names of Ivan's provinces that he was expected to recite, though provocatively he refused to do so: Berry and Crummey (eds), *Rude and Barbarous Kingdom*, p. 265.

Chapter Thirty-Nine

1 Fennell (ed.), *Correspondence*, p. 73.

2 Ivan was crowned on 16 January 1547; Edward on 20 February.

3 De Madariaga, *Ivan the Terrible*, pp. 33–4.

4 Fennell (ed.), *Correspondence*, p. 95.

5 Fennell (ed.), *Correspondence*, p. 95.

6 Fennell (ed.), *Correspondence*, p. 237.

7 Bogatyrev, *The Sovereign and his Counsellors*, p. 21; Miller, 'The Viskovatyi Affair', p. 304.

Chapter Forty

1 Scheyfve to the Bishop of Arras, 10 April 1553. Later embassies brought specimens of crafted silver, like the large, shallow drinking cup, decorated with leaves and classical figures, brought by Anthony Jenkinson soon afterwards. On this occasion, though, they had not known their destination, let alone the Tsar's liking for silver objects. See Dmitrieva and Abramova (eds), *Britannia & Muscovy: English Silver at the Court of the Tsars*, pp. 60–1.

2 A similar symbolism was understood from being the first to dismount from a horse, and ambassadors reported what now seem ludicrous stand-offs in which a visitor and his Russian contact strained to hold a posture half off their

horse, feet hovering over the ground, anxious not to be the first to touch down: Hakluyt, *Principal Navigations*, 2, p. 254.

3 Hakluyt, *Principal Navigations*, 1, pp. 429–30 and 2, p. 104.

4 Kudriavtseva, 'Ambassadorial Ceremony at the Tsar's Court', p. 57.

5 Campbell, 'Gold, Silver and Precious Stones', p. 156.

6 De Madariaga, *Ivan the Terrible*, pp. 55–6; Hughes, 'The Courts of Moscow and St Petersburg', p. 296.

7 Fennell (ed.), *Correspondence*, p. 25.

8 De Madariaga, *Ivan the Terrible*, pp. 68–71, p. 140.

9 De Madariaga, *Ivan the Terrible*, p. 87, quoting Kurbsky letter.

10 De Madariaga, *Ivan the Terrible*, p. 44.

11 Fennell (ed.), *Correspondence*, p. 27, p. 59 (the repetition of 'suppression' is in the translation).

Chapter Forty-One

1 The English guests would not have been particularly surprised. The 'mute' swan had been considered a royal bird in England since well before this was reaffirmed by the 1482 Act of Swans, but its flesh was a regular at the royal table.

2 Kudriavtseva, 'Ambassadorial Ceremony at the Tsar's Court', p. 58.

3 Hakluyt, *Principal Navigations*, 1, p. 421. Account of Osip Napea voyage by Robert Best.

4 Ibid.

Chapter Forty-Two

1 Took, *Running with Reindeer*, p. 170.

2 Henry Lane wrote of Willoughby 'entering into a River immediately frozen up' upon a 'desert coast in Lappia'. Hakluyt, *Principal Navigations*, 2, p. 265.

3 Hakluyt, *Principal Navigations*, 1, p. 228.

Chapter Forty-Three

1 Ives, *Lady Jane Grey*, p. 248.

2 Ives, *Lady Jane Grey*, p. 249.

3 Edwards, *Mary I*, p. 131.

4 Williamson, *Maritime Enterprise*, p. 170. For details of the procession, Edwards, *Mary I*, pp. 125–8.

5 See Wooding, 'The Marian Restoration and the Mass'.

6 Edwards, *Mary I*, pp. 114–16.

7 Regarding her marriage plans see Loades, *Mary Tudor*, pp. 201–3 and Kamen, *Philip of Spain*, pp. 54–7.

8 Edwards, *Mary I*, pp. 172–3.

9 Quoted in Ives, *Lady Jane Grey*, pp. 267–8.

10 The last hours of Jane's life are recounted in Ives, *Lady Jane Grey*, pp. 271–7. See the letter sent by Robert Swyft to the Earl of Shrewsbury, Lodge, *Illustrations of British History*, vol. 1, p. 235.

Chapter Forty-Four

1 Hasse's account is in Hakluyt, *Principal Navigations*, 1, pp. 294–9.

2 See Tiberg, *Moscow, Livonia and the Hanseatic League, 1487–1550*.

3 Berry and Crummey (eds), *Rude and Barbarous Kingdom*, p. 30.

4 Hakluyt, *Principal Navigations*, 1, p. 422 (Robert Best account).

5 Ostrowski, *Muscovy and the Mongols*, p. 51.

6 Hakluyt, *Principal Navigations*, 1, p. 423.

7 Berry and Crummey (eds), *Rude and Barbarous Kingdom*, p. 27. Unusually, Chancellor does seem to have bought this exaggerated claim. The Russian army of the time was very large by western European standards, but is thought to have been around 150,000-strong.

8 Not until later in the sixteenth century was the metropolitan of Moscow officially hailed as Patriarch of the Russian Orthodox Church, but already, since the fall of Constantinople to the Ottomans, he was esteemed as the Orthodox Church's most revered figure.

9 See Hakluyt, *Principal Navigations*, 1, p. 415 and pp. 424–5.

10 Kudriavtseva, 'Ambassadorial Ceremony at the Tsar's Court', p. 60.

11 In their veneration of St George Russians and Englishmen were at one. The dragon he battled with represented a variety of enemies: evil, paganism, the Roman Empire or other anti-Christian forces.

12 It was the twentieth year of Ivan's governance only if the years of his minority are included.

13 De Madariaga, *Ivan the Terrible*, pp. 119–20.

Chapter Forty-Five

1 Hakluyt, *Principal Navigations*, 1, p. 254.

2 Hakluyt, *Principal Navigations*, 2, p. 265.

3 Hakluyt, *Principal Navigations*, 1, p. 236.

4 Nordenskiold, *The Voyage of the Vega*, p. 62 for instance.

5 Or they might, like Martin Frobisher later on his voyages in search of a north-west passage, have carried it with them.

6 For this argument see Gordon, 'The Fate of Sir Hugh Willoughby and his Companions'.

Chapter Forty-Six

1 The phrase 'Merchant Adventurers of England' comes from the charter granted by Philip and Mary, Hakluyt, *Principal Navigations*, 1, p. 319. Arber (ed.), *First Three English Books*, p. 59.

2 It took Stephen Borough's son Christopher two months over a quarter of a century later. Subsequent voyages did not depart until July, returning in September or even October, but the crew would surely have been anxious, this first time, to set out.

3 Hakluyt, *Principal Navigations*, 2, pp. 264–9.

4 Quoted in Willan, *Early History*, p. 45.

5 It is true that much company paperwork has not survived, after its archive was destroyed over a century later during the Great Fire of London.

6 Scammell, 'Manning the English Merchant Service', pp. 134 and 139.

7 Simon Renard to the Emperor, Blois, 4 February 1551.

8 Andrews, 'The Elizabethan Seaman', p. 250.

9 Fury, *Tides in the Affairs of Men*, pp. 22–6.

10 Andrews, *Trade, Plunder and Settlement*, chapter 7 passim; Senior, *A Nation of Pirates*.

11 Williamson, *Maritime Enterprise*, pp. 365–7; see also Andrews, *Trade, Plunder and Settlement*, pp. 27–8.

12 Scammell, 'Manning the English Merchant Service', p. 131.

13 Scammell, 'European Seamanship in the Great Age of Discovery', p. 368.

Chapter Forty-Seven

1 Hakluyt, *Principal Navigations*, 1, p. 333.

2 S. Purchas, *Hakluytus Posthumus or Purchas, His Pilgrimes*, quoted in Cotton, 'Stephen Borough, the Navigator' and in Mayers, *North-East Passage*, p. 76.

Chapter Forty-Eight

1 The outline of Scandinavia and northern Russia on the surviving map of 1544 with which Cabot was involved is wildly inaccurate. The original is in the Bibliothèque Nationale de France. The British Library has a facsimile.

2 Hakluyt, *Principal Navigations*, 1, pp. 239 and 254.

Chapter Forty-Nine

1 Brennan, *Sidneys of Penshurst*, p. 23.

2 Brennan, *Sidneys of Penshurst*, pp. 24–5.

3 Brennan, *Sidneys of Penshurst*, pp. 24–5.

4 Hannay, *Philip's Phoenix*, p. 10. A general pardon, as was customary, was issued on Mary's coronation, to which there were forty-seven named exemptions along

with anyone imprisoned at the command of Mary and her Council. See Kesselring, *Mercy and Authority*, pp. 66–7.

5 Brennan, *Sidneys of Penshurst*, p. 25. Edwards, *Mary I*, pp. 179–81. Sir Henry Sidney, DNB. Bedford is mentioned as being in Santiago de Compostela when Philip signed the contract on 25 June. For Bedford's early involvement see 1555 charter, Hakluyt, *Principal Navigations*, 1, p. 318.

6 Kamen, *Philip of Spain*, p. 56.

7 Edwards, *Mary I*, p. 182.

8 Edwards, *Mary I*, pp. 183–5.

9 Edwards, *Mary I*, p. 187.

10 Edwards, *Mary I*, p. 190.

11 Edwards, *Mary I*, p. 197.

Chapter Fifty

1 Hakluyt, *Principal Navigations*, 2, p. 67.

2 See Willan, *Early History*, p. 6 footnote 5.

3 Hakluyt, *Principal Navigations*, 2, p. 66. The royal licence is Cotton MSS. Faustina CII, f.110.

4 Hakluyt, *Principal Navigations*, 2, p. 66. Act of Incorporation 1566. Quoted in Willan, *Early History*, p. 6.

5 Edwards, *Mary I*, p. 197.

6 Hakluyt, *Principal Navigations*, 1, p. 254.

7 Hakluyt, *Principal Navigations*, 1, p. 295.

8 Hakluyt, *Principal Navigations*, 1, pp. 296–7.

9 Hakluyt, *Principal Navigations*, 1, p. 294. Of course no member of Mary's Council was sent back to Russia in 1555.

10 Quoted in Turner, *The History of England*, Vol. 11, p. 298.

Chapter Fifty-One

1 Edwards, *Mary I*, p. 213; Kamen, *Philip of Spain*, p. 58; Whitelock, *Mary Tudor*, pp. 243, 246. Michael Surian, the Venetian ambassador, also agreed: see his letter home of 3 April 1557.

2 J. Pratt and J. Stoughton (eds), *The Acts and Monuments of John Foxe*, Vol. 6, p. 572.

3 Edwards, *Mary I*, p. 223.

4 Duffy, *The Voices of Morebath*, p. 94.

5 Duffy, *The Voices of Morebath*, p. 94.

6 Sir John Cheke, DNB.

7 See Duffy, *The Voices of Morebath*, pp. 72–8.

8 Quoted in Knighton, 'Westminster Abbey Restored', p. 82.

9 Quoted in Picard, *Elizabeth's London*, p. 47.

10 Page (ed.), *Victoria History of the County of Kent*, Vol. 2, pp. 194–8.

11 Michiel, 4 November 1555.

12 Webb, *The Records of St Bartholomew's Priory*, 1, p. 277.

13 These were repealed under Edward VI, who was not, of course, a paragon of tolerance. He may have planned a comparable persecution of those who spurned his Protestant vision, but death deprived him of the chance.

14 Baldwin Smith, *Fools, Martyrs, Traitors*, chapter 8.

Chapter Fifty-Two

1 The charter is printed in Hakluyt, *Principal Navigations*, 1, pp. 318–29. It is in *Calendar of Patent Rolls, 1554–55*, pp. 55–9. The original is now in C66/883 at the National Archives.

2 Willan, *Muscovy Merchants*, pp. 14–16. Different copies of the charter give slightly varying numbers of members. Mayers, on p. 115, for instance, cites 213 men.

3 Gerson, *Studies in the History of English Commerce*, p. 37.

4 Also included among the aldermen in some lists is Mrs Margaret Kyrtom (or Kirton), though she is not mentioned by Willan.

5 Thornbury, 'St Bartholomew's Hospital', in his *Old and New London*, Vol. 2, pp. 359–63.

6 Nichols (ed.), *Diary of Henry Machyn*, p. 7 (10 July 1551). Rappaport, *Worlds within worlds*, p. 50.

7 Elizabeth Wilford, DNB; Katherine Lomnour, Willan, *Muscovy Merchants*, p. 110. See also the document in M.A.E. Green, *Calendar of State Papers, Domestic Series, of the Reign of Elizabeth, 1601–03 with Addenda 1547–65* (original document reference SP 15/7 f.115).

8 Willan, *Muscovy Merchants*, p. 9. The charter granted by Queen Mary is in Hakluyt, *Principal Navigations*, 1, pp. 318–29.

9 See coin at British Museum – illustration. http://www.britishmuseum.org/explore/highlights/highlight_image.aspx?image=ps289219.jpg&retpage=20841

Chapter Fifty-Three

1 The name Buckland was sometimes written as Backhand. Like Chancellor and Stephen Borough, Buckland was an investor as well as a company employee. See Willan, *Muscovy Merchants*, p. 83.

2 Hakluyt, *Principal Navigations*, 1, p. 380.

3 Hakluyt, *Principal Navigations*, 1, p. 303.

4 Whitelock, *Mary Tudor*, p. 253.

5 See Arber (ed.), *First Three English Books*, pp. xxxix, 46, 50–60. None of this

prevented Eden being arrested and deprived of office, charged with heresy.

6 Edwards, *Mary I*, p. 267; L. Porter, *Mary Tudor: The First Queen*, p. 338; Whitelock, *Mary Tudor*, p. 255.

7 Edwards, *Mary I*, p. 267 footnote. The Privy Council order is reproduced in The Society of Antiquaries of London, *Archaeologia or Miscellaneous Tracts relating to Antiquity*, Vol. 18 (1817), p. 182.

8 Kamen, *Philip of Spain*, pp. 62–3.

Chapter Fifty-Four

1 Michiel, 21 May 1555.

2 Hamel, *England and Russia*, pp. 87–8. Henry Lane records that Willoughby et al. were found by Russian fishermen in the summer of 1554 in his letter to William Sanderson, Hakluyt, *Principal Navigations*, 2, p. 265.

3 Giovanni Michiel to the Venetian Doge and Senate, 4 November 1555, Rawdon Brown (ed.), *Calendar of State Papers relating to English Affairs in the Archives of Venice, Vol. 6 Part 1 1555–1558*, p. 240.

4 Hamel, *England and Russia*, pp. 87–8.

5 Hakluyt, *Principal Navigations*, 2, p. 267.

Chapter Fifty-Five

1 Kerner, *The Urge to the Sea*, p. 39.

2 Hakluyt, *Principal Navigations*, 2, p. 81 and p. 173.

3 Hakluyt, *Principal Navigations*, 1, p. 239. See Orme, *Early British Swimming*, p. 49 and *passim*.

4 For Christopher Hudson, or Hoddesdon see Willan, *Early History*, pp. 34–5.

5 Hakluyt, *Principal Navigations*, 1, p. 407.

6 On Lane see Willan, *Early History*, p. 25. On Best, ibid., p. 36 (note 5) but Willan is surely mistaken that he was sent from England into Scotland, since Hakluyt is sure he was in Moscow with Chancellor.

Chapter Fifty-Six

1 Baldakin was an ornate fabric made of gold and silver.

2 The letter from Philip and Mary is printed in Tolstoy, *First Forty Years*, pp. 9–10.

3 The 'And the Son', or 'Filioque', clause in the Nicene Creed lay at the heart of the schism between East and West which solidified in 1054. The authority of the Pope in Rome was another cause of disagreement, and here, of course, the dispute was rather too close to home given the similar rejection of Rome by Protestants in England, which had been, of course, a common bond between London and Moscow – though no more.

4 At a distance of thirty-one years, Lane had got the names slightly wrong; as Kill-

ingworth no doubt remembered more accurately, Arthur Edwards had stayed in
Vologda, while Edward Price and Robert Best joined the party in Moscow.

5 See Henry Lane letter: Hakluyt, *Principal Navigations*, 2, p. 267. See also De
Madariaga, *Ivan the Terrible*, pp. 84–5.

Chapter Fifty-Seven

1 See also the list of cloths given as sent in 1557, Hakluyt, *Principal Navigations*, 1,
pp. 381–2.

2 Hakluyt, *Principal Navigations*, 1, pp. 380–91.

3 Hakluyt, *Principal Navigations*, 2, p. 220. Norris, *Tudor Costume and Fashion*, p.
345.

4 Plesco is known now as Pskov, and is a city in the far west of European Russia.

5 Hakluyt, *Principal Navigations*, 1, p. 416.

6 Hakluyt, *Principal Navigations*, 2, p. 139.

7 Martin, *Medieval Russia*, pp. 393ff.

8 There is a useful short summary of the situation in Hosking, *Russia and the
Russians*, pp. 117–19.

9 This was Dr Joseph Hamel, whose work was published initially in German in
1847. See Quinn (ed.), *The Hakluyt Handbook*, p. 162 footnote 2. The version in
Hakluyt is in *Principal Navigations*, 1, pp. 313–18.

10 See the discussion in Willan, *Early History*, pp. 11–14.

11 If there is any truth in the claim, later made, that Willoughby's suit of clothes
survived at his family home of Wollaton, then his body must, in all likelihood,
have sailed home with the *Philip and Mary*. Hamel, *England and Russia*, p. 94.

12 Hamel, *England and Russia*, p. 146.

Chapter Fifty-Eight

1 See John Incent's account: Hakluyt, *Principal Navigations*, 1, p. 356–64 (although Hamel, p. 146, gives 2 August).

2 Willan, *Early History*, pp. 52–3 and see reference in footnote.

3 For their names see Hakluyt, *Principal Navigations*, 1, p. 366. Hamel, *England
and Russia*, pp. 146–7.

4 Hakluyt, *Principal Navigations*, 1, p. 381.

5 Henry Lane to William Sanderson, Hakluyt, *Principal Navigations*, 2, pp. 264–
9.

6 Hakluyt, *Principal Navigations*, 1, p. 380.

Chapter Fifty-Nine

1 Hakluyt, *Principal Navigations*, 1, p. 380.

2 Hakluyt, *Principal Navigations*, 1, p. 381.

3 Nichols (ed.), *Diary of Henry Machyn*, p. 127 (27 February 1557).

Chapter Sixty

1 John Incent account, Hakluyt, *Principal Navigations*, 1, p. 361. Nichols (ed.), *Diary of Henry Machyn*, p. 127 (27 February). How little was generally known of the distant realm from which this man came is suggested by the fact that Holinshed, in his chronicle, referred to Napea's master as 'the emperor of Cathay, Muscovy and Russeland': Holinshed, *Chronicles*, Vol. 6, p. 1132 (This is transcribed and analysed online at the Holinshed Project: http://www.cerns.ox.ac.uk/holinshed/).

2 Nichols (ed.), *Diary of Henry Machyn*, p. 127. See the references to plate at the wedding feast of Philip and Mary, Edwards, *Mary I*, p. 191.

3 Nichols (ed.), *Diary of Henry Machyn*, p. 127 (27 February). Admittedly this was not always then an exclusively nocturnal garment: Norris, *Tudor Costume and Fashion*, p. 262.

4 Hakluyt, *Principal Navigations*, 1, p. 381.

5 Michiel Surian, 3 April 1557.

6 Whitelock, *Mary Tudor*, pp. 277–81.

7 Nichols (ed.), *Diary of Henry Machyn*, pp. 129–30 (20–31 March).

8 Giovanni Michiel, 29 July 1555.

9 Michiel Surian, 3 April 1557. Surian took over from Giovanni Michiel in the spring of 1557.

10 Gerson, *Studies in the History of English Commerce*, pp. 55–6. The letter, in Latin, is printed in full in Tolstoy, *First Forty Years*, pp. 13–14.

11 Hakluyt, *Principal Navigations*, 1, p. 379.

12 See Alcock's letter describing his experiences, Hakluyt, *Principal Navigations*, 1, pp. 395–7. Also see the further accusations and rationale in Gerson, *Studies in the History of English Commerce*, p. 56.

13 Emperor Ferdinand to Queen Elizabeth, 17 August 1559.

14 Gerson, *Studies in the History of English Commerce*, p. 57.

15 Whitelock, *Mary Tudor*, p. 277.

16 Slack, 'Mortality Crises and Epidemic Disease in England, 1485–1610', p. 31. Strype, *Ecclesiastical Memorials*, 2, pp. 156–7. Fisher, 'Influenza and Inflation in Tudor England', pp. 126–7.

17 See Knighton, 'Westminster Abbey Restored', pp. 77–123.

18 Nichols (ed.), *Diary of Henry Machyn*, pp. 131 and 137 (6 April and 28 May).

19 Giovanni Michiel, 4 Nov 1555.

20 Whitelock, *Mary Tudor*, p. 287.

21 On Calais' perceived importance to the English see Michiel's report made in 1557.

22 Giovanni Michiel, 13 May 1557.

23 Nichols (ed.), *Diary of Henry Machyn*, p. 130 (31 March 1557).

24 Hakluyt, *Principal Navigations*, 1, pp. 390–1.

Chapter Sixty-One

1 He had certainly been in contact with men in Spain, like Alonso de Santa Cruz, who attempted to measure longitude this way: see Portuondo, *Secret Science*, p. 69. And there were others too; see Taylor, *Tudor Geography*, p. 66.

2 Arber (ed.), *First Three English Books*, p. xlvii. The comment was included by Eden in the dedication he wrote to his translation of John Taisner's *De natura magnetis &c.*

3 Skelton, 'Sebastian Cabot'.

Chapter Sixty-Two

1 Hakluyt, *Principal Navigations*, 1, p. 465.

2 Hakluyt, *Principal Navigations*, 2, p. 268.

3 It was not long before the company was equipping its ships to hunt whales in these northern waters, cutting them up on deck and boiling their blubber to produce oil. A careful list in 1575 described the necessary equipment, including javelins, great and small, harping irons, 'great hooks to turn the Whale', pulleys, tackles, huge baskets and knives: Hakluyt, *Principal Navigations*, 2, pp. 162–3.

4 Hakluyt, *Principal Navigations*, 1, p. 375.

5 Arber (ed.), *First Three English Books*, p. xliii.

6 Hakluyt, *Principal Navigations*, 1, p. 398.

7 Account of Christopher Borough, Hakluyt, *Principal Navigations*, 2, p. 181. For a general survey see Andrews, *Trade, Plunder and Settlement*, pp. 79–86.

Chapter Sixty-Three

1 Arber (ed.), *First Three English Books*, pp. 290 and 292. The comments were originally made by Sebastian Munster and John Faber.

2 Hakluyt, *Principal Navigations*, 1, p. 384.

3 Hakluyt, *Principal Navigations*, 1, p. 399.

4 Hakluyt, *Principal Navigations*, 1, p. 400.

5 Arber (ed.), *First Three English Books*, p. 297, quoting Jacobus Ziglerus.

6 Hakluyt, *Principal Navigations*, 1, p. 383.

7 Baldwin, *Sumptuary Legislation*, p. 213 and pp. 216–20, quoted in Willan, *Early History*, p. 55.

8 Hakluyt, *Principal Navigations*, 1, pp. 401–2.

9 Detailed instructions for this rope-walk are in the letter of Thomas Hawtrey to Henry Lane, Hakluyt, *Principal Navigations*, 1, p. 392. Willan, *Early History*, p. 40.

10 Morris, 'Naval Cordage Procurement in Early Modern England', p. 88, quoting Hakluyt.

11 Willan, *Early History*, pp. 55–6; Anderson, *Britain's Discovery of Russia*, p. 5.

12 Hakluyt, *Principal Navigations*, 1, p. 401.

13 Hakluyt, *Principal Navigations*, 1, p. 384. Willan, *Early History*, p. 38.

14 Hakluyt, *Principal Navigations*, 1, p. 405. Willan, *Early History*, p. 39.

15 Land which Sir Hugh Willoughby believed he had seen in 1553 was known in England long after as Willoughby's Land and was depicted as an island on numerous late 16th century and early 17th century maps, such as Mercator's map of the north pole published in 1595, before it was established that no such island actually existed.

16 Nicholas Chancellor's account of the voyage was included by Hakluyt in his first edition of 1589 though he removed it from his fuller edition of ten years later. See the facsimile edition of the 1589 text introduced by D.B. Quinn and R.A. Skelton and published by the Hakluyt Society, pp. 476–82.

17 In 1565 Anthony Jenkinson argued that the discovery of a unicorn's head (that of a narwhal, presumably), on the island of Vaigach, showed a passage did exist to 'the Lands of Cathay, China and other Oriental Regions', Anderson, *Britain's Discovery of Russia*, p. 6. See the doubts of Sir Humphrey Gilbert: Quinn (ed.), *Voyages and Colonising Enterprises*, p. 157.

18 Willan, *Early History*, pp. 41–2. Hakluyt, *Principal Navigations*, 1, pp. 384–5.

19 Hakluyt, *Principal Navigations*, 1, p. 402.

Chapter Sixty-Four

1 Quoted in Whitelock, *Mary Tudor*, p. 291.

2 Edwards, *Mary I*, p. 325.

3 Giovanni Michiel had been the Venetian ambassador in England from May 1554. His final letter, with its full report on the state of England, was dated 26 January 1557. R Brown (ed.), *Calendar of State Papers Relating to English Affairs in the Archives of Venice, Vol. 6: 1555–1558*, pp. 1041–95. Whitelock, *Mary Tudor*, p. 297.

4 Edwards, *Mary I*, p. 333. Whitelock, *Mary Tudor*, p. 306.

5 Nichols (ed.), *Diary of Henry Machyn*, p. 178 (17 November).

Chapter Sixty-Five

1 Fennell (ed.), *Correspondence*, pp. 19, 41.

2 Morgan and Coote, *Early Voyages and Travels*, 2, p. 284.

3 De Madariaga, *Ivan the Terrible*, p. 229 for Kurbsky 'children of darkness' quote.

4 Hosking, *Russia and the Russians*, p. 123. Crummey, 'Reform under Ivan IV', pp. 19–22.

5 De Madariaga, *Ivan the Terrible*, p. 193. Bogatyrev, 'Ivan IV', p. 259. On the description also by other western European observers of the horrors committed see Poe, 'A Distant World: Russian Relations with Europe Before Peter the Great', pp. 14–15.

6 Willan, *Early History*, p. 101. Morgan and Coote, *Early Voyages and Travels*, 2, pp. 256–7.

7 Morgan and Coote, *Early Voyages and Travels*, 2, pp. 335–40.

8 De Madariaga, *Ivan the Terrible*, pp. 182–3, 194–5.

9 Morgan and Coote, *Early Voyages and Travels*, 2, pp. 281–2; Willan, *Early History*, p. 98.

10 Willan, *Early History*, p. 119. See also Anderson, *Britain's Discovery of Russia*, pp. 5–6.

11 Willan, *Early History*, p. 80.

Chapter Sixty-Six

1 Purchas, *Hakluytus Posthumus*, xiii, p. 5. Willan, *Early History*, p. 3.

2 Andrews, *Trade, Plunder and Settlement*, p. 73. Scammell, 'Hakluyt and the economic thought of his time', p. 22.

3 Andrews, *Trade, Plunder and Settlement*, pp. 9–10.

4 Hakluyt, *Principal Navigations*, 1, pp. 267, 237–9 (instructions nos 21 and 28).

5 Arber (ed.), *First Three English Books*, p. 285.

6 Lamb, 'Science by Litigation: A Cosmographic Feud', p. 40.

7 F. Godwin, *Annals of the Reign of Queen Mary*, p. 354.

8 Ballad by Thomas Churchyard. Quoted in Taylor, *Tudor Geography*, p. 41 and Stefansson, *The Three Voyages of Martin Frobisher*, 2, p. 231.

BIBLIOGRAPHY

Primary

Arber, E. (ed.), *The first three English books on America* (Edinburgh: Turnbull & Spears, 1885).

Barlow, R., *A Brief Summe of Geographie* (London: The Hakluyt Society, 1932).

Berry, L.E. and Crummey, R.O. (eds), *Rude and Barbarous Kingdom: Russia in the Accounts of Sixteenth-Century English Voyagers* (Wisconsin: University of Wisconsin Press, 1968).

Crossley, J. (ed.), *Autobiographical Tracts of John Dee* (Manchester: Chetham Society, 1851).

Dasent, J.R. (ed.), *Acts of the Privy Council, 1556–1558* (London: Stationery Office, 1890–).

Fennell, J.L.I. (ed.), *The Correspondence between Prince A.M. Kurbsky and Tsar Ivan IV of Russia, 1564–1579* (Cambridge: Cambridge University Press, 1955).

Fennell, J.L.I. (ed.), *Prince A.M. Kurbsky's History of Ivan IV* (Cambridge: Cambridge University Press, 1965).

Fletcher, G., *Of the Russe common wealth* (London: T.D. for T. Charde, 1591).

Gairdner, J. and Brodie, R.H. (eds), *Letters and Papers, Foreign and Domestic, Henry VIII* (Great Britain, Public Records Office. London: Longman, Green, Longman and Roberts (1862–1932)).

Garcie, P., *The Rutter of the Sea with the Havens, Rodes, Soundings, Kennings, Windes, Floods, and Ebbes, daungers and coastes of divers regions with the lawes of the Ile of Auleron, and the judgements of the Sea* (trans. Robert Copland) (London: John Awdeley for Antony Kytson, 1560).

Hakluyt, R., *The Principal Navigations, Voyages, Traffiques & Discoveries of the English Nation: made by sea or overland to the remote and farthest distant quarters of the earth at any time within the compass of these 1600 years.* Unless otherwise stated, references are to the 8-volume edition (London: J.M. Dent & Sons, 1927). Occasional reference is also made to the 12-volume edition (Glasgow: MacLehose, 1903–5) and to the facsimile of the 1589 edition introduced by D.B.

Quinn and R.A. Skelton (Cambridge: University Press for The Hakluyt Society and the Peabody Museum of Salem, 1965).

Hay, D. (ed.), *The Anglica Historia of Polydore Vergil* (London: Royal Historical Society, 1950).

Holinshed, *Chronicles of England, Scotland and Ireland/ with a new introduction by Vernon F. Snow* (6 vols, New York: AMS Press, 1976).

Hume, M.A.S. and Tyler, R. (eds), *Calendar of State Papers, Spain. Vol. 9: 1547–1549* (London: Longman, Green, Longman & Roberts, 1862–1954).

Jordan, W.K. (ed.), *The Chronicle and Political Papers of King Edward VI* (London: George Allen & Unwin, 1966).

Knighton, C.S. and Loades, D., *The Anthony Roll of Henry VIII's Navy: Pepys Library 2991 and British Library additional MS 22047 with related documents* (London: Navy Record Society, 2000).

Latham, R. (ed. and trans.), *The Travels of Marco Polo* (London: Penguin, 1958).

Lemon, R. and Green, M.A.E. (eds), *Calendar of State Papers, Domestic Series, of the reigns of Edward VI, Mary, Elizabeth* (7 vols, London: Public Record Office, 1856-72).

Morgan, E.D. and Coote, C.H., *Early Voyages and Travels to Russia and Persia by Anthony Jenkinson and other Englishmen* (London: The Hakluyt Society, 1886).

Nichols, J.G. (ed.), *The Diary of Henry Machyn: Citizen and merchant-taylor of London from AD 1550 to AD 1563* (London: Camden Society, 1848).

Picard, B. and Grundy, J.B.C. (eds), *Description of Moscow and Muscovy, by Sigmund von Herberstein* (London: J.M. Dent & Sons, 1969).

Pratt, J. and Stoughton, J. (eds), *The Acts and Monuments of John Foxe* (London: The Religious Tract Society, 1877).

Purchas, S., *Hakluytus Posthumus or Purchas, His Pilgrims* (20 vols, Glasgow: MacLehose, 1905).

Stow, J., *A Survey of London. Reprinted from the text of 1603, with introduction and notes by Charles Lethbridge Kingsford* (2 vols, Oxford: Clarendon Press, 1908; 1971).

Strype, J., *Life of the Learned John Cheke, Kt, first instructor, afterwards Secretary of State, to King Edward VI: One of the great restorers of good learning and true religion in this kingdom* (Oxford: Clarendon Press, 1821).

Strype, J., *Ecclesiastical memorials: relating chiefly to religion, and the reformation of it, and the emergencies of the Church of England* (3 vols, Oxford: Clarendon Press, 1822).

Tyler, R. (ed.), *Calendar of Letters, despatches and state papers relating to the negotiations between England and Spain, preserved in the Archives at Vienna, Brussels, Simancas and elsewhere. Vol. 10: 1550–1552* (London: HMSO, 1914).

Wallis, H. (ed.), *The maps and text of the Boke of Idrography presented by Jean Rotz to Henry VIII, now in the British Library* (Oxford: The Roxburghe Club, 1981).

Warner, J.C. (ed.), *John Bale's Catalogue of Tudor Authors* (Tempe, Arizona: Arizona Center for Medieval and Renaissance Studies, 2010).

Yule, H. (ed.), *Cathay and the way thither; being a collection of medieval notices of China, with a preliminary essay on the intercourse between China and the western nations, previous to the discovery of the Cape route* (London: The Hakluyt Society, 1866).

Secondary

Abulafia, D., *The Discovery of Mankind: Atlantic Encounters in the Age of Columbus* (New Haven and London: Yale University Press, 2008).

Adamson, J. (ed.), *The Princely Courts of Europe, 1500–1750* (London: Weidenfeld & Nicolson, 1999).

Adlard Coles, K. and Blake, P., *Heavy Weather Sailing* (London: Adlard Coles Nautical, fourth edition, 1991).

Anderson, M.S., *Britain's Discovery of Russia, 1553–1815* (London: Macmillan, 1958).

Andrews, K., *Trade, Plunder and Settlement: Maritime Enterprise and the Genesis of the British Empire* (Cambridge: Cambridge University Press, 1984).

Ash, E.H., *Power, Knowledge and Expertise in Elizabethan England* (Baltimore and London: John Hopkins University Press, 2004).

Aslet, C., *The Story of Greenwich* (London: Fourth Estate, 1999).

Bagrow, L. and Skelton, R.A., *History of Cartography* (London: C.A. Watts & Co., 1964).

Baker, T.F.T. (ed.), *A History of the County of Middlesex: vol.XI* (Oxford: Oxford University Press, 1998).

Baldwin, F.E., *Sumptuary Legislation and Personal Regulation in England* (Baltimore: John Hopkins University Press, 1926).

Baldwin Smith, L., *Fools, Martyrs, Traitors: The Story of Martyrdom in the Western World* (New York: Alfred A. Knopf, 1997).

Ball, J.N., *Merchants and Merchandise: The Expansion of Trade in Europe, 1500–1630* (New York: St Martin's Press, 1977).

Baron, S.H., *Explorations in Muscovite History* (London: Variorum, 1991).

Beazley, C. R., *John and Sebastian Cabot* (London: T. Fisher Unwin, 1898).

Billington, J.H., 'The Projection and Celebration of Power', in B. Shifman and G. Walton (eds), *Gifts to the Tsars 1500–1700: Treasures from the Kremlin* (New York; London: Harry N. Abrams, 2001).

Block, L., *To Harness the Wind: A Short History of the Development of Sails* (Annapolis: Naval Institute Press, 2003).

Bogatyrev, S., *The Sovereign and his Counsellors: Ritualised Consultations in*

Muscovite Political Culture, 1350s to 1570s (Helsinki: Suomalainen Tiedeakatemia, 2000).

Bogatyrev, S., 'Ivan IV', in M. Perrie (ed.), *The Cambridge History of Russia Volume 1: From Early Rus' to 1689* (Cambridge: Cambridge University Press, 2006), pp. 240–64.

Bowden, P.J., *The Wool Trade in Tudor and Stuart England* (London: Macmillan, 1962).

Bradley, P., *British Maritime Enterprise in the New World: From the Late Fifteenth to the Mid Eighteenth Century* (Lewiston; Lampeter: E. Mellen Press, 1999).

Brennan, M.G., *The Sidneys of Penshurst and the monarchy, 1500–1700* (Aldershot: Ashgate, 2006).

Brenner, R., *Merchants and Revolution: Commercial Change, Political Conflict, and London's Overseas Traders, 1550–1653* (London: Verso, 2003).

Brun, M.C., *Universal geography, or, A description of all the parts of the world* (Edinburgh: Adam & Charles Black, 1834).

Burwash, D., *English Merchant Shipping, 1460–1540* (Toronto: University of Toronto Press, 1947).

Bushkovitch, P., 'The Moscow Kremlin and its History', in O. Dmitrieva and N. Abramova (eds), *Britannia & Muscovy: English silver at the court of the Tsars* (New Haven and London: Yale University Press, 2006).

Campbell, M., 'Gold, Silver and Precious Stones', in J. Blair and N. Ramsay, *English Medieval Industries* (London: Hambledon Press, 1991).

Carus-Wilson, E.M., *Medieval Merchant Venturers* (London: Methuen, 1954).

Carus-Wilson, E.M. and Coleman, O., *England's export trade 1275–1547* (Oxford: Clarendon Press, 1963).

Channon, J. and Hudson, R., *The Penguin Historical Atlas of Russia* (London: Penguin, 1995).

Chettle, G.H., *The Queen's House, Greenwich* (Greenwich: National Maritime Museum, 1937).

Cipolla, C.M., *Guns and Sails in the early phase of European expansion, 1400–1700* (London: Collins, 1965).

Connell-Smith, G., *Forerunners of Drake: A study of English trade with Spain in the early Tudor period* (London: Longmans, Green & Co., 1954).

Cooper, J., *Scottish Renaissance army 1513–1550* (Oxford: Osprey, 2008).

Couper, H. and Henbest, N., *The Story of Astronomy: How the Universe Revealed its Secrets* (London: Cassell Illustrated, 2012).

Crane, N., *Mercator: The Man who Mapped the Planet* (London: Weidenfeld & Nicolson, 2002).

Crone, G.R., *Maps and their Makers* (London: Hutchinson University Library, fourth edition, 1968).

Crone, G.R., 'Richard Hakluyt, geographer', in D.B. Quinn (ed.), *The Hakluyt Handbook*, Vol. 1 (London: The Hakluyt Society, 1974), pp. 8–14.

Cross, C., 'The English Universities, 1553–1558', in Duffy and Loades (eds), *The Church of Mary Tudor*, pp. 57–76.

Crummey, R.O., *The Formation of Muscovy, 1304–1613* (London: Longman, 1987).

Crummey, R.O., 'Reform under Ivan IV: Gradualism and Terror', in R.O. Crummey (ed.), *Reform in Russia and the USSR: past and prospects* (Urbana: University of Illinois Press, 1989), pp. 12–27.

Dalton, H., 'Negotiating Fortune: English merchants in Early Sixteenth Century Seville', in C. Williams (ed.), *Bridging Early Modern Atlantic Worlds: People, Products and Practices on the Move* (Aldershot: Ashgate, 2009), pp. 57–73.

Davis, R., *English Overseas Trade, 1500–1700* (London: Macmillan, 1973).

De Madariaga, I., *Ivan the Terrible: First Tsar of Russia* (New Haven and London: Yale University Press, 2005).

Deacon, R., *John Dee: Scientist, Geographer, Astrologer and Secret Agent to Elizabeth I* (London: Frederick Muller, 1968).

Dmitrieva, O., '"The Golden Chain of Traffic": The First Hundred Years of Anglo-Russian Relations', in O. Dmitrieva and N. Abramova (eds), *Britannia & Muscovy: English Silver at the Court of the Tsars* (New Haven and London: Yale University Press, 2006).

Dmitrieva, O., 'From Whitehall to the Kremlin: The Diplomacy and Political Culture of the English and Russian Courts', in O. Dmitrieva and T. Murdoch (eds), *Tudors, Stuarts and the Russian Tsars: Treasures of the Royal Courts* (London: V&A Publishing, 2013), pp. 13–35.

Duffy, E., *The Stripping of the Altars: Traditional Religion in England 1400–1580* (New Haven and London: Yale University Press, 1992).

Duffy, E., *The Voices of Morebath: Reformation and Rebellion in an English Village* (New Haven and London: Yale University Press, 2003).

Duffy, E. and Loades, D., *The Church of Mary Tudor* (Aldershot: Ashgate, 2006).

Dulles, F.R., *Eastward Ho! The First English adventurers to the Orient* (London: John Lane, 1931).

Dunnett, D., *The Ringed Castle* (London: Century Hutchinson, 1983).

Edwards, J., *Mary I: England's Catholic Queen* (New Haven and London: Yale University Press, 2011).

Elliott, J.H., *The Old World and the New, 1492–1650* (Cambridge: Cambridge University Press, 1970).

Elliott, J.H., *Empires of the Atlantic World: Britain and Spain in America, 1492–1830* (New Haven and London: Yale University Press, 2006).

Esser, R., 'Germans in Early Modern Britain', in P. Panayi (ed.), *Germans in Britain since 1500* (London: Hambledon Press, 1996).

Feingold, M., *The Mathematicians' Apprenticeship: Science, universities and society in England, 1560–1640* (Cambridge: Cambridge University Press, 1984).

Fernández-Armesto, F., *1492: The Year Our World Began* (London: Pearson Education, 2011).

Filatov, N. et al., *White Sea: Its Marine Environment and Ecosystem Dynamics Influenced by Global Change* (Chichester: Praxis, 2005).

Fletcher, H., 'A Note on Two Words in Milton's *History of Moscovia*', in B. Maxwell et al. (eds), *Studies in Honor of Hardin Craig* (Stanford: Stanford University, 1941), pp. 309–19.

Fox Bourne, H.R., *English Merchants* (London: Chatto & Windus, 1886).

French, P., *John Dee: The World of an Elizabethan Magus* (London: Routledge & Kegan Paul, 1984).

Fury, C.A., *Tides in the Affairs of Men: The Social History of Elizabethan Seamen, 1580–1603* (Westport, Conn.; London: Greenwood Press, 2002).

Fury, C.A., 'Health and Health Care at Sea', in C. A. Fury (ed.), *The Social History of English Seamen, 1485–1649* (Woodbridge: Boydell, 2012), pp. 193–227.

Gerson, A.J., *Studies in the History of English Commerce in the Tudor Period. Volume I: The Organisation and Early History of the Muscovy Company* (New York: D. Appleton & Co., 1912).

Gibson, M. (ed.), *Witchcraft and Society in England and America, 1550–1750* (Ithaca, New York: Cornell University Press, 2003).

Girouard, M., *Life in the English Country House: A Social and Architectural History* (Harmondsworth: Penguin, 1980).

Godwin, F., *Annals of the Reign of Queen Mary* (J. Hughes trans., London: Brab. Aylmer etc., 1706).

Griffiths, P.J., *A Licence to Trade: The History of English Chartered Companies* (London: E. Benn, 1974).

Hadfield, A., *Literature, Travel, and Colonial Writing in the English Renaissance, 1545–1625* (Oxford: Clarendon Press, 1998).

Hair, P.E.H., and Alsop, J.D., *English Seamen and Traders in Guinea, 1553–1565: The New Evidence of their Wills* (Lewiston, New York; Lampeter: E. Mellen Press, 1992).

Hall, P., *Cities in Civilisation* (London: Weidenfeld & Nicolson, 1998).

Hamel, J., *England and Russia: Comprising the voyage of John Tradescant the Elder, Sir Hugh Willoughby, Richard Chancellor, Nelson and Others to the White Sea* (London: Richard Bently, 1854).

Hamy, E.T., 'Jean Roze, Hydrographe Dieppois', in E.T. Hamy, *Études Historiques et Géographiques*, No. X (Paris: Ernest Leroux, 1896), pp. 229–39.

Hannay, M.P., *Philip's Phoenix: Mary Sidney, Countess of Pembroke* (Oxford: Oxford University Press, 1990).

Haring, C.H., *Trade and Navigation between Spain and the Indies in the Time of the Hapsburgs* (Cambridge: Harvard University Press, 1918).

Harris Sacks, D., *The Widening Gate: Bristol and the Atlantic Economy, 1450–1700* (Berkeley; Oxford: University of California Press, 1991).

Hosking, G., *Russia and the Russians* (Cambridge, Mass.: Belknap, 2001).

Hughes, L., 'The Courts of Moscow and St Petersburg c.1547–1725', in J. Adamson (ed.), *The Princely Courts of Europe: Ritual, Politics and Culture under the* Ancien Régime *1500–1750* (London: Weidenfeld & Nicolson, 1999).

Hume Brown, P., *History of Scotland* (3 vols, Cambridge: Cambridge University Press, 1911).

Ives, E.W., *Lady Jane Grey: A Tudor Mystery* (Chichester: Wiley-Blackwell, 2011).

Jennings, C., *Greenwich: The Place Where Days Begin and End* (London: Little, Brown & Co., 1999).

Johnson, D. and Nurminen, J., *The History of Seafaring: Navigating the World's Oceans* (London: Conway, 2007).

Johnson, F.R., *Astronomical Thought in Renaissance England: A study of the English scientific writings from 1500–1645* (Baltimore: John Hopkins University Press, 1937).

Jordan, W.K., *Edward VI. Volume I: The Young King* and *Volume 2: The Threshold of Power* (London: Allen & Unwin, 1968 and 1970).

Kamen, H., *Philip of Spain* (New Haven and London: Yale University Press, 1997).

Kemp, P. (ed.), *The Oxford Companion to Ships and the Sea* (Oxford: Oxford University Press, 1976).

Kerner, R.J., *The Urge to the Sea: The Course of Russian History: The role of rivers, portages, ostrogs, monasteries, and furs* (Berkeley and Los Angeles: University of California Press, 1942).

Kesselring, K.J., *Mercy and Authority in the Tudor State* (Cambridge: Cambridge University Press, 2003).

Knighton, C.S., 'Westminster Abbey Restored', in Loades and Duffy (eds), *The Church of Mary Tudor* (Aldershot: Ashgate, 2006), pp. 77–123.

Knighton, C.S., and Loades, D., *The Navy of Edward VI and Mary I* (Burlington, Vt.; Farnham: Ashgate for the Naval Records Society, 2011).

Kudriavtseva, A.G., 'Ambassadorial Ceremony at the Tsar's Court', in B. Shifman and G. Walton (eds), *Gifts to the Tsars 1500–1700: Treasures from the Kremlin* (New York; London: Harry N. Abrams, 2001).

Lach, D.F., *Asia in the making of Europe* (2 vols, Chicago; London: University of Chicago Press, 1965).

Lamb, U., 'Science by Litigation: A Cosmographic Feud', in Ursula Lamb, *Cosmographers and Pilots of the Spanish Maritime Empire* (Aldershot: Variorum, 1995), pp. 40–57. Lamb, U., 'Cosmographers of Seville: Nautical Science and Social

Experience', in Ursula Lamb, *Cosmographers and Pilots of the Spanish Maritime Empire* (Aldershot: Variorum, 1995), pp. 675–86.

Landes, D., *The Wealth and Poverty of Nations* (London: Little, Brown and Co., 1999).

Lloyd, T.H., *The English wool trade in the Middle Ages* (Cambridge: Cambridge University Press, 1977).

Lloyd, T.H., *England and the German Hanse, 1157–1611: A study of their trade and commercial diplomacy* (Cambridge: Cambridge University Press, 1991).

Loades, D., *Mary Tudor: A Life* (Oxford: Basil Blackwell, 1989).

Loades, D., *The Tudor Navy: An administrative, political and military history* (Aldershot: Scolar, 1992).

Loades, D., *The Reign of King Edward VI* (Bangor: Headstart History, 1994).

Loades, D., *John Dudley, Duke of Northumberland, 1504–1553* (Oxford: Clarendon Press, 1996).

Loades, D., 'The Personal Religion of Mary I', in Duffy and Loades (eds), *The Church of Mary Tudor*, pp. 1–29.

Loades, D., 'The English Maritime Community, 1500–1650', in C. Fury, *The Social History of English Seamen, 1485–1649* (Woodbridge: Boydell, 2012), pp. 5–26.

Lobel, M.D. and Carus-Wilson, E.M., 'Bristol', in M.D. Lobel (ed.), *The Atlas of Historic Towns*, Vol. 2 (London: Scolar, 1975).

Lodge, E., *Illustrations of British history, biography, and manners, in the reigns of Henry VIII, Edward VI, Mary, Elizabeth, & James I, exhibited in a series of original papers, selected from the manuscripts of the noble families of Howard, Talbot, and Cecil . . .* (3 vols, London: John Chidley, 1838).

Loudon, J.C., *Arboretum et Fruticetum Britannicum; Or the trees and shrubs of Britain, native and foreign, delineated and . . . described, etc.* (8 vols, London: J.C. Loudon, 1838).

Lubimenko, I., *Les Relations Commerciales et Politiques de l'Angleterre avec la Russie avant Pierre le Grand* (Paris: Librairie Ancienne Honoré Champion, 1933).

Martin, J., *Medieval Russia, 980–1584* (Cambridge: Cambridge University Press, 2007).

Matthew, H.C.G. and Harrison, B. (eds), *Oxford Dictionary of National Biography* (Oxford: Oxford University Press, 2004).

Maxwell, B. et al. (eds), *Renaissance Studies in honor of Hardin Craig* (Stanford: Stanford University, 1941).

Mayers, K., *North-East Passage to Muscovy* (Stroud: Sutton Publishing, 2005).

Morison, S.E., *The European Discovery of America: The Northern Voyages, AD 500–1600* (New York: Oxford University Press, 1971).

Nordenskiold, N.A.E., *The Voyage of the Vega round Asia and Europe* (2 vols, London: Macmillan, 1881).

Norris, H., *Tudor Costume and Fashion* (Mineola, New York: Dover Publications, 1997).

Oppenheim, M., 'Maritime History', *Victoria History of the County of Somerset* (Exeter: University of Exeter, 1968).

Oppenheim, M., *A History of the Administration of the Royal Navy and of merchant shipping in relation to the Navy from 1509–1660* (Aldershot: Temple Smith, 1988).

Orme, N., *Early British Swimming 55 BC–AD 1719* (Exeter: University of Exeter, 1983).

Osselton, N.E., 'Hakluyt's Language', in D.B. Quinn (ed.), *The Hakluyt Handbook*, Vol. 1 (London: The Hakluyt Society, 1974), pp. 23–30.

Ostrowski, D., *Muscovy and the Mongols: Cross-cultural influences on the steppe frontier, 1304–1589* (Cambridge: Cambridge University Press, 1998).

Page, W. (ed.), *The Victoria History of the County of Kent* (London: Archibald Constable, 1908).

Paine, L.P., *Warships of the World to 1900* (Boston, Mass.: Houghton Mifflin Harcourt, 2000).

Parker, J., *Books to Build an Empire: A Bibliographical History of English Overseas Interests to 1620* (Amsterdam: N. Israel, 1965).

Parks, G.B., *Richard Hakluyt and the English Voyages* (New York: American Geographical Society, 1928).

Parks, G.B., 'Tudor Travel Literature: A Brief History', in D.B. Quinn (ed.), *The Hakluyt Handbook*, Vol. 1 (London: The Hakluyt Society, 1974), pp. 97–132.

Parry, J.H., *The Age of Reconnaissance: Discovery, Exploration and Settlement 1450–1650* (London: Cardinal, 1973).

Parry, J.H., 'Hakluyt's view of British History', in D.B. Quinn (ed.), *The Hakluyt Handbook*, Vol. 1 (London: The Hakluyt Society, 1974), pp. 3–7.

Penrose, B., *Travel and Discovery in the Renaissance 1420–1620* (Cambridge, Mass.: Harvard University Press, 1952).

Picard, L., *Elizabeth's London: Everyday Life in Elizabethan London* (London: Phoenix, 2004).

Pike, R., *Aristocrats and Traders: Sevillian Society in the Sixteenth Century* (Ithaca; London: Cornell University Press, 1972).

Pipes, R., *Russia under the Old Regime* (London: Penguin, 1995).

Planché, J.R., *A Cyclopedia of Costume. Vol.II: A General History of Costume in Europe* (London: Chatto and Windus, 1876–9).

Poe, M. (ed.), *Early Exploration of Russia* (12 vols, London: Routledge Curzon, 2003). Poe, M., 'A Distant World: Russian Relations with Europe Before Peter the Great', in C.H. Whittaker (ed.), *Russia Engages the World, 1453–1825* (Cambridge, Mass.; London: Harvard University Press, 2003), pp. 3–23.

Porter, L., *Mary Tudor: The First Queen* (London: Portrait, 2007).

Porter, S. (ed.), *Survey of London vols 43 & 44: Poplar, Blackwall and the Isle of Dogs: the Parish of All Saints* (London: Athlone, 1994).

Portuondo, M.M., *Secret Science: Spanish Cosmography and the New World* (Chicago and London: University of Chicago Press, 2009).

Quinn, D.B. (ed.), *The Voyages and Colonising Enterprises of Sir Humphrey Gilbert* (London: The Hakluyt Society, 1940).

Quinn, D.B., 'Sailors and the Sea', in N.A. Allardyce (ed.), *Shakespeare in his Own Age* (Cambridge: Cambridge University Press, 1964), pp. 21–36.

Quinn, D.B., *England and the Discovery of America, 1481–1620* (London: George Allen, 1974).

Quinn, D.B., 'Hakluyt's reputation', in D.B. Quinn (ed.), *The Hakluyt Handbook*, Vol. 1 (London: The Hakluyt Society, 1974), pp. 133–52.

Ramsay, G.D., *England's Overseas Trade in the Centuries of Emergence* (London: Macmillan, 1957).

Ramsay, G.D., 'Hakluyt's Use of the Materials Available to him: Northern Europe', in D.B. Quinn (ed.), *The Hakluyt Handbook*, Vol. 1 (London: The Hakluyt Society, 1974), pp. 155–60.

Ramsay, G.D., *The English Woollen Industry, 1500–1750* (London: Macmillan, 1982).

Rappaport, S., *Worlds within worlds: structures of life in sixteenth-century London* (Cambridge: Cambridge University Press, 1989).

Richey, M.W., 'Astronomy and Astrology', in S.A. Bedini (ed.), *The Christopher Columbus Encyclopaedia*, Vol. 1 (London: Macmillan, 1992), pp. 49–51.

Richey, M.W., 'Navigation: Art, Practice and Theory', in S.A. Bedini (ed.), *The Christopher Columbus Encyclopaedia*, Vol. 2 (London: Macmillan, 1992), pp. 505–12.

Romaniello, M.P., *The Elusive Empire: Kazan and the Creation of Russia, 1552–1671* (Madison, Wisconsin: University of Wisconsin Press, 2012).

Rubio, J.P., *El Piloto Mayor de la Casa de la Contratación de Sevilla: Pilotos Mayores, Catedráticos de Cosmografía y Cosmógrafos* (Seville: Escuela de Estudios Hispano-Americanos de Sevilla, 1950).

Sadler, J., *Border Fury: England and Scotland at War, 1296–1568* (Harlow: Pearson Education, 2005).

Scammell, G.V., 'Hakluyt and the economic thought of his time', in D.B. Quinn (ed.), *The Hakluyt Handbook*, Vol. 1 (London: The Hakluyt Society, 1974), pp. 15–22.

Scarisbrick, J.J., *Henry VIII* (London: Eyre Methuen, 1968 reprinted 1983).

Scott, W.R., *The Constitution and Finance of English, Scottish and Irish Joint-Stock Companies to 1720* (3 vols, Cambridge: Cambridge University Press, 1910–12).

Senior, C.M., *A Nation of Pirates: English Piracy in its Heyday* (Newton Abbot: David and Charles, 1976).

Shirley, R.W., *The Mapping of the World: Early Printed World Maps 1472–1700* (London: New Holland Publishers, 1993).

Simmons, J.S.G., 'Hakluyt's Use of the Materials Available to him: Russia', in D.B. Quinn (ed.), *The Hakluyt Handbook*, Vol. 1 (London: The Hakluyt Society, 1974), pp. 161–7.

Skelton, R.A., *Explorers' Maps: Chapters in the Cartographic Record of Geographical Discovery* (London: Routledge & Kegan Paul, 1958).

Skelton, R.A., 'Hakluyt's maps', in D.B. Quinn (ed.), *The Hakluyt Handbook*, Vol. 1 (London: The Hakluyt Society, 1974), pp. 48–69.

Skidmore, C., *Edward VI: The Lost King of England* (London: Weidenfeld & Nicolson, 2007).

Slack, P., 'Mortality Crises and Epidemic Disease in England, 1485–1610', in C. Webster (ed.), *Health, Medicine and Mortality in the 16th Century* (Cambridge: Cambridge University Press, 1979), pp. 9–59.

Spies, M., *Arctic Routes to Fabled Lands: Olivier Brunel & the Passage to China and Cathay in the Sixteenth Century* (Amsterdam: University of Amsterdam Press, 1997).

Stefansson, V., *The Three Voyages of Martin Frobisher* (2 vols, London: The Argonaut Press, 1938). Stephen, L. and Lee, S. (eds), *The Dictionary of National Biography* (London: Oxford University Press, 1973).

Stevens, C.B., 'Banditry and Provincial Order in Sixteenth-century Russia', in A.M. Kleimola and G.D. Lenhoff (eds), *Culture and Identity in Muscovy, 1359–1584* (Moscow: ITZ-Garant, 1997).

Strickland, A., *Lives of the Queens of Scotland and English Princesses, connected with the Regal Succession of Great Britain* (Edinburgh and London: Blackwood, 1854).

Taylor, E.G.R., *Tudor Geography, 1485–1583* (New York: Octagon Books, 1930; 1968).

Taylor, E.G.R., *Later Tudor and early Stuart Geography, 1583–1650* (London: Methuen, 1934).

Taylor, E.G.R., *Original Writings and Correspondence of the two Richard Hakluyts* (2 vols, London: The Hakluyt Society, 1935).

Taylor, E.G.R., *The Mathematical Practitioners of Tudor & Stuart England* (Cambridge: For the Institute of Navigation at the University Press, 1970).

Thomas, H., *Rivers of Gold: The Rise of the Spanish Empire* (London: Weidenfeld & Nicolson, 2003).

Thomas, K., *Religion and the Decline of Magic* (Harmondsworth: Penguin, 1973).

Thomas, K., *Man and the Natural World: Changing Attitudes in England 1500–1800* (London: Penguin, 1984).

Thornbury, W. (ed.), *Old and New London* (6 vols, London: Cassell & Co., 1879–85).

Tiberg, E., *Moscow, Livonia and the Hanseatic League, 1487–1550* (Stockholm: Almqvist & Wiksell International, 1995).

Tolstoy, G., *First Forty Years of Intercourse between England and Russia* (New York: Burt Franklin, 1875).

Took, R., *Running with Reindeer: Encounters in Russian Lapland* (London: John Murray, 2003).

Trevor-Battye, A.B.R., *Ice-Bound on Kolguev: A Chapter in the Exploration of Arctic Europe* (London: Constable & Co., 1895).

Turner, S., *The History of England from the earliest period to the death of Elizabeth*, Vol. II (London: Longman, Orme, Brown, Green, and Longmans, 1839).

Vanes, J., *The Port of Bristol in the Sixteenth Century* (Bristol: Bristol Historical Association, 1977).

Voyce, A., *The Moscow Kremlin: Its history, architecture, and art treasures* (London: Thames & Hudson, 1955).

Waters, D.W., *The Art of Navigation in England in Elizabethan and Early Stuart Times* (London: Hollis and Carter, 1955).

Webb, E.A., *The Records of St Bartholomew's Priory, and of the church and parish of St Bartholomew the Great, West Smithfield* (2 vols, Oxford: Oxford University Press, 1921).

Weinreb, B. and Hibbert, C. (eds), *The London Encyclopaedia* (London: Macmillan, 1983).

Whitelock, A., *Mary Tudor: England's First Queen* (London: Bloomsbury, 2010).

Willan, T.S., *The Muscovy Merchants of 1555* (Manchester: Manchester University Press, 1953).

Willan, T.S., *The Early History of the Russia Company, 1553–1603* (Manchester: Manchester University Press, 1956).

Williams, P., *The Later Tudors, 1547–1603* (Oxford: Clarendon Press, 1995).

Williamson, J.A., *Maritime Enterprise, 1485–1558* (Oxford: Clarendon Press, 1913).

Williamson, J.A., *The Cabot Voyages and Bristol Discovery under Henry VII – with the cartography of the voyages by R.A. Skelton* (Cambridge: Cambridge University Press, 1962).

Wilson, F., *Muscovy: Russia through foreign eyes, 1553–1900* (London: Allen & Unwin, 1970).

Wilson, I., *John Cabot and the Matthew* (Bristol: Longdunn Press, 1996).

Wooding, L., 'The Marian Restoration and the Mass', in Loades and Duffy (eds), *The Church of Mary Tudor*, pp. 227–57.

Woolley, B., *The Queen's Conjuror: The Life and Magic of Dr Dee* (London: Flamingo, 2002).

Zagorodnaya, I., 'English Diplomats at the Court of the Tsars', in O. Dmitrieva and N. Abramova (eds), *Britannia & Muscovy: English silver at the court of the*

Tsars (New Haven and London: Yale University Press, 2006).

Zell, M. (ed.), *Early Modern Kent, 1540–1640* (Woodbridge: Boydell Press, 2000).

Theses

Bratchell, M.E., 'Alien Merchant Communities in London 1500–1550' (Ph.D., University of Cambridge, 1975).

Johnston, S., 'Making Mathematical Practice: Gentlemen, Practitioners and Artisans in Elizabethan England' (Ph.D., University of Cambridge, 1994).

Jones, E.T., 'The Bristol Shipping Industry in the Sixteenth Century' (Ph.D., University of Edinburgh, 1998).

Articles

Alef, G., 'The Origin and Early Development of the Muscovite Postal Service', *Jahrbücher für Geschichte Osteuropas*, Neue Folge, Bd 15, H. 1 (March 1967), pp. 1–15.

Andrews, K.R., 'The Elizabethan Seaman', *Mariner's Mirror*, 68 (1982), pp. 245–62.

Ash, E.H., '"A Note and a Caveat for the Merchant": Mercantile Advisors in Elizabethan England', *The Sixteenth Century Journal*, Vol. 33, No. 1 (Spring 2002), pp. 1–31.

Baron, S.H., 'Ivan the Terrible, Giles Fletcher and the Muscovite Merchantry: A Reconsideration', *The Slavonic and East European Review*, Vol. 56, No. 4 (October 1978), pp. 563–85.

Baron, S.H., 'Herberstein and the English "Discovery" of Muscovy', *Terra Incognita*, 18 (1986), pp. 43–54.

Bindoff, S.T., 'A Kingdom at Stake, 1553', *History Today*, Vol. 3, No. 9 (September 1953), pp. 642–8.

Bogatyrev, S., 'Reinventing the Russian Monarchy in the 1550s: Ivan the Terrible, the Dynasty, and the Church', *The Slavonic and East European Review*, Vol. 85, No. 2 (April 2007), pp. 271–93.

Brenner, R., 'The social basis of English commercial expansion, 1550–1650', *The Journal of Economic History*, 32 (1972), pp. 361–84.

Carter, R. and Mendis, K.M., 'Evolutionary and Historical Aspects of the Burden of Malaria', *Clinical Microbiology Reviews* (October 2002), pp. 564–94.

Casimir, N., Baron de Bogoushevsky, 'The English in Muscovy during the Sixteenth Century', *Transactions of the Royal Historical Society*, Vol. 7 (1878), pp. 58–129.

Cavendish, R., 'Kazan falls to Ivan the Terrible', *History Today*, Vol. 52, Issue 10 (2002), p. 54.

Connell-Smith, 'English Merchants Trading to the New World in the Early Sixteenth Century', *Bulletin of the Institute of Historical Research*, Vol. 23, Issue 67 (May 1950), pp. 53–66.

Cotton, R.W., 'Stephen Borough, the Navigator', *Transactions of the Devonshire Association*, 12 (1880–81), pp. 332–60.

De Roover, F.E., 'Early Examples of Marine Insurance', *The Journal of Economic History*, Vol. 5, No. 2 (November 1945), pp. 172–200.

Deane, C., 'The Mappemonde of Sebastian Cabot', *Science*, Vol. 1, No. 3 (February 1883), pp. 62–5.

Deane, C. et al., 'February Meeting, 1891: Cabot's Mappe-Monde', *Proceedings of the Massachusetts Historical Society*, Second Series, Vol. 6 (Vol. 26 of continuous numbering) (1890–91), pp. 285–350.

Esper, T., 'Russia and the Baltic, 1494–1558', *Slavic Review*, Vol. 25, No. 3 (September 1966), pp. 458–74.

Esper, T., 'A Sixteenth-Century anti-Russian Arms Embargo', *Jahrbücher für Geschichte Osteuropas*, Neue Folge, Bd 15, H. 2 (June 1967), pp. 180–96.

Fisher, F.J., 'Influenza and Inflation in Tudor England', *The Economic History Review*, new series, Vol. 18, No. 1 (1965), pp. 120–9.

Friel, Ian, 'Guns, Gales & God: Elizabeth I's "Merchant Navy"', *History Today*, Vol. 60, Issue 1 (January 2010).

Gordon, E.C., 'The Fate of Sir Hugh Willoughby and His Companions: A New Conjecture', *The Geographical Journal*, Vol. 152, No. 2 (July 1986), pp. 243–7.

Gwyn, D., 'Richard Eden: Cosmographer and Alchemist', *The Sixteenth-Century Journal*, Vol. 15, No. 1 (Spring 1984), pp. 13–34.

Harrisse, H., 'Did Cabot Return from His Second Voyage?', *The American Historical Review*, Vol. 3, No. 3 (April 1898), pp. 449–55.

Hunt, P., 'Ivan IV's Personal Mythology of Kingship', *Slavic Review*, Vol. 52, No. 4 (Winter 1993), pp. 769–809.

Jones, E., 'Alwyn Ruddock: "John Cabot and the Discovery of America"', *Institute of Historical Research*, Vol. 81, No. 212 (May 2008), pp. 224–54.

Jones, E., 'Henry VII and the Bristol expeditions to North America: the Condon documents', *Institute of Historical Research*, Vol. 83, No. 221 (August 2010), pp. 444–54.

Kropotkin, P.A., 'Novaya Zemlya', in *Encyclopedia Britannica* (London and Edinburgh: A. and C. Black, 1902–3)

Menken, J., 'Ivan the Terrible', *History Today*, Vol. 3, No. 3 (March 1953), pp. 167–73.

Meyendorff, 'Anglo-Russian Trade in the 16th Century', *The Slavonic and East European Review*, Vol. 25, No. 64 (November 1946), pp. 109–21.

Miller, D.B., 'The Viskovatyi Affair of 1553–4: Official Art, the Emergence of

Autocracy, and the Disintegration of Medieval Russian Culture', *Russian History*, 8, part 3 (1981), pp. 293–332.

Morris, M., 'The Rise of the English Sailcloth Industry, 1565–1643: Coastal trade records as an indicator of import substitution', *Mariner's Mirror*, 84 (1998), pp. 139–51.

Morris, M., 'Naval Cordage Procurement in Early Modern England', *International Journal of Maritime History*, 11 (1999), pp. 81–99.

Newton, A.P., 'An Early Grant to Sebastian Cabot', *The English Historical Review*, Vol. 37, No. 148 (October 1922), pp. 564–5.

Nicholls, J.F., 'The Royal Grammar School of Bristol, and the Thorns, its Founders', *Transactions of the Royal Historical Society*, 1872 . . .

Paul, M.C., 'The Military Revolution in Russia, 1550–1682', *The Journal of Military History*, Vol. 68, No. 1 (January 2004), pp. 9–45.

Robertson, J., 'The First Russian Embassy to England', *The Archaeological Journal*, No. 49 (March 1856), pp. 77–80.

Ruddock, A.A., 'The Earliest Records of the High Court of Admiralty (1515–1558)', *Bulletin of the Institute of Historical Research*, 22, part 66 (November 1949), pp. 139–51.

Ruddock, A.A., 'John Day of Bristol and the English Voyages across the Atlantic in 1497', *The Geographical Journal*, 132 (1966), pp. 225–33.

Ruddock, A.A., 'The Reputation of Sebastian Cabot', *Bulletin of the Institute of Historical Research*, 42 (1974), pp. 95–9.

Sandman, A. and Ash, E.H., 'Trading Expertise: Sebastian Cabot between Spain and England', *Renaissance Quarterly*, Vol. 57, No. 3 (Autumn 2004), pp. 813–46.

Scammell, G.V., 'Manning the English Merchant Service in the Sixteenth Century', *Mariner's Mirror*, 56 (1970), pp. 131–54.

Scammell, G.V., 'Shipowning in the Economy and Politics of Early Modern England', *Historical Journal*, 15 (1972), pp. 385–407.

Scammell, G.V., 'European Seamanship in the Great Age of Discovery', *Mariner's Mirror*, 68 (1982), pp. 357–76.

Skelton, R.A., 'Sebastian Cabot', *Dictionary of Canadian Biography Online*.

Taylor, E.G.R., 'Roger Barlow: A New Chapter in Early Tudor Geography', *The Geographical Journal*, Vol. 74, No. 2 (August 1929), pp. 157–66.

Taylor, E.G.R., 'John Dee and the Map of North-East Asia', *Imago Mundi*, Vol. 12 (1955), pp. 103–6.

Wallis, H., 'England's Search for the Northern Passages in the Sixteenth and Early Seventeenth Centuries', *Arctic*, Vol. 37, No. 4 (December 1984), pp. 453–72.

Watt, J., 'Some forgotten contributions of naval surgeons', *Journal of the Royal Society of Medicine*, Vol. 78 (September 1985), pp. 753–62.

Acknowledgements

I have loved history since I was young and grew to love writing and telling a story. I am grateful to the history department at Oriel College, Oxford, and to my D. Phil supervisor, Dr Mark Almond, for instilling a conviction that the first duty of historical writing is to be a pleasure to read. I hope that I have succeeded.

Subsequently, making historical documentaries for television, I have jumped between periods and subjects, in search of a good story, and particularly of one illustrating a wider point. It was while working with one master of popular (as well as good) history, Niall Ferguson, that I first read about the voyage made by Sir Hugh Willoughby and Richard Chancellor in 1553. I looked for the popular account of what seemed at once an extraordinary story, the perfect illustration of an important, wider change, and one served unusually well by the documents which survived. When I realised, to my surprise, that there wasn't one, I resolved to try to write it. I am grateful to James Runcie for his firm insistence at the time that I should do so.

I am lucky to live close to both the British Library and to the London Library. Both are marvellous institutions, as all who use them know, and I could not have written this book without them. Through them I have acquired debts to other authors too numerous to mention – though repeated reference to them will be found in my notes and bibliography. I would, however, like to pay particular tribute to the work of T.S. Willan and E.G.R. Taylor as well as, more fundamentally still, to the sixteenth-century editor Richard Hakluyt, without whom this story, like many others, could simply not be told in the same way.

My thanks are due to Lord Middleton for permission to photograph the family portrait of Sir Hugh, to Lady Cara Willoughby for her help in doing so, and to Richard Flint, who did the photography. For the portrait of Robert Thorne, I am grateful to Nicola Pearce, the assistant archivist at Bristol Grammar School, for photographing it, as well as to Anne Bradley, the archivist, and Pete Jakobek, the assistant head, for their help.

On the map on p. x I have used and gratefully acknowledge the course of the *Bona Esperanza* and the *Bona Confidentia*, approximately plotted by Kit Mayers, an experienced sailor, on p. 65 of his book *North-East Passage to Muscovy*.

Professor David Loades has provided invaluable help simply through his prolific study of Tudor politics and maritime life, but he also read this book in manuscript, providing very useful feedback and pointing out some factual inaccuracies. Any errors that remain are of course my own.

I owe enormous thanks to my publisher, Weidenfeld & Nicolson, for their enthusiasm and support, and particularly to my wonderful editor, Bea Hemming, who has improved my initial efforts dramatically by deft questions and suggestions. I am very grateful to my copy editor, Linden Lawson. And I owe a great deal too to my agent, Ben Mason, who believed in me and took me on, and who showed me the way to turn an idea into reality. Jo Cantello read a draft proposal early on, introduced me to Ben, and has been so supportive and encouraging throughout.

Deep thanks are due to both of my parents, for their endless love and support, and to my father, in particular, for reading and commenting on these chapters in their first draft. My small children, Thea and Guy, have provided very welcome love and distraction. Last and anything but least, my largest debt is to my wife Nicola, who has read chapters, put up with countless weekends of solitary childcare and remained enormously loving, patient and supportive, about a book she had every right to resent. I am more grateful than I can say.

INDEX